SOULFUL ORGANIZATIONAL LEADERSHIP

by

Arthur William McVey

En Route Books and Media, LLC

St. Louis, MO

⊕ENROUTE
Make the time

En Route Books and Media, LLC
5705 Rhodes Avenue
St. Louis, MO 63109

Cover credit: Dr. Sebastian P. Mahfood, OP

Library of Congress Control Number: 2020952953

ISBN-13: 978-1-952464-47-8

Acknowledgments

I WISH TO THANK PETER A. REDPATH MY EXTRAORDINARY TEACHER AND FRIEND, Eduardo Bernot, who brought me through this journey in so many ways and at critical moments, Curtis Hancock who inspired my return to Aquinas, and Linda my patient, supportive, and loving wife.

Grant that I may
through justice
be subject to You,
avoid the beguilements of the devil,
through temperance
exercise restraint,
and through fortitude
endure adversity with patience.

Order me inwardly through a good life,
that I may do
what is right
and what will be
meritorious for me
and a good example for others.

Grant that I may
never crave to do things impulsively,
never disdain to do what is burdensome,
Lest I begin things before I should
or abandon them before finishing.

Amen

St. Thomas *AQUINAS, Prayer to Acquire the Virtues*

Contents

Introduction

The Problem

This book is a study and application of Thomistic soulful organizational leadership based on a metaphysics of organization and a faculty-behavioral-psychology of the soul. It applies to a broad definition of organizations, i.e. profit, nonprofit, government, religious and volunteering. Since our study of soulful leadership is of an organizational context, the dissertation focuses largely on the executive function of organizational leadership. The primary reason for a study of soul organizational leadership is to comprehend and apply the executive function and diffusion of leadership powers at work in a soulful organization. Therefore, it is essential to our dissertation that we must initially focus on the function of the executive and his/her character as a leader.

The Soulful Quest Situation

In the executive summary of "Rediscovering the Corporate Soul," William SIDEMAN, Ph.D., and Michael MCCAULEY propose that some organizations show passion, commitment and achieve success because they have a soulful quality.[1] They claim that there is a feel, buzz, and a noticeable and memorable quality, as compared to disorganized, unfocused, and unproductive soulless organizations. Furthermore, they maintain that organizations with soulful leaders, called soul keepers, incorporate new employees easily into a soul culture. Soulful organizations form teams more easily, reduce stress, produce higher quality

---

[1] William SEIDMAN and Michael MCCAULEY, "Rediscovering the Corporate Soul," www.cerebyte.com 2003

i

products and services, sales and profits are enhanced and greater customer satisfaction.

The authors put forth their definition of a corporate soul:

> Corporate Soul? Is this some kind of new wave business psychology? Hardly, but it is a new way to think about organizational performance.

The dictionary defines soul as:

> An entity which is regarded as being an immortal or spiritual part of the person and, though having no physical or material reality, is credited with the functions of thinking and willing hence determining all behavior.[2]

They state that in their work with top performers, there is an observable level of performance beyond the mission statement or corporate vision. There is some type of profound drive beyond the mental model of the goals and objectives. There is just some exceptional difference to great performing companies. They conclude the following:

> We spent years collecting data and searching for understanding. We had almost given up when, quite by chance, we found that we were looking for in a dictionary. The dictionary defines "soulful" as "full of or showing deep feeling" and "soulless" as "lacking soul, sensitivity, or deepness of feeling; without spirit or inspiration." These definitions hinted at the explanation that we had been looking for. They effectively accounted for all the reactions that we were observing. Something profound was occurring and this underlying phenomenon was indicative of "soulful" and of "soulless" behaviors.
>
> However, this is hardly a satisfactory description of something so critical to an organization as its soul. In fact, far from ending our search, this line of thinking led us to ask several follow up questions. How does everyone seem to know when a company is soulful or soulless? Where does the company's soul

---

[2] Ibid., 2.

come from? How can a company proactively develop a corporate soul? […] In sum, these organizations have an almost spiritual quality of faith in their goodness and individuals within the organization behave with that faith.[3]

These authors seem to define and defend their metaphorical concept of "soulfulness" by means of an exercise in organizational, philosophical anthropology. They start with the assumption that company X is a successful company; therefore, it is successful because of certain apparent activities. Based on these observed activities they develop the indicators of "Soulfulness and Soullessness."[4]

They suggest that it is the corporate CEO or founder who is *The Keeper of the Corporate. Soul,* as they explain:

Who best exemplifies the corporate soul? Most textbooks, as well as many popular business books will tell you that it's the chief executive officer or company founder. We're not going to say that the CEO has no part to play in establishing the corporate soul. When a CEO acts in a soulful way, he/she has an impact on everyone else's behavior. Conversely, it is difficult for an organization to overcome a completely soulless CEO.[5]

Since the nineties, there has been a growing interest in the nature of soulful leadership by professional organizational consultants and recently some more scholarly approaches to the subject. We briefly review some of these approaches from the article "Soul Work in Organizations," in *Organization Science* by Philip H. MIRVIS. He examines the efforts to build bridges between secularity and spirituality in organizations. Therefore, he considers various efforts in this direction as theoretical probes of the study and practice of "soul work in organizations." We present some of his descriptions of organizational soul work.

---

[3] Ibid., 3–4.

[4] Ibid., 5–6.

[5] Ibid., 7.

The organization becomes soulful to the extent that a deep sense of community comes about with a "spiritual slant".[6]

1) The "soul at work" is a matter of consciousness of the self and other as the two cornerstones of community. It is the deep connection to community in seeing ourselves in the other and the other in ourselves. Also, conscious is a deep shared awareness of the capacity to see the system as a whole.[7]

2) Soulfulness begins when individuals discover that spirituality is different from religion. It is when the individual crafts "fine distinctions between my rejection of God 'out there' and willingness to apprehend God 'within'. Religion is about answers, and spirituality is about questions."[8]

3) Soul work is being aligned with the spirit. It is a sense of being in harmony with what William James calls the "unseen order of things."[9]

4) The sense of deep community and soul work go together. The psychological sense of community encompasses emotive connectedness of empathy with others sharing values, rituals, and common purpose.[10]

Ian I. MITROFF is a respected management scientist who has given scholarly attention and research to the topic of the soulful organization. In Chapter Four, we focus on some of his research as it applies to soulful leadership. From his research we are able to gather a sense of authors who contribute definitions of the soul required for an empirical investigation of the subject domain of the nature of soulful leadership, such as J. HILLMAN, *The Soul's Code*,[11] T. MOORE, *Care of The*

---

[6] PHILIP H. MIRVIS, "Soul Work in Organizations," *Organization Science* https://doi.org/10.1287/orsc.8.2.,192.

[7] Ibid., 194.

[8] Ibid., 195.

[9] Ibid., 195, 199.

[10] Ibid.

[11] J. HILLMAN, *The Soul's Code: In Search of Character and Calling* (New York: Random House, 1996).

Soul,[12] L. G. BOLMAN and T.E. DEAL, *Leading with Soul,*[13] A. BRISKIN, *The Stirring of Soul in the Workplace,*[14] and T. CHAPPELL, *The Soul of Business.*[15]

Methodology and Principles

We will use a methodology of engaging in a trading zone between a Thomistic faculty-behavioral-psychology and other schools of psychology and organizational studies that pertain to the nature of organizational soulful leadership. This trading zone methodology, it is important to note, is not an attempt to construct a synthesis on the organizational meaning of soulful leadership with other organizational empirical psychologists or consultants, as much as it is an effort to develop a transitional genus on particular topics, practices, and solutions with other disciplines on the principles and behavioral activities of soulful organizational leadership.

Yet, grounded on a metaphysics of organization and a Thomistic organizational psychology, we will, when required, clearly engage in a Thomistic critical analysis of "yes, it is most informative what others propose about the soul, leadership, and the organization, but there is always something most profoundly essential and critical missing when discussing the nature of the organizational leadership and the soul without a metaphysics of organization and a faculty of the soul psychology." Basically, in a Thomistic dissertation on soulful organizational leadership, we start at the beginning with proper first principles.

However, we stress that this dissertation is chiefly a study of the practical function of the executive soulful leader and the diffusion and emulation of exemplar leadership throughout an organization. Fundamentally, it is a study of the executive function as a practice of exemplar virtuous character. We argue that

---

[12] T. MOORE, *Care of the Soul: A Guide for Cultivating Depth and Sacredness in Everyday Life* (New York: Harper Perennial, 1994).

[13] L.G. BOLMAN and T.E. DEAL, *Leading with Soul: An Uncommon Journey of Spirit* (San Francisco: Jossey-Bass, 1996).

[14] A. BRISKIN, *The Stirring Soul in the Workplace* (San Francisco: Jossey-Bass, 1996).

[15] T. CHAPPELL, *The Soul of a Business: Managing for Profit and the Common Good* (New York: Bantam Books, 1994).

exemplar leadership is best comprehended and practiced from the perspective of a Thomistic practical understanding of a faculty-behavioral-psychology.

The soul is, in Thomistic psychology, real. It is as true a reality of human existence as is oxygen, as stated below in principle number one. We do not consider the soul as a type of descriptive and poetic metaphor for the best expression and unifying power of organizational shared values and spiritual feelings. We will follow an Aristotelian-Thomistic definition of the soul. Also, we will approach leadership within the context of an organizational whole. We will also develop a Thomistic faculty-behavioral-psychology that is an application of, as Peter Redpath has defined, a "Faculty Psychology of the Human Person".[16] Therefore, a Thomistic methodology requires that we must begin this endeavor by establishing the necessary first principles necessitated by the subject matter of the organizational, faculty, behavioral psychology of soulful leadership that the soul is the form of the body.

In this Thomistic dissertation, we begin by pointing out that the interpretation of the writings of Thomas Aquinas on the metaphysics of organization and a faculty-behavioral-psychology are grounded primarily on the foundational works of Peter A. REDPATH, namely *A Not–So–Elementary–Metaphysics*, *The Moral Psychology of St. Thomas,* and other quoted writings.[17]

Principle Number One: The soul (a form that gives being and species to the body)

By "soul" we understand that by which a living thing is alive; it is understood, therefore, as existing in a subject, taking "subject" in a broad sense to include not only those actual beings which are subjects of their accidental modifications, but also bare matter or potential being. On the other hand, the body that receives life is more like a subject and a matter than a modification existing in a subject.

---

[16] Peter A. REDPATH, *The Moral Psychology of St. Thomas: An Introduction to Ragamuffin Ethics* (St. Louis: En Route, 2017), 72.

[17] PETER A. REDPATH, *A Not-So-Elementary Christian Metaphysics, Volume One* (St. Louis, MO 63109: En Route Books & Media, 2015)

Since, then, there are three sorts of substance: the compound; matter; and form; and since the soul is neither the compound—the living body itself; nor its matter—the body as the subject that receives life; we have no choice but to say that the soul is a substance in the manner of a form that determines or characterizes a particular sort of body, i.e. a physical body potentially alive.[18]

Principle Two: Virtual quantity (perfection of the form and its operations)

Quantity is twofold. There is quantity of 'bulk' or dimensive quantity, which is to be found only in corporeal things, and has, therefore, no place in God. There is also quantity of 'virtue', which is measured according to the perfection of less, not some nature or form: to this sort of quantity, we allude when we speak of something as being more, or, forasmuch as it is more or less, perfect in heat. Now this virtual quantity is measured firstly by its source—that is, by the perfection of that form or nature: such is the greatness of spiritual things, just as we speak of great heat on account of its intensity and perfection. And so, Augustine says (*De Trin.* vi, 18) that 'in things which are great, but not in bulk, to be greater is to be better', for the more perfect a thing is the better it is. Secondly, virtual quantity is measured by the effects of the form. Now the first effect of form is being, for everything has being by reason of its form. The second effect is operation, for every agent acts through its form. Consequently, virtual quantity is measured both in regard to being and in regard to action: in regard to being, forasmuch as things of a more perfect nature are of longer duration; and in regard to action, forasmuch as things of a more perfect nature are more powerful to act.[19]

Principle Three: The whole soul is diversely in the multiple parts of the body

Since matter exists for the sake of form, form gives an act of existing and species to matter inasmuch as matter is disposed for the operations of the form.

---

[18] St. Thomas AQUINAS, *Commentary on Aristotle's De anima* 2, Lecture 1, nn. 220–221.

[19] St. Thomas AQUINAS, *Summa Theologiae* I, q. 42, a. 1, ad 1.

And therefore, the soul, even though it is one and simple in its essence, perfects the parts of the body in different ways, because the body, which is capable of being perfected by the soul, requires diversity in its parts in order that it may be disposed for the different operations of the soul.

Since the soul exists in a part of the body in the manner just described, no part of the soul is found outside the soul which is in this part of the body. However, it does not follow that no part of the soul exists outside this part of the body, but rather than no part of the soul exists outside the whole body which the soul perfects as a principle.[20]

Principle Four: What is First in a Genus is its Measure, Exemplar and Rule
The leader is like the first part of the body, its brain and heart. And whatever is first and most simple and perfect in a genus (i.e., that in which the nature of the genus is found in a most perfect way)[21] is called the common measure, exemplar,[22] rule,[23] of all things that are in that genus, because each thing is known to have more of the truth of a genus inasmuch as it approaches it; and it is thus that something is known to be more perfect.[24]

Chapter One: The Behavioral Soul

With the awareness that in order to study the nature of organizational soulful leadership we must approach the challenge from the perspective of a metaphysics of organization and a Thomistic Faculty-Behavioral-Psychology. In chapter one, we focus on establishing the approach of a Thomistic faculty-behavioral-psychology as being foundational to the development of a more applied organizational psychology of soulful leadership. It is best to consider the challenge of the dissertation as the development of an applied psychology of organizational

---

[20] St. Thomas AQUINAS, *Disputed Questions on the Soul*, a. 10, ad 2–3.

[21] St. Thomas AQUINAS, *De veritate*, q. 23, a. 7.

[22] St. Thomas AQUINAS, *Summa Contra Gentiles* 3, c. 24, n. 8.

[23] St. Thomas AQUINAS, *Summa theologiae* I-II, q. 90, a. 1.

[24] See especially See AQUINAS, *Commentary on the Metaphysics of Aristotle*, Book 10, lect. 2, nn. 1937–1960; *Super De causis*, lect. 16.

soulful leadership. However, it is only possible to put forth a Thomistic solution to the issue of organizational leadership, if the solution is grounded on a well-developed Thomistic faculty-behavioral-psychology. Therefore, we begin chapter one with a proposed, behavioral, soul psychology as foundational to the study and practice of soulful leadership.

Chapter Two: The Dark Soul

We deliberately begin with an examination of "the Dark Soul." Unfortunately, we seldomly think in terms of organizations as domains of soulfulness. The history of the relationship of leaders and workers in organizations is, as a rule, one of pejorative connotations. It is more frequently expressed and believed that organizations, especially business and government, are perceived as being soulless as opposed to soulful. We examine the reasons for such perceptions and attitudes and suggest that the sense of workers feeling discontented with their organizational existence is more often than not justified. We argue that the main reason for soulless organizational discontent is the result of dark soulless leadership. We contend that the primary reason for soulless leadership is caused by the lack of appropriate executive leadership. Therefore, we begin in this chapter and throughout the issue addressing the issue of the dark soul organizational syndrome as a lack of executive soulful leadership.

Chapter Three: The Virtual Soul

It is necessary that the study of organizational soulful leadership must be grounded on metaphysical principles and a faculty psychology of the powers and acts of the soul. It is in this chapter that we turn our attention to the issue of metaphysics. Unfortunately, it is not usual to draw attention to metaphysics as foundational to the study of organizational leadership. We will, to the contrary, maintain that metaphysics is fundamental to the understanding and practice of organizational leadership, particularly the topic of organizational soulful leadership. The main task of this chapter is to articulate concisely a new respect for metaphysics by executives who act as truly soulful leaders. We began in chapter two and continue in three to define the executive soulful leader as the exemplar of the organization whose soulful character is emulated by the members of the organization. We argue by means of practical examples and metaphysical principles of organization that the exemplar soulful leader diffuses and amplifies the virtuous powers and perfection of the organization. This process of virtual intensity of organizational power must begin with the soulful executive who has a metaphysical sense of organizational perfection.

Chapter Four: The Sensemaking Soul

We examine the evidence that models of traditional bureaucratic organizational leadership are being challenged for various reasons. We examine some of the reasons for the breakdown of the hierarchical authoritarian model of organizational leadership. More specifically, we give attention to the growing interest in the relationship between leadership and spirituality. Increasingly, it has become acceptable to refer to leadership in terms of spirituality and the soul at work. It seems to represent a discontent with the impact of enlightenment philosophy upon Western organizational concepts of leadership. We argue in the search for more spiritual and soulful modes of leadership that a Thomistic organizational practical psychology of soulful leadership is highly appropriate for the disruptive age in quest of the soul. One of the more interesting phenomena developing in the education of present-day organizational leaders is the attention given to the evolving discipline of leadership and sensemaking. There is a recognition that leaders must have highly developed sense making abilities in modern day leadership. On this issue we argue that empirical psychology and leadership education has an inadequate understanding of the intellect and intuition. We propose based on the faculties of the soul a much more accurate understanding of sensemaking based on premodern induction and the sensing and resting of principles in the soul.

Chapter Five: The Estimative Soul

We concentrate more on organizational soulful leadership as a practical science and art. If there is one dominant power of the soul essential to a practical art of leadership, it is the Thomistic estimative power of the soul. The task, therefore, becomes twofold: First, we explain that soulful organizational leadership is exercised in a real-world environment. As any leader knows leadership is about achieving the organizational aim. Every successful leader is a realist because he/she has real goals and objectives. However, the organizational environment is not predictable. Every student of business learns quickly that he/she must lead under the tension of a desired order and an emerging order. Every organizational leader must daily to some extent confront variation and is responsible for the response and control of variation. Leading an organization in conditions of desired and emerging order requires that a leader has a highly developed estimating sense of the soul. This power of the estimating soul is the result of a confluence of internal powers of the soul. We define this confluence of estimative powers as an estimative intelligence which is essential to the practical art of soulful organizational leadership.

Second, the ability to lead by means of the confluence of the estimative powers of the soul also requires a mastery of the soul. Organizational leadership is challenging on a daily basis and over extended arduous periods of time. The demands of decision making and risk taking require mastery of the passions. We suggest that the estimating soul and mastery of the passions is a much more important factor for soulful leadership than emotional intelligence.

Chapter Six: The Big Soul

In the Big Soul, we continue the practical art of organizational soulful leadership. The exemplar as a wise leader with a magnanimous character is a Big Soul leader. It is the exemplar leader who is the organizational role model of virtuous habits. In this chapter, we explain the behavioral dynamics of the moral virtues that enhance a leader's capacity for rational and moral decision making, problem solving, strategic planning, tactical execution, and operational activities.

As opposed to an imposed Kantian type of management top-down ethics of duty and human resource monitoring, we present an everyday faculty-behavioral-psychology of soulful leadership based on a unity of the intellectual and moral virtues. We complete, from the Behavioral Soul of chapter one, the trading zone relationship between a Thomistic faculty-behavioral-psychology with the work of the neo-behaviorist William Baum and his theory of behavior and the observation of molar behavior as compatible with a Thomistic faculty-behavioral-psychology. Most important, we will apply this concept of the observation of molar behavior and nesting activities to the moral virtues. We will conclude by giving cases and practical examples of the moral virtues and nested behavior.

1.

The Behavioral Soul

The aim of this chapter is to establish an Aristotelian-Thomistic foundation for a faculty-behavioral-psychology that is applied to the study and practice of organizational soulful leadership. Faculty is used in the Aristotelian-Thomistic understanding of "the faculties of the soul."

The rudimentary concept of the trading zone is taken from Robert KUGELMANN in his pivotal historical study of psychology, *Neo-Scholasticism, and Catholicism: Contested Boundaries.*[1] KUGELMANN is a psychologist and researcher at the University of Dallas. He also has devoted much of his research and publishing on the contested boundaries between scientific psychology and neo-scholastic rational psychology. Using KUGELMANN's historical study of Catholic psychology and the search for boundaries with empirical psychology, we will divide the quest into three periods: 1) Period One, 1879-1950, 2) Period Two, 1950 to 2000 and 3) Period Three, the present pursuit of the Thomistic behavioral option and neuropsychology ascendancy.

1.1 Period One (1879-1965), Neo-Scholastic Rational Psychology

KUGELMANN clearly spells out how the first period of Catholic psychology and neo-scholastic rational psychology started with Pope Leo XIII and Cardinal Desire Felicine-Francois Joseph MERCIER's classic work *The Origins of Contemporary*

---

[1] Robert KUGELMANN, *Neo-Scholasticism, and Catholicism: Contested Boundaries* (Edinburgh: Cambridge University Press, 2011).

Psychology, spanning to the 1950s. MERCIER was appointed in 1882 by Leo XIII to head the Institute Superior de Philosophie at the University of Louvain to engage in an effort to integrate the findings of natural science with Thomistic thought, and MERCIER was most committed to integrating Thomistic rational psychology with the emerging science of experimental school of psychology founded by Wilhelm WUNDT. MERCIER describes WUNDT's ambitions as the following:

> To study facts, psychological facts; to observe them by themselves, to press them closely, to disentangle their elements, and to measure these alike in their intensity and in their duration to study the "psychic compounds" formed by them and revealed to us by experience under the form of representations and emotions, to fix the empirical laws of their association and recurrence; such is the dominant interest of him who was, if not the creator, yet surely the most vigorous promoter of psycho-physiology.[2]

MERCIER described WUNDT as, "if not the creator, yet surely the most vigorous promoter of psycho-physiology."[3] WUNDT is seen by MERCIER as a scientist who is the product of enlightenment schools of philosophy, i.e. DESCARTES, LOCKE, BERKELEY, and most of all Immanuel KANT. As a physiologist, he is a Kantian idealist who does not exclude a certain type of realism. It is impossible, WUNDT taught, that we must not "deny the objects of our thoughts a certain being of their own […] the subject matter of psychology is the data of experience, as provided immediately to the intuition of consciousness."[4] It is as a Kantian that MERCIER primarily describes WUNDT:

> The world is only made up of our representations and when at last he asks himself what the psychology of the future might be and ought to be, he lays upon it this condition-that it is never to contradict the ideological and critical

---

[2] Desire Felicien Francois Joseph MERCIER, *The Origins of Contemporary Psychology* (New York: P.J. Kenedy & Sons, 1918), 125–126.

[3] Ibid., 126.

[4] Ibid., 128.

theory to which he is inviolably true [...] hence the immediate data of experience are real. But the concrete data of experience imply two inseparable but distinct elements: the content, and the apprehension of such content, the object of consciousness, and the conscious subject. The subjective point of view is that of the natural sciences. [...] Thus, psychology is, by definition, the strictly immediate science of the concrete data of consciousness.[5]

In Period One, Catholic psychology attempted to form a Thomistic synthesis between rational and scientific experimental psychology. The intention of Neo-Scholastic psychology was rooted in the desire to blend the faculties of the soul with experimental testing methodology. This desire for a blending of the method of experimental psychology with Neo-Scholastic psychology is apparent in chapter 8, Thomism of Mercier's *The Origins of Contemporary Psychology* where he looks with enthusiasm for the integration of Thomistic rational and experimental psychology.

We should love science and cultivate it in our schools of philosophy more energetically than ever. The Aristotelian philosophy lends itself better than any other to the interpretation of the facts of experimental psychology. [...] Aristotelian animism, which connects psychology with biology, is the only plausible metaphysical conclusion to be drawn from experimental psychology. [...] On the other hand, if the soul be nothing but mind, if it subsists of itself independently of the living body, and is directly and solely observable through consciousness, a laboratory of experimental psychology becomes inconceivable, for it presupposes a claim to make the soul the subject of experimentation and to weigh it and test its forces etc., it presupposes the material character of the soul.

But if with, Aristotle and all the teachers of the School, we admit that man is a composite substance made up of matter and an immaterial soul that his higher functions are really dependent upon his lower functions, that not one of his

---

[5] Ibid., 127–129.

inward acts is without its physical correlative, not one of his volitions without its representations, not one of his volitions without sensible emotion, at once concrete phenomenon presented to consciousness gets the note of a combination which is both psychological and physiological. It depends both upon conscious introspection and upon biological and physiological observation. In short, we have a clear indication of the raison d'etre of a science of psychophysiology.[6]

The path to this integration will prove difficult because, driven by a spirit of anti-modernism, the Neo-Scholastics are dedicated to apologetical criticism of the philosophical foundations of scientific psychology. For example, the Neo-Scholastic Edward PACE captures an essential aspect of Neo-Scholastic thought when he spoke of the desire "to pierce through the manifold of appearance to the ultimate reality beneath as this passion of unity."[7] As KUGELMANN points out the Neo-Scholastics sought to achieve a synthesis in a metaphysical system of truths discovered by positive sciences. KUGELMANN, in his historical study of the contested boundaries, points out:

> What this meant in practice was chiefly a repeated critique of the inadequate philosophical bases of psychology and reinterpretation of research along Neoscholastic lines. Synthesis existed as an ideal, one that proved elusive to actualize.[8]

1.2 Period Two (1965 to Present), after Vatican II

KUGELMANN documents that Catholic philosophy is no longer Thomistic, and Catholic psychology is no longer Neo-Scholastic rational psychology. Catholic psychology was influenced by continental psychology and moved to a synthesis with

---

[6] Ibid., 339.

[7] KUGELMANN, *Neo-Scholasticism and Catholicism*, 82–83; E.A. PACE, "St. Thomas and modern thought," *Catholic University Bulletin* (2), 188-197.

[8] Ibid. 83

existential phenomenology, psychoanalysis, and humanistic psychology. Catholic psychology moved from a strong Neo-Scholastic foundation of principles and faculties of the soul to a Thomistic pursuit of a dynamic personal self.

After Vatican II, Thomistic philosophy is no longer the official philosophical foundation of Catholicism, and the search is on for a new foundation. Catholic psychologists look for the foundation in the wave of scientific psychology. Coming into the seventies, Catholic universities' departments of philosophy and psychology become completely separated. Scientific empirical psychology is no longer interested in the faculties of the soul and especially the nature of the internal senses. Catholic philosophical and practical psychology becomes engaged in the pursuit of a humanistic personality integration methodology.

We see major mistakes in Period One and Two. Period One attempted the synthesis with the faculties of the soul and mostly scientific experimental psychology. Period Two attempted to redefine the soul as a process of introspective consciousness, personal identity, and discovery of Dasein. We argue that we are coming into a Period Three born-again period of Thomistic psychology—in many ways a return to Period One without the influence of Cartesian transcendental and analytical Thomists.

1.3 Emerging Period Three Thomistic Psychology

In a third period, Thomistic psychology breaks cleanly from the synthesis with experimental measurement psychology and phenomenological *epoche*, i.e., transcendental reduction. Thomistic rational psychology becomes a Thomistic behavioral psychology grounded on a well-defined foundation of the faculties of the soul, metaphysical principles of one and the many (genus and species), creation and participation, particular reason, and a trading zone with behavioral methodological observation of individual and social behavior in the process of coping with life, striving for a continuous sense of the soul as the behavioral organizer of personal and communal identity and habits of behavioral activity.

This Trading Zone methodology is explained in KUGELMANN's chapter One, From Neo-Scholastic Psychology to a Thomistic Rational Behavioral Psychology.

The trading zone is concerned with what happens at disciplinary boundaries. KUGELMANN turns to Peter GALISON's metaphor of "trading zone." Between different cultures and applied to different sciences as working on a common project such as the development of radar or of nanotechnology. Anthropologists have been most interested in "trading zones." As KUGELMANN explains,[9] one of the most remarkable domains of such investigations has been in the field of anthropological linguistics surrounding the problems of pidginization and creolization. Both refer to languages at the boundary between groups. A pidgin is a simplified form of communication that is not a full-fledged language, whereas creole is a language, for example, Modern English began as a creole between Norman French and Anglo-Saxon. GALISON provides an example of a 1960 era textbook in quantum mechanics that attempts to create a stable pidgin language for an audience outside the subculture of theorists that is for the subculture of experimentalist in physics.

> [F]or example, [...] cognitive science came from a variety of backgrounds: artificial intelligence, linguistics, neuroscience, philosophy, and psychology. The places where the exchanges occurred were journals, university departments, and professional organizations; however, conferences "are probably the closest analog to intercultural trading zones, as people from various disciplines and countries gather to exchange ideas."[10]

KUGELMANN claims that the point of intellectual trading zones is the exchange of ideas that the trading zone exchange has made it possible for some subcultures in psychology to engage in exchange with religious communities and traditions.[11] He adds, however:

> Some subcultures, in particular the more narrowly defined experimental ones, have no interest in exchanges, nor do the religious groups seem interested in their wares. But [...] in both theoretical and applied areas of psychology there

---

[9] Ibid., 352.

[10] Ibid., 352–353.

[11] Ibid., 353.

has been lively interest in the boundaries, and much interest in what the other side has. In these trading zones, there are many crossings and exchanges.[12]

Yet Thomistic psychology must exercise serious caution in trading zone exchanges. In a bold confrontation with the basic failure of scientific psychology, the influential Thomistic psychologist Robert Edward BRENNAN in 1941 warned that scientific psychology does not have the answers to the existential pursuit of meaning, purpose, spirituality, and the cure of mental illness. BRENNAN, in his formative work *Thomistic Psychology: A Philosophical Analysis of the Nature of Man*, concludes in the final chapter *Modern Psychology Modern Psychology and The Thomistic Synthesis* with an intrepid apologetical assertion:

> Without a soul, psychology is like a temple without a deity or a home without a family spirit. […] It is difficult to see, then, how the investigator can avoid assuming some definite philosophic attitude toward the subject matter which he is studying. In this case, the subject matter is man, regarding whom there can be but only one satisfactory attitude. It is the position which recognizes in every human being, regardless of race or age, a creature possessed of soul and body; a cosmic entity made out of spirit and matter, an organism quickened with a principle of rational life; a corporeal substance that not only vegetates with plants and senses with the animals but also, and more importantly, reflects on its own intellectual nature and stretches out, by its faculty of divine love, toward a Good that is supremely perfect.[13]

Of course, slowly from the modern to postmodern period the straightforward problem is that scientific psychology has increasingly eliminated the soul and replaced it with consciousness.

We suggest that we must take BRENNAN'S warning about entering a "trading zone relationship," especially in Period Three development of Thomistic psychology.

---

[12] Ibid.

[13] Robert Edward BRENNAN, *Thomistic Psychology: A Philosophical Analysis of the Nature of Man* (New York: MacMillan, 1941), 364.

We define Period Three as really beginning in 1949 with D.O. HEBB's book, *The Organization of Behavior: A Neuropsychological Theory.*[14] The term, "neuropsychological," was undefined. In 1957, the term became a recognized designation for a subfield of the neurosciences when Heinrich KLUVER, in *Behavior Mechanisms in Monkeys,* suggested the book would be of interest to neuropsychologists. In 1960, the term was given wide publicity when it appeared in Karl LASHLEY's *The Neuropsychology of Lashley.*[15] Therefore, we select 1960 as when psychology became the science of human behavior based on the function of the brain. Neuropsychology aided by advanced brain scanning technology, e.g., functional magnetic imaging (MRI), positron emission psychology (PET) promised the science of psychology as the final response to B.F. SKINNER's challenge to non-behavioral psychology that it is possible to study behavior by entering the black box of the mind. Neuropsychology has become confident that a new age of human psychology is here because we can study neural networks by means of various extremely advanced methods of brain imaging.

As RACHLIN explains, Neuropsychology of the present, in a way, is a return to the Renaissance science that began to explain many aspects of the world in purely physical terms, e.g., discovery of the circulation of blood and the function of the heart as a mechanical pump was the most successful example of this widespread movement. DESCARTES was a contributor to this movement. He expanded the concept of involuntary behavior to include the behavior of all non-human animals and some of the behavior of humans. Involuntary behavior consisted of automatic, relatively simple motions: sneezing, puling one's foot from the fire, focusing one's eyes, and so forth. Such behavior was explained by DESCARTES in terms of causal chains (later called "reflexes") originating in the environment (and ultimately in God as the creator of the world). DESCARTES' reflexive behavior worked as:

---

[14] Bruce Darry, "On the Origin of the Term Neuropsychology," *Neuropsychologia,* 23 (6), (1985) 813-814

[15] Spencer, Karl, *The Neuro Psychology of Lashley. Selected Papers of K.S. Lashley,* ed. Frank Beach ((New York: McGraw Hill, 1960)

A stimulus, such as a hot flame (A) on a boy's foot (B) tugged at a thin string within a nerve (C); the string opened a valve (D) in a chamber (F) in the center of the brain and allowed animal spirits (a vitalistic gas distilled in the boy's heart and fed into his brain) to flow down the tube and inflate the muscle; the inflation contracted the muscle and moved the boy's foot out of the fire.[16]

In the case of voluntary behavior, the opening and closing of valves in the chamber at the center of the brain were caused by minute movements of the pineal gland, which in turn were controlled directly by the boy's will. Thus, the ultimate cause of involuntary human behavior was placed by DESCARTES inside the behaving person, directly knowable by that person but not observable by anyone else.[17]

Johannes MULLER (1850-1858) was the foremost authority on physiology of his day. His law of nerve energies (LOSNE) extended DESCARTES conception of the mind as prisoner within the body to nineteenth-century physiology. He formulated "the law of specific nerve energies" that stated the mind communicates not with objects in the outside world but only with our nerves. LOSNE says that our sensations, perceptions, thought, and so on, have no qualities in common with things in the world, but serve only as arbitrary signs or markers or representations of objects. As E.G. BORING points out, "The central and fundamental principle of the doctrine is that we are directly aware not of objects, but of our nerves themselves; that is to say, the nerves are intermediaries between perceived objects and the mind and thus impose their own character on the mind."[18] Although MULLER was a vitalist, it was not the case with his students. BORING says:

In 1845 […] four young, enthusiastic, and idealistic physiologists, all pupils of the great Johannes Muller, all later to be very famous, met together and formed a pact. […] They were in order of age, Carl Ludwig, who was then twenty-

---

[16] RACHLIN, *The Escape of The Mind* (New York, NY: OXFORD, University Press, 2014) 37.

[17] Ibid., 36–38.

[18] E.G. BORING, *A History of experimental psychology*, second edition (New York: Appleton, 1957), 82.

nine, Emil du Bois-Reymond, Ernst Brucke and Herman von Helmholtz, then twenty-four. They were joining forces to fight vitalism, the view that life involves forces other than those found in the interaction of inorganic bodies. The great Johannes Muller was a vitalist, but these men were of the next generation. DuBois and Brucke [later to become Freud's teacher] even pledged between them a solemn oath that they would compel the acceptance of this truth: "No other forces than common chemical ones are active within the organism."[19]

We could say that the beginning of neuropsychology, cognitive psychology and introspective psychiatry really begins with "Muller's law that our conscious experience of the stimuli is directly due to the place in the brain where nerves end and not all to the stimuli themselves."[20] As RACHLIN explains, for MULLER a blow to the head stimulates the visual nerves and we "see stars" or auditory nerves and we "hear chimes." But there are no sounds or lights within our bodies—only nervous energy. MULLER held that our minds have access only to this nervous energy:

> From this energy, plus whatever innate tendencies our minds possess (according to Muller the Kantian categories: space, time, moral sense, and so forth), they must construct the world. How our minds, manage this construction became the business of all psychology for the next hundred years and of non-behavioristic psychology, even up today.[21]

As RACHLIN explains, MULLER's students were identity theorists who believed that the construction of the world from nervous energy took place in the physical brain rather than in a non-physical mind. HELMHOLTZ's identity theory, as well as modern neural identity theory, recognized the existence of the unconscious mind. The neural identity theory neatly separates the mental from the conscious and opens psychological investigation to methods other than conscious introspection. As

---

[19] Ibid., 708.

[20] RACHLIN, *The Escape of The Mind*, 46.

[21] Ibid.

RACHLIN suggests, "the project of modern neural identity theory may be likened to the study of an unknown computer-neuroscientists opening it up in an attempt to discover its hardware, psychologists operating its keys and mouse and observing the results on its screens in an attempt to discover its program."[22]

We suggest that it is obvious why the desired synthesis between scholastic rational psychology and the experimental psychology of MULLER, HELMHOLTZ and WUNDT was never a possibility. For example, assistant professor of psychology at St. Louis University Francis L. HARMON, in his classic textbook of 1938, *Principles of Psychology*, writes in the introduction:

> The psychologist observes, describes, and classifies; then attempts to organize his data and to formulate hypotheses and laws of nature. This constitutes the first step in psychology; because it is based upon the actual experience of mental phenomenal or empirical psychology.
>
> The second phase of psychological investigation emphasizes the exercise of reasoning rather than direct observation. Rational psychology, as the study is called, is concerned with the nature of the mind. Starting with the conclusions established through observation, the inquirer applies these conclusions to the solution of such problems as attributes of the soul, its union with the body, the nature of intellectual activity and freedom of the will. Although both observation and reasoning necessarily play a part in rational as well as empirical psychology, the ultimate test of the latter is the adequacy of observation; of the former, logicality of inference-presupposing, of course, that the data have been noted accurately and completely.
>
> In practice it is a mistake to attempt too sharp a separation between empirical and rational psychology. Knowledge of the one is but a steppingstone to an understanding of the other. If psychology is to be called the study of human nature, this study must be carried through to its completion, which, as we have remarked, involves the recognition of the soul itself as the final animating principle of human life. Thus, while the emphasis in this book will be primarily upon the observation of mental life as manifested

---

[22] Ibid., 48–49.

in man's conscious experience and behavior, we shall not hesitate, where the occasion demands, to draw necessary conclusions as to the nature of man himself.[23]

Obviously, HARMON follows in the tradition of period one Neo-Scholastic Rational Psychology. As a 1930s Catholic hybrid experimental/rational psychologist, he boldly and convincingly holds that "knowledge of the one is but a steppingstone to an understanding of the other." In other words, it is a synthesis waiting to happen. He is not really looking so much for a "trading zone" between empirical and rational psychology because a trading zone is an exchange of ideas and methods between psychological traditions for, as a rule, research in mutual areas of concern, e.g., research in marriage counseling, addiction treatment, etc. HARMON, and the Period One tradition, assume the synthesis is possible based on an inevitable and emerging empirical rational meta-psychology. It should be noted more specifically that it is really a synthesis with the principles and methods of 19th experimental psychology. In fact, it seems as if there is the possibility of an eventual empirical-rational genus of the science of the mental life "as manifested in man's conscious experience and behavior."

Robert KUGELMANN's historical study is about the contested boundaries of psychology and Catholic teaching. In the nineteenth century Neo-Scholastic period the boundaries are clearly defined based on the superseding boundary. It is the issue of the soul as KUGELMANN explains:

The Neoscholastic solution to the problem of science and religion lay in granting science its proper autonomy and situating it within a hierarchy of knowledge. At the summit gained by human reason unaided by Divine Revelation lay metaphysics, which studies the ultimate causes of things. This partitioning and hierarchical arrangement gave room for scientific psychology

---

[23] Francis L. HARMON, *Principles of Psychology* (Milwaukee: The Bruce Publishing Company, 1938), 5.

to develop. The nature of the human soul, however, remained both the pole star and a stumbling block for Neoscholastic psychologists.[24]

However, as Vatican II began to call for a renewal of a more progressive and ecumenical theology, Thomistic philosophy assumed less of a clear and defined boundary line between Catholic teaching and science. Notably, in terms of the boundaries between Catholics and psychology, Neo-Scholastic considerations of the soul changed as well. KUGELMANN writes:

> Catholic psychologists, drawing on Jung and others still explicitly spoke of the soul, for the most part the discourse changed to the person, the self, the I-Thou relationship, and concepts such as existence and Dasein. These concepts, while still keeping psychologists focused on the uniquely human aspects of psychology and thus countering reductionistic tendencies, do not have the theological denotations that soul carries. They thus fostered the development of a psychology that deals with religious and spiritual aspects of life without being tied to a specific religious tradition as was Neo-Scholasticism. While psychology and religion remained knotted together in many ways, the soul as a stumbling block was removed along with Neo-Scholasticism.[25]

The problem is that Neo-Scholastic and Catholic empirical psychologists attempted an impossible task, i.e., forming a synthesis with nineteenth century empirical psychology that had no desire to understand the soul and the faculties of the soul as the very foundation of a science of human behavior, as did ARISTOTLE and AQUINAS. How is it possible to form a meta-psychology with the disciples of MULLER who had taken an oath that no other forces than common chemical ones are active within the organism? The attempt at this synthesis could only end with a type of Faustian bargain where the soul becomes an existential spiritual metaphor for empirical psychology, and Thomistic psychologists must sell their nobility for modern academic recognition. What else could be expected when Neo-Scholastics

---

[24] KUGELMANN, *Neo-Scholasticism and Catholicism*, 116;

[25] Ibid., 117.

sought a synthesis with the nineteenth century and modern identity theorists who held the science of behavior is based on a scientific cult myth of "common chemicals active within the organism," as opposed to the Thomistic tradition of matter and form and human nobility, as AQUINAS teaches:

> But we must observe that the nobler a form is, the more it rises above corporeal matter, the less it is merged in matter, and the more it excels matter by its power and its operation; hence we find that the form of a mixed body has another operation not caused by its elemental qualities. And the higher we advance in the nobility of forms the more we find that the power of the form excels elementary matter; as the vegetative soul excels the form of the metal, and the sensitive soul excels the vegetative soul. Now the human soul is the highest and noblest of forms. Wherefore it excels corporeal matter in its power by the fact that it has an operation and a power in which corporeal matter has no share whatever. The power is called intellect.[26]

1.4 The Behavioral Trading Zone

As explained above, a trading zone is where we cross over to other disciplines and exchange theories and practices with very specific targets in mind. We could say that we are interested in learning and borrowing for the sake of problem solving within complementary disciplines. The initial idea of a trading zone relationship with behavioral psychology came from the larger-than-life modern Aristotelian-Thomistic philosopher Mortimer J. ADLER, who was known in popular parlance as a critical realist. It was his book on the mind and the limitations of the brain in terms of defining the nature of a person, *Intellect: Mind over Matter*. ADLER treats the basic issues regarding the boundaries between classical philosophy and a neuropsychology of the brain, such as 1) Is the mind observable, 2) Is our intellect unique, 3) Is the intellect immaterial, 4) Artificial Intelligence, 5) Extraterrestrial intelligence. It is important to note that ADLER's first PhD was in experimental psychology. He soon

---

[26] AQUINAS, *Summa Theologiae* I, q. 76 a. 2.

began to realize that scientific psychology was not providing answers to the fundamental questions about the pursuit of truth, moral good, education, political order, and the nature of human happiness. Consequently, he turned to classical philosophy, particularly common-sense realism. This transition is obvious in *Intellect: Mind over Matter* as he treats the primary obstacle between classical metaphysics and postmodern scientific psychology, i.e., the dematerialized intellect.

> In antiquity, the word "soul" (in Greek, psyche; in Latin, anima) was used to signify whatever it was in living organisms that made them alive, active without being acted upon. Since plants are living organisms, they too, have souls, conferring on them the vegetative powers of nourishment, growth, and reproduction. Animals have souls that confer upon them additional powers-the powers of sense, of appetite or desire, and of locomotion. In addition to endowing man with all the vital powers possessed by plants and other animals, the human soul gives man his distinctive power of conceptual thought, the power of judging and reasoning and the power of free choices.[27]

The concept of an Aristotelian-Thomistic philosophical apologetics seems to describe most of ADLER's writings, but *Intellect: Mind over Matter* is vitally important in the confrontation between metaphysics and scientific neuropsychology. ADLER begins his defense of the importance of the dematerialized human being in the tradition of psychology and points to the source of scientific psychology's beginnings and meta-traditions. He develops a metaphysical defense of the dematerialized nature of a human being based on a philosophical psychology of methodological behaviorism.

> I will try to explain at length why, like behaviorists of this century, beginning with John B. Watson, I reject the whole tradition of introspective psychology that had its beginnings in early modern times with Thomas Hobbes and John Locke. [...] If the supposed introspectively observed contents of the mind—its percepts, memories, images, and thoughts, concepts, or ideas—called attention

---

[27] Mortimer J. ADLER, *Intellect: Mind Over Matter* (New York: MacMillan,1990), 10.

to themselves, they would necessarily distract our attention from the objects that we consciously experience. If they drew attention to themselves exclusively, such attention would exclude those objects entirely from our conscious experience.

The objects, consciously experienced, are of two sorts: private and public. Private are all bodily feelings and emotions—feelings of pleasure and pain, of hunger and thirst, of fear and anger. These private objects of consciousness belong exclusively in the experience of this individual or that individual. Public are the objects that we and others apprehend in common and being the same objects experienced by two or more individuals can be talked about by them.

This distinction between public and private objects of our conscious experience calls for a parallel distinction between two kinds of mental processes: cognitive and affective. The affects are directly experienced bodily feelings and emotions. They are always that which we experience, never that by which we experience something. In sharp contrast, cognitions—perceptions, memories, imaginations, and thoughts—are always that by which we experience the objects they make present to our minds. They are never the experienced objects themselves, never that which is apprehended by the mind.

In denying an introspective awareness of the cognitive contents of the mind, I would describe myself as a methodological behaviorist. I agree with Professor JOHN B. WATSON that, apart from subjectively experience bodily feelings, the contents of the mind cannot be introspectively observed. At the same time, I disagree with his metaphysical materialism—his assertions that only bodies, and their motions exist and his denial that anything mental exist.

To be a methodological, but not materialistic, behaviorist is to take the position that whatever can be said about the mind and its contents, or its processes and products, neither of which can be directly observed must be inferred from behavior that is directly observed. From the observable fact that you and I are discussing a painting on the wall, I need not infer that each of us perceives it, for that is an act of our minds that each of us can introspectively observe. But I must infer that there is in my mind a percept and in your mind a percept-product of our acts of perceiving that by which the painting has become an object we can discuss with one another.

That is the first inference I must make as a methodological behaviorist. A second inference is that each of us, being reflexively aware of the acts of his or her own mind, can infer that minds have certain generic powers and also as many different specific powers as there are distinct types of mental acts that we are able to perform. On what basis do we distinguish the diverse powers of our mind or the diverse acts the basis of inferring the existence of these powers.[28]

The other major issue that ADLER addresses is the principle of the sufficiency and insufficiency of scientific materialistic neuro brain psychology. In his chapter on "Is the Intellect Immaterial?"[29] he develops his apologetics of insufficiency. The basic argument is that the brain is necessary for the understanding of the human intellect, but it is not sufficient. The argument then reaches its conclusion in a first principle of an Aristotelian-Thomistic behavioral psychology.

Our concepts are universal in their signification of objects that are kinds or classes of things rather than individuals that are particular instances of these classes or kinds. Since they have universality, they cannot exist physically or be embodied in matter. But concepts do exist in our minds. They are there as acts of our intellectual power. Hence that power must be an immaterial power, not one embodied in a material organ such as the brain.

The action of the brain, therefore, cannot be the sufficient condition of conceptual thought, though it may still be a necessary condition thereof, insofar as the exercise of our power of conceptual thought depends on the exercise of our powers of perception, memory, and imagination, which are corporeal powers embodied in our sense-organs and brain.[30]

Therefore, it appears obvious, from reading KUGELMANN's *Neo-Scholasticism and Catholicism: Contested Boundaries* and *Adler's Intellect: Mind Over Matter*, if

---

[28] Ibid., 13; 21–22.

[29] Ibid., 50.

[30] Ibid.

Thomistic psychologists are looking for trading zone relationships with empirical psychology, then it is best to look for dealings in behavioral psychology. It is possible to construct a "trading zone crossover" exchange with the non-radical Skinnerian brand of behavioral psychologists, e.g., Howard RACHLIN, Edwin B. HOLT, and William H. BAUM. As we engage in a "trading zone crossover" exchange with behavioral psychologists somewhat compatible with Thomistic psychology, we must heed the warning of BRENNAN that without a soul, psychology is like a temple without a deity or a home without a family spirit. We might expand BRENNAN's insight and say that an organizational psychology without a foundation of the faculties of the soul would be a Thomistic faculty- behavioral psychology like a temple without a deity.

We are, however, not entering into a trading zone crossover with cognitive or a cognitive behavioral psychology. Cognitive psychology is most often the preferred school with organizational psychologists, especially for techniques in organizational learning and skill development.[31] We hold that it is a psychology based on a philosophy of mentalism.

Cognitive psychology began in the 1950s as a reaction against behaviorism.[32] Behaviorists rejected studying the mind because internal mental states cannot be

---

[31] See, for example, James L. BOWDITCH and Anthony F. BUONO, *A Primer on Organizational Behavior* (New York: John Wiley & Sons, 2000), 2: "Thus, learning by experience, which involves practicing a skill (such as decision making under uncertainty) in a simulated situation (such as the classroom), is thought to improve an individual's ability to perform on the job. Within this context, many OB instructors attempt to develop such key management skills as working in teams, effective listening, problem solving, managing conflict, delegating tasks, giving directions, and motivating and leading others. Although there are differences of opinion as to which of these approaches is indeed the most effective, it seems that a combination of cognitive learning and skill development is the key to management education. This book provides the foundation for a *cognitive understanding* of OB. [...] the book is intended to be part of an *integrative approach* to learning about behavior in organizations."

[32] Perhaps the most formative person in the school of cognitive psychology movement of the 50s is Norbert WIENER. His major work is *Cybernetics or Control and Communication in Animals & Machine* (Cambridge, Massachusetts, 1948 and 1961). The cognitive approach

observed and objectively measured. Cognitive psychologists considered it essential to look at the mental processes of an organism and how these influence behaviors. As a result, cognitive psychology defined humans as information processors, arguing information processing in humans resembles that in computers, and is based on transforming information, storing information, and retrieving information from memory.

> The computer information-processing theories assume that humans, like computers, process information serially. That is processed one step after another. Some aspects of human cognition may indeed be explained in terms of serial processing, but psychobiological findings and other cognitive research seem to indicate other aspects of human cognition. These aspects involve parallel processing, in which multiple operations go on all at once.[33]

We have, therefore, defined in this chapter a Thomistic faculty-behavioral-psychology that we apply to the art of organizational soulful leadership. It is called a faculty-behavioral-psychology because it is grounded on an Aristotelian-Thomistic understanding and application of the faculties of the soul to the issue of organizational soulful leadership. At times throughout this dissertation we refer to the study as a *psychology of soulful leadership*; however, it is the same construct as a *Thomistic faculty-behavioral- psychology*. It is in chapters five and six that we develop in detail the principles and methods of a Thomistic faculty-behavioral-psychology as a practical psychology of soulful leadership in terms of behavioral principles and organizational applications.

---

is probably the most dominant approach in psychology today and has been applied to a wide range of practical and theoretical contexts. Cognitive psychology combines with other methods. behaviorism, social learning, organizational learning, cognitive behavioral coaching, social learning, evolutionary psychology, cognitive neuroscience and especially the rapid interests in artificial intelligence.

[33] STERNBERG ROBERT J. *Cognitive Psychology* (Belmont, CA:Wadsworth,2009) 329

2.

The Small Dark Soul

The aim of this chapter is to present the opposite of organizational soulful leadership with the concept of the dark soul. It is a metaphor used to describe dysfunctional organizational pathology that is the result of dark soul executive leadership. We introduce the Thomistic soulful solution to dark soul executive leadership with the concept and function of the exemplar executive organizational leader.

2.1 The Dark Soul of Executive Organizational Leadership

An accepted foundational text in organizational psychology is *Organizational Psychology* by Edgar H. SCHEIN.[1] The field began in 1965 with the first edition of *Organizational Psychology* and was structured around "three key thematic concepts, including (1) managerial assumptions about human nature, (2) the psychological contract, and (3) the organization as a dynamic, open, coping, developing system."[2] The discipline rapidly became "interdisciplinary with contributions from various psychologists, sociologists, anthropologists, scientists and systems theorists interested in understanding the organizational phenomena."[3] As the field developed, SCHEIN identified the multiple perspectives of organizational psychology:

---

[1] Edgar H. SCHEIN, *Organizational Psychology* (Upper Saddle River: Prentice-Hall, 1994).

[2] Ibid., Preface xiv.

[3] Ibid., 3.

The effective utilization of people in any organized effort has always been a pressing problem in society. The pharaoh building a pyramid faced problems fundamentally similar to those faced by the corporation executive or a university president today. Each must figure out (1) what he or she is basically trying to accomplish; (2) how to organize the work to achieve the goals selected; (3) how to recruit, train, allocate work to, and manage the human resources (workers and managers) available to do the work; (4) how to create work conditions and reward and punishment systems that will enable morale to remain effective over long periods of time; (5) how to change the organization in response to the pressures that arise from technological and social change, both in the external environment and within the organization itself; and (6) how to cope with the competition and other forces which derive from other organizations, from units within the organization such as unions, from regulatory agencies, and ultimately from its own "growing pains." These and many other questions which lie at the heart of any "organization" have had to be faced and resolved by politicians, managers, bureaucrats, and leaders throughout history.

Such organizational questions can be viewed from at least two major perspectives: (1) the perspective of the individual employee who depends upon the organization as a source of work, economic livelihood, membership, identity, social contact, and the basic life routines, acknowledging the fact that most people most people in modern society spend the bulk of their waking hours in some form of organization; and (2) the perspective of the manager of the organization who is acting on behalf of the organization, creating policies and making decisions which affect the day to day routines of large numbers of individuals and which ultimately affect the destiny of the organization as a whole. This latter perspective is a kind of "organizational" perspective but should not be construed to mean that the organization acts as an abstract entity; rather, it acts through the individual behavior of certain key members in crucial managerial or leadership roles.[4]

---

[4] Ibid., 4.

SCHEIN in his foundational text in organizational psychology divided the discipline into four major divisions of equal importance to scientific research and practical application. The proposed divisions for scientific inquiry are: 1) The Individual and the Organization, 2) Motivation and Assumptions About Human Nature, 3) Leadership and Participation, 4) Groups in Organizations, and 5) Organizational Structure and Dynamics. This dissertation will focus primarily on the subject division of leadership and participation as the most important in a science of organizational psychology. Since a Thomistic Organizational Psychology finds it necessary to apply principles and practices from a metaphysics of organization, the function of executive soulful leadership and participation is selected as the main topic of this dissertation. It is, therefore, necessary to emphasize from the beginning that a Thomistic organizational psychology, unlike empirical organizational psychology, is grounded on a defined Aristotelian-Thomistic metaphysics of organization.

SCHEIN states that organizational psychology is the perspective of the individual employee whose livelihood, personal and social identity and the bulk of his waking hours is shaped by his/her organizational involvement. What is missing in this perspective is the extent that a work organization shapes our existential spiritual identity and impacts our moral identity.

The influence of corporate business culture upon the modern American lifestyle and moral values is vividly portrayed in SLOAN WILSON'S novel, *The Man in the Gray Flannel Suit.*[5] His novel and his central character Tom Rath is the epitome of the influence of the powerful effect of the corporate cultural on the lifestyle of the 1950s cultural identity of a rational and moral organizational conformity. *The Man in the Gray Flannel Suit* is a metaphor for the Durkheim's culture of modern anomie and the erosion of traditional moral values of family, community, and public responsibility.

> Durkheim thus saw anomie as the erosion of moral restraint, releasing in a person's restless, insatiable cravings—unbridled acquisitiveness—whose inevitable consequence is frustration, stress, and depression. "One does not advance when one proceeds toward no goal," he wrote, "or—which is the same

---

[5] Sloan Wilson, *Man in the Gray Flannel Suit* (Cambridge, MA: DaCapo Press, 1958)

thing—when the goal is infinity. To pursue a goal which is unattainable is to condemn oneself to a state of perpetual unhappiness. The theory of anomie as decay or abandonment of moral stricture is usefully applied to the timely problem of corporate malfeasance, placed in high relief by the American corporate governance and accounting scandals of 2001–02 (Enron, WorldCom, Adelphia, and so on). A common interpretation of the ethical/legal lapses that proliferated in this period is that the implicated firms were imbued with a gun-slinging "cowboy culture," or worse, a "culture of corruption." The implicit subtext is that, had they not been immersed in such strong but errant cultures, the managers of those companies might have behaved less badly.[6]

Tom Rath, as described by DIAMOND SHARP,[7] is the metaphor for the corporate men wearing a tailored Gray suit, wingtip shoes and regimental tie, catching the early Connecticut train and living the American dream of the suburban values of consumption and the getting ahead, self-reliant individualist. Gregory Peck plays Tom Rath in the film adaptation of the novel *The Man in The Gray Flannel Suit*, a story of post-World War Two America's new ideological cultural war that pits communism against free market individualism. Rath returns from the war and struggles with his family to make ends meet. He has fought for freedom but now returns to struggle to make it with a low- paying and unfulfilling job.

Tom is a Harvard graduate working for a charitable organization and by means of a personal contact gets a job at the United Broadcast Corporation. The President is Ralph Hopkins, played by Fredric March, who has sacrificed his family life and especially his tarnished relationship with his daughter, who hires and mentors Rath. Tom learns well the demands of success at the UBC ego-driven, hedonistic, and competitive agency, and he is a man caught in the tension between the authentic goals of family, marriage and trying to do something meaningful with one's life and yet the challenge of having to serve a corporate ethos and someone else's goals to make a

---

[6] James R. LINCOLN and Didier GUILLOT, "Durkheim and Organizational Culture," *IRLE Working Paper*, 108–04 (2004), 13.

[7] DIAMOND SHARP, "SLOAN, MAN IN THE GRAY FLANNEL SUIT," *READING JOURNAL*, WORDPRESS.COM/2012/28

living. The following quotes from Sloan WILSON's novel describe the existential anomie of the emerging modern corporate world:

> But when you come right down to it, why does he hire me? To help him do what he wants to do-obviously that's why any man hires another. And if he finds that I disagree with everything he wants to do, what good am I to him? I should quit if I don't like what he does, but I want to eat, and so, like a million other guys in a gray flannel suit, I'll always pretend to agree, until I get enough to be honest without being hurt. That's not being crooked, it's just being smart... How smoothly one becomes, not a cheat, exactly, not really a liar, just a man who'll say anything for pay.[8]
>
> The trick is to learn it's a disconnected world... where Thou Shalt Not Kill and the fact that one has killed a great many men means nothing, absolutely nothing, for now is the time to raise legitimate children, and make money, and dress properly, and think of oneself as what? That makes no difference, he thought—I'm just a man in a gray flannel suit.[9]

Edgar H. SCHEIN, in his seminal work on the nature of organizational psychology, established the multiple perspectives for the development of the field of study, e.g. the definition and development of an organization, recruitment and training of personnel, utilization of resources, integration of functions and divisions, the need for sociological situational perspective, behavioral contingency theories, rational-social, self-actualization assumptions, the structure of groups and intergroup problems, formal and informal organization, organization as rational natural and complex open systems and organizations and effective coping. SCHEIN's perspective on organizational behavior like other empirical organizational psychologists is an application of various cognitive behavioral models based mostly on research of behavior traits, interpersonal relationships, reward systems, teamwork dynamics and,

---

[8] Sloan WILSON, *The Man in the Gray Flannel Suit* (Cambridge, Ma.: Dacapo Press, Perseus Books,1995), 183.

[9] Ibid., 98.

since the 1980s, the formal and non-formal organization, best practices, leadership coaching and evolving organizational.

2.2 Finding the Soul

From the standpoint of a Thomistic organizational psychology of the function of executive leadership, it is argued that this basically strong cognitive behavioral approach to organizational psychology is necessary but not sufficient. The psychiatrist Mar ÁLVAREZ SEGURA and psychologists Martín F. ECHAVARRÍA and Paul C. VITZ speak to the fact that "the rupture between philosophy and psychology, especially moral philosophy, has brought on the idea that personality itself is the result of either biological or social conditions. The underlying connection between ethics and psychology has not been explicitly addressed."[10]

In the above quote Tom Rath states, "The trick is to learn it's a disconnected world." Herein lies the glaring issue of the cause of anomie that Tom the organizational soulless man must learn to live in a disconnected world. It is an issue of an individual and organizational sense of being in a state of disconnectedness. Tom is suffering from a loss of a sense of an integrated personality.

We might look at Tom Rath from the perspective of Karen HORNEY as the prototype of organizational neurotic traits. HORNEY's school of psychoanalysis is uniquely applicable to an organizational understanding of the rational, moral, and

---

[10] Mar ÁLVAREZ, Martín F. ECHAVARRÍA and Paul C. VITZ, "A psycho-ethical approach to personality disorders: The role of volitionality," *New Ideas in Psychology*, 47 (2017), 49–56. This combined authorship points to the rupture between psychology and ethics that has led to an oversimplification of the study of personality disorders. They claim that a more integrated perspective including the dimension of volitionality and the similarity with classical moral philosophy concept of vicious character and how vicious cognition develops is approached from a psychological and ethical perspective. In this work attention is drawn to a major insufficiency of the psycho-ethical approach to current studies of PD is "This is why Millon, Blaney and Davis (1999, chap. 4, p. 551) stated, no other area in the study of psychopathology is fraught with more controversy than the PDs." In all this process, the interaction between social factors with biological influences has been studied, little or no attention has been paid to the participation of the human will in PD development.

psychological limitations of leadership. In any organization, the executive function and any level of leadership brings heavy responsibility and stress. Especially in business the livelihood of the leader depends on his/her ability and willingness to accept the responsibility and the stress for their own livelihood and all the employees, the owners, and contractual relationships with customers.

HORNEY maintains, "Neuroses thus represents a peculiar kind of struggle for life under difficult conditions. Their very essence consists of disturbances in the relation to self and others and conflicts arising on these grounds."[11] Under the heavy responsibilities and stress of leadership, neurotic trends are exaggerated, and the leader must struggle to maintain or regain a rational, emotional and moral center of gravity. Tom, the organizational neurotic, says, "… time to raise children, and make money and dress properly and think of oneself as what?" Magda B. Arnold, a psychologist of major importance in the development of Thomistic psychology writes:

> For the man who simply drifts, whose self-ideal is the whim of the moment, who follows all his impulses and inclinations, there may be no obvious emotional disturbance… In these cases, there is a disturbance of self-organization, but no disease, his own actions, even though he cannot see the connection. It is never an isolated problem to which he cannot find the answer which disturbs his normal living, it is his whole life pattern that is disturbed and must be reorganized-and this pattern, as we have seen, is formed, and implemented by himself and must be changed by himself.[12]

---

[11] Karen HORNEY, MD, *New Ways in Psychoanalysis* (W. W. Norton: London, 1939), 68–74. Horney, because of her study of the complex relationship between culture and neurosis, is readily compatible with organizational psychological constructs especially her understanding of narcissism. She held that the narcissist who is self-centered, perfectionist, unemphatic, manipulative is the personality type of our time, particularly in authoritarian bureaucracies and competitive corporate settings. It is Robert JACKAL, in *Moral Mazes: The World of Corporate Managers* (New York: Oxford University Press, 1988) who is the most current scholar on the issue of organizational neurotic traits as a phenomenon of the modern corporate milieu.

[12] Magda B. ARNOLD, John A. GASSON, *The Human Person an Approach to An Integral Theory of Personality* (New York: The Ronald Press Company, 1955), 498.

Conrad BAARS is the renowned psychiatrist who revised psychoanalysis from a Freudian foundation to an in-depth Thomistic psychotherapy of psychic wholeness and healing.[13] He developed his school of psychotherapy on a solid and applied Thomistic faculty psychology of the soul. BAARS would diagnose Tom Rath as suffering from an energy neurosis. The easiest way to explain the energy neurotic is his inability emotionally to connect with others in his work environment. The energy neurotic is afraid of his/her feelings. In other words, he/she is afraid of the feelings of guilt and shame that are repressed for various feelings of inadequacies. It is the fear of having to experience and reflect upon these feelings of the fear of failure in a challenging competitive environment. The energy neurosis is the egocentric defense strategic mechanism against the irrational fear of feeling failure. Tom Rath represses his fear of being unable to integrate his personal character and the stress of his external organizational environment. In turn, it forces him to live in his idealized castle of emotional and moral disconnectedness. In an organizational setting the "energy neurotic" is a hard-driving and goal-driven leader who functions well in command and control authoritarian structures. It is mainly the characteristic of self-control that determines his attitude toward others.

> The energy neurotic is a lonely individual, but his rigid self-control has caused him to be preoccupied with himself that he is not even aware of his loneliness. He readily displays an air of coldness, even of hardness, toward his fellowmen. All emotions, even those of others, are interpreted in a sober, dispassionate matter of fact manner, and although this may be entirely reasonable, man is not merely an intellectual being. He remains separated by an unbridgeable chasm.[14]

In terms of being an organizational man, Tom Rath expresses a high degree of egocentricity. It occurs in an organization usually under the guise of just having to play corporate politics to survive. Of course, there is always the need for a certain

---

[13] Conrad W. BAARS, *Psychic Wholeness and Healing: Using All the powers of the Human Psyche* (Eugene: Wipf and Stock Publishers, 1982).

[14] Ibid., 74

necessary amount of political awareness required. It is expected of the executive at that level as a basic requirement. So often in organizations the line of political machinations is crossed and leads to irrational and immoral behavior. Then an executive, leader or any employee must engage in some extremely deep moral reflection and decision-making. There are various rational and moral options open to the employee. Later in the dissertation, we will address the issue of rational and moral options in an organizational environment from the perspective of a virtue psychology of prudence, and the unity of virtue.

In the case of Tom Rath, he completely disconnects and says, "The fact that one has killed a great many a man means nothing, absolutely nothing." He is displaying what Martín F. ECHAVARRÍA, following Thomas Aquinas, discusses as the configuration of personality in the context of virtues. ECHAVARRÍA declares that many neurotic disorders are accompanied by the absence of the fundamental virtues that prop up personality:

> Virtue in this case is understood in Aquinas' terms: *ultimum potentiae*, the highest a person can aim at, in other words, the achievement of human possibilities in both the natural and supernatural realms. They amplify the determining motives of our behavior beyond what we conceive through our normal psychological capacities. Every act and decision under the effect of the virtues liberates the person still for greater flourishing.[15]

Tom Rath experiencing the stress, role playing politics and competition of the corporate environment finds that his only existential goal becomes survival: "Raise legitimate children, make money and think of oneself as what?" He lacks any ultimate goal other than being just a man in a gray flannel suit. We could say that Tom Rath has become the soulless executive. ECHAVARRÍA might refer to him, quoting Aquinas, as "the pusillanimous person who withdraws from his true potential by refusing the

---

[15] Mar ÁLVAREZ, Martín F. ECHAVARRÍA and Paul C. VITZ, "Re-conceptualizing Neurosis as a Degree of Egocentricity: Ethical Issues in Psychological Theory," *Journal of Religion and Health* (October 2015), 7–8.

tendency toward what is proportionate to his potential."[16] His organizational success is grounded on an egocentric defense mechanism that leads to his self-loathing. His cynical self-centered soulless philosophy is no more than an exercise in intellectual pride. As ECHAVARRÍA points out, pride is the opposite of humility and the lack of humility produces a distortion of self-knowledge and "a fictional self and an eagerness to be superior to others."[17]

In launching the discipline of organizational psychology, SCHEIN comes up against a major problem as he enunciates a theoretical foundation of *Leadership and Participation and the Complexity of Human Nature*. In *Organizational Psychology*, he is aware that "Organization and management theory has tended toward simplified and generalized conceptions of human motivation. Empirical research has consistently found some support for the simple generalized conception but only some."[18] He is, in fact, focusing on the Max Weber analysis of the bureaucratic iron cage, as concisely articulated by Stewart R. Clegg:

> As Western corporate organizations, especially American business, in the 50's undergo a fusion of Max Weber bureaucratic organizational world that Stewart R CLEGG describes as: 1) specialization, 2) authorization of organizational action, 3) a tendency toward hierarchization, 4) a contractualization of organizational relationships, 5) credentialization in organizations, 6) a tendency toward careerization (striving to be bigger cogs in the machine) within organizations, 7) a process of stratification in the organization, 8) a tendency toward a specific configuration of authority within the structure, 9) a tendency toward a formalization of rules in the organization, 10) a tendency toward standardization, 11) a tendency toward centralization, 12) a tendency toward legitimization of organizational action, 13) a tendency toward officialization of organizational action, 14) a tendency toward impersonali-

---

[16] Ibid., 8.

[17] Ibid.

[18] SCHEIN, *Organizational Psychology*, 93.

zation of organizational action, 15) a tendency toward a disciplinization of organizational action.[19]

Specifically, as we examine SCHEIN's organizational psychology, we see the need for a Thomistic Organizational Psychology. Quite simply, it is because human nature is complex, and organizational behavior and leadership is uncontrollably complex when it is comprehended without an organizational faculty psychology. A faculty psychology is required because organizational leadership and especially the executive function "cannot be reduced to an organizational psychology that is a series of prescriptive rules, procedures, and models and fails to address vital questions about the inner world of leaders."[20] Roger LEWIN and Birute REGINE in *The Soul at Work, Embracing Complexity Science for Business Success* quote Alan BRISKIN, an author and Business consultant, who, in turn, quotes a manager from a large conglomerate:

> We're so busy moving people around, trying to meet our deadlines, trying to influence people to believe in what we're doing, that we just don't want to really look into anybody's eyes and see they have souls. We should start with the premise that we have souls. But souls are difficult to manage. And even if we talked about people having souls, it would probably be from a corporate viewpoint. The manager's last point is that making "soul" into some kind of company slogan would be worse than not recognizing the existence of worker's souls in the first place.[21]

At the proceedings of an international conference, *Renewing the West by Renewing Common Sense,* a Thomistic scholar Peter MANGO, PhD, presented a paper *Philosophical Tensions among Leadership* (2014) Gray, *Efficiency, Community-and What It Means for the Academy.* MANGO, in that paper, draws attention to the vital

---

[19] Stewart R. CLEGG, *Modern Organizations: Organization Studies in the Postmodern World,* (London: Thousand Oaks; New Delhi: Sage Publications, 1990), 39–40.

[20] Manfred F.R. Kets DE VRIES, *Leaders, Fools, and Impostors: Essays in the Psychology of Leadership* (Lincoln: iUniverse, 1993), 4.

[21] Roger LEWIN and Birute REGINE, *The Soul at Work* (New York: Simon & Schuster, 2000), 22–23.

questions about a dysfunctional style of organizational leadership that he calls "Toxic Leadership." He writes:

Yet according to Goleman, today we are increasingly confronted with the workplace narcissism of what others have called the toxic leader. The U.S. Army defines toxic leaders as those who put their own needs first, micromanage subordinates, and periodically behave in a mean-spirited manner, and display poor decision-making.

One of the first things one notices about a toxic leader is how he or she may feel subjectively that everything is "on" him or her to perform; and thus, he or she may feel a crushing sense of responsibility to something -or, more to the point, to someone. Yet what is noteworthy is that this sense of all-encompassing responsibility- and that distrust of subordinate collaborators that so often accompanies this sense of responsibility-is itself a manifestation of ego-centricity; of a kind of self-imposed isolation from subordinates, professional peers, or external advisors; and of a failure to trust deeply or perseveringly in any higher power for assistance.

Whereas so called "task-oriented" leaders are usually unconcerned with catering to group members, and more centered with working out a solution to meeting a concrete goal, they can ensure certain deadlines are met, but their group members' well-being may suffer. Relationship oriented leaders, by contrast, focus on updating their team members' skills, and enhancing the relationships within the team by soliciting honest feedback.

In the end-whether he is fully conscious of it or not-the health of an institution in the toxic leader's eyes of others is merely the health of the leader's own reputation, in his own eyes, and in the eyes of others be they subordinates, peers, clients, or all three. This in its turn leads to what are called "CWB" or "counterproductive workplace behaviors," which result when toxic leaders feel pressured or threatened-which is fairly regularly, Management analyst Gillian Flynn has described a toxic leader as one who at least periodically "bullies, threatens, yells. Whose mood swings determine the climate of the office or any given workday. Who forces employees to whisper in sympathy in cubicles and hallways?[22]

MANGO, in his concept of "toxic leadership," describes a dysfunctional syndrome that is really a strong expression in an organizational cultural environment of pathological leadership behavior of feelings happening on a regular basis and impossible to control.

It is the behavior that is tolerated, if not nurtured, as in *The Man in the Gray Flannel Suit*. For six seasons on American television the series *Mad Men* was a popular weekly success. The series was a 2007–2015 adaptation of SLOAN's *The Man in the Gray Flannel Suit*; as with the original story, the new Tom Rath is Don Draper of the advertising agency of Sterling Cooper Draper Pryce who relives the story of organizational "toxic leadership." The series is set in the 1960s, and it reminds the viewer of the way business was in the 60s into the late 70s. Yet it is more than a TV media walk down memory lane. As audiences watched the series, they were attracted to the intrigue of the dysfunctional toxic leadership behavior of the agency. It is the story of MANGO's bullies, threats, yelling and mood swings. Most of all, it is a story of the immoral conduct of the agency's senior executives in their work, personal, and marital behavior.

Throughout the seasons of *Mad Men*, the viewing audience comes to learn of the soulless character of the agency executive team. In the language of contemporary organizational psychology, the series *Mad Men* points to the lack of emotional intelligence and moral self-control. It is what Harvard University's Dr. Daniel GOLEMAN calls "emotional intelligence" that refers to a super focused management style. They exercise a command and coerce leadership strategy. They simply give orders and command respect. Even though it is not the intention of MANGO's paper on toxic leadership, it seems to explain in part why TV audiences from 2007–2015 were glued weekly to their TV sets watching the *Mad Men* of Sterling Cooper Draper Pryce. The series explained that the men in the gray flannel suits were still holding executive positions of leadership in 1990s and into the business crash of 2008. MANGO

---

[22] Peter J. MANGO, "Philosophical Tensions among Leadership, Efficiency, Community- and What It Means for the Academy," *Studia Gilsoniana*, 3 (2014), 567–568.

cites Daniel GOLEMAN on contemporary ominous organizational leaders sporting a myopic leadership style:

> Create a toxic climate, one that dispirits those they lead. Such leaders may get short-term results through personal heroics… but do so at the expense of building their organizations… Such leaders don't listen, let alone make decisions by consensus. They don't spend time getting to know the people they work with day in and day out but relate to them in one-dimensional roles. They don't help people develop new strengths or refine their abilities but dismiss their need to learn as a failing. They come off as arrogant and impatient.[23]

2.3 The Organizational Soulless Psycho-Ethics of Winning

Another TV type popular morality play, in the motif of *The Man in the Gray Flannel Suit* and *Mad Men*, is the 2016 series *Billions*. It brings the viewing audience to the post-recession financial crisis of 2006–2009 world. As described in *Business Insider*,[24] the mortgage market was comprised of thousands of highly intelligent and financially brilliant people, but their minds had been closed to the coming cataclysmic subprime failure. They were persons who had graduated from elite business and financial schools. Furthermore, for the greater part, they saw themselves as master of competition in the financial industry. They were confident of their intelligence and skills because their incomes and lifestyle verified their competitive status. They were the financial victorious competitors of the investment game. Yet, right to the highest executive ranks of banks, insurance companies, rating agencies, hedge funds and SEC regulators, the financial crisis and ensuing great recession of 2008 were missed. What happened with all these bright investment people who appeared as the elite masters

---

[23] Ibid., 564.

[24] CARRIE WITTMER, "BUSINESS INSIDER," www.businessinsider.com/what-is-billions-show-about-2017-3

of investment competition? Investment bankers, the analysts, the traders, and government regulators committed, what the Greeks called the sin of hubris. They believed that they were more than masters of competition; instead they began to believe that they were the master of reality. Even more insane, they believed that they had become the masters of the financial universe.

Billions is a recent popular television series about the antagonistic culture of the post great 2008 financial recession and the increase in government regulation of the financial industry. It is, however, not just a matter of increased regulation of the financial industry, it is about the fanatic regulatory reform and enforcement spirit of the Federal Justice Department. Chuck Rhoades (played by Paul Giamatti) is the U.S. attorney for the Manhattan, New York office, and he is fervently focused on Bobby "Axe" Axelrod (played by Damian Lewis) who is the hedge fund billionaire.

Axe is a graduate of Hofstra College who came from a working-class family, and now lives in an 84-million-dollar home in Long Island. He is a multi-billionaire, hedge fund genius who still plays to the reputation of being a homegrown hero who after the 9/11 crisis continues to pay for the college education of children of his partners who were killed in the New York Twin Towers collapse. As a hedge fund manager, he has a gifted sense of making brilliant and highly profitable arbitrage buy outs, stock offerings and leverage purchases moves. The elixir of the hedge fund entrepreneur is information on stock values of corporations and the opportunities for early purchase, acquisition and selling short.

Although Axe is brilliant as an analyst and fearless as a decision maker and risk taker, he will do anything to acquire the right information and beat his competitors to the next enormous hedge fund play. Axe is not an amoral debauched *Wolf of Wall Street* man. He is extremely faithful to his family and children, and he is a well-respected philanthropist. Yet, when it comes to making business decisions, it is as if Axe has drunk some type of soulless concoction that says the high morality of family is one thing, but business is another thing. In the world of hedge fund business, anything goes.

Chuck Rhoades, the U.S. Attorney, is Axe's nemesis who is determined that Axe must go to prison. Rhoades is a hard-driven justice department attorney, but he is mostly driven by his own career. Bobby Axelrod is Chuck's Moby Dick obsession; he must destroy this recognized enlightened master of the hedge fund world that he perceives as being the most corrupt of the hedge fund crooks of Wall Street. Rhoades is more than a federal prosecutor; rather, he sees himself as the Wyatt Earp of Wall Street pursuing the biggest symbol of the run amok wheeler dealers of Wall Street. His pursuit of Axe is not driven by a pristine respect for the laws of free trade. He has a deep-rooted, personal hatred of Bobby Axelrod, and he sees the take-down of Axelrod as a steppingstone to his political career. It is this Moby Dick obsession that even begins to erode his personal relationship with his wife. He is ambitious and is totally focused on his career and will go to any lengths and cross any moral or legal line to win.

More so than Axelrod, he lacks emotional mastery, and he is the classic toxic leader in that his own personal career, anger and fear of failure and the need for prestige needs drive him. The Thomistic psychiatrist Conrad BARRS would describe Rhoades as the "highly-driven task-oriented" energy neurotic who is unconcerned about his team of attorneys or his family relationships.[25] He ignores his bad and immoral behavior because he has a crushing desire to protect the free market from the likes of Bobby Axelrod. He is the type of leader who hides behind the truth of a perceived righteous cause to rationalize his emotional and moral failings. It is his wife Wendy who adds fuel to his vendetta against Axelrod because she is a psychiatrist working for Axe Capital. A big part of Rhoades' family income and lifestyle comes from Wendy's salary. Furthermore, Axe is a handsome, macho and GQ magazine image billionaire, and Chuck is an overweight, unattractive geek.

What is most interesting about the series *Billions* is that Axe Capital has hired a full-time psychiatrist. It is Wendy Rhoades, the wife of Chuck Rhoades. Wendy had been a personal psychiatrist to Axe for some years. She has counseled him through the competitive stress and the often-moral decisions with emotional consequences of the hedge fund world. She has a critical function in Axe Capital with the team of bright traders and analysts. Wendy, as a psychiatrist, treats them, when they question their grit and confidence, as a superstar in the hedge fund trader business. The purpose of her intervention is that they may find within themselves, by means of a style of rational cognitive behavior, the power to win. She also helps them overcome any sense of

---

[25] Anna A. TERRUWE & Conrad W. BARRS, *Psychic Wholeness & Healing: Using All the Powers of the Human Psyche* (Eugene: Wipf and Stock Publishers, 1981), 71–85.

shame or irrational guilt over the financial decisions made and the consequences of the decisions. She practices a type of "you do what it takes to win, you never give up taking a risk, you have courage and you will be rich" therapy, but it is based on a bold, hedonistic, moral psychology.

There is, in each of these three melodramas of corporate power at the executive level, a manner of psychology and moral conduct that appears unique to the American business world from the 1940s to the present. It is indigenous to the American business culture; it is a psychology and ethics of the Bluffing Game. Albert Z. CARR recommended this game of moral psychology as foundational to competitive business leadership. In 1968 his essay was published in the Harvard Business Review: "Is Business Bluffing Ethical?" It was extremely controversial and has been debated for years. He examined business ethics from the analogy of the competitive game of poker.

> Poker's own brand of ethics is different from ethical ideals of civilized relationships. The game is based on distrust of the other fellow. It ignores the claim of friendship. Cunning deception and concealment of one's own strength and intentions, not kindness and open heartedness, are vital in poker. No one thinks any worse of poker on that account. And no one should think any the worse of the game of business because its standards of right and wrong differ from the prevailing traditions of morality in our society.[26]

His advice for success to business executives is to discard the ethics of the Golden Rule. He writes:

> Most businessmen are not indifferent to ethics in their private lives, everyone will agree. My point is that in their office lives they cease to be private citizens;

---

[26] Albert Z. CARR, "Is Business Bluffing Ethical?", *Harvard Business Review*, January 1968, https://hbr.org/1968/01/is-business-bluffing-ethical, 4

they become game players who must be guided by a somewhat different set of ethical standards.[27]

In business, CARR teaches that it is best to ignore the golden rule:

> …so long as a businessman complies with the laws of the land and avoids telling malicious lies, he's ethical. If the law as written gives a man a wide-open chance to make a killing, he'd be a fool not to take advantage of it. If he doesn't, somebody else will. There's no obligation on him to stop and consider who is going to get hurt.[28]

CARR wrote *Business as a Game* as a knowing guide for executives on the way up. In this work, he presents a blunt perspective on the competitive game of business and the need for pragmatic competitive skills to achieve higher levels of leadership. He does not examine strategic methods of competitive business strategy. He speaks to persons in business who aspire of rising to top levels of management and executive positions:

> But it is not my intention to deal with the game of business as played by corporations. This book is not a guide for top management in planning the competitive strategies of their companies. It is aimed primarily at the middle and lower echelon executives on their way up, at trainees for executive jobs, and at students planning on executive careers. The need for game strategy is common to all who look for good incomes, a degree of prestige, and economic security.[29]

It is important to note that Albert CARR's article on "Business and the Ethics of Bluffing" was published in the prestigious *Harvard Business Review*. In this journal of

---

[27] Albert Z. CARR, *Business as a Game: A Knowing Guide for Executive on the Way Up* (New York: New American Library, 1968), Foreword, xii-xiv.

[28] Ibid.

[29] Ibid.

scholarly applied business research, he suggests that the topic was worthy of serious consideration within the science of business administration. CARR's thoughts on business as a competitive game; and using the metaphor of a poker game, he aroused a quick response from the business and academic community. They argued against his position on business and ethical bluffing as a plea for an ethical immunity from any form of rational moral standards on business conduct in a competitive marketplace. Although there are many ways to respond to CARR's ethical theory, it is beyond the intention or scope of this dissertation.

CARR's controversial thinking of the 60's is presented rather as an example of a culturally tolerable corporate psychology of playing the competitive game of "you do what it takes to win" unique ethical minimalism grounded on an organizational psychology of how to win in the competitive game of commerce. CARR is accused of being a cynic about human nature, and he responds, "Aren't you taking a cynical position in saying business is a game... You might as well say life is a game... After all, business is a way of life?"[30] His response is that business is basically requires a certain type of psychological personality construct to play the important game, and he continues to defend his position that a unique necessary psychological character of business requires a unique ethics:

> To be sure business is incomparably more important than any recreational game. But buying, producing, and selling, although they are America's dominant occupations, are not part of the biological mainstream of life. Business does not have the resources to deal with our deep instinctual needs for health, love, sex, parenthood, and self-expression. Its purpose has all the characteristics of a game of strategy within life, a game played with economic chips. That as a game of great intricacy and subtlety is obvious, but game it is, as Ralph Waldo Emerson long ago perceived when he wrote, "Commerce is a game of skill, which every man cannot play, which few man plays well."

> Men who recognize the game character of business and who learn to play the game well armor themselves against many of the stings of the competitive business world. Those, on the other hand, who keep trying to apply lofty

---

[30] Ibid xiii

standards to human relations in business may well experience a good deal of emotional turmoil. Business cannot realistically be expected to live up to ideals formed in churches, schools .and homes, in literature and philosophy. No game of strategy gives prizes for ethics.

If, as a company employee, you suffer on making the discovery that your associates are indifferent to your convictions about the way people should behave toward each other, the fault is not in business; it is in your misconception of the nature of business.[31]

If we compare Peter MANGO's description of the highly task-focused psychology of the "toxic leader" to CARR's requirements for success as a business leader, then it is possible to look upon the game culture as a fertile breeding ground for toxic leadership. We also find the examples of *The Man in the Gray Flannel Suit*, *Mad Men*, and *Billions* which represent a dark side of powerful leadership and the bureaucratic executive function of any organization. We are using "the dark soul of an organization" as a metaphor to describe a severe state of crippling dysfunctional pathological behavior that permeates organizational culture which receives little, if any, serious attention in empirical psychological cognitive behavioral studies of organizational psychology.

2.4 Thomistic Organizational Psychology as a Science of Executive Leadership

At the Huntington, New York, Aquinas Leadership International 2014 Inaugural World Congress on *Renewing the West by Renewing Common Sense*, Peter MANGO presented his paper on "Toxic Leadership." Another paper on organizational leadership was put forth by A William MCVEY: *Thomistic Scientific Leadership and Common-Sense Organizational Harmony*. It was argued that a Thomistic science of organizational leadership is based on a habit of wonder and a psychology of power, i.e. a Thomistic faculty psychology. The Thomistic understanding of the habit of wonder is of paramount importance to a Thomistic organizational psychology,

---

[31] CARR, *Business as a Game*, Foreword, xiii-xiv.

especially as an applied science of organizational leadership where Thomistic Organizational Psychology is approached as an art and science:

> St. Thomas's teaching is chiefly about existential judgments, not about ideas. The emotions are crucial in all forms of judging and reasoning, judging to forming every emotion. In fact, we can have no emotion without forming judgments related to ideas. St. Thomas considered business activity in the highest form to be a practical or productive science. He would view any kind of modern corporation in the same way. Like every practical activity, it starts in wonder. Wonder is an activity moving away from the emotion of fear through hope to escape from fear. Since all art, science, philosophy starts in wonder, it starts in total conviction or hope of being able to satisfy a desire, ending the desire in intellectual, volitional, and emotional satisfaction. A human aim, or end, is to simply a hope or conviction-filled hope of being able to satisfy a desire, ending the desire in intellectual, volitional, and emotional satisfaction. The object of that hope or conviction is the final act that stops the movement of desire, puts it to rest, and satisfies it. Good leaders lead by instilling conviction filled, hope-filled friendship, desire in a multitude: creating professional friendships.[32]

The three melodramas of *The Man in the Gray Flannel Suit, Mad Men,* and *Billions* are really tragedies about modern organization's dark soul. These are corporations that on the surface appear to be successful corporations; yet there is a dark soulless side that bespeaks a deep dysfunctionality. It is a psychology of game leadership that is promulgated by the executive leadership of an organization. It is

---

[32] A William McVey, "Thomistic Scientific Leadership and Common-Sense Triad of Organizational Harmony," *Studia Gilsoniana,* 3 (2014), 586. This was a description of Thomistic leadership that Peter Redpath, PhD, metaphysics of organization significantly contributed to this article. Throughout this dissertation we shall return to the concepts in this definition as essential to a Thomistic Organizational Psychology, especially the sections dealing with organizational decision making and strategy. Attention to the Thomistic concepts organizational wonder, intellectual, volitional, and emotional rational sense making and the organizational cadence of her and hope.

really a dark type of moral psychology easily detected from the perspective of a Thomistic Organizational psychology. A Thomistic Organizational psychology is a rational moral psychology that will be treated in more detail in following chapters. Since its conception in the 1960s, organizational psychology, as a rule, studies executive leadership in terms of personality traits and values. For example, SCHEIN observes three kinds of relevant executive leadership competence:

1) Analytical—the ability to identify, analyze and solve problems (task competence)

2) Interpersonal competence—the ability to work under, with, and through other people and in group

3) Emotional competence—the ability to make tough decisions either in the task or interpersonal area[33]

2.4.1. Organizational Executive Leadership Is Not a Soulless Instrumental Psychology

Empirical Organizational Psychology is a multi-perspective discipline on the nature of the human psyche in the organizational setting, but it is not grounded on any type meta-psychology (metaphysical) foundation. Whereas, a Thomistic Organizational Psychology maintains that it is not possible to construct a true organizational psychology of leadership without a metaphysics of organization. Without such a metaphysics of organization, organizational psychology and executive leadership become a discipline of skill set instrumentalism. Without a premodern Aristotelian-Thomistic metaphysics of organization, the concept of executive leadership competence becomes a matter of executive competence defined as skill sets. Instrumentalism generally portrays individuals' and groups' strategic expertise in reaching their goals as independent of the kinds of persons they are. Strategies, techniques, methods, skill sets and so on are spoken of as tools that can be acquired by anyone with the resources to do so. Blaine J. FOWERS, in *Virtue and Psychology,*

---

[33] Edgar H. SCHEIN, *Organizational Psychology*, 131-132.

explains the detachment of an instrumental psychology from an ethics of virtuous character of internal goodness:

> In an instrumental framework, communication skills, leadership skills, interviewing skills, diagnostic skills are no different from house painting skills or driving skills. These technical capabilities are separate from the quality of the person possessing them. In fact, one of the attractive features of an instrumental approach is the possibility of enhancing individuals' lives through training them in skill sets that will help them to attain their goals [...] There are many paths to wealth, including hard work, innovation, luck, inheritance, marrying someone wealthy, fraud, theft, exploitation of others, and so forth. Any of these approaches is equally valuable in terms of the sheer possession of wealth, as long as it is successful. Individuals have used all of these strategies. From a purely strategic point of view, theft or exploitation can be at least as effective as hard work or invention. If an individual successfully obtains wealth through immoral means, the wealth is no different than wealth attained in any other way. Of course, our conventional moral codes and laws make a relatively clear distinction here between legitimate and illegitimate wealth acquisition, but instrumentalism generally views these moral or legal considerations only as strategic impediments (i.e., theft may be less efficacious because it may lead to legal difficulties and loss of acquired wealth). Indeed, moral, and legal codes are often seen as necessary to curb the "natural" instrumentality of humans in choosing the most efficacious goals. Within instrumentalism, the reason that theft is not a good strategy is that it is likely to lead to negative consequences, not that it is inherently wrong... The difficulty is that instrumentalism has become so pervasive in the way people think in the modern West and in psychology that we can scarcely conceive of an alternative. Within the perspective of instrumentalism, external goods are the only type that have any firm reality. Although a good deal of human activity is instrumental in nature, we must recognize that some actions are inherently tied to goals individuals

seek and are therefore valuable in themselves. Such actions are required to pursue internal goods.[34]

2.5 The Necessity of Moral Rectitude

In this dissertation, it is contended that Thomistic organizational psychology initially observes an organization from the perspective of the function of leadership based on rational and moral principles. The reason for this position will become clear, after we present in chapter Three a metaphysics of organization and participation. Throughout this dissertation, we shall also use extensively the philosophical perspective of Chester I. BARNARD (1886–1961) on the organization and the function of executive leadership. We will discuss in chapter Three that the metaphysics of organization and BARNARD's philosophy of the organization is most compatible with a Thomistic metaphysics of organization and a rational sensing moral psychology.

BARNARD was the Chief Executive officer of a major American public service company, the United Service Organization in the 1940s and President of the Rockefeller foundation from 1948–52. He taught at the Harvard School of Business. He was influenced by the works of the sociologist Talcott PARSONS and maintained a close working relationship with PARSONS. His major work is *The Functions of the Executive*.[35] It is perhaps one of "the 20th century's most influential books on management and leadership."[36] In his work BARNARD emphasizes his view on relevant executive leadership competence, moral authority, rational stewardship, professionalism, and a systems approach.[37]

---

[34] Blaine J. FOWERS, *Virtue and Psychology* (Washington, DC: American Psychological Association, 2005), 56–57.

[35] Chester I. BARNARD, *The Functions of the Executive* (Cambridge, Massachusetts and London, England: Harvard University Press, 1938 and 1968).

[36] Andres GABOR and Joseph T. MAHONEY, "Chester Barnard and the Systems Approach to Nurturing Organizations" https://business.illinois.edu/working_papers/papers/10-0102.pdf, published: 2010.

[37] Ibid. Commenting on the importance of BARNARD's book and its contribution to posterity they wrote, "The book emphasizes competence, moral integrity, rational stewardship, professionalism, as a systems approach, and was written for posterity. For generations, *The*

In chapter three, we will define a Thomistic rational sensing moral psychology based on a metaphysics of an organizational whole as most compatible with BARNARD's views on the sensing of the whole. BARNARD in his personal executive role, his writing, public lecturing, and teaching at the Harvard School of Business Administration sensed a coming intellectual and spiritual crisis of the twentieth century.

His views on organizational ethics are diametrically opposed to the Bluffing Ethics of Albert Z. CARR. He articulated a defense of managerial capitalism based on a high moral authority of stable organizational habits of goodness, as expressed in the moral habitual behavior of the higher levels of the organization that set the example for an organizational living and dynamic moral code.

From *The Functions of the Executive* by Chester I. BARNARD, the definition of the executive function and practice of leadership is different than is found in present texts on organizational psychology and much more extensive than the three-relevant executive leadership competencies of Edgar H. SCHEIN. This definition points to the need in coming chapters for a rational sensing moral psychology based on a metaphysics of organization and a metaphysical-based moral psychology. BARNARD clearly states:

> In short, neither men of weak responsibility nor those of limited capability can endure or carry the burden of many simultaneous obligations of different types. If they are "overloaded," either ability, responsibility, or morality, or all three, will be destroyed. Conversely, a condition of complex morality, great activity, and high responsibility cannot continue without commensurate ability. I do not hesitate to affirm that those whom I believe to be the better and more able executives regard it as a major malefaction to induce or push men of fine character and great sense of responsibility into active positions exceeding their

---

Functions of the Executive proved to be an inspiration to the leading thinkers in a host of disciplines. Perrow writes that 'This… remarkable book contains within it the seeds of three distinct trends of organizational theory that were to dominate the field for the next three decades. One was the institutional theory as represented another was the decision-making school as represented by Herbert Simon; the third was the human relations school'."

technical capacities. Unless the process can be reversed in time, the result is destructive. [...] Executive positions are (a) imply a complex morality, and (b) require a high capacity of responsibility (c) under conditions of activity, necessitating (d) commensurate general and specific technical abilities as a moral factor and in addition there is required (e) the faculty of creating morals for others.[38]

The movement to a Thomistic organizational psychology is highlighted by putting forth two opposed executive moral psychologies of a business organization. One is the Albert Z. CARR of Business and Ethical Bluffing, as expressed in American literature and media from the 1940s to the present. Two is Chester BARNARD in 1938. He calls for a business organization, or any organization, to be grounded on a moral psychology. Furthermore, BARNARD argues that the lasting power of an organization is dependent upon the executive levels of the organization setting by personal moral habit and organizational policy of high standards of moral behavior. BARNARD is explicit on the issue of the relationship of executive leadership and proper moral behavior:

> Organizations endure, however, in proportion to the breadth of the morality by which they are governed. This is only to say that foresight, long purposes, high ideals are the basis for the persistence of cooperation.
>
> The endurance of the organization depends on the quality of leadership; and that quality derives from the breadth of the morality upon which it rests. High responsibility there must be even in the lowest, the most immoral organizations; but if the morality to which the responsibility is low, the organizations are short lived. A low morality will not sustain leadership long, its influence quickly vanishes, it cannot produce its own succession.[39]

The psychologist MANFRED F.R. KETS DE VRIES, an organizational psychologist who focuses on the psychodynamics of the executive function and leadership, puts

---

[38] BARNARD, *The Functions of the Executive*, 272–273.
[39] Ibid., 282-283.

forth a psychoanalytical observation that traditional western approaches to organizational leadership are one-dimensional and mechanical descriptions. He argues that usual overly rational management mistakenly ignores that rational beings are also driven by emotions, aspirations or fantasies that influence how they function as executives and leaders daily in a concrete organizational existential environment.

> Our leaders, whether heroes or villains, are rewarded with reproductions of themselves in literature, newsprint, and analysis. The study of leadership itself, which is at least as ancient as Plato's *Republic,* continues almost to overburden the pages of historical, political, and business journals. Unfortunately, too many management theorists have reduced the study of leadership to a series of prescriptive rules, procedures and models and have failed to confront some of the most vital and interesting questions raised by the subject: what determines who will become our leaders? What is the intrapsychic theater like?
>
> Leadership in action is characterized as much by its complications and subtleties as by its dramatic success or failure stories. These stories fill the best seller shelves in bookshops and are much more attractive to those interested in leadership than dull, scholarly studies, notwithstanding the best sellers' frequent superficiality and lack of conceptualization.[40]

DE VRIES in his approach to organizational psychology of leadership explores the origins and manifestations of dysfunctional leadership. He observes leadership under the stress of executive rational and moral responsibility and their struggles with the addiction to power coupled with the fear of failure are inclined to narcissistic behavior, cyclothymic mood swings and lack of moral integrity and executive character. In other words, DE VRIES analyzes the impact of the "dark side" of leadership upon the organization as an issue beyond the acumen of traditional organizational psychological methods to explain the executive function such as rational-economic assumptions of managerial behavior, such as:[41]

---

[40] DE VRIES, *Leaders, Fools, and Impostors*, 4–5.

[41] SCHEIN, *Organizational Psychology*, 50–57.

1920s Trait theory (Great man theory of common traits and characteristics), Behavior Theory of the 1940s (Ohio & Michigan studies task-oriented and relationship-oriented leadership), and Contingency Theory (Situational leadership, transactional/transformational, Servant leadership Value-based leadership and Authentic leadership).[42]

DE VRIES refers to the dark side of leadership as the Darth Vader aspect of leadership which grows out of personality traits such as narcissism, self-deceit, and abuse of power that leaders are unwilling to face and acknowledge their weaknesses.[43]

2.6 Organizational Pathology

The argument of a culture of dark soulless leadership is approached by BOARDMAN and PONOMARIOV with an organizational pathology construct based on a broad concept that encompasses any internal aspect of the organization that threatens organizational survival:

> Specifically, the concept analogizes organizational differentiation to vital organs and systems thereof in a human, organizational formalization to biologic systems like circulation and respiration, organization centralization to the brain, strategic and operational planning to synaptic firing in the brain, appendages, and orifices to resource-dependent ties to the external environment, and organizational culture to personality and mental health.[44]

These authors use the analogy of an organization as an organism that proves as a most suitable way to look at, in their studies of public organizations, complex living systems (e.g. a biologic organism). The advantage of this approach is that like in a

---

[42] David R. KOLZOW, *Leading from Within: Building Organizational Leadership Capacity* (ideconline.org client uploads, 2014).

[43] DE VRIES, *Dysfunctional Leadership*, https://flora.insead.edu/fichiersti_wp/inseadwp2003/2003-58.pdf.

[44] Craig BOARDMAN and Branco PONOMARIOV, "Organizational Pathology," *Global Encyclopedia of Public Administration, Public Policy, And Governance* (January 2017), 1.

biologic organism replete with a brain, other vital organs, circulatory and respiratory and digestive systems the organization is susceptible to internal and external pathological attacks. It is these pathological attacks, unless treated, slowly and at times abruptly, corrode the fitness for organizational success.

Vital organs are the vertically and horizontally subunits that fulfill the core function or functions of an organization.

The brain is the function and responsibility for a of rational moral sense making, a moral psychology of individual and organizational flourishing, rational moral sensing strategic and operational decision making. The executive function is to exercise vigilance for expressions and any formalization of organizational pathology.

Sustenance appendages are like arms and hands and legs and are analogous to the individuals and/ or organizations in the external environment that are in possession of necessary resources vital to the fitness of the organization. It is important to note that an organization is extended in a logistical and supply chain of relationships with vendors. If a pathological or illegal relationship develops in this network, it has a destructive viral impact on the organization. This issue of pathology in sustenance appendages is extremely important given that organizational activity is part of a digital network where virus protection must be constant.

Psychological factors, like human organisms, an organization's psychology or culture are much more difficult to observe empirically than are other internal aspects of the organization. Organizational cultures typically become pathological due to multiple other pathologies occurring elsewhere in the organization, e.g. in a subunit, in managerial and supervisory leadership, human relations. If behavioral dysfunctional pathologies go unaddressed or addressed but persist and remain, then they become the most serious threat to the fitness and success of the organization. If psychological pathologies are not remedied symptoms increased, such as turnover, increased absenteeism, decreased organizational commitment, decreased worker motivation, decreased job satisfaction, delinquent supplier begin to become increasingly apparent.

BOARDMAN and PONOMARIOV, based on their research, give clear examples of formalized organizational pathologies e.g.:

- Leader-member exchanges that engender suspicion rather than trust

- Leadership that fails to provide guidance for difficult tasks
- Leadership that provides too much oversight for the investigation of complex problems
- Bureaucratic personalities that obfuscate collective and /or individual performance
- Formalization that fails to fulfill its intended function
- Formalization that fulfills a defunct function that impedes extant functions
- Organizations differentiation that impedes coordination and communication across subunits
- Decision making that takes too long to adapt to contingencies
- Decision making that goes uninformed by expertise
- Worker expectations for behaviors that diverge from those of management and leadership
- Leadership and management that fails to ensure that the organization has the resources it needs to fulfill core functions[45]

2.7 The Art of Sensing the Whole

In this dissertation we are not arguing that business leadership is fundamentally built on an immoral, toxic, and dysfunctional behavior. We are, however, suggesting that a Thomistic organizational psychology examines the nature of the executive function of an organization as having the major responsibility of creating a culture of rational and moral behavior. In turn, this becomes the main cause, as BARNARD argues, for the long-term success of the organization. Even though, we give careful attention to business organization in this study, we hold that a Thomistic organizational psychology of the executive function of leadership applies to any manner of organization. Again, similar to BARNARD's approach to the organizational executive function and leadership of an organization "is defined as a system of consciously coordinated personal activities of forces."[46]

---

[45] Ibid., 2–4.

[46] BARNARD, *The Functions of the Executive*, 72.

Based on this definition, an organization is similar whether applied to a military, a religious, an academic, a manufacturing, a service industry, a software industry, a nonprofit, a fraternal cooperation, even though the social environment, the number and kinds of persons and the purpose and bases of their relation to the organization will be widely different. Basically, a Thomistic organizational psychology of soulful leadership being established on a rational moral sensing psychology applies to any "formal organization as a system of consciously coordinated activities or forces of two or more persons."[47] BARNARD is the philosopher of coordination, "At first thought it may seem that the element of communication in organization is only in part related to authority; but more thorough consideration leads to the understanding that communication, authority, specialization, and purposes are all aspects comprehended in co-ordination."[48]

Even in the Weberian bureaucratic management of the 1940s, he is given to the driving theme of the executive function of coordination of rational and moral behavioral habits of character. He designates two types of specific personal abilities for leadership. There are those who are the talented supervisors with "general abilities, involving general alertness, comprehensiveness of interest, flexibility, faculty of adjustment, courage, etc. Leaders in higher positions of authority must have general abilities."[49] He states, "we do not develop general executives well by specific efforts, and we know very little about how to do it."[50]

Yet, the operation of such systems of a complex organization requires the highest development of executive arts. The various forms and techniques are most definitely exemplified in the most successful in terms of longevity such as the armies and navies of the major powers, Bell Telephone system, the great railway system and he selects the Catholic Church as an exemplar of organizational successful executive leadership.[51] It is important to note that BARNARD's concept of the executive function is based mostly on a fundamental habit of the art of sensing the whole.

---

[47] Ibid., 73.

[48] Ibid., 184.

[49] Ibid., 222.

[50] Ibid.

[51] Ibid., 84.

Control from the view of the effectiveness of the whole organization is important and is sometimes of critical importance; but it is in connection with efficiency, which in the last analysis embraces effectiveness, that the viewpoint of the whole is necessarily dominant…the common sense of the whole is not obvious, and in fact often is not effectively present. Control is dominated by a particular aspect—the economic, the political, the religious, the scientific, the technological, with the result that efficiency is not secured, and failure ensues or perpetually threatens. No doubt the development of a crisis due to the unbalanced treatment of all the factors is the occasion for corrective action on the part of the executives who possess the art of sensing the whole. A formal and orderly conception of the whole is rarely present perhaps even rarely possible, except to a few men of executive genius, or a few organizations the personnel of which is comprehensively sensitive and well-integrated.[52]

Even back in the 1940s, he is a forerunner in what today would be the cultural school of organizational behavior:[53] "The coordination of efforts essential to a system of cooperation requires, as we have seen, an organization system of communication.

---

[52] Ibid., 238.

[53] Henry MINTZBERG, Bruce AHLSTRAND and Joseph L. LAMPEL, *Strategy Safari: A Guided Tour Through the Wilds of Strategic Management* (New York: Free Press, 2005). The authors present ten schools of organizational strategy that have developed since the 1950s: 1) The Design School: strategy formation as a process of conception, 2) The Planning School: strategy formation as a formal process, 3) The Positioning School: strategy formation as an analytical process, 4) The Entrepreneurial School: strategy as a visionary process, 5) The Cognitive School: strategy formation as a mental process, 6) The Learning School: strategy formation as an emergent process, 7) The Power School: strategy formation as a proves of negotiation, 8) The Cultural School: strategy formation as a collective process, 9) The Environmental Process: strategy formation as a reactive process, 10) The Configuration School: strategy formation as a process of transformation. The authors describe and analyze the principles and methods of each of these ten schools and conclude with a meta-analysis of organizational strategic formation. As we establish a Thomistic metaphysics of organization and the executive function of leadership in the next chapter, we, in turn, analyze this meta-analysis. The argument is then made that a Thomistic common sense concept of the organization is most compatible with a combination of the visionary and learning schools of organization.

Such a system of communication implies centers or points of interconnection and can operate as these centers are occupied by persons who are called executives."[54] In his writings on the executive function BARNARD calls for a scientific development of his proposed science of executive function and leadership:

> In the common-sense leadership, every day, practical knowledge necessary to the practice of the arts, there is much that is not susceptible of verbal statement—it is a matter of know-how. It may be called behavioral knowledge. It is necessary to doing things in concrete situations. It is nowhere more indispensable than in the executive arts. It is acquired by persistent habitual experience and is often called intuitive.[55]

We will continue in successive chapters to extend BARNARD's philosophy into an examination of Thomistic metaphysical organizational principles and executive organizational psychology of character of excellence. Specifically, we will give attention to BARNARD's insight about the nature of the art of sensing the whole. Although the issue of the "art of sensing the whole" will be addressed in more detail in chapters three and four, we will define in Aristotelian-Thomistic terms the art of sensing the whole as the executive function of inductive reasoning. The Aristotelian-Thomistic concept of induction is different from the modern definition and approach to inductive reasoning. In his seminal works *A Not-So-Elementary Christian Metaphysics* and *The Moral Psychology of St Thomas Aquinas: An Introduction to Ragamuffin Ethics*, PETER A. REDPATH has emphatically stressed the importance of the Aristotelian-Thomistic concept of inductive reasoning, as it applies to organizational science and psychology:[56]

> Aristotle begins to talk about *the fact the proper method of study in practical science is to examine the nature of things for their utility*, not to understand the

---

[54] BARNARD, *The Functions of the Executive*, 215.

[55] Ibid., 290.

[56] Peter A. REDPATH, *The Moral Psychology of St. Thomas: An Introduction to Ragamuffin Ethics* (St. Louis: En Route, 2017)

natures exhaustively and speculatively. The proper method of study is to seek chiefly to identify the causes considered as such, *that this or that is the cause*, not to probe the cause's nature considered as such, but considered as useful for generating this or that activity!

Whether our chief aim is to examine the nature of things to understand the causes of those natures in depth and considered as such, or for their utility, all human reasoning, including philosophical/scientific reasoning starts with a generic knowledge (induction) we have of the nature of something, of some organizational whole (a one existing in a many). All reasoning, right as well as wrong, starts with, presupposes, some organizational whole that we know; with an induction of some chief relation that harmonizes, orders, some disparate multitude into being parts of a whole that we immediately, recognize!

Despite popular and widespread contemporary misunderstandings of the nature of induction as a logical process of reasoning from a concrete particular to an abstract universal idea, strictly speaking, induction, in the form of: 1) initially recognizing the nature of something, or 2) philosophical/scientific induction is no process at all; especially not a logical or non-logical one of reasoning, or in the case of philosophical/scientific induction, *induction is an instantaneous act of understanding, immediately apprehending, in terms of the parts that harmonize to constitute, it, the generic kind of organizational whole that a person is intellectually grasping.*

For example, in the two cases referred to in the paragraph immediately above, induction is no logical process and it does not require numerous acts of 'empirical experience' of sense data about which we logically reason to achieve. How complicated the act of induction needs to be essentially depends upon 1) the intellectual excellence of individual human being who is doing the inducing; 2) the more or less complicated nature of the organizational whole which that person is attempting to understand; and 3) the extent and depth of familiarity with that organizational whole that person has.

Essentially, the act of induction involves instantaneously apprehending the chief principle of unity (a one) *that exists within a multitude (a many) that harmonizes orders, that multitude into being parts of this or that kind of a whole!* Essentially, induction involves being able to grasp the chief principle that essentially causes: 1) organizational harmony, order; 2) some multitude to be unified as harmoniously connected (ordered) so as to generate this or that kind of whole and the acts which that whole naturally inclines to cause (the organization's chief aim: cooperatively to accomplish numerically-one act).

For example, within moments of walking into a business organization, school, church, military or medical facility, charitable foundation, political party, or orchestral performance and sensing how it operates, an intelligent person with extensive experience working with one or more of these organizations just mentioned can immediately induce its nature, and determine whether its activities are healthy or unhealthy, strong, or weak. For such a person, doing so requires no extensive process of empirical verification, logical reasoning, or mathematical testing for the simple reason *that the inductive skill resides within the high-quality of harmonious cooperation existing between the organization being experienced and the estimative sense faculty, cogitative reason, and virtuously trained intellect of the expert.*[57]

2.8 Systems Thinking, Knowledge and Thomistic Psychology of Executive Leadership

This above lengthy explanation of inductive reasoning is vital to the nature and methodology of a Thomistic organizational psychology of the executive function and leadership. It also fundamentally differentiates the method and practical application of Thomistic organizational psychology from scientific psychology. Since we have presented this important distinction, we will use throughout this thesis REDPATH's terminology of "philosophical/scientific" organizational psychology as differentiated from scientific organizational psychology. It is amazing that REDPATH, a Thomist, writing on a Thomistic Metaphysics of Organization in 2017 relates directly to BARNARD's executive issue on cooperation. REDPATH states in the above paragraph, "skill resides within the high-quality of harmonious cooperation existing between the

---

[57] Ibid., 214–216.

organization being experienced and the estimative sense faculty, cogitative reason and virtuously trained intellect of the expert."[58]

BARNARD states in 1938, "The questions which we ask ourselves are straightforward, simple, direct, easy to ask-but difficult to answer. They are: 1) Why or when is cooperation effective? 2) What are the objects of cooperative processes? 3) What are the limitations of cooperation? 4) What are the causes of instability in cooperative systems? 5) What effect has cooperation upon the ends sought?"[59] In the coming chapters we will continue not only the comparison of Barnard's philosophy of executive function and organizational leadership with Redpath's metaphysics of organization and moral psychology, but we will, also, introduce the thought and management principles of inductive reasoning and Japanese knowledge management.

In the late seventies and early eighties, America was losing badly in the world of manufacturing and hit hard by Japan's sudden amazing mastery of total quality management. Especially in the automotive industry, American quality control had become outmoded considering Japanese competition, and panic had set in big time. Of course, it provided a promising opportunity for various schools of quality control consultants. It was W. Edwards DEMING who had gone to Japan and introduced them to quality management. Basically, he introduced them to the work of Walter A. SHEWART in statistical methods and quality control. As a tribute to DEMING, the Japanese to this day award the Deming Prize medal of quality to companies of excellence. DEMING was far more than a consultant in statistical methods of measurement of quality: he had rediscovered Aristotelian causation. It was a philosophy of practical knowledge based fundamentally on Aristotelian causation (material, formal, efficient, and final).

Primarily, DEMING called for a return to the Aristotelian principle of teleology in the management of any organization dedicated to the satisfaction of the end user of a product, good or service. The founder of the quality movement held emphatically two Aristotelian principles. One, the relation of parts to whole in organizational structures is essentially teleological since an organization needs machinery, manpower, material, and methods to perform the functions for which they are designed, i.e. the end user

---

[58] Ibid.

[59] BARNARD, *The Functions of the Executive*, 23.

satisfaction. Two, mechanical efficiency and teleological purpose must be continuously reconciled throughout the organization. It is the task of management to optimize the organization by maintaining the mutual compatibility of these two forces. Based on the relation of part to whole and teleological purpose, Deming defines business from the perspective of an interactive and interdependent system, and it is here that he begins to sound like a Thomist.

> A system must create something of value, in other words, results, the intended results, along with consideration of recipients and of cost, mould the aim of the system. It is thus management's task to determine those aims, to manage the whole organization toward accomplishment of those aims. It is important that an aim never be defined in terms of a specific activity or method. It must always relate to a better life for everyone.[60]

Like Barnard, Deming followed in the tradition that the main trait of a leader is to understand how the work of a group fits the aim of the company. Like Redpath and Barnard, Deming taught, "A system does not manage itself."[61] To do this, the executive leader must seek to understand the system he or she is attempting to manage. Without this understanding, the system cannot be managed or improved. Optimization of the parts does not optimize the whole. As we will develop in a metaphysics of organization, Deming like Barnard builds on the basic organizational principle that "system optimization requires coordination and cooperation of the parts, which requires leadership."[62] Deming's foremost contri-

---

[60] W. Edwards Deming, *The New Economics: For Industry, Government, Education* (Cambridge, Massachusetts and London, England: MIT Press, 1994), 52.

[61] Brooks Carder, PhD, and Marilyn Monda, MA, "Deming's Profound Knowledge and Leadership, We Are Still Not 'Out of the Crisis'" *Human Leadership and Development Division ASQ* (2013), 2–4.

[62] W. Edwards Deming, *Out of Crisis* (Cambridge: Massachusetts Institute of Technology, 1982), 309–371. It is in chapter eleven Deming presents his teaching on the central problem in management and in leadership. In the words of his colleague Lloyd S. Nelson, it consists in failure to understand information in terms of variation. He argues that leadership that takes aim at people that are below average in production, or above average in mistakes, is wrong,

bution to the systems approach to management is that a system can only be improved if it is in control, i.e. when the variation inherent to every system is predictable. This principle provided the statistical foundation for the systems view of organizational improvement.

DEMING was hailed in the eighties as the founder of the Total Quality Movement, and it was a title he rejected. He proclaimed in his writings and in his worldwide public four-day seminars on his 12 principles of transformation that he was teaching a philosophy of management based on "Profound Knowledge" comprised of four elements, i.e. an appreciation of a system, knowledge of variation, theory of knowledge and an understanding of psychology. It is beyond the scope or the demands of this thesis to examine in depth DEMING's theory of knowledge. Yet, his belief was that the executive function is to perceive the organization as fundamentally a learning culture.

He held that learning is a continuous process running throughout and at every level of the organization, i.e. "organizations learn only when people in them learn."[63] Deming introduced to organizational and management science a philosophy of knowledge that was extremely influenced by his background as a PhD mathematical statistician who approached the knowledge acquisition of an organizational system as primarily a methodology of statistical process control and continuous testing and improving of the system using an inductive method known as the Shewart Cycle of testing.

DEMING brought quality control methods to Japanese manufacturing after World War II when General McArthur was rebuilding the Japanese economy. He was one of the consultants selected for the reconstruction of their manufacturing base. He had been educated in quality control by Leslie Shewart of Bell Labs who was the major founder of statistical process control. In the 1950s and 60s, Japanese manufacturing was well known for poor quality products. DEMING taught their executives and

---

ineffective, costly to the company; that the same holds for a leader that supposes that everyone could be an achiever. He would understand why it is that costs decrease as quality improves. It is essential, however, in industry and in science to understand the distinction between a stable system and an unstable system, and how to plot points and conclude rational methods whether they indicate a stable system (309–310).

[63] DEMING, *The New Economics*, 106.

engineers statistical methods of quality control that American companies were not using. His efforts were monumentally successful, and, in turn, he became the leading presenter of the Total Quality Movement of the 1980s. This DEMING transformation continues as a major force in global manufacturing to the present day in new movements like "Six Sigma and "ISO 9000." Although DEMING made major contributions to the Japanese method of quality control, he was also impressed with the general approach to their style of management. As a result, DEMING attempted to introduce his followers somewhat to the Japanese concept of knowledge management with his theory of profound knowledge.[64]

He was less successful at this effort and began to state that the entire process of organizational transformation was basically an issue of psychology. Deming had really no idea of an organizational psychology, although he was most concerned about worker motivation and a trust relationship between the worker and management.[65] The problem is that DEMING was really looking for an organizational moral psychology. It is BARNARD who had recognized in the 1930s the true sustaining factor of a successful organization is a moral psychology:

> Thus, the endurance of an organization depends upon the quality of leadership and that quality derives from the breadth of the morality upon which it rests. High responsibility there must be even in the lowest, the most immoral, organizations; but if the morality to which the responsibility relates is low, the organization is short lived. A low morality will not sustain leadership long, its influence quickly vanishes, it cannot produce its own succession.[66]

The other problem is that DEMING introduced the concept of profound knowledge driven basically by a statistical method of inductive reasoning. It was a management approved method of testing of a process by means of defined statistical control measurement. For DEMING, it is the responsibility of executive leadership to

---

[64] William MCVEY, "Thomistic Scientific Leadership," *Studia Gilsoniana*, 3 (2014), 585.

[65] Brooks CARDER, PhD, and Marilyn MONDA, MA, "Deming's Profound Knowledge for Leadership," *Human Development Leadership Division* (2013), 10–12.

[66] BARNARD, *The Functions of the Executive*, 282–283.

install a culture of predictive leadership at all levels. In other words, it is a fundamental organizational principle that executive leadership understands that management is prediction. Prediction does not come from tests of statistical inference; rather it comes from theory. This theory, for DEMING, begins with a "hunch" that is tested by means of the SHEWART method of Plan-Do-Study-Act. It is a structured cycle to test if a theory is viable. If the theory does not bear out, then there is a need to change and test again. Should the test verify the hunch then the action is to improve the process tested. It is the cycle of continuous improvement. DEMING's concept of theory construction is somewhat like the Peircean concept of abduction, but he does not develop this line of thought. However, he does reject the idea that it is possible to predict future occurrences by means of statistical confidence interval levels.

It is the Japanese organizational scientists Ikujiro NONAKA and Hirotaka TAKEUCHI who present in the 1990s a knowledge management approach based on a concept of inductive reasoning similar to the Redpath's Aristotelian-Thomistic definition of induction described in previous paragraphs.[67] Western view of organizational management knowledge is primarily explicit knowledge. Meaning that, organizational knowledge is best expressed in the form of hard data, scientific formula, and codified procedures. In the Western approach to knowledge management, the words *data*, *information* and *knowledge* are used interchangeably. Deming's inductive reasoning was limited to an explicit and sequential cycle of testing over time.

Japanese companies, however, have a very different understanding of knowledge. They recognize that the knowledge expressed in words and numbers represents only the beginning. They view knowledge as being primarily *tacit*—something not easily visible and expressible. Tacit knowledge is highly personal and hard to formalize, making it difficult to communicate or to share with others. Subjective insights, intuitions, and hunches fall into this category of knowledge. Furthermore, tacit knowledge is deeply rooted in an individual's action and experience, as well as in the ideals, values, or the emotions he or she embraces.

---

[67] Ikujiro NONAKA and Hirotaka TAKEUCHI, *The Knowledge-Creating Company: How Japanese Companies Create the Dynamics of Innovation* (New York and Oxford: Oxford University Press, 1995).

At the same time tacit knowledge contains an important cognitive dimension. It consists of schemata, mental models, beliefs, and perceptions so ingrained that we take for granted. The cognitive dimension of tacit knowledge reflects our image of reality (what is) and our vision for the future (what ought to be). Though they cannot be articulated very easily, these implicit models shape the very way we perceive the world around us.

The distinction between explicit knowledge and tacit knowledge is the key to understanding the differences between the Western approach to knowledge and the Japanese approach to knowledge. Explicit knowledge can be easily transmitted electronically, can be easily processed by a computer, transmitted electronically, or stored in databases. But the subjective and intuitive nature of tacit knowledge makes it difficult to process or transmit the acquired knowledge in any systematic logical way.[68]

There are three key characteristics of Japanese knowledge creation:

1) use metaphor and analogy to express the heavy reliance on figurative language and symbolism. We could call it a method of knowledge by inductive elicitation by means of figurative ideas, feelings, and hunches, 2) elicitation from personal to organizational knowledge. An individual cannot create knowledge on their own. There must be interaction and dialogue that takes place that is amplified in a group by means of dialogue, experience sharing and observation, 3) Ambiguity and redundancy—it is difficult for Western managers to grasp the concept of redundancy because of the emphasis in Western organizations on bottom line management against unnecessary duplication and waste. Redundancy is important because it encourages frequent dialogue and communication. It creates a common ground, both in the formal and informal organization, for the transfer of tacit knowledge, and allows members of the organization to share over lapping information.[69]

---

[68] Ibid., 8–9.
[69] Ibid., 12–14.

Executive leadership's responsibility is to promote a tacit/explicit knowledge culture. Middle managers serve as a bridge between visionary ideals of the top and the often-chaotic reality of those on the front line of business. Middle managers mediate between the *what should be* mindset of the top and the *what is* mindset of the front-line employees by creating mid-level business and product concepts. As team leaders of the product development team, for example, middle managers are able to remake reality according to the company's vision. Middle managers play a key role in the knowledge-creation process. They synthesize the tacit knowledge of front-line employees and senior executives, make it explicit, and incorporate it into products and techniques. The Japanese knowledge creation concept of oneness of body and mind, knowledge spiral and middle-up-down management style may seem strange sounding to Western executives, managers, and supervisors. As we develop an Aristotelian-Thomistic metaphysics of organization and a rational sensing moral psychology in the following chapters, we find that an Aristotelian-Thomistic framework is compatible with the Japanese rejection of the mind and body dualism of Cartesian and Kantian epistemology.[70]

It is interesting that BARNARD saw that Catholic Church as a fine paradigm of executive interconnection and coordination. In his model, the interconnection points are not only positions of leadership, rather an intersection point has a great deal of independence in decision making, in procurement, in personnel selection, in logistics, and supply chain management. Most of all, the executive intersection point must have a strong trust relationship with the Chief Executive Officer and a bond of loyalty to the organizational culture. He/she must, also, have high rational and moral habits of character and is able to interact with ease with the formal and informal social structure of the organization. Issues of coordination are increasingly important in the emerging vanishing bureaucratic organizations demanding intersection point executive type leaders capable of particular-concrete contextual rational and moral decision making supportive of the organizational universal purpose and vision of excellence.

---

[70] Ibid., 13–15.

2.9 A Case Study of Executive Function Transformational Cultural Leadership

Since we are not restricting this dissertation to the topic of a Thomistic organizational psychology of business and the executive function of leadership, we will turn our attention to Chester BARNARD's paradigm to a non-business organization, namely the Catholic Church. Usually, the Catholic Church identifies itself as an institution. Sociologists define an institution as a system of behavioral relationship patterns that are densely interwoven and enduring and function across an entire society. They order and structure the behavior of individuals by means of their normative character. Institutions, from the perspective of sociology, in the domain of culture, media and religion are responsible for the transmission of contexts of meaning, value orientations and symbolic codes. For centuries, religious institutions had a monopoly here. In the twentieth century, institutions in the spheres of mass media and cultural production began to convey values, norms, and symbolic codes, reaching broad segments of the population.[71] The drastic cultural global impact on family, religious, commerce, government and social institutions (especially beginning in the later part of the twentieth century) has been caused by multi-cultural factors; but there are two socio-culture factors that have had a dominant impact on organizational culture: a psychology of self-realization and a secular spiritual psychology.

In his work, *The Fourth Great Awakening & the Future of Egalitarianism*, the winner of the 1993 Nobel Prize, economist Robert William FOGEL analyzes the drastic change in American culture from the 1730s to 1960 and the transformation in economic standards, cultural values and religious practices and affiliation. There is one amazing insightful fact that explains much of the change in particularly American culture toward institutional religion in the United States, although his observations may apply to most of Western European culture as well. The ability of an

---

[71] Roland VERMIEBE, https://www.soz.ukdnivie.ac.at/fileadmin/user_upload/inst_soziologie/Personen/Institutsmitglieder/Verwiebe/Social-Institutions-in-Encyclopedia-of-Quality-of-Life-Research.pdf

organization's survival over time is of the key criteria in assessing the competence of the executive function and leadership. An executive function of the organization is concerned with more than internal co-ordination and leadership, the executive function must also respond continuously to the environmental changes impacting on the stability and the growth of the organization. In FOGEL's discussion on technological change, cultural transformations, and political crises, he draws attention to the rise in higher education and college education and the impact on institutions and organizations.

Undergraduate enrollment at colleges and universities increased more than fourfold between 1870 and 1900, when it stood at 230,000. It increased again by fourfold during the thirty years, reaching 1.1. million in 1930. The huge growth in enrollment resumed after World War II, going from 2.8 million in 1960 to 13.7 times in 1990.

Because of this expansion in higher education, professional occupations in 1997 counted for about 33 percent of the labor force, and the composition of these occupations had changed from a century before. The clergy, which had dominated intellectual life in the 1890s, represented in 1997 less than 1 percent of the professional class. In 1997 journalist, social and natural scientists, college and university teachers, and mathematicians each outnumbered the clergy. As if an answer to the appeals of modernists, a secular class of experts on the natural and social worlds has usurped the monopoly that theologians once had on these domains.

The new professionals have played three important roles in the establishment and perpetuation of the egalitarian state. They provide most of the personnel who manage the egalitarian state, both as designers and as implementers of policy. The governments today employ one-fifth of all physical scientists, one-third of all life scientists, three-eighths of all mathematicians, and more than a quarter of all social scientists. Even cabinet posts, once filled almost exclusively by politicians and businessmen, are increasingly claimed by professionals.[72]

In the coming chapters, we shall return to thoughts of FOGEL and others on cultural change, as we develop the concept of a Thomistic rational sensing moral psychology and the concept of self and the being of the "organizational person." We will use FOGEL's terminology and other cultural and organizational scientists of the premodern, modern, and postmodern organization. This terminology is not used to explain or defend any philosophical system. It is rather an effective way to set boundaries of observable categories of change in the understanding of the emerging sense of an organization in a global information society and the impact of spiritual and moral leadership on the organizational philosophy of management. Fogel describes the postmodern egalitarian culture in the developed world as one of a quest for self-realization.

The problem of self-realization has distinct aspects, and different solutions, for the young and the aged, for ethic and racial minorities, and for women, yet all fuel the moral crisis that is the hallmark of our age and the greatest threat to the survival of society. To achieve self-realization, each individual must have an understanding of life's opportunities, a sense of which opportunities are most attractive to him or her at each stage of life, and the requisite educational, material, and spiritual resources to pursue these opportunities. In the era that is unfolding, fair access to spiritual resources will be as much a touchstone of egalitarianism as an access to material resources was in the past. Spiritual resources are not limited to those found in the sacred realm but include the whole range of immaterial commodities that are needed to cope with emotional

---

[72] Robert William FOGEL, *The Fourth Great Awakening & The Future of Egalitarianism* (Chicago and London: The University of Chicago Press, 2000), 72–73. FOGEL's work portrays American culture as a transformation of four great awakenings. His theory of social economic transformation of American culture is based on religious and political reforms to achieve spiritual equity. He defines spiritual assets such as self-esteem, a sense of discipline, a vision of opportunity, and a thirst for knowledge as an essential part of the sociocultural transfer at a very young age.

trauma and that, more often than not, are transferred between individuals privately, rather than through the market. Such resources include a sense of purpose, a sense of opportunity, a sense of community, a strong family ethic, a strong work ethic and high self-esteem. Although the majority of Americans, especially those over forty, find many of these resources in the ethics and creeds of their religion, there are numerous other codes of behavior and theories of life that inspire virtue and lead to success in coping with the challenges and pitfalls of modern life. Various quasi-religious organizations and movements have developed-the nature and content are widely debated by scholars. Severe inequality in the distribution of spiritual resources results in part from changes in the structure of the economy and to the social institutions through which immaterial resources are transferred. Spiritual deprivation is due in part to the glorification of hedonistic impulses and instant gratification by the media and advertising; this has diverted many children and adolescents from the quest for self-realization.[73]

FOGEL portrays an American cultural transformation of four great awakenings. It is a sweeping historical cultural economic analysis of an America society driven by a spiritual and moral value system of egalitarianism. Gradually in his analysis, he puts forth the theory of the emergence of a new socio-cultural postmodern agenda of the Fourth Great Awakening.

Now at the dawn of the new millennium, it is necessary to address such postmodern concerns as the struggle for self-realization, the desire to find a deeper meaning in life than the endless accumulation of consumer durables and the pursuit of pleasure, access to miracles of modern medicine, education not only for careers but for spiritual values, methods of financing an early and fruitful, and long-lasting retirement, and increasing the amount of quality time available for family activities.[74]

---

[73] Ibid., 72–73.

[74] Ibid.

What is most applicable to this thesis is that we are exploring the changing nature of the postmodern organization, corporate executive function of leadership and the motivational psychology worker self-realization, participation, and self-organization.

We have introduced FOGEL because of the importance of his theory of the postmodern culture of self-realization and its relationship to new types of religious pursuit, especially in free market and consumer purchase motivated societies. Given BARNARD's admiration for the executive function and leadership of the Catholic Church and its survival over centuries, we will examine its executive function, especially as the executive leadership confronts the need for transformational change in a postmodern culture of self-realization and the appearance of new cultural expressions of nontraditional spirituality. It is suggested that FOGEL in many ways explains why we hear statements like, "I am religious but not spiritual. I want nothing to do with organized religion. I think that institutional religion does more harm than good, etc."

David R. KOLZOW in *Leading from Within: Building Organizational Leadership Capacity* describes six leadership styles, i.e. Authoritarian vs. Democratic Leadership, Power and Leadership, Charismatic Leader, Transactional Leadership, Transformational Leadership, The Servant Leader, and The Situational Leader. An organizational leader may have characteristics that fit with anyone of these styles of leadership. Over time, especially at the executive level, these styles aid in developing a leadership philosophy at the highest levels and throughout organization, while at the same time allowing for and blending a diversity of leadership styles. In a case study of Pope Francis, we have chosen to examine from the perspective of an executive leader who engages in a style of transformational leadership. It is the style of leadership that seems a good fit with the radical changes that the Church is encountering in a global culture of self-realization and multiple forms of non-institutional religious expressions.

Transformational leadership grows out of the assumption that people will follow a leader who inspires and motivates them. The leader motivates and inspires by developing a compelling vision, selling that vision, and focusing on developing relationships with followers as teacher, mentor, and coach. Transformational leadership focuses on the big picture and on concern for people and their individual needs. Four main components (the four "I s") of transformational leadership striving are:

> Idealized Influence—a leader is to instill pride and trust among followers so that they will emulate the leader and his/her ideals.

> Inspirational Motivation—leader must create a sense of team spirit, passion, and optimism for the organization's vision. It is the function of leadership to provide a culture of inspiration for achievement.

> Intellectual Stimulation—the leader must question old assumptions, cast problems in a new light, encourage creativity and innovation, and look at more effective ways to make decisions. The leader solicits ideas and nurtures and develops people who think independently and who value learning.

> Individual Consideration—The leader pays attention to the needs of individuals, and seeks to develop followers by supporting, mentoring, and coaching employees to reach their full potential. A concern exists to keep lines of communication open so that followers feel free to share ideas in this supportive environment. This type of leader also makes a strong effort to recognize followers for their unique contributions.[75]

BARNARD argues that organizational endurance comes from an executive function driven by foresight, high ideals, and persistence of cooperation. For centuries, the Catholic Church has existed with the executive function of the Pope, the Vatican, and a Roman Magisterium. The executive leadership of communication and coordination depends on distributed leadership points of interconnection, namely the national Cardinals and local bishops throughout the world. Yet, even the executive function of the Catholic Church admired by Barnard is being severely tested by, in FOGEL's analysis, a postmodern culture of self-realization and the secularization of religion. We can, somewhat briefly, scrutinize this present postmodern executive

---

[75] KOLZOW, *Leading from Within*, 43–47.

function of Rome by means of an insightful interview of Jorge Mario Bergoglio (Pope Francis) who is responsible for the executive coordination of the Catholic Church during a period of organizational adaptation.

2.9.1 A Case Study of Executive Function Transformational Leadership

The interview was conducted by Antonio SPADARO, S.J. "A Big Heart Open to God: An Interview with Pope Francis."[76] This interview is studied not from a theological dogmatic, philosophical, or canonical perspective; rather it is a study of Pope Francis in his role as the Chief Executive Officer who is responsible for the necessary transformation of the organizational culture in response to the impact of the postmodern self-realization culture and nontraditional, often referred to as anti-organizational religion, spirituality. We will apply to this Transformational leadership a framework of Thomistic organizational psychological insight. Such insights will be more developed in later chapters. We will refer to Antonio SPADARO as Father SPADARO.

> Father Spadaro asks: "Who is Jorge Mario Bergoglio?" The Pope stares at me in silence. I ask him "if this is a question that I am allowed to ask…" He nods that I am, and he tells me.

> Pope Francis answers: "I am a sinner. It is the most accurate definition. It is not a figure of speech, a literary genre, I am a sinner."

> Father Spadaro: The Pope continues to reflect and concentrate, as if he did not expect this question, as if he were forced to reflect further.

> Pope Francis: "Yes, perhaps I can say that I am a bit astute, that I can adapt to circumstances, but it is true that I am a bit naïve. Yes, but the best summary, the

---

[76] Antonio SPADARO, S.J. "A Big Heart Open to God: An Interview with Pope Francis," *American Jesuit Review* (2017), https://www.americamagazine.org/faith/2013/09/30/big-heart-open-god-interview-pope-francis.

one that comes more from the inside and I feel most true is this: I am a sinner whom the Lord has looked upon." And he repeats: "I am the one looked upon by the Lord. I always felt my motto. Miserando atque Eligendo [By Having Mercy and by Choosing Him] was very true for me."

[The motto is taken from the Homilies of Bede the Venerable, who writes in his communion on the Gospel of the calling of Matthew:] Jesus saw a publican, and since he looked at him with feelings of love and chose him, he said to him, 'Follow me'." The Pope adds, "I think the Latin gerund Miserando is impossible in both Italian and Spanish. I like to translate it with another gerund that does not exist: misericordiando ['mercy-ing'] …I always stayed in [the neighborhood of] Via della Scrofa. From there I often visited the Church of St. Louis of France, and I went there to contemplate the painting of The Calling of St. Matthew by Caravaggio."

"The Calling of Saint Matthew," by Caravaggio

Father Spadaro asks I begin to intuit what the pope wants to tell me.

Pope Francis answers: "That finger of Jesus, pointing at Matthew. That's me. I feel like him. Like Matthew. It is the gesture of Matthew that strikes me: he holds on to his money as if to say, 'no, not me! No, this money is mine.' Here, this is me, a sinner on whom the Lord has turned his gaze. And this is what I said when they asked me if I would accept the election as Pontiff…I am a sinner, but I trust in the infinite mercy and patience of our Lord Jesus Christ, and I accept in a spirit of penance."

Executive Leadership Observation: It is argued in the coming chapters that there are substantial areas in the subject matter of organizational psychology, where it is possible and advantageous for Thomistic psychology to engage in an exchange of concepts on the theory and practice of the organizational executive function and leadership with scientific organizational psychology. Simultaneous to this cross-boundary exchange, a Thomistic organizational psychology must define its unique identity based on metaphysical, moral, and spiritual principles. In this chapter, we have begun with the principle that organizational leadership requires facing the potential dark soul of executive leadership. In Pope Francis, we find a person called to an incredibly high position of leadership in the Catholic Church, and his first instinctual habit as an executive is to engage in a rational and moral reflection of, "I am a sinner." In other words, he is a leader who is fully aware of his dark soul and enters his executive position with humility. He will lead with the habit of humility.

We have, thus far, argued that it is a necessary first principle of a Thomistic organizational psychology to recognize that the reality of degrees of neurotic egocentric leadership exists within an organization and it is the task of the executive leadership to establish a systemic sense of rational and moral behavior, i.e. a policy and practice of organizational moral rectitude. As we look at Pope Francis, in his executive capacity, we learn before he is prepared to carry out his leadership, as he is intensely aware of the potential dark side of his behavior as he answers the question, "Who is Jorge Mario Bergoglio?", and he answers, "This is the most accurate definition. It is not a figure of speech, a literary genre. I am a sinner." Then he explains how this habit of soul has developed over the years.

Father Spadaro asks: "What does it mean for a Jesuit to be Bishop of Rome? What element of Ignatian spirituality helps your life your ministry"

Pope Francis replies: "Discernment is one of the things that worked inside St. Ignatius. For him it is an instrument of struggle in order to know the Lord and follow him closely. I was always struck by a saying what describes the vision of Ignatius: non coerceri a maximo, sed contineri a minimo divinum est (not to be limited by the greatest and yet to be contained in the tiniest-this is the divine)." I thought a lot about this phrase in connection with the issue of the different role in the government of the church, about becoming the superior of somebody else: it is important not to be restricted by a larger space, and it is important to be able to stay in restricted space. The virtue of the large and the small is magnanimity. Thanks to magnanimity, we can always look at the horizon from the position where we are. That means being able to appreciate the small things inside large horizons, those of the kingdom of God.

This discernment takes time. For example, many think that changes and reforms can take place in a short time. I believe that we always need time to lay the foundations for real, effective changes. And this is the time for discernment.

But I am always wary of decisions made hastily. I am always wary of the first decision, that is, the first thing that comes to my mind if I have to make a decision. This is usually the wrong thing. I have to wait and assess, looking deeply into myself, taking the necessary time. The wisdom of discernment redeems the necessary ambiguity of life and helps us find the appropriate means, which do not always coincide with what looks great and strong.

Father Spadaro asks: "What do you think about the Roman dicasteries [the various departments that assist the pope in his mission.]

Pope Francis answers: "The dicasteries of the Roman Curia are at the service of the Pope and the bishops, and when they are not functioning well, they run the risk of becoming instruments of censorship. It is amazing to see the denunciations for lack of orthodoxy that come to Rome. I think the cases should be investigated by local bishops' conferences, which get valuable assistance from Rome. These cases, in fact, are much better dealt with locally. The Roman congregations are mediators; they are not middlemen or managers."

Father Spadaro asks: "Do we have to be optimistic? What are the signs of hope in today's world?"

Pope Francis answers: "I do not like to use the word optimism because it is about a psychological attitude...I like to use the word hope instead."

Leadership Observation: Even this small selection of dialogue from Antonio SPADARO, S.J. article indicates the organizational executive talents of Pope Francis, especially as a transformational leader under a difficult historical period in church history. His goal is to instill pride and trust among his followers so that they emulate his ideals. He is a passionate and optimistic leader in the confusing and difficult historical period of transformation. He stimulates the soul to ask questions and question old assumptions. He wants to solicit new ideas and look for more effective ways to make decisions. Finally, in terms of individual considerations he calls for the need to pay attention to the needs of the followers at the local level with pastoral prudence. He seeks to improve lines of communication in order to solve the problems of his followers more efficiently and effectively. Then as any organizational executive he sets a clear transformational organizational vision.

Father Spadaro asks: "What does the Church need most at this historic moment? Do we need reforms? What are your wishes for the church in the coming years? What kind of church do you dream of?"

Pope Francis answers: "The thing the church needs most today is the ability to heal wounds and to warm the hearts of the faithful; it needs nearness, proximity. I see the church as a field hospital after battle."

2.10 It is More Than a Code of Ethics; It is About Character

Thomistic metaphysical psychological illumination enables leaders who opt seriously to wonder about the nature of executive levels of leadership to observe and explain organizational life considered in an entirely assumption-less manner. It is not a system of empirical measurement or logic. It is a habit of knowing first principles (including powers of the human person) essential to explaining the proper navigation of his/her personal and organizational life as a leader.

Peter DRUCKER (1909–2005) has been considered the most prominent thinker in the field of business and a major shaper of management thought. Marcia KURZYNSKI wrote an important and insightful article "Peter Drucker: modern day Aristotle for the business community." Even though, this dissertation is on Thomistic organizational psychology, we will develop in the coming chapters that Thomas AQUINAS rational moral psychology is a development of ARISTOTLE's psychology of the soul, and especially AQUINAS's commentary on *ARISTOTLE's Nicomachean Ethics*. Marcia KURZYNSKI identifies the following Aristotelian themes in DRUCKER's philosophy of management and the executive function of organizational leadership.

> Drucker criticized contemporary business ethics as a form of "casuistry" which permitted a special code of ethics for people of power. He held that there is really just one ethic, which should apply to all, regardless of status or function. Drucker did indeed recognize the importance of understanding right and wrong as an indispensable feature of executive decision making and effectiveness. Drucker's criticism of business ethics, as it has been adapted by business ethicists and the contemporary business organization, stemmed from his belief that the traditional principle-based theories of ethical business behavior are not sufficient to guide business character. This is not that he discounted the need for moral principles, only that there is little moral foundation for reliance on principles based strictly on subjective interpretation. He believed that contemporary philosophical analysis of management ethics had been loosely derived from rational absolutes determined by the secular society of the eighteenth century, which focused on society, and not on the

individual moral responsibility. As a result, Drucker turned to Aristotelian philosophy for illumination as he developed his science of management.

Drucker's works reveal that there is much in his management philosophy that is analogous with Aristotle's moral philosophy in the Nicomachean Ethics and to some degree his political philosophy as delineated in Aristotle's Politics. Drucker's concepts of community, the idea of purpose (what Aristotle called telos), and the importance of character, in creating a good life for oneself and others are similar Aristotle's teachings. Aristotelian philosophy and Drucker's theory of management share a common vision of eudemonia, to live the good life, in fact, the best life, which is achievable through the practice of virtue. Drucker did not use the classical word, telos, as did Aristotle, nor does his idea of telos have exactly the same meaning in Drucker's management philosophy. Nevertheless, Drucker emphasized the importance of character for the manager seeking to accomplish business-oriented goals. Drucker prioritized integrity of character as the wellspring of managerial effectiveness and success. The connection between effectiveness and integrity implies that the manager can be counted to think things through, to act consistently according to a high standard of principle, to choose consistently the right course of action to achieve results hat are good for the community, for all who might be affected by the action.

Both Aristotle and Drucker underscored the concept of character in their respective theories. Aristotle maintained the idea that good character is essential for living a good life and Drucker asserted that integrity of character is the essential quality for managerial success. With respect to their thinking on the concept of character, to some extent the similarities stop at this point, for Aristotle moral theory is extensively developed, and Drucker's is not. Drucker was never able to discover a uniform profile of leadership traits yet insisted that character was the essential quality for being a good manager. Drucker employed Aristotle's concept of character more fully in the concrete practices of management, while Aristotle was less clear, did not illustrate with many concrete examples, and so remains more abstract.

Drucker held management to high standards of excellence and living a good life. Like the way Aristotle's theory of virtue ethics centers on moral character and how a good character can help one reach the telos of living a good life, as a responsible member of society, Drucker's ideas about management locate integrity of character as the wellspring of good management and effective management.[77]

We started this chapter on the nature of a Thomistic organizational psychology and the function of executive leadership by discussing the "the dark soul" of leadership. We began with this issue because there is a need to differentiate a Thomistic organizational philosophical/psychological analysis of leadership from an empirical organizational psychology treatment of leadership. The fundamental reason for the main differentiation is that Thomistic organizational psychology analyzes the issue from the perspective of a faculties psychology, i.e. the faculties of the soul. We did note that even in a non-Thomistic study of leadership by Roger LEWIN and Birute REGINE, the issue of soul is used as a critical metaphor to express the dark side of leadership: "…that we just don't want to really look into anybody's eyes and see they have souls. We should start with the premise that we have souls."[78]

The concept of the dark soul of leadership is that organizations so easily and naturally are organized ignoring the principle that workers or volunteers in profit and nonprofits or government services have souls. According to St. Thomas human nature no longer exists within its pristine condition of perfect organizational harmony sometimes called "the state of original justice," consequently there is always the ever present "dark soul" of organizational leadership. It means, therefore, that "the light of wisdom within nature became increasingly dulled as the emotional appetites became increasingly stronger."[79]

In the next chapter, we will explain that a Thomistic metaphysics of organization and moral psychology is required to study the functions of executive leadership. In constructing a psychology of the functions of executive leadership, we will use principles and methods from other schools of psychology. As we did in this first

---

[77] Marcia KURZYNSKI, "Peter Drucker: modern day Aristotle for business community," *Journal of Management History*, 5 No. 4 (2009) 361–365.

[78] LEWIN and REGINE, *The Soul at Work*, 23.

[79] REDPATH, *The Moral Psychology of St. Thomas*, 68–69.

chapter, as a rule, the psychological principles, and methods of Thomistic psychology will be used. Psychologists used will be mostly from a background in Aristotelian-Thomistic neo behavioral theory. At the same time, we will include principles and methods from molar behavioral psychology.

Karen HORNEY's neo psychoanalytical construct of culture neuroses is compatible with the issues of executive leadership and the "dark soul" because of her attention to the issue of general hostile intensions and fear of envy in cases of culture and career success, contempt for failure, and lack of self-confidence. HORNEY addresses a problem most related to organizational leadership that individuals in an organizational culture are not prepared for the hostilities and struggles for success and the avoidance of failure in a competitive organizational environment. The major interest, however, in this dissertation, will be to study the issue of the function of executive leadership from the organizational and moral psychology of St. Thomas AQUINAS from the recent and pivotal work of Peter A. REDPATH, *The Moral Psychology of St. Thomas*. We will also blend with REDPATH's Aristotelian-Thomistic psychology compatible psychological empirical theory from teleological and molar neo behaviorists and current Aristotelian virtue psychology.

In this dissertation, when necessary, we will examine scientific studies on leadership traits and types, but always maintain our focus on a Thomistic concept of a psychological metaphysical foundation of: 1) the one and the many, 2) the executive leadership function of command and control, 3) the executive function of blending contrary organizational forces, 4) a psychological metaphysical executive sense of organizational vision and the emulation and diffusion of executive leadership as a collective participation in the vision, and 5) the development of an organizational spiral of Aristotelian-Thomistic speculative and practical knowing and doing, as it applies to desired and emergent order in evolving organizational environments. Finally, it is necessary to describe clearly the meaning of the function of executive leadership.

First, from BARNARD, we are "not restricted to the executive functions in industrial or commercial organizations. On the contrary, all classes or types of formal organizations are within the scope of observation for our purpose. The nature and processes of such organizations determine what the executive functions are and how they are to be performed."[80]

Second, we are using BARNARD's meaning of the executive organization and leadership.

> In a unit organization there are executive functions to be performed, but not necessarily by a single individual continuously. They may be performed alternatively by the several persons who contribute to the organization. In complex organizations, on the other hand, the necessities of communication result almost invariably in the localization of the executive functions of the subordinate unit organizations normally in one person.[81]

BARNARD's description of the executive function is somewhat difficult to explain; therefore, we will return to it in the following chapters. His concept is difficult because he has a rather wide application of the executive function throughout the organization. His ideas of a functioning executive leader are like present organizational methods in leadership empowerment and self-directed work teams.[82]

---

[80] BARNARD, *The Functions of the Executive*, 7.

[81] Ibid., 136–137.

[82] See BOWDITCH and BUONO, *A Primer on Organizational Behavior*. One way to conceptualize the idea of team-centered as opposed to leader center decision making and work direction is R. TANNENBAUM and W. H. SCHMIDT's classic continuum of leadership behavior, "How to Choose a Leadership Pattern: Retrospective Commentary," *Harvard Business Review* 51, no.3 (1973), 162–175, 178–180. Work related decisions can range from those in which the manager has complete control to those in which the decision-making process is centralized in the group. The idea of worker and team empowerment emphasizes a move away from leader's dominance and expert problem solving to a system where the organizational members, as the new experts, are continuously involved in organizational decision processes. While traditional models of power and authority were based on position and status, empowerment and self-directed teams emphasize the involvement of all organizational members in efforts to continuously improve work systems and outcomes. As a growing body of research indicates, especially for complex tasks, directive leadership is relatively ineffective when compared with the efficacy of work experience and training of members of close-knit, self-directed teams.

Third, we will adhere closely to concept of Warren BENNIS' definition of a leader, since it is extremely compatible with Thomistic organizational psychology of leadership: "Leaders are people who do the right thing; managers are people who do things right."[83] BENNIS in *Why Leaders Can't Lead* claims, "This study also reinforced my earlier insight-that American organizations (and probably those in much of the rest of the industrialized world) are under led and overmanaged. They do not pay enough attention to doing the right things, while they pay too much attention to doing things right."[84]

Fourth, considering the arguments in this chapter from the framework of a Thomistic organizational psychology regard the "dark soul" of leadership and organizational pathology. The virtue of humility is proposed as the rational moral antibiotic, by way of metaphor, for executive neurotic behavior and endemic pathological organizational behavior. Given that the habit of humility is a function of executive leadership, the habit of this virtue must be distributed throughout all levels of permanent, temporary, and emerging organizational leadership.

Fifth, when we use the term executive exemplar soulful leadership, we are always basically referring to a mode of leadership empowered by the Aristotelian-Thomistic psychology of the faculties (powers) of the soul and expressed in actions.

2.11 The Executive Function of Leadership and the necessity of the Virtue of Humility

It is interesting when SPADARO asks Pope Francis about his executive responsibilities, he answers, "I am a sinner." When Francis states that he is a sinner, he is as an executive practicing the habit of humility. It is a habit based on a power to act that is necessarily related to the executive function of leaders. It could be said that it is essential to the character of a good executive. When we think of the exercise of executive power, as a rule we do not think of a humble leader. The most common understanding of humility is of a monkish character, i.e. a saintly person who is

---

[83] Warren BENNIS *Why Leaders Can't Lead: The Unconscious Conspiracy Continues* (San Francisco: Jossey-Bass Publishers, 1989), 18.

[84] Ibid.

known for his/her humbleness of character and at times self-abasement. It is an unfortunate understanding of the virtue of humility because humility as a virtue is a power of the soul. Any leader, especially an executive leader, must have the insight of his/her intellectual and emotional strengths and weaknesses. In terms of a Thomistic organizational psychology it is the habit of humility that guards a leader from the egocentric dark soul organizational character.

The function of executive leadership is to will the rational and moral good of the organization. Most often, the executive leader is under grave responsibilities and stress, as he/she makes decisions for the good of the organization. AQUINAS's teachings on the virtue of humility are most applicable to such leadership situations. In recent years in organizational behavior, there has been much discussion on the importance on emotional intelligence. The issue of Thomistic mastery of the emotions is an integral part of AQUINAS's rational sensing moral psychology and a virtue psychology.

AQUINAS in his treatment of humility in the *Summa Theologiae*, on humility as a virtue holds that humility allows a leader to master his/her traits of egocentricity and turn to the rational estimative powers of the soul. He identifies the two emotions that an organizational leader experiences as he/she is drawn to difficult decisions regarding the good of the organization. The executive is a being moved by the feelings of hope and despair. It is in these intense existential decision-making situations, the leader must exercise caution, and there is the need of a moderating and restraining moral virtue.

Thus, Aquinas teaches:

There is a need, on the part of the appetite, of a moral virtue to strengthen it and urge it on. Wherefore a twofold virtue is necessary with regard to the difficult good: one, to temper and restrain the mind, lest it tend to high things immoderately; and this belongs to the virtue of humility; and another to strengthen the mind against despair and urge it on to the pursuit of great things according to right reason; and this is magnanimity. Therefore, it is evident that humility is a virtue.[85]

---

[85] Thomas AQUINAS, *Summa Theologiae* II-II, q. 161, a. 1.

It could be said that the purpose of the virtuous habit of humility is to check and moderate the decision making, strategy and goal setting of executive leadership. Humility is a virtue that in a sense cautions executive leadership from tending to egocentric sudden, rash, impetuous and unnecessary behavior when making strategic decisions, goal setting and policy procedures:

> In so far as a man restrains the impetuosity of his soul, from tending with the appetite, from tending inordinately to great things: yet its rule is in the cognitive faculty, in that we should not deem ourselves to be above what we are. Also, the principle and origin of both these things is the reverence we bear to God. Now the inward disposition of humility leads to certain outward signs in words, deeds, and gestures, which manifest that which is hidden within, as happens also the other virtues. For a man is known by his look, and "a wise man, when thou meetest him by his countenance" (Ecclus. 19:26).[86]

Executive leadership, furthermore, must have the habit of humility for the pursuit of great things. Humility controls the emotions of the dark soul and calms the mind for accomplishing great deeds. The character of the executive leader is about the intermingling of the virtuous habit of humility and magnanimity which "by it very name denotes stretching forth the mind to great things."[87]

---

[86] Ibid., a. 6.

[87] Ibid., q. 129, a. 1: "I answer that, Magnanimity by its very name denotes stretching forth of the mind to great things. Now virtue bears a relationship to two things, first to the matter about which is the field of its activity, secondly to its proper act, which consists in the right use of such matter. And since a virtuous habit is denominated chiefly from its act, a man is said to be magnanimous chiefly because he is minded doing some great act. Now an act may be called great in two ways: in one way proportionately, in another absolutely. An act may be called great proportionately, even if it consists in the use of some small or ordinary thing, if, for instance, one makes a very good use of it: but an act is simply and great when it consists in the best use of the greatest thing. The things which come into man's use are external things, and among these honor is the greatest simply, both because it is the most akin to virtue, since it is an attestation to a person's virtue, as stated above (Question [103], Articles [1],2); and because

However, we must state a principle of paramount importance to a Thomistic understanding of executive leadership and virtue that will be developed in later chapters, especially chapters five and six. We will contend that, by means of exemplar executive leadership, a Thomistic organizational psychology begins to immunize the organization against dark-soul leadership psychological disorder. We will define the exemplar executive as a leader responsible for rational, moral goodness in all organizational affairs. In turn, the exemplar becomes the virtuous role model for emulation by members of the organization. We will put forth and explain that, beyond the other cardinal moral virtues of temperance, courage, and justice, the virtue of prudential and organizational self-understanding (that, by nature generates personal and organizational humility and opposes personal and organizational arrogance, hubris) is the most important virtue for an executive exemplar to develop.

We have been identifying throughout this first chapter the "dark side" of the organization leadership. We have made this argument because it is purpose of a Thomistic organizational psychology of the executive function of leadership to answer the issue mentioned above by Roger LEWIN and Birute REGINE, where is the soul within organizations.

> Actually, most people want to be part of their organization's purpose; they want to make a difference. When the individual soul is connected to something deeper-the desire to contribute to a larger purpose, to feel they are part of a greater whole, a web of connection. When this connection develops, people begin to openly acknowledge the need for others, to see their independence, and their desire to belong-their tribal instinct awakens. The soul at work is also a collective soul-the transformation of the protean spirit of the organization in all its shades and hues-from trauma to hope, to infinite possibilities. The collective soul at work is a journey aligning abilities and values with the collective, shared purpose, an unfolding identity that is constructed and reconstructed

---

it is offered to God and to the best; and again because, in order to obtain honor even as to avoid shame, men set aside all other things. Now a man is said to be magnanimous in respect of things that are great absolutely and simply, just as a man is said to be brave in respect of things that are difficult simply. It follows therefore that magnanimity is about honors."

continually by the people, who are part of the system. And it is this collective soul at work that is most capable of intelligent, humane action that benefits the whole.

How, then, to engage the soul at work? There are no simple solutions. But it begins with altering our perspective. To engage the soul is to see people as people, not as employees. It is to assume an intention of goodwill on their part, and that it is better to err in trusting too much than not enough…To engage the soul at work is to focus not only on a plan of action but also to be alert to unfolding and unexpected directions and outcomes that are inherent in complex systems…To engage the soul at work is to realize that talking to people, listening to them, responding to them is not a waste of time. Rather, this is creating a context where people are more willing to change and to adapt, which in turn makes the organization more adaptable.[88]

When the "dark soul" of the executive function of leadership and expressions of neurotic leadership are ignored, as established above by BOARDMAN and PONOMARIOV, an organization becomes a pathological culture. BARNARD argues that it is the primary responsibility of executive leadership to intensify rational and moral leadership in the organizational whole. DURKHEIM's concept of anomie influences BARNARD's executive psychology of leadership as mentioned in the opening paragraphs of this chapter. One does not advance when one proceeds toward no goal. To pursue a goal which is unattainable is to condemn oneself to a state of perpetual unhappiness. The theory of anomie as decay or abandonment of moral stricture is usually applied to the timely problem of organizational malfeasance.

Bruce NOLOP the former chief financial officer of Pitney Bowes Inc. and E*Trade in "Four Qualities of Successful Executives" contends:

A combination of decisiveness, confidence, flexibility, and humility-I believe that this is the recipe for superior executive leadership. He, then, adds, Humility: Most important, and a seeming paradox, great executives are humble; they recognize the need to listen to alternative points of view and to trust the judgments of others. It's like the scene in 'Hoosiers where Hickory is playing in

---

[88] LEWIN and REGINE, *The Soul at Work*, 27–28.

the championship game and, in the words of Jim Valvano, is in a position to win. When Coach Dale diagrams the final play-which will determine whether the team wins or loses-he is met with grimaces and an awkward silence; the team clearly would prefer that star, Jimmy, to take the final shot. Finally, Jimmy breaks the silence, saying quietly 'I'll make it.'

Rather than sticking doggedly to his plan, the coach trusts the team's judgment and changes the play. This is leadership at its best; 'I get misty-eyed just thinking about it.'[89]

For BARNARD, an organization is dedicated to purpose, and therefore, the "concrete object of action is necessary to social satisfactions."[90] The lack of concrete objectives of action is a condition of social complexity and uncoordinated action. Without the organizational purpose related to the concrete object of action. This may induce a sort of paralysis of action through inability to make choice, or it may be brought about by conflict of obligations. It leads to Durkheim's anomie. This I take to be a state of individual paralysis of social action due to the absence of effective norms of conduct.[91]

Again, we draw attention to the fact that BARNARD presented in *The Functions of the Executive* in 1938; still in many ways his insights hold in organizational science. He realized that moral leadership at the highest level and the expression of moral character by leaders is far more than just writing a moral code, a policy statement or human resource monitoring. For example, he held:

> The activities of individuals necessarily take place within local immediate groups. The relation of a man to a large organization, or to his nation, or to his church, is necessarily through those with whom he is in immediate contact. Social activities cannot be activities at a distance. This seems not to have been sufficiently noted. It explains, or justifies, a statement made to me that

---

[89] Bruce NOLOP, "The Experts," https://blogs.wsj.com/experts/2014/04/29/four-qualities-of-successful-executives/.

[90] BARNARD, *The Functions of the Executive*, 118.

[91] Ibid.

comradeship is much more powerful than patriotism etc., in the behavior of soldiers. The essential need of the individual is association, and that requires local activity or immediate interaction between individuals.[92]

Douglas GRIFFIN, a leading organizational scholar on leadership and self-participation foresees organizations in the digital economy are changing drastically from top down pyramids to networks requiring a drastic rethinking of the nature of organizational leadership. There is one concept that describes the current organizational transformation, especially in business, and it is the distributed leadership organization. We are moving toward the distributed organizational culture driven by "an increasing agreement that he world has become more complex, fast paced, hazardous and unpredictable. Economies in crisis, war, nuclear proliferation, global warming, starvation, and disease-the list is long and daunting. For companies, fears might include shrinking revenues, increasingly competitive markets, or a never-ending race for new product development."[93] It is a movement from authoritarian-bureaucratic to participatory distributed organizations. It is a transition from authoritarian bureaucratic command and control to organizations built on extremely strong bonds of trust, loyalty, shared vision and push for ownership and decision making deeper into the organization as a network of communication, co-operation, and co-ordination:

What is distributed leadership? It involves leadership practices that are more collaborative, open and decentralized--designed to mesh more effectively with new forms of work and new technologies which is difficult. And while it is difficult to leave behind the models of the pyramid with the omniscient, omnipotent leader at the top, organizations are beginning to view leadership not as an individual characteristic, but as a system involving networks of

---

[92] Ibid., 119.

[93] Deborah ANCONA and Elaine BACKMAN, "From Pyramids to Networks: The Changing Leadership Landscape," *MIT Leadership Center*, Massachusetts Institute of Technology (2010), https://mitsloan-php.s3.amazonaws.com/leadership_wp/wp-content/uploads/2015/06/Distributed-Leadership-Going-from-Pyramids-to-Networks.pdf.

leaders-some formal and other informal-operating at all levels of an organization and often across organizational boundaries. The result is that organizations can more effectively mobilize the collective intelligence, motivation and creative talent of their employees, partners, and customers.[94]

Douglas GRIFFIN, in his 2002 work *The Emergence of Leadership: Linking Self-Organization and Ethics*, reaffirms Barnard's principle that moral beliefs at the concrete daily interactions and operations demands distributed leadership of the highest rational and moral character. "Leaders act and leadership is action. This immediately means that a theory of leadership is also a theory of ethics. Ethical values emerge in interaction as a reflection of the emergence of leaders. Large-scale organizational and cultural events emerge everyday social interaction through participation in local events."[95]

What BARNARD and GRIFFIN are calling for is a leadership that is a concrete, practical and action oriented based on an organizational moral psychology. Such a leadership demands communication, cooperation, coordination habits of doing the next right thing in all the organizational interpersonal, interactive, and operational activities. Curtis HANCOCK succinctly defines *habit* as:

> 'operational structures,' a phrase at once that expresses that habits exercise powers toward action and yet do so in a way that involves ease, constancy, and purpose. As an acquired operational tendency, a habit is not identical with knowledge or appetite. For we can know things without needing skill to do so, and we can desire things in a random and unproductive way. Nor is a habit identical with the activity toward which it is directed, for we retain our acquired abilities even when we are not performing those actions at a given moment [...] Consequently, a habit is related to a power by giving it a limiting qualitative ability and aim (an operational, determinate structure, as it were) and is related to an activity by enabling it to occur quickly and with comparative ease and

---

[94] Ibid.

[95] Douglas GRIFFIN, *The Emergence of Leadership: Linking Self-Organizing and Ethics* (London: Routledge, 2002), 213.

proficiency. In this light, we see that habit actuates (by giving structure or form) a power within definite limits while an activity actuates a habit. Accordingly, a habit is related to a power as act to potency; a habit is related to an activity as potency to act.[96]

It is a distributed style of leadership that uses the practical talents of the soul to discern the true good of the individual in terms of the common good of the whole in every circumstance. It is the willingness and ability to measure short-term gain against long-term gain. It looks at the destination of the organizational vision and appraises in the present operational context. It is shared metaphysical illumination that is implanted in the collective soul of the organization and workers.

A philosophical/scientific Thomistic organizational psychology of leadership is differentiated from a scientific organizational psychology based a principle of a metaphysical illumination meaning:

> All human reasoning, in one way or another, involves a power to put things in proper places, to put things where they belong [...] Now for human beings to be able to position their activities in ways as we have been describing, they have to have some sense of part/whole relationships. That is, they have to see the bits of action which they are joining together as parts of some bigger plan. It is in light of the bigger plan, of action to be completed, of the finished whole, that the parts are compared to another and are judged to fit together or not fit together. It is light of the action to be completed that people hesitate and argue with themselves, that they weigh alternatives, develop strategies, seek help from friends, and try to figure out how they should direct their movements to complete the action they desire.[97]

---

[96] Curtis L. HANCOCK and Peter A. REDPATH, *Recovering a Catholic Philosophy of Elementary Education* (Mount Pocono: Newman House Press, 2006), 82–83.

[97] REDPATH, *The Moral Psychology of St. Thomas*, 6.

3.

The Virtual Soul

The aim of this chapter is to introduce the importance of the relationship between an organizational psychology of soulful leadership and a metaphysics of organization. It is argued that the executive exemplar must have a masterful sense of metaphysical organizational principles. As this metaphysical sense and wisdom is defined and applied to practical cases, the chapter concludes with a significant description of an executive soulful virtual leader and the diffusion of the virtual intensity of leadership throughout the organizational whole. The soulful exemplar has the character of a: 1) discoverer, 2) teacher who instills hope and drives out fear, 3) builds confidence, 4) energizes, and 5) calms emotions.

3.1 A Foundational Metaphysics of Organization

In the last chapter, we treated the issue of the "dark soul" of organizational leadership, and we learned that it is a foremost responsibility of executive leadership to practice the virtue of humility. We will now turn our focus to an organizational psychology grounded on a Thomistic metaphysical organizational foundation. We will examine the nature of organizational leadership in the modern and the so-called "postmodern" eras. Careful to note is that the following is not intended to be a critical analysis of the impact of philosophical "postmodern" movements on culture. Nonetheless, the argument is made that a need exists for a "real postmodern" Thomistic organizational psychology grounded on a return to an Aristotelian-Thomistic philosophical metaphysics. The position is taken from REDPATH's *Not-So-Elementary Christian Metaphysics:*

We cannot look to modern or contemporary "philosophy" or "science" for an adequate solution. Such a solution must be a philosophical metaphysics. And modern and contemporary "philosophers," "scientists," do not have the foggiest idea, much less a clear and distinct one, of just what the nature of such a study might be. [...]

We cannot turn to most students of classical metaphysics to solve this problem because most of them have no idea what metaphysics, or philosophy, is. And we cannot simply return to the classical notion of natural law, or even to the classical understanding of the human person as a "rational animal" to help us. Modernity in its fully developed and rotting state (postmodernism falsely so-called) has largely twisted these ideas beyond recognition, divorced them from connection with reality in which we live our daily lives.

To reunite wisdom and science in a new understanding, we need a real postmodernism essentially rooted in a new understanding of the human person. And we need to recover a proper understanding of the nature of philosophy and science, a real modern philosophy; not one falsely so called.[155]

---

[155] REDPATH, *A Not-So-Elementary Christian Metaphysics*, 63-64. In this work, in chapter One, *Why Care about Metaphysics*, REDPATH focuses on three philosophers of the enlightenment who have had extreme influence in the development of modern and postmodern organizational philosophy and psychology i.e. Jean-Jacques ROUSSEAU, Immanuel KANT and David HUME. ROUSSEAU was influenced by DESCARTES' attempt "to construct his scientific system by maintaining that only two substances exist, mind and matter; and these substances cannot communicate. Descartes considered matter to be totally inactive and mind, or spirit, to be the only thing that acts. Rousseau recognized that, in the real world, matter and mind communicate. Since Descartes could not explain this communication between substances of mind, or spirit, and matter, Rousseau resigned to overcome this failure by accepting a position Descartes had rejected. He declared 'modern philosophy's principles' to be 'essentially, dualist, animistic and obscure'. [...] He thought that only spirit exists and even 'apparently inanimate beings, like stones, are animate.' [...] Rousseau constructed an elaborate fairy tale: *a utopian history about nature and origin that replaced metaphysics with history as the means to explain the nature and development of true science, philosophy*" (ibid., 18–19).

3.2 A Proper Understanding of Common Sense

We will briefly summarize the new concept of the modern psychology of leadership as opposed to the evolving postmodern psychology of leadership. We will examine the executive leadership of Southwest Airlines as the opposite of the dysfunctional bureaucratic style of leadership discussed in the previous chapter. Furthermore, Southwest Airlines' leadership model is dedicated to immunizing against expressions of destructive pathological behavior. Southwest airlines started in 1971 and grew into the fourth largest airline in the United States, with 30 consecutive years of profitability, in an industry in which no other company had been profitable for more than five years. Total shareholder returns were almost double the returns for the S&P 500. It managed to accrue a market capitalization larger than the rest of the American airlines combined.

Southwest executive leadership is grounded on the personalism and character of the founder Herb Kelleher as described in the book *Nuts! Southwest Airline Recipe for Business and Personal Success* by Kevin FREIBURG and Jackie FREIBURG. The book is a necessary read on the nature of the function of executive leadership, organizational harmony, and the concept of distributed leadership. Collen Barrett, one of the original founders with Kelleher, describes Southwest as an organization of common sense:

> Let common sense prevail. Southwest employees know from history that when they use common sense to do what they think is right, the company will support them. We never jump on employees for leaning too far in the direction of the customer. They have to know that we stand behind them, and we do. The only time we come down on them pretty hard is when they fail to use common sense. Common sense may sound easy enough, but it's a hard thing to define. When we say we are going to be an on-time airline and we are not holding planes for anybody period, we have to use good judgment. We once had a situation where we slammed the door to a jet because we wanted to push the plane on time. But when the passenger coming down the ramp is a paraplegic and can be seen by the operations

agent in the jet way and has to sit in a wheelchair for four and a half hours for the next flight—that's not common sense.[156]

From the earliest days, Southwest was founded as a practical-reasoning-and-moral organization. For example, Colleen Barrett maintains "Southwest employees know from history that when they use common sense to do what they think is right, the company will support them. Common sense may sound easy enough but is a hard thing to define." Barrett presents here the issue of the responsibility of the function of Southwest executive leadership to establish an organizational culture that facilitates distributed leadership down to the daily and concrete basic units of the operation.

The flight crew team and the team leader share in the belief of "common sense." The problem is that in an organization everyone believes that they understand "common sense."

In the case, the gate attendant could think that we have a rule, company policy of planes must leave on time. The attendant might think, "That's the norm and I am just doing my job. If there is any hassle or complaint, then I can say I was just following policy. I was being a good employee!"

Here exists the need for an organizational whole cultural embodiment of a rational sensing moral psychology. ADLER would suggest that the above case of the gate attendant is more than a practical common-sense decision.[157] In terms of a Thomistic rational sensing moral psychology, the situation is not just an organizational practical problem like any other daily on- the-job practical problem. It is essentially a moral problem that becomes a "common-sense real problem" when the gate attendant thinks, "What is really good for the organization and the passenger? What really is the higher good for the airline and passenger?" In the coming chapters, we will gradually establish that this situation, described by Collen Barrett, is not addressed by universal ethical norms and organizational codes, instead it requires an organizational Thomistic rational sensing moral psychology.

---

[156] Kevin FREIBURG and Jackie FREIBURG, *Nuts! Recipe for Business and Personal Success* (Austin: Brad Press, 1996), 287–289.

[157] Mortimer J. ADLER, *The Time of Our Lives* (New York: Fordham University Press, 1996), 160.

3.3 Embedded Habits of Leadership

Southwest is a culture of habits of distributed leadership embedded in the organizational whole by means of tacit and explicit knowledge Herb Kelleher establishes his concept of leadership on the virtuous habit of love:

> If you are careful about hiring people, it should come as no surprise that acts of love and generosity will naturally spill out of them. It should come as no surprise that when you get enough people with these attributes the same company, a corporate character is created that practices love as a way of doing business.[158]

Kelleher looks to recruit persons who are willing to express their capacity to love in relation to other employees and customers. AQUINAS teaches that acts and habits are specified by their objects and the proper object of love is the good so that wherever there is a special aspect of good, there is a special kind of love.[159] For Kelleher, the primary function of the executive leadership of Southwest is that "acts of love and generosity spill out of them." If we follow this definition of AQUINAS, it means the employees are not working just for a paycheck. They are working at Southwest because it is a culture that allows them to develop the virtue of love by doing acts of goodness to others.

Chester I. BARNARD felt large complex organizations are characterized by an obvious lack of complete understanding and acceptance of general purposes or aims. It is a major problem because each unit of the organization must know and accept the organizational main purpose as its own. It is the challenge of leadership to instill the belief that the more a unit or individual understand "what the whole objective is, the intensity of its action will ordinarily be increased. It is the belief in the cause rather than intellectual understanding of the objective which is of chief importance. Understanding by itself is rather a paralyzing and divisive element."[160]

---

[158] FREIBURG and FREIBURG, *Nuts! Recipe for Business and Personal Success*, 216

[159] AQUINAS, *Summa Theologiae* II-II, q. 23, a. 4, ad 1.

[160] BARNARD, *The Functions of the Executive*, 138.

Kelleher taught from the conception of Southwest that there was a simple strategy based on three objectives that required extreme disciple and intensity of focus:

> We basically said to our people, there are three things that we are interested in. The lowest costs in the industry—that can't hurt you, having the lowest costs. The best customer service—that's a very important element of value. We said beyond that we're interested in intangibles—a spiritual infusion—because they are the hardest things for your competitors to replicate. The tangible things your competitors can go out and buy. But they can't buy your spirit. So, it's the most powerful thing of all.[161]

In the previous chapter, we put forth the importance of the executive leadership practice of the virtue of humility and the cultural practice of humility at all levels of organizational leadership. Kelleher was asked in an interview, "One of your values in the mission statement is humility as a corporation. With all your wonderful results, is Southwest really humble?" He responded:

> No question. I constantly have warned our people over the years that, as we became bigger and more successful, our primary potential enemy was ourselves, not our competitors. Getting cocky, getting complacent, thinking that the world was our oyster, disregarding our competitors, both new and old. I think humility is very important in keeping your eye on the carrot, keeping focused outwardly instead of inwardly, and knowing when you have to change. An investor in the airline industry some years ago that I was talking to said, "Southwest Airlines is the most humble and disciplined airline that I deal with." I said, "The two go together."[162]

---

[161] Chuck LUCIER, "Herb Kelleher: The Thought Leader Interview," https://www.strategy-business.com/article/04212?gko=8cb4f.

[162] Ibid.

We began our construction of a Thomistic organizational psychology identifying the critical issue of the "dark soul" of leadership. In the executive leadership of Southwest, one of the most successful business organizations from the 1970s to the present, we learn that the virtue of humility is written into the mission statement of the organization. The mission statement of Southwest Airlines is written basically as an inspirational statement of belief for employees, investors, and customers. Mission statements are not worth the paper they are written on unless the statement is put into daily and concrete action. The mission statement must lay forth well-founded beliefs based on principles that will lead to success. Kelleher makes it clear that the belief in the practice of humility is essential to greatness.

3.4 Diffusion of a Sense of Unity

In 1938, BARNARD, with tremendous foresight, realized that the function of executive leadership will require a science of cooperation and organization. He maintained that "executive arts are highly developed in the fields called technological; they are well developed in the technical commercial fields; they are least developed in the techniques of human interactions and organization."[163] BARNARD, somewhat like Peter DRUCKER, did not believe that the integration of organizational activity is achieved by implementation of policy statements or elitist rational ethical systems. It does appear that he was foreseeing the need for a rational sensing moral psychology:

> The ethical ideal upon which cooperation depends requires the general diffusion of willingness to subordinate immediate personal interest for both ultimate personal interest and the general good, together with a capacity of the individual responsibility. The senses of what will be for the ultimate personal interest and of what will be for the ultimate interest and of what will be for the general good both must come from outside the individual. They are social, ethical, and religious values. For their general diffusion they depend upon both intelligence and inspiration. Intelligence is necessary to

---

[163] BARNARD, *The Functions of the Executive*, 292.

the appreciation of the interdependence of peoples in a crowded world on their combined technological competence—an intelligence that perhaps will be derived from experience in cooperation rather than from anything suggestive of formal education. Inspiration is necessary to inculcate the sense of unity, and to create common ideals. Emotional rather than intellectual acceptance is required. No one who reads, or who observes the events of our times, but will recognize, it seems to me, the supreme importance of belief in ideals as indispensable to cooperation.[164]

In the 30s, it was BARNARD who identified the need for a less bureaucratic authoritative style of executive leadership and a rational, emotional, and moral intelligence. It was Kelleher at Southwest Airlines in the 70s who totally rejected any manner of the traditional bureaucratic top-down psychology of executive leadership. Southwest marks a revolutionizing impact on organizational leadership, and it is a revolution that did not come from the academic halls and organizational consultants. We get a glimpse of the personalistic psychology behind this psycho-ethical revolution in some of Southwest's Kelleher's quotes:

1) "Power should be reserved for weightlifting and boats, and leadership really involves responsibility."
2) "A company is stronger if it is bound by love rather than by fear."
3) "We will hire someone with less experience, less education, and less expertise, than someone who has more of those things and has a rotten attitude."
4) "You must be very patient, very persistent. The world isn't going to shower gold coins on you just because you have a good idea. You're going to have to work like crazy to bring that idea to the attention of people."
5) "I forgive all personal weaknesses except egomania and pretension."
6) "One piece of advice that always stuck in my mind is that people should be respected and trusted as people."

---

[164] Ibid., 293–294.

7) "It is my practice to try to understand how valuable something is by trying to imagine myself without it."

8) "I've found that many of the greatest ideas surface in bars because that's where many people cultivate inspiration."[165]

In an interview to new CEOs looking for success. Kelleher gave a straightforward word of advice. It really marks the change in executive leadership beginning in the 70s.

> First of all, they have to focus intently upon what's important, not be trapped in bureaucracy. Be results and mission oriented. Keep it as simple as they possibly can, so that the values and the destination of the organization are well understood by all the people that are part of it so that they can feel that they are truly participants in it.[166]

3.4.1 Executive Sense of Metaphysical Wisdom

There are many possible ways to describe Herb Kelleher as a successful executive entrepreneur. He could be called a business genius, a brilliant entrepreneur, an innovative Chief Executive Officer, an executive of outstanding marketing insight and strategic brilliance. In chapter Two, Chester I. BARNARD argues that there is a type of aesthetic and moral sense that is an essential function of executive leadership:

> What is required is the sense of things as a whole, the persistent subordination of parts to the total, the discrimination from the broadest standpoint of the strategic factor from among all types of factors—other executive functions, technology, persuasion, incentives, communication, distributive efficiency. Since there can be no common measure for the

---

[165] ABRAHAM OLMSTEAD, "8 Herb Kelleher Quotes That Will Teach You Everything You Need To Know About Life," *https://www.freeenterprise.com/8-herb-kelleher-quotes-will-teach-you-everything-you-need-know-about-life/*, March 21, 2014.

[166] LUCIER, "Herb Kelleher: The Thought Leader Interview."

translation of the physical, biological, economic, social, personal, and spiritual factors of creative cooperation is a matter of sense, of feeling of proportions, of the significant relationship of the heterogeneous details to a whole.

This general executive process is not intellectual in its important aspect; it is aesthetic and moral. Thus, its exercise involves the sense of fitness, of the appropriate, and that capacity which is known as responsibility—the final expression of the achievement of cooperation.[167]

We are turning our attention in this chapter to an organizational metaphysics of participation. It is not common to find in modern psychological and sociological studies of organizational leadership the pursuit of a metaphysical foundation. This lack of dedication to the relationship between metaphysics and a psychology is missing. Contemporary psychology, organizational psychology and the social sciences have rejected for the greater part any metaphysical spiritual understanding of the human person. As Peter A. REDPATH states, "It is a metaphysical and moral clash between the ancient and modern West […]. Since the time of Descartes, 'science' falsely-so-called has divorced itself from any essential connection to wisdom, virtue, and human happiness, a human soul, human habits, and a creator-God (from all human good), and classical common sense."[168]

In other words, "philosophical inquiry is not a method of a logical-analytical investigation, rather it is a state of an agent engaging in a state of wonder. There exists a hope of being able to satisfy a desire; it is an existential fulfillment of a desire resulting in an intellectual volitional and emotional satisfaction."[169] From the viewpoint of a Thomistic organizational psychology of leadership, it is contended that there are certain individuals with the genius for executive leadership like Herb Kelleher who have a natural sense of metaphysical wisdom.

---

[167] BARNARD, *The Functions of the Executive*, 256–257.

[168] Peter A. REDPATH, "The Nature of Common Sense," *Studia Gilsoniana*, 3 (2014), 479.

[169] MCVEY, "Thomistic Scientific Leadership and Common-Sense Triad of Organizational Harmony," 131–132.

Therefore, in terms of a Thomistic organizational psychology of the executive leadership, we look at a leader like Kelleher as a person who has a natural sense of metaphysical wisdom. BARNARD believed the executive process is not intellectual in its important aspect; it is aesthetic and moral. It is Peter A. REDPATH who completes BARNARD's natural sense of metaphysical wisdom:

> While the origin of all species (operational organizations) is a genus (organization) and its chief aim, and while each science studies a species of organization (same species within a genus), no specialized science studies the nature and chief aim of the genus (organization) that causes all species of organization within creation. Consequently, a person who possesses wisdom, who knows the causes of all the essential part/whole relationships (organizational relationships) that generate this or that organization can, at best, possess wisdom in some respect: cannot be totally wise.
>
> In any specialized science, the wise person knows the essential principles (part/whole relations) that generate this or that organization, its chief aim, and its chief act; but such a person cannot be absolutely wise, or wise absolutely considered (in some way, wise about everything). He or she can only be wise related to this or that organization and its operations. In contrast, the absolutely wise person, the wise person absolutely considered, knows the organizational plan of operations (principles) that causes all organizations and all actions that flow from considered generically, simply as organizations.[170]

3.4.2 A Wise Executive Touches the Soul

Given the natural metaphysical sense of wisdom of the wise executive, we look at Herb Kelleher who is an entrepreneurial-executive style with a sense of a genus (organizational whole) from conception to the emergence of an extremely successful business organization. Again, we return to his interview in the *Strategy + Business interview*:

---

[170] REDPATH, *The Moral Psychology of St. Thomas*, 46.

We used to have a corporate day. Companies would come in from around the world and they were interested in how we hired, trained, that sort of thing. Then we'd say, "Treat your people well and they'll treat you well," and then they'd go home disappointed. It was too simple. Or too hard—because it's a vast mosaic with thousands of pieces that you have to keep putting in place every day. It's not a programmatic thing. It can't be. It has to come from the heart, not the head. If it's programmatic, everybody will know that and say, "Hell, they're not sincere; they don't really care, they're just telling us that they care." It has to be a continuous stream of one-on-one communication, not like you sit down and say, "Boy communication is pretty important. Let's really communicate for the next six months and then move on to what is really significant. It has to be of your fabric it has to do with something that you do really as a product of your soul.[171]

Kelleher states, when other organizational leaders come to observe the functions of executive leadership at Southwest, they cannot understand the airline's organizational success. It seems either too simple or the demands of such an intense personalistic organizational psychology are too hard. Of course, it is hard to comprehend unless an observer has a sense of metaphysical wisdom. Kelleher says that "it has to be of your fabric [...] a product of your soul."

Kelleher does not give any metaphysical explanation of his understanding of the soul. He describes what we have called a sense of metaphysical wisdom, as a habit of understanding the organization on a daily basis as "a vast mosaic with thousands of pieces that you keep putting in place every day."[172] He uses the metaphor for the soul: "It has to be of your fabric." The metaphor of the fabric is used to express a special type of knowledge. It is the same issue that Chester BARNARD encounters when he attempts to explain the intellectual capabilities of executive leadership. It is not a formal education; rather, it is inspirational knowledge and gives one a sense of unity.

Joe SACHS has written a notable translation of ARISTOTLE's, *On the Soul* and *Memory and Recollection*. In the introduction he describes the meaning and

---

[171] CHUCK LUCIER, "Herb Kelleher: Thought Leader Review"

[172] Ibid.

intention of ARISTOTLE's word for the soul "psyche" that explains perhaps Kelleher's need to use a metaphor of the soul to explain his organizational wisdom. SACHS presents an explanation of ARISTOTLE's *On the Soul* in his section *Recognizing the Soul*:

> To the simple and unsophisticated among us, or perhaps to all of us at unguarded moments, there is a certain comfort in the fact that we share the world with so many varieties of beings that are so much like ourselves. To commune with nature means to recognize something in ourselves by its reflection in something outside us. We do this when we stare into a fire, when we listen to waves breaking on a shore, or when we drink in with our eyes any unspoiled formation of the earth. The peacefulness that comes when such things absorb us is a way of being at home, of discovering, that we have a place. But the same sort of peaceful rest is enhanced by the still greater kinship we feel in being among plants and trees, and especially in understanding encounters with animals. They recall us to what we are; they remind us that we have souls.
>
> I believe that I am here using the word soul in exactly the sense that Aristotle uses the word psyche. Much can be written about these words and the connotations each has collected by association with various beliefs that have come and gone in the course of time, but there is a primary meaning at the root of each. That meaning precedes anything that can be read or written and is found only in experience. I have tried to evoke that experience in the preceding paragraph. When Aristotle sets out to define the soul, he is not saying 'let us agree to use this word this way," but making a step toward understanding our common experience of an aspect of the world.
>
> In the physics, though, that almost is crucial, as nature unfolds itself between two poles. Nature is predominantly living nature, but it is also the ordered cosmos that sustains life and ensures its possibility. The focus of physics is on what is shared by living things and the elemental universe, but the recognition of nature that the inquiry presupposes must include, and cannot be present without, the recognition of soul.

But what kind of recognition is this? Is it, for instance, clear and distinct? If we are vague about what constitutes the soul, and apt to confuse it with other things, it may be that it is nothing at all, or only some sort of illusion [...] The place to begin is with what is familiar, which is bound to be confused and indistinct. Clarity and distinctiveness prematurely arrived at might be imposed on things or invented by us in our impatience. The clarity and distinctiveness that are worth attaining are those that merge through the honest examination of what we encounter most worth examining might be just exactly that have some mystery about them, some hidden depth.[173]

3.5 Organizational Genus, Wise Man, Executive Genius

We have described Kelleher as the wise executive who possesses the natural sense of metaphysical wisdom. In other words, we could say that he is an organizational genius, but what is a genius? In terms of a Thomistic definition of an organizational genius, the original concept of being capable of bringing into being seems a most fitting description of an executive-entrepreneurial organizational leadership. Perhaps the description of genius that comes closest to a Thomistic rational sensing psychological comprehension of organization genius is the eighteenth-century description of Jean-Francois de SAINT-LAMBERT:

Genius is the expansiveness of the intellect, the force of imagination and activity of the soul [...] The man of genius is affected by the object itself, it is by the memory of it; however, in the man of genius, the imagination goes farther, it remembers with more a striking feeling than when it received them, because to these ideas are attached a thousand others which appropriately give rise to the feeling.[174]

---

[173] JOE SACKS, *Aristotle's On the Soul and On Memory and Recollection* (Santa Fe, New Mexico: Green Lion Press, 2001) 1-3

[174] Jean-Francois de SAINT-LAMBERT, *The Encyclopedia of Diderot & d'Alembert Collaborative Translation Project*, Trans. John S.D. (Ann Arbor: Michigan Publishing University of Michigan Library, 2007), entry "genius."

From the viewpoint of a Thomistic metaphysical psychology, it is the capability of a wise person that allows a person to sense and develop an organization; it is an intellectual and sensing faculty.

> According to St. Thomas, Aristotle and *the Many* say wise man know order, that his office, business, duty is to know the order existing in things in both speculative and practical ways: to recognize and establish order in things.[175][…]
>
> Hence, St. Thomas understands the office of the wise man essentially to involve understanding the divine rule of government that exists as the proximate principle of unifying and harmonizing all the parts of creation as one of the best order of the parts involved. Because St. Thomas considers the

---

[175] St. Thomas AQUINAS, *Summa contra gentiles*, Chapter 1, "The usage of the multitude, which according to the Philosopher is to be followed in giving names to things, has commonly held that they are to be called wise who order things rightly and govern them well. Hence, among other things that men have conceived about the wise man, the Philosopher includes the notion that 'it belongs to the wise man to order'. Now, the rule of government and order for all things directed to an end must be taken from the end. For, since the end of each thing is its good, a thing is then best disposed when it is fittingly ordered to its end. And so, we see among the arts that one functions as the governor and the ruler of another because it controls its end. Thus, the art of medicine rules and orders the art of the chemist because health, with which medicine is concerned, is the end of all the medications prepared by the art of the chemist. A similar situation obtains in the art of ship navigation in relation to shipbuilding, and in the military art with respect to the equestrian art and the equipment of war. The arts that rule other arts are called architectonic, as being the ruling arts. That is why the artisans devoted to these arts, who are called master artisans, appropriate to themselves the name of wise men. But, since these artisans are concerned, in each case, with the ends of certain particular things, they do not reach to the universal end of all things. They are therefore said to be wise with respect to this or that thing; in which sense it is said that 'as a wise architect, I have laid the foundation' (1 Cor. 3:10). The name of the absolutely wise man, however, is reserved for him whose consideration is directed to the end of the universe, which is also the origin of the universe. That is why, according to the Philosopher, it belongs to the wise man to consider the highest causes."

order of creation to consist in parts *fitting, proportionately*, harmoniously arranged to guarantee maximization of their qualitative performance resulting from maximization of their qualitative organization, he maintains that arts that study the created order are essentially architectonically arranged according to an analogously proportionate, corresponding perfection of order, or organization.[176][...]

Given his acceptance of evident truth of architectonic nature of the relationship between performance and production arts and sciences, St. Thomas realizes that each art, science, is a habit of soul concerned with understanding the part/whole relationships that exist within one or another qualitatively different kinds of parts qualitatively different and unequally different kinds of parts. He calls such composite whole (wholes generated by uniting qualitatively different and unequally perfect parts into a harmonious unit) a "genus." Consequently, when St. Thomas says that the chief job of the wise man is to know the order that exists within things, he is simply saying that the chief job of a wise person is to be able to know: 1) the nature of organizations (what constitutes their essential parts and how multitudes

---

[176] AQUINAS, *Summa Theologiae* I, q. 1, a. 5, "I answer that, since this science is partly speculative and partly practical, it transcends all others speculative and practical. Now one speculative science is said to be nobler than another, either by reason of its greater certitude, or by reason of the higher worth of its subject-matter. In both these respects this science surpasses other speculative sciences; in point of greater certitude, because other sciences derive their certitude from the natural light of human reason, which can err; whereas this derives its certitude from the light of divine knowledge, which cannot be misled: in point of the higher worth of its subject-matter because this science treats chiefly of those things which by their sublimity transcend human reason; while other sciences consider only those things which are within reason's grasp. Of the practical sciences, that one is nobler which is ordained to a further purpose, as political science is nobler than military science; for the good of the army is directed to the good of the State. But the purpose of this science, in so far as it is practical, is eternal bliss; to which as to an ultimate end the purposes of every practical science are directed. Hence it is clear that from every standpoint, it is nobler than other sciences."

have to be qualified and related to become parts that compose organizations and 2) how to create organizations.[177]

3.6 Sensing the Inkling of the Genus (Organizational Generic Nature)

Therefore, we can say given the above description of an organizational whole that the concept of genius explains the ability to sense the dynamics of organizational whole. When Herb Kelleher states that the executive understanding and leadership of the organization "has to be of your fabric [...] the product of soul," he is stating the medieval metaphysical maxim, "Whatever is received into a receiver is received according to the capacity of the receiver."[178] We looked at, in chapter Two, the Japanese school of knowledge management concept of tacit knowledge and Michael POLANYI's philosophy of "we can know more than we can tell." The Japanese knowledge management approach to the functions of executive leadership and the tacit knowledge principle of POLANYI is somewhat similar to the medieval metaphysical maxim:

> It is commonplace that all research must start from a problem. Research can be successful only if the problem is good; it can be original only if the problem is original. But how can one see a problem, any problem, let alone a good and original problem? For to see a problem is to see something that is hidden. It is to have an intimation of the coherence of hitherto not

---

[177] REDPATH, *The Moral Psychology of St. Thomas*, 41–44.

[178] AQUINAS, *Summa theologiae* I, q. 75, a. 1, ad 2, "The likeness of a thing known is not of necessity actually in the nature of the knower; but given a thing which knows potentially, and afterwards knows actually, the likeness of the thing known must be in the nature of the knower, not actually, but only potentially; thus, color is not actually in the pupil of the eye, but only potentially. Hence it is necessary, not that the likeness of corporeal things should be actually in the nature of the soul, but that there be a potentiality in the soul for such a likeness. But the ancient philosophers omitted to distinguish between actuality and potentiality; and so, they held that the soul must be a body in order to have knowledge of a body; and that it must be composed of the principles of which all bodies are formed in order to know all bodies."

comprehended. The problem is good if this intimation is true; it is original if no one else can see the possibilities of the comprehension that we are anticipating. To see a problem that will lead to a great discovery is not just to see something hidden, but to see something the rest of humanity cannot have seen an inkling.[179]

Composite wholes are "generated by uniting qualitatively different and unequally perfect parts into a harmonious unit a genus."[180] Therefore, it is the responsibility of executive leadership to have a sense of the genus and generate the organizational whole by uniting qualitatively different and unequally perfect parts of the organizational whole. An executive leader like Kelleher is most interesting as a paradigm of the functions of executive leadership because he and his early partners as a team had an inkling (metaphysical sense of a genus) of an opening for a new type of service in the airline industry and were able to develop and bring the genus into existence and successfully maintain and strive for excellence.

It is a remarkable story of entrepreneurial genius that Kelleher, with a small team of partners in 1971, sensed the genus of something hidden to the airline industry and would decide to enter into a business market in which no other company had been profitable for even five straight years. Total shareholder returns during that period were almost double the returns of the S&P 500. Southwest managed to accrue a market capitalization larger than that of the rest of the American airlines combined. Kelleher was asked if he had a vision for the whole thing thirty-five years ago: "Did you write that we're going to become the largest airline with the lowest cost?" Kelleher answers:

Oh, no. We didn't write it down because when you write things down you confine yourself. That's why we never used the fancy titles for empowerment, total quality, etc. Every time you talk jargon you find that people assume that they have the same thing in mind when they really don't.

---

[179] Michael POLANYI, *The Tacit Dimension* (Chicago and London: The University of Chicago Press, 1966), 21-22.

[180] REDPATH, *The Moral Psychology of St. Thomas*, 41–44.

We don't apply labels to things because they prevent you from thinking expansively.

Basically, what we said 35 years ago was that Texas was captive: Braniff had a monopoly among the larger cities; Trans Texas had monopoly among the smaller cities. The fares were very high. Because the short-haul passenger was merely an addendum to long-haul service, the short-haul passenger was, being totally neglected. In other words, a flight from San Antonio to Dallas were scheduled in terms of what your arrival was in Seattle or Paris. It looked like an opportunity to do something a lot better: provide higher-quality air service at lower fares.

One of the things that people, I think, didn't understand is that we started out saying we're going to give you more for less, not less for less. We're going to give new airplanes, not old airplanes. We're going to give you the best on-time performance. We're going to give you the people who are the most hospitable.

We've never done the long-range planning that is customary in many businesses. When planning became big in the airline community, one of the analysts came up and said, "Herb, I understand you don't have a plan." I said that we have the most unusual plan in the industry: Doing things. That's our plan. What we do by way of strategic planning is we define ourselves and then we redefine ourselves.[181]

In the selected interview passages and quotes of Kelleher, we learn that the function of executive leadership is to sense an organizational whole in the perfection of its parts. We will refer to this sensing of the perfection of the organizational whole as the sensing of the continuous excellence of the genus. When Kelleher says that they did not start out with any long-term market plan or competitive strategy, we suggest that he is referring to a powerful sense of an organizational whole and a commitment to perfection. He says, "Strategic planning is we define ourselves and then we redefine ourselves". It is an organizational psychology of defining the unity and harmony that the organization requires as a continuous practice.

---

[181] LUCIER, "Herb Kelleher: The Thought Leader Interview."

3.7 Executive Leadership and Equality of Inequality

The major contribution of the genius of W. Edwards DEMING is his focus on an organizational whole defined by a constancy of purpose, "Create constancy of purpose toward improvement of product and service, with the aim to become competitive and to stay in business, and to provide jobs."[182] DEMING was a statistical physicist by education who approached organizational executive leadership with a call for a return to the Aristotelian principle of teleology in the management of any organization dedicated to the satisfaction of the end user of a product, good or service.

As the founder of the quality movement of the 80s, he held emphatically to Aristotelian principles of causation that must be understood and applied throughout the organization. One, the harmonious unity of parts to the whole of the organizational structure is essentially teleological since machinery, material, manpower, and methods have to perform the functions for which they are designed (end user satisfaction). Two, causal "efficiency and effectiveness" and teleological purpose of management must be continuously defined, tested, and improved throughout the organization.[183]

It is the responsibility of executive leadership to promote by means of training a leadership capable of achieving organizational perfection:

Aim of leadership. The aim of leadership should be to improve the performance of man and machine, to improve quality, to increase output, and simultaneously to bring pride of workmanship to people. Put in a negative way, the aim of leadership is not merely to find and record failures of men, but to remove the causes of failure: to help people to do a better job with less effort. Actually, most of this book is involved with leadership.

---

[182] DEMING, *Out of Crisis*, 23.

[183] See ibid., Chapter One, page 34. It is here that we learn that both DEMING and BARNARD thought in terms of an organization as a system. However, DEMING was much more given to organizational systems theory than BARNARD. Yet, DEMING did not express a type of mechanical systems view. It was much more of a system as one of measurement within the context of knowledge management.

Nearly every page heretofore and hereafter states a principle of good leadership of man and machine or shows an example of good or bad leadership.[184]

It was a fundamental principle of DEMING that transformational leadership was only possible if it had the complete support of the highest executive levels of the organization. DEMING wrote his second work, *The New Economics: For Industry, Government, Education,* because by that time he had gained national and international recognition as a prominent figure in the total quality movement. He conducted four-day seminars that attracted very large numbers of attendees from various types of organizations and industries. His teaching was originally focused on the manufacturing industry, but his final work was dedicated, especially, to service industries, government, and non-profits. His final work was not as statistical as *Out of Crisis* and placed greater emphasis on the issue of knowledge management, psychology, and principles of organizational executive leadership:

Where is quality made? The answer is by the top management. The quality of the output of a company cannot be better than the quality determined at the top.

Job security and jobs are dependent on management's foresight to design product and service that will entice customers and build a market; to be ready, ahead of the customer, to modify product and service.[185]

A manager understands and conveys to his people the meaning of a system. He explains the aims of the system. He teaches his people to understand how the work of the group supports these aims.

1) He helps his people to see themselves as components in a system, to work in cooperation with preceding stages and with following stages toward optimization of the efforts of all stages toward achievements of the aim.

---

[184] Ibid., 248.

[185] DEMING, *The New Economics*, 18.

2) A manager of people understands that people are different from each other. He tries to create for everybody interest and challenge, and joy in work. He tries to optimize the family background, education, skills, hopes, and abilities of everyone.[186]

Psychology helps us to understand people, interaction between people and circumstances, interaction between customer and supplier, interaction between teacher and pupil, interaction between a manager and his people and any system of management. People are different from one another. A manager of people must be aware of these differences and use them for the optimization of everybody's abilities and inclinations.[187]

Leadership in an organization whole (genus) is dependent on a rational sensing psychology of intensity of participation of the organizational purpose. We will come to an explanation of this psychology of intensity by examining DEMING's teaching on the executive function, and then return to the Thomistic principle of equality of inequality, i.e. "the opposition between unity and plurality is the first principle of all other opposition and is the principle into which all others are reduced and made intelligible."[188] This principle of equality of inequality within the

---

[186] Ibid., 125.

[187] Ibid., 108.

[188] REDPATH, *A Not-So-Elementary Christian Metaphysics*, 154. See ibid., 173–174, "Aristotle held that we derive all our conceptions, definitions, and first cognitions of first principles by privative negations of the way we sensibly perceive them as composite beings. He thought of unity as the most primary privation, consisting of negation in a subject. Since Aristotle maintained that plurality stems from unity, and causes diversity, difference, and contrariety, he viewed diversity, difference, and contrariety to be effects of unity's pluralization, and claimed that we know first principles negatively in reference to the way we perceive their contraries. Hence, Aristotle said that 'all things are contraries or composed of contraries, and unity and plurality are the starting points of all contraries' [...] This means that contrariety consists in the greatest distance of difference, or inequality, between extremes of species within a genus [...] if Aristotle is correct, as Charles Bonaventure Crowley (Charles Bonaventure Crowley, O.P., edited with a prescript Peter A. Redpath, Aristotelian-Thomistic Philosophy of Measure the International System of

organizational whole (genus) is extremely important because we will point out later that there is in postmodern organizational theories of leadership and self-participative organization ignorance of this self-evident metaphysical principle of organization. It does appear that DEMING in his metaphysical psychological sense respects the principle of "equality of inequality" as foundational.

As the US automotive industry influenced by DEMING bounced back from the loss of market dominance due to Japanese competition, DEMING became highly recognized for his views on organizational leadership in the new economy of global competition. It is a new world where people no longer live in global isolation. In chapter one, we discussed the postmodern culture of self-realization that Deming simply described thus:

> Anybody wishes to live like somebody else. Anybody else lives better, so everybody presupposes. How many people live as other people live? People blame their plight on to the government and its leaders, or to management and its leaders. They may be correct. But what change in leadership will assure better living? What if the new leaders are no better?
>
> What characteristics ought a leader to possess? Will best efforts bring improvement? Unfortunately, no. Best efforts and hard work, not guided by new knowledge will only dig deeper the pit that we are in.[189]

It is interesting that DEMING had a rather simple definition for quality, "What is quality? The basic problem anywhere is quality. What is quality? A product or a

---

Units (SI), (New York. Lanham: University of America Press, 1996)) rightly recognized, the principles of similarity, equality, and sameness and their opposites and contraries (dissimilarity, inequality, and difference) are the first principles of all per se accidents and of relative first principles of all philosophy and science for all time. This must be the case because they constitute the most fundamental oppositions between unity and plurality. The opposition between unity and plurality is the first principle of all other oppositions and is the principle into which all others are reduced and made intelligible."

[189] DEMING, *The New Economics*, 1.

service possesses quality if it helps somebody and enjoys good and sustainable market. Trade depends on quality."[190]

It is the function of executive leadership to determine not only the quality of the product or service, but also the quality of excellence of the organizational whole. DEMING holds firmly that "quality is determined by top management. Moreover, an essential ingredient that I call profound knowledge is missing. There is no substitute for knowledge. Hard work, best efforts and best intentions will not by themselves produce quality nor a market."[191] It should be mentioned that DEMING's concept of profound knowledge is completely influenced by the pragmatist Clarence Irving LEWIS, *Mind and The World Order, Outline of a Theory of Knowledge*, P.W. BRIDGMAN, *The Logic of Modern Physics* and Walter A. SHEWART, *Statistical Method from the Viewpoint of Quality Control.*[192] There is no need to explore the philosophical foundation of these philosophers, and indeed it would demand a separate study.

We can say that DEMING was a scientific pragmatist who expresses the core of his concept of knowledge in his work *Out of Crisis* in chapter nine, *Operational Definitions, Conformance, and Performance*:

> What is an operational definition? An operational definition puts communicable meaning into a concept. Adjectives like good, reliable, uniform, round, tired, unsafe, unemployed have no communicable, meaning until they are expressed in operational terms of sampling, test, and criterion. The concept of a definition is effable; it cannot be communication to someone else. An operational definition is one that reasonable men can agree on.[193]

---

[190] Ibid., 2.

[191] Ibid., 17.

[192] Clarence Irving LEWIS, *Mind and The World Order, Outline of a Theory of Knowledge* (New York: Dover Publications, 1929); P.W. BRIDGMAN, *The Logic of Modern Physics* (New York: Macmillan, 1928); Walter A. SHEWHART, *Statistical Method from the Viewpoint of Quality Control* (Washington, D.C.: Graduate School of the Department of Agriculture, 1939; New York: Dover Publication, 1986).

[193] DEMING, *Out of Crisis*, 277.

DEMING's theory of knowledge is best summarized in his expression that profound knowledge is about the temporal spread of knowledge, and it is taken directly from chapter Six, *The Relativity of Knowledge* of LEWIS's work, "Knowledge does not copy anything presented; it proceeds from something given toward something else. When it finds that something else, the perception is verified."[194] However, DEMING is a dedicated pragmatist who depicts the function of executive leadership as a rational scientific elitist who is the designer of the organizational whole (genus). Other than teaching workers methods of inductive testing and verification, he does not seem to treat the issue of diffusion and participation of leadership throughout the genus. Although, it is interesting when DEMING in his work and four-day seminars gives an example of a perfect system, he picks:

> St. Paul understood a system. Excerpts from 1 Corinthians 12: 14-21. A body is not one single organ, but many. Suppose that the foot should say, "Because I am not a hand, I do not belong to the body," it does belong to the body none the less. Suppose that the ear were to say, "Because I am not an eye, I do not belong to the body," it does still belong to the body. How could it hear? If the body were all ear, how could it smell… there are many different organs, but one body. The eye cannot say to the hand, "I do not see you."[195]

As DEMING published his final work, *The New Economics*, he began to give attention to the need for an organizational motivational psychology. DEMING was a devout and deeply spiritual traditional high church Anglo-Catholic, who believed that something more than an extrinsic reward system is required to motivate employees to strive for perfection:

> Extrinsic motivation may indirectly bring positive results. For example, a man takes a job and receives money. Money is extrinsic reward. He arrives

---

[194] LEWIS, *Mind and The World Order*, 167.

[195] DEMING, *The New Economics*, 65. DEMING's footnotes: "Called to my attention by Dr. Backaitis at Westminster Abbey, 11 July 1990, this passage being in the second lesson appointed for Evensong for 11th day of the month, as it has been for centuries."

at work on time, and comes in a clean shirt, and discovers some of his abilities, all of which helps his self-esteem.

Some extrinsic motivation helps to build self-esteem. But total submission to extrinsic motivation leads to destruction of the individual. Joy in learning is submerged in order to capture top grades. On the job, under the present system, joy in work, and innovation, become secondary to a good rating. Extrinsic motivation in the extreme crushes motivation.

A bonus for high rank in the ranking of people, teams, divisions, regions, brings demoralization to all the people concerned, including him that receives the bonus.

I repeat here Norb Keller's famous statement made on 8 November 1987 in a meeting in General Motors: "If General Motors were to double the pay of everybody commencing the first of December, performance would be exactly what it is now."

He was, of course, talking about pay above that needed to maintain quality of life. He also meant to include everybody, not a select group.

Some of his friends told him afterward that they would be willing to take part in an experiment in double pay, but they acknowledged in the same breath that double pay would make no difference in their performance.[196]

We are giving attention to DEMING's understanding of executive leadership because of its instrumental impact on theories of organizational leadership in the 1980s and 90s. However, as DEMING came to realize, it was incomplete in its lack of a developed psychology of motivation. We are, therefore, suggesting that DEMING's desire to transform the concept of the functions of executive leadership required an Aristotelian-Thomistic comprehension of genus as one and the many and a Thomistic psychology of virtue. It is apparent in his examples of a system that he did sense the nature of a genus, e.g.:

An example of a system, well optimized, is a good orchestra. The players are not there to play as prima donnas, each one trying to catch the ear of the

---

[196] Ibid., 108–109.

listener. They are there to support each other. Individually, they need not be the best players in the country.

Thus, each of the 140 players in the Royal Philharmonic Orchestra of London is there to support the other 139 players. An orchestra is judged by the listeners, not so much by the illustrious players, but by the way they work together. The conductor, as manager, begets cooperation between the players, as a system, every player to support the others. There are other aims for an orchestra, such as joy in work for the players and for the conductor.[197]

It is obvious that DEMING had a sense of an organization as a system, but he did not understand the organization as a dynamic genus that moves to perfection to the extent the members are committed to the perfection of the genus. DEMING was limited by his lack of a metaphysical understanding of a genus since he was grounded in the conceptual pragmatism of LEWIS who holds:

The nature of mind in general is a fundamental and complex problem of metaphysics, including much with which we are not concerned. While it is not possible to avoid such metaphysical problems altogether, the attempt will be to restrict the discussion to the point in hand—that is, to explain the possibility of the mind's knowledge of itself, compatible with the conception that the knowledge of a real object is through interpretation of something given in experience, and that element of interpretation in knowledge is due to mind.[198]

3.7.1 The Person Knows, Senses, and the Soul Touches, the Genus

In the framework of a Thomistic metaphysics of organization, the genus results from something given in experience. The soul touches the genus, as previously stated "Whatever is received into a receiver is received according to the capacity of the receiver." The organizational whole (genus) is not an interpretation of the

---

[197] Ibid., 96–97.
[198] LEWIS, *Mind and The World Order*, 413.

mind; the genus is sensed by a knower who "uses abstract reasoning initially to grasp his formal object, he always views this formal object concretely and as existentially related, as a causal principle of real species."[199]

Jim COLLINS and Jerry I. PORRAS in *Built to Last, Successful Habits of Visionary Companies*, based on an extremely broad study of highly successful business organizations, discovered the success of visionary companies comes from:

> Underlying processes and fundamental dynamics embedded in the organization and not primarily the result of a single idea or some great, all-knowing, godlike visionary who made great decisions, had great charisma, and led with great authority. If you're involved in building and managing a company, we're asking you to think less in terms of being a brilliant product visionary or seeking the personality characteristics of charismatic leadership, and to think more in terms of being an organizational visionary and building the characteristics of a visionary company.[200]

An incredibly important principle from Peter A. REDPATH, as it relates to the above, is the knower of the genus (organizational whole) is concretely related to the organizational whole (genus) as a causal principle. REDPATH clarifies that, for St. Thomas that "it is the person, not the that intellect knows; and neither the senses nor intellect grasp the existence or essence of anything without the assistance of another faculty."[201] Or, as GILSON contends, that for St. Thomas "the existing man, the individual person not the intellect or senses, grasps the existence (esse) of anything; and we sense with our intellects and intellectualize with our sense."[202] It seems that COLLINS and PORRAS have this Thomistic sense of an underlying fundamental dynamic vision embedded in the organizational whole diffused throughout the organization.

---

[199] REDPATH, *A Not-So-Elementary Christian Metaphysics*, 167.

[200] Jim COLLINS and Jerry I. PORRAS in *Built to Last, Successful Habits of Visionary Companies* (New York: Harper Business, 1994), 41.

[201] REDPATH, *A Not-So-Elementary Christian Metaphysics*, 147

[202] Etienne GILSON, *Thomist Realism and the Critique of Knowledge*, trans. Mark A. Wauck (San Francisco: Ignatius Press, 1986), 172-173.

Robert William FOGEL's description, of a postmodern Western economy examines how the number of earned hours from dedication to organizational pay labor will decrease caused by technological innovation. Consequently, "to some extent currently and more so in the future, as the average workweek declines toward twenty-eight hours and retirement routinely begins at age fifty-five, work will increasingly mean activity under the compulsion of earning income regardless of whether the effort is manual or mental."[203] It means that as the new increased time for leisure economy rapidly grows, individuals will become more involved in volunteer organizations. FOGEL suggests that we will have to think in terms of earn-work and vol-work.

We mention this because it is argued that an understanding of Thomistic organizational psychology provides a most suitable framework for volunteer organizational leadership, e.g., church, community-based volunteers, special cause organizations, sports, and adult learning, etc. In order to explain why these organizations will need a Thomistic organizational psychology we will use an example somewhat similar to DEMING's example of the Royal Philharmonic Orchestra, except we are using the example of a small volunteer-based organization. Here it should be mentioned that most contemporary theories on executive leadership are constructed from the standpoint of large business, government, military, or major nonprofit organizations. In coming chapters, we will focus, as a rule, on the function of executive leadership in small business and nonprofit organizations. We argue that the principles of Thomistic organizational leadership are much more evident in concrete everyday activities and existentially as causal principles in smaller organizations.

3.8 Case Study of a Volunteer Community Organizational Whole (Genus)

3.8.1 A Community All Volunteer Symphonic Band

Many large and small communities in the United States have an all-volunteer community symphonic orchestra or a symphonic band. A symphonic band does

---

[203] FOGEL, *The Fourth Great Awakening*, 187.

not have a string section and is more like a college marching band. This study of organizational leadership pertains to an all-volunteer symphonic band in a small Midwest community adjacent to a large metropolitan community. It is comprised primarily of retired individuals, although there are some members who hold full time jobs in the community. We will, therefore, refer to this symphonic band as vol-work organizational whole (genus). For sake of brevity, we will name this organization the *Volunteer Symphonic Band Genus* (VSBG) and refer to the musical director and the executive leader as the same individual, the "Director."

History: The VSBG was formed in the mid-1960s in the community known as Raytown. It had been a fast-growing community after the war years with a school system known for one of the finest high school music programs in the country. Coming into the eighties, the community changed from a lower upper-class community to a middle to lower income community. The community demographics changed gradually from younger families to an aging and retiring community. Also, the racial and ethnic identity of the community changed from predominantly Caucasian to African American and Latino.

It was a community that responded somewhat harmoniously to the changing economics and a new middle to lower income, racially integrated community. One of the reasons for the smoothness of the transition was there was a strong presence of churches in the community with various social outreach programs. The community also had always been known for the excellence of its grade and high school music programs. Several graduates of these programs entered college music programs or opted for a minor in music. After graduation, some of these graduates returned to the community to teach music in the local school system.

The emergence of the VSBG: Increasingly, a population of retired schoolteachers who had opted to maintain residence in the community became interested in forming a community symphonic band. Four of these retired teachers began seriously to discuss among themselves forming this community symphonic band. Of the original four, three were retired high school music directors, three had Master of Arts degrees in music and one was a retired multi gifted musician female business executive. Soon, a fifth retired person heard of the idea and joined the group, but he had moved about fifty miles outside the community. This fifth person was the retired music director nationally known for taking his high school bands to major wins in state individual and band music competitions. He had his PhD in music, was retired and was working as a music consultant to two school districts.

3.8.2 Emerging Sense of Purpose

This fifth person eventually became the director of the emerging volunteer organization. He began to sense an emerging vague purpose for the volunteer group. One, there were several retired musicians in and outside the community who missed playing in a symphonic setting. Two, many of the musicians had not been practicing for a long time and their playing and reading skills were weak. Three, there were furthermore even non-retired musicians without the skill level as a musician that allowed them to play in a professional symphony menu. Four, there was a strong belief that an VSBG would bring Caucasian, African American and Latino musicians together which would contribute to racial integration of the community.

3.8.3 Emerging Executive Function

The PhD retired consultant was most excited about the concept and he was willing to serve as the director and conductor of the symphonic band. He also would contact retired musicians with whom he had a personal and career relationship about joining in the venture. The retired female executive offered her services in planning and accounting. She was highly known and respected in the community as a musician and for her dedication to community organizations. The other three musicians were excited and promised to contact retired and non-retired amateur musicians. Furthermore, the new Director and the retired executive assumed the responsibilities of co-ordination and contacting local churches for a time and place to practice and local businesses for donations to purchase music sheets.

3.8.4 Purpose

It was agreed the purpose of the VSBG was to allow retired and amateur musicians to have the opportunity to continue to enjoy their art and love of participating on a symphonic organization. Furthermore, it would give the musicians an opportunity to perform at various yearly community events that would continue the community's image of commitment to music and cultural events.

3.8.5 The Aim

With the clear aim of the organizational whole established, the organization whole came together effectively and efficiently over a short period of time and has survived for approximately thirty years. It has remained an all-volunteer organization, the original conductor served in this position for twenty-seven of those years and three of the original founders still play with the VSBG.

3.8.6 Operation

The director selected the music for the performance, often with the recommendations of band members. A musician and volunteer secretary handled all co-ordination with community events, the church where rehearsals were held, local press relationship, social media, email communication and funding for music sheets.

As mentioned, the particular challenge of a volunteer symphonic band is the range of talent and skills from musicians who could perform and read in a forty-member band to amateur musicians who had low to moderate skill levels. It would be here that the character of the conductor and some of the advanced musicians was critical. The director and the initial founders adopted the policy that individuals would be accepted with a low skill level, and it would be the challenge of the lead musicians of the wind and percussion sections to mentor those volunteers with a low skill set.

After and before rehearsals, the conductor, would spend time with the new members in their first years. If he recognized the required raw talent, he would work with them. He would build hope by constantly reminding them if they practiced that by the third year, they would feel confident. During the two years of mentoring by the director and section lead musicians, the volunteers' progress was continuously reinforced.

3.9 Constancy of Organizational Purpose and the Form of the Genus

W. Edwards DEMING's teachings on quality and transformational management had a profound impact on Japanese industry and eventually in the 1980s the American quality movement. He introduced a construct of transformational management based on 14 Principles for the transformation of western management. It has been argued that DEMING's management theory of organizational causation is compatible with Aristotelian-Thomistic understanding of causation.[204] It is his foundational first principle that deserves the most serious attention of a Thomistic organizational psychology:

> Create constancy of purpose for improvement of product and service. There are two problems: (i) problems of today; (ii) problems of tomorrow, for the company that hopes to stay in business. Problems of today encompass maintenance of quality of product put out today, regulation of output so as not to exceed immediate sales by too far, budget, employment, profits, sales, service, public relations, forecasting, and so forth. It is easy to stay bound up in the tangled knot of the problems of today, becoming ever more and more efficient in them, as by (e.g.) acquisition of mechanized equipment for the office.
>
> Problems of the future command first and foremost constancy of purpose and dedication to improvement of competitive position to keep the company alive and to provide jobs for their employees. Are the board of directors and the president dedicated to quick profits, or to the institution of

---

[204] MCVEY, "Thomistic Scientific Leadership and Common-Sense Triad of Organizational Harmony," *Studia Gilsoniana*, 3(2014), 579-593

constancy of purpose? The next quarterly dividend is not as important as existence of the company 0, 20, or 30 years are from now.[205]

We have previously drawn attention to DEMING's realization that the diffusion throughout the organizational whole requires a diffusion of the rational sense of a constancy of purpose. From the framework of Thomistic organizational psychology achieving an organizational diffusion of a rational sense of purpose requires an executive understanding of the Thomistic concept of "the organizational form," i.e., the generic purpose. This is a critical principle in Thomistic psychology, and it will be given greater attention in chapter Four as we develop the meaning of a rational "sensing" psychology. Because of the importance of the principle, we will describe the meaning of form in terms of a rational sensing moral psychology from Peter A. REDPATH's *Moral Psychology*, chapter seven, *The Nature of Moral Science and Its Relation to Happiness*:

> According to St. Thomas, in the finite order: 1) only the human intellect, human reason, knows the order of one thing to another and 2) a twofold order exists within things: of parts to parts, and of parts to a whole and the whole to an end through a highest part.
>
> He claims that this second order constitutes one in which: 1) the action of the whole and of the parts are identical; 2) a combined, or cooperative action (what today, we would commonly call an "organizational" or "corporate" act) constitutes numerically-one act (like an entire army attacking an enemy or all the parts of a crew harmoniously rowing together). The first order (of parts to parts) resembles departmental actions that occur within contemporary corporations in which the actions of this or that department do not constitute that of the whole corporation. [...]
>
> St. Thomas cites Aristotle as maintaining that *a common agreement exists about happiness being the best of things, the ultimate end and best and self-sufficient good. Using this commonly held agreement* (what the *Many* and the *Learned* say) about the nature of happiness as an induction of a generic definition from which to start further inquiry and specification,

---

[205] DEMING, *Out of Crisis*, 23–24.

Aristotle induces the genus of happiness by examining this commonly held agreement in relation to the chief aim of human nature considered as an organizational whole. In so doing, Aristotle is inducing the nature of happiness as a final cause, a chief first principle through which to identify the chief organizational activities of human beings pursued through the perfective exercise of human faculties: the chief action of the whole nature of man, the action that all human faculties naturally incline to generate.

With this chief aim in mind, St. Thomas says that *the final good of every composite whole or organization is its ultimate perfection* (that is, an organizational whole's qualitatively greatest act). The form, however, is an organizational whole's first perfection (the intrinsic first principle that generates an organizational whole's final perfection: perfect organizational operation). *The formal perfection of an organizational whole is perfectly harmonious operation*, the first principle of which is the organization's form, or nature (the qualified part/whole relations that generate harmonious organizational activity in relation to perfect execution of numerically-one act [for example, the skills possessed by the members of the more or less perfectly harmonious operation of the crew members]).[206]

The founding members of this VSBG with advanced degrees in music were accomplished amateurs; two founders were also semiprofessional musicians; and four of the five had been music teachers. It was the original Director who had a state and national reputation as a conductor and teacher. Besides having a PhD in music, he played six different instruments. It was his task to take volunteers of various musical talents, skill levels and the ability to read music readily, with ease and confidence.

Quickly, the symphonic genus grew to forty plus members. These were volunteers, like the founders, who shared a passionate love for music and participated as part of a performing organization. When a musician is performing with such an organization there is a tremendous sense of pleasure as the skills begin to blend together into a harmonious whole, especially as more difficult compositions are mastered. The creation and development of the genus required the talent and

---

[206] REDPATH, *The Moral Psychology of St. Thomas*, 200–212.

knowledge of the Director, the director/conductor and the secretary and flutist, who served as the community liaison person.

The success of this enterprise depended on the early founders who established a character of leadership based on a rational sense of the organizational form of amateurs capable of possible symphonic performance of an appropriate level of perfection. With this rational sense of form, they, then, were capable of executing the required habits to attract volunteers who possessed a love and capacity for performing in a symphonic community volunteer organization. In the framework of a Thomistic organizational psychology, attention increasingly will be given to the concept of character and the habits of virtuous leadership. It has been necessary before we enter into this phase of organizational psychology to establish the importance of the concept of the constancy of purpose of the organizational whole as the genus, i.e., the generic nature of the organization. Consequently, Thomistic organizational psychology observes the nature of the executive function by examining the virtuous habits of executive leadership and the equality/inequality diffusion of such virtuous habits within the genus.

Looking again, at the example of VSBG, we observe that five founders had an idea and a sense from years of experience of playing in symphonic bands and orchestras. The founders had experience, but they had never played in an all-volunteer community band comprised of retired and amateur musicians who had a wide range of variation in skill levels. It was a genus of a skill variation from more to less accomplished musicians who must blend together harmoniously to achieve within the limits of the capacity of skill of the musicians to generate the musical perfection given the limitations of the genus. As AQUINAS states:

> When a thing has a proper operation, the good of a thing and its well-being consist in that operation. Thus, the good of a flute player consists in his playing, and similarly the good of the sculptor and of every artist in their respective activity. The reason is that the final good of everything is its ultimate perfection, and the form is its first perfection while its operation is the second.[207]

---

[207] St. Thomas AQUINAS, *Commentary on Aristotle's Nicomachean Ethics*, Trans. By C.J. Litzinger, O.P. (Notre Dame: Dumb Ox Books, 1964), Book 1, n. 119.

3.9.1 Principles of Similarity, Equality, Sameness and Their Opposites and Contraries of the Genus

We defined Thomistic organizational psychology in chapter two as an art and a philosophical science, meaning it is chiefly about existential judgments. Moreover, the emotions are crucial in all forms of judging and reasoning. A community symphony band starts with the artistic wonder and moves to a total conviction that the formation of the symphonic band is doable. The aim is the final good of the genus, and it is the form of the genus that defines the generating power of the performing symphonic band. The generating power of the VSBG strives for excellence of performance as a volunteer amateur organization.

Given the nature of the genus, the founders must be aware of the strengths and limitations of the musicians. The founding members wisely selected the Director and the secretary for the executive function of co-ordination, but the Director agreed to serve as the conductor of the new organizational whole. The Director was selected because he was recognized as the most gifted musician willing to serve as the conductor. It is the conductor-director who conducts from the master composition sheets for all the parts of the whole. He must select the musical compositions that are within the capacity of the symphonic band as a genus. He must know who the lead musicians in each of the wind and percussion sections are. In order to have a high performing symphonic band, the conductor must build a repertoire of compositions within a range of limitations of the genus, i.e., the conductor and the musicians with the most to the least skills.

The Director of the VSBG had several years of experience as a musician performing in symphonic ensembles and as a conductor and music teacher. He was recognized by the founding associates as the person most capable of holding the executive function with one assistant of the VSBG. It was also because of his reputation as a conductor, teacher and his character that retired musicians in and from outside the community wanted to become a member of the ensemble led by a person recognized as a maestro. He was known as a kind and patient teacher. For example, a person would join the symphonic organization, and he would assess their skill level. If it was weak, he was more concerned about their willingness to work with a mentor and to practice. He would then tell the new musicians nervous about their playing and music reading skills that if they were prepared to work hard, then by year three they would feel confident and begin to experience joy playing in a symphonic band.

We have selected this case of a VSBG because it serves as a metaphorical description of six critical Thomistic principles of organizational psychology: similarity, equality, sameness and their opposites and contraries (dissimilarity, inequality, and difference). In the genus of a symphonic orchestra, understanding these 6 principles and how they oppose or harmonize with each other, is a function of executive leadership. In the community symphonic band, strictly speaking, the Director/Conductor has (or should have) the greatest musical sense of the organizational whole in terms of the selected compositions; symphonic, musical repertoire capabilities; capabilities of each instrumental section; and the musicians. The estimative sense of compositions of the music must be selected, and each of the musician's skills and capabilities of participating, more, or less, in the musical performance as part of the whole must be precisely determined.

The Director who must understand and blend the parts (the participating members) to maximize the perfection of performance of the whole. Every member of the genus has a proportionately equal moral challenge to share with their fellow musicians. While an inequality of musical ability, talent, exists within the orchestra because of musical good, beauty, and truth exists among professional acting as professionals, throughout the genus each member strives for a performance of excellence.

3.9.2 Organizational Virtual Quantity and the Form of Perfection of the Organizational Whole

In chapter two, we defined virtue based on Aquinas as the *ultimum potentiae*:

> It is a habit of the soul that motivates properly to achieve excellence: Virtue in this case is understood in Aquinas's terms: *ultimum potentiae*, the highest a person can aim at, in other words, the achievement of human possibilities in both the natural and supernatural realms. They amplify the determining motives of our behavior beyond what we conceive through our normal

psychological capacities. Every act and decision under the effect of the virtues liberates the person still for greater flourishing.[208]

In coming chapters, we will give more attention to the Thomistic concept of character and the diffusion of leadership. We will also focus on the contemporary interest in the issue of character and on first principles of a sense making organization. Presently, we are examining virtue as it relates to the maximization of perfection within an organizational whole, particularly in the case of the Director/Conductor and the maximization of performance perfection of a community band.

The Director has the function of continuously sensing with the musicians the perfection of the symphonic band, as they continuously strive for individual musical perfection. The conductor blends the musicians into an increasing level of a greater perfection in playing the artistically demanding repertoire in the performance of the musical ensemble. We have defined the director and the musicians motivated to excellence to exceed their normal capacities and amplify the intensity of perfection within the organizational whole.

ARISTOTLE defines virtue by drawing attention to a common quality of virtue that makes its possessor and the possessor's work good. For example, ARISTOTLE teaches that "the virtue, power, and the excellence of an eye of a horse make them excel at their proper act. We judge or measure power or virtue of the thing by 1) the best thing that it can do, 2) its excellent performance and 3) its perfect operation."[209] In the example of the Symphonic Band, the audience by their applause and the monetary contributions from the community are the judges and measurement of the excellence of their powerful performance. It is the measurement that allows the director who is the executive leader to maintain and monitor a stable level of perfection of performance.[210]

---

[208] ÁLVAREZ, ECHAVARRÍA and VITZ, "Re-conceptualizing Neurosis as a Degree of Egocentricity: Ethical Issues in Psychological Theory," 7–8.

[209] REDPATH, *The Moral Psychology of St. Thomas*, 236–237.

[210] REDPATH in chapter eight, *Moral Virtue Considered in General*, explains (ibid., 237) AQUINAS's expansion of the generic definition of virtue within the framework of Virtual Quantity: "St. Thomas adds that virtue deals with three things, the 1) more, 2) less, and 3)

Thomistic organizational psychology is a rational-sensing moral psychology of perfection, the executive leadership. In terms of an organizational rational sensing moral psychology, the executive function is to have a rational sense of the intensity of organizational limits of perfection. The executive rational-moral-sense of the organizational mean that has the following qualities:

> *In its specific nature as an intensive quantity, quality, or right proportion, moral virtue is beautiful and a mean.* In the way it acts, it is an extreme between too much and too little; an extreme that, because it is beautiful, is a perfect measure to which nothing can be added and from which nothing can be subtracted.[211]

A Thomistic organizational soulful psychology of the function of executive leadership, as established in chapter two, focuses on the rational and moral responsibilities of leadership. Therefore, the primary function of executive leadership is a rational moral sense making of the perfect and good as applied to the organizational whole.

> According to St. Thomas, what makes something perfect is what makes it beautiful, whole with a maximum qualitative intensity (or intensive quantity greatness). The perfection of a being's act of existing (the qualitative in which a being acts) determining within it a qualitative limit (measure) of possession

---

the equal in continuous, and divisible matters according to dimensive and intensive quantity. In relation to those three things, he maintains that the equal holds a midpoint between more (excess, too much) and less (defect, too little) according to both absolute quantity between accidents and things and by intensity and in distinctness of quality (that is, according to intensive quantity) in a subject. He adds that the mean according to absolute quantity is the equal taken from things compares, from the quantity of the thing, while the mean relative to us is the mean proportioned, suitable, to our power (the mean according to us, like the size of a shoe relative to the size of the person's foot that it fits or does not fit) and is not the same for all. Because he has a healthy estimative sense and, as a result, has a good sense of personal capabilities and, as a result, has s good sense of personal capabilities, the virtuous, prudent, man seeks and knows the mean relative to him.

[211] Ibid., 239.

of virtue (a virtual quantity maximum of possession [limit of qualitative greatness] of its existence), makes a being desirable.[212]

3.9.3 Organizational Virtual Intensity Measurement of Perfection and an Existential Metaphysics of Participation

We saw in the interview of Herb Kelleher of Southwest Airlines, who is a respected lifetime business and organizational strategist, when asked, "Did you have a vision for the whole thing thirty-five years ago? Did you write we're going to become the largest airline with the lowest cost?" He responded:

We didn't write it down because when you write things down you confine yourself. That's why we never used the fancy titles for empowerment, total quality, etc. Every time you talk jargon you find that people assume that they have the same thing in mind when they really don't. We don't apply labels because they prevent you from thinking expansively...I said that we have the most unusual plan in the industry: Doing things, that's our plan. What we do by the way of strategic planning is define ourselves and then we redefine ourselves.[213]

---

[212] Ibid., 50. See AQUINAS, *Commentary on the Metaphysics of Aristotle*, Bk. 5, Lect. 18, n. 1037: "The reason why a thing is said to be perfect in the line of its particular ability is that an ability is a perfection of a thing. For each thing is perfect when no part of the natural magnitude which belongs to it according to the form of its proper ability is missing. Moreover, just as each natural being has a definite measure of natural magnitude in continuous quantity, as is stated in Book II of *The Soul*, so too each thing has a definite amount of its own natural ability. For example, a horse has by nature a definite dimensive quantity, within certain limits; for there is both a maximum quantity and minimum quantity beyond which no horse can go in size. And in a similar way the quantity of active power in a horse has certain limits in both directions. For there is some maximum power of a horse which is not in fact surpassed in any horse; and similarly, there is some minimum which never fails to be attained."

[213] LUCIER, "Herb Kelleher: The Thought Leader Interview."

As has been suggested, entrepreneurial-executive leaders have a metaphysical sense of an organizational whole. More so, as argued in this chapter, they have a rational sense of the form of the organizational whole, defined previously as:

> Everything we know we apprehend in terms of being some kind of composite whole or organization, we identify the attractive good within an organizational whole to be that it has all of the parts needed to be a composite whole, harmoniously arranged proportionately one to another, in terms of the suitability of the parts qualitatively to unite (that it is able to execute a fitting organizational action, thereby making it maximally an organization: beautiful). Hence, when we desire something as good, we desire it precisely because we recognize it to have some sort of perfecting quality about it; we desire it because it is beautiful.[214]

In terms of a metaphysics of an organization.

> There is a quantity of virtue (*quantitas virtutis*), which is measured according to the perfection of some nature of form. It is this sort of quantity we allude to when we speak of something as being more or less hot; in as much as it is more or less perfect in heat.[215]

It is Charles Bonaventure CROWLEY, O.P., who contends that "there is no contradiction between the principles of classical Thomistic metaphysics and the principles of modern experimental science, but there is actually a correlation between the principle of unity convertible with being contained within this metaphysics with something which he calls the principles of a philosophy of measure and with the principles of both of these studies and the laws of modern

---

[214] . REDPATH, *The Moral Psychology of St. Thomas*, 51

[215] Charles Bonaventure CROWLEY, *Aristotelian-Thomistic Philosophy of Measure, and the International System of Units (SI)* (Lanham, New York, London: University Press of America, 1996), 249.

experimental science and the measuring principles and artifacts of the current International System of Units."[216]

CROWLEY's explanation, it could be said, of *quantitas virtutis* as measurable (his philosophy of measurement) is the responsibility of the function of executive leadership. For example, DEMING taught in his famous four-day seminars his 97/10 principle that executive management is responsible for 90% of the output of quality products. It is management who controls all the decisions about the utilization and co-ordination of worker, training, recruitment, proper equipment, rational and moral expectations, strategies, and tactics. A Thomistic organizational soulful psychology of executive leadership likewise views executive leadership as responsible for developing the proper entwinement of a psychology of excellence and a measurement of the mean of organizational perfection. It is, according to CROWLEY, a measuring of quality as virtual quantity:

> Speaking this way, a quality as virtual quantity is **measured firstly** by its source, that is by the perfection of that form or nature, just as we speak of great heat on account of its intensity and perfection. [...]
>
> Secondly, virtual quantity is **measured** by the effects of the form. Now, the first effect of form is **being,** for everything has been by reason of its form. The second effect is **operation**, for every agent acts through its form. Consequently, virtual quantity is measured both in regard to being and in regard to action. In regard to being, insofar as things of a more perfect nature are of longer duration; and in regard to action inasmuch as things of a more perfect nature are more powerful to act.
>
> Thirdly, the more powerful the effect, the more powerful is the act that produced it; and the more powerful the act, the more powerful is the principle of that activity; and the more powerful the principle of the action is, the more powerful the nature is, in which that principle resides—for everything is measured by that upon which it depends.[217]

---

[216] Ibid., xii.

[217] Ibid., 259. See AQUINAS, *Commentary on the Metaphysics of Aristotle*, Bk. 5, Lect. 17, n. 1027: "Hence, they are not said to be relative because of something which pertains to them, such as quality, quantity, action, or undergoing, as was the case in the foregoing

Returning to the example of the Community Volunteer Symphonic Band, the effects of the form measure the virtual quantity. The form is the playing of musical scores to perfection in performance. It is the task of the director to continuously measure the performance level of the band as more or less perfect. Furthermore, each of the musicians must measure their participation in the form of a perfect performance. Everything, such as the demands of rehearsals, individual practice of the musical charts and the reading and playing skills and constantly recruiting new capable musicians must be exercised more or less to the defined and measurable oneness of the organizational form.

3.10 Thick Measurement and Thin Measurement

In a *Harvard Business Review* article *What Can't be Measured*, Larry PRUSAK quotes the prominent psychologist ROBERT STERNBERG: "Society needs to move beyond narrow conceptions of the skill needed for life success and to correct its gross under-emphasis on wisdom and ethical qualities." PRUSAK then states,

---

relations, but only because of the action of other things, although these are not terminated in them. For if seeing were the action of the one seeing as extending to the thing seen, as heating extends to the thing which can be heated, then just as what can be heated is related to the one heating, so would what is visible be related to the one seeing. But to see and to understand and actions of this kind, as is stated in Book IX (1788) of this work, remain in the things acting and do not pass over into those which are acted upon. Hence what is visible or what is knowable is not acted upon by being known or seen. And on this account, these are not referred to other things but others to them. The same is true in all other cases in which something is said to be relative because something else is related to it, as right and left in the case of a pillar. For since right and left designate starting points of motion in living things, they cannot be attributed to a pillar or to any nonliving thing except insofar as living things are related to a pillar in some way. It is in this sense that one speaks of a right-hand pillar because a man stands to the left of it. The same holds true of an image in relation to the original; and of a denarius, by means of which one fixes the price of a sale. And in all these cases the whole basis of relation between two extremes depends on something else. Hence all things of this kind are related in somewhat the same way as what is measurable and its measure. For everything is measured by the thing on which it depends."

In business, the emphasis naturally lands on the kind of value that can be set by a market. This is why knowledge made it on to management's agenda; it can be measured somewhat in terms of education and experience. Good judgment is another important virtue—if not the most important one (as Aristotle thought). Like love, it so far defies measurement. But we ignore it as a critical factor in organizational life at our peril.[218]

A famous quote of Peter DRUCKER is, "What gets measured gets improved." But, from the perspective of an organizational psychology of *quantits virtutis*, we would better say: "What gets measured the right way gets improved." In organizations, it is necessary to measure the progress of an organization in terms goals and objectives, revenue stream (cash flow success) quality control. CHRISTIAN MADSBJERG in Sensemaking, the *Power of the Humanities in the Age of the Algorithm*, proposes that in organizations, especially business and finance, there is a fascination with thin data as opposed to thick data.[219] He contends that thin data is used to measure organizational processes, human resource issues, accounting procedures, etc. Thin data measures processes in terms of successful effective and efficient functioning, but it is thick data that measures the participation of the organizational whole in perfection of the form.

MADSBJERG describes a conversation with the economist Robert Johnson to explain his description and distinction between thick and thin data:

Robert Johnson studied economics at MIT and completed his PhD at Princeton—but he thrived under Soros's management style—the culture of humanities thinking at Soros. The culture of humanities thinking at Soros Fund Management demanded that he seek out the cultural context of data. Robert Johnson explained their unique process to me: "The data was not numbers mostly. It was not all quantifiable on spreadsheets. It was

---

[218] Larry PRUSAK, "What Can't Be Measured," https://hbr.org/2010/10/what-cant-be-measured.

[219] Christian MADSBJERG, *Sensemaking, The Power of the Humanities in the Age of Algorithm* (New York, Boston: Hachette Books, 2017).

experiences, newspaper articles, stories about how people were reacting, conversations. Narrative data.

This is what I call thick data. What makes it thick? And what does it matter when machine learning gives us a surfeit of thin data?[220]

MADSBJERG gives another concise description of the thick data-thin data issue from the perspective of the historian Isaiah Berlin who spent much his academic career studying politics and leadership:

Berlin found out that great political leaders had a set of personal skills that he called "perfectly ordinary, empirical, and quasi-aesthetic." These skills were characterized by an engagement with reality founded on experience, empathic, understanding of others, and sensitivity to the situation. It's the extraordinary ability to synthesize "a vast amalgam of constantly changing, multicolored, evanescent, perpetually overlapping data, too many, too intermingled to be caught and pinned down and labeled so many individual butterflies."[221]

If we follow Berlin's argument that a vast ocean of data, impressions, facts, experiences, opinions, and observations is gathered, then these patterns are connected into a single unifying insight, i.e., thick data. In his mind this requires a "direct almost sensuous contact with the relevant data," an "acute sense of what fits with what, what springs from what, what leads to what."[222]

We can measure processes, estimate profit and loss, quarterly reports, categorize large databases with thin numbers because thin data is necessary for organizational efficiency and effectiveness. On the other hand, when the VSBG wants to measure the more or less of the perfection of the measurable mean performance, i.e., their participation in the form, then it becomes a matter of thick data. How did the audience applaud? What did members of audience who were fellow respected musicians say about the performance, were their reviews in the

---

[220] Ibid., 70.

[221] Ibid., 80–81.

[222] Ibid., 81

newspaper, how did the musicians and the director evaluate their performance and offer recommendations to improve the level of perfection?

3.11 A Case Study of Organizational Perfection and Touching the Divine

Peter A. REDPATH in *The Moral Psychology of St. Thomas* writes:

> Whatever moves, changes, in any way, gets its initial impulse to move, change from a determinate agent: one with an act *proportionate in intensive quantum greatness to the faculty or habit it activates, proportionate to this faculty's or habits qualitative, receptive capacity* (its intensive quantum greatness *to receive an act proportionate to its power:* to receive an act that has been able to establish an organizational [generic] relation: unity with it). [...]
>
> It is a state of *being* within an organizational whole, a genus that has become unified into a perfect, composite whole (like the harmonization of unity of specific parts within the crew of a rowing team or business organization).[223]

The following case study speaks to the relationship of the coordinated powerful movement of a crew as a participation in the intensive quantum greatness of a form. Our case study, therefore, is about the "perfect and good that a finite being must have some receptive power, i.e., a capacity to receive a form to be unified as an organizational whole."[224] Our case study is about an extraordinary story of a competitive team and the philosophy of one of their coaches. We use this case study because the coach and the team organizational motivational psychology is really a study in the Thomistic organizational psychology of form and virtual quantity.

---

[223] REDPATH, *The Moral Psychology of St. Thomas*, 478–479.

[224] Ibid., 478.

The case story is from the novel *Boys in The Boat* by Daniel James BROWN.[225] The novel celebrates the 1936 U.S. men's Olympic eight-oar rowing team. Brown describes the nine working class boys who stormed the rowing world, transformed the sport of rowing, and galvanized the attention of millions of Americans. It was during the Depression years, and they were the sons of loggers, shipyard workers, and farmers from the American West. The boys took on and defeated echelons of privilege and power. They vanquished the sons of bankers and senators rowing for elite eastern universities. They defeated the sons of British aristocrats' rowing for Oxford and Cambridge. And finally, in an extraordinary race in Berlin, they stunned the Aryan sons of the Nazi state as they rowed for gold in front of Adolf Hitler.

Against the grim backdrop of the Great Depression, they reaffirmed the American nation that merit, in the end, outweighs birthright. They reminded the country of what can be done when everyone quite literally pulls together. And they provided hope that in the titanic struggle that lay ahead, the ruthless might of the Nazis would not prevail over American grit, determination, and optimism.

Besides the collective team effort, it is also the heartwarming story of one young man in particular: Joe Rantz, who was cast aside by his family at an early age, abandoned and left to fend for himself. It is this Joe Rantz who rows not just for glory, but to participate in a team effort that moves his soul, especially by the guidance of two coaches, Al Ulbrickson and George Yeoman Pocock.

Al Ulbrickson was the head coach of the University of Washington rowing program and was a stickler for detail. He had the build of a perfect oarsman and all the natural talent and had won national championships in 1924 and 1926. He was a highly disciplined man of few words, as Daniel BROWN says, "He was a tall, muscular, broad shouldered, and distinctly Nordic in his features, with high cheek bones, a chiseled jaw line and cold-slate gray eyes. They were the kind of eyes that shut you up fast if you were a young man inclined to challenge something he had just said."[226]

---

[225] Daniel James BROWN, *Boys in The Boat: Nine Americans and Their Epic Quest for Gold at the 1936 Olympics* (New York: Penguin Books, 1951).

[226] Ibid., 15.

The other coach is George Yeoman Pocock who was a leading designer and builder of racing shells in the 20th century. Pocock shells, known for excellence, began to win U.S. Intercollegiate Rowing Association championships in 1923. Besides being an assistant coach, he achieved recognition for providing the shell for the 1936 Olympics. Pocock was also known as an author and philosopher on the sport of rowing and the pursuit of perfection in the art of rowing. His teachings on rowing and perfection are interspersed throughout the chapters of BROWN's novel:

1) It's a great art, rowing. It's the finest art there is. It's a symphony of motion. And when you're rowing well, why it's nearing perfection. And when you near perfection, you're touching the Divine. It touches the you of yours. Which is your soul.[227]

2) In sport like this—hard work, not much glory, but still popular in every century—well, there must be some beauty which ordinary men can't see, but extraordinary men do.[228]

3) Having rowed myself since the tender age of twelve and having been around rowing ever since, I believe I can speak authoritatively on what we may call the unseen values of rowing—the social, moral, and spiritual values of this oldest of chronicled sports in the world. No didactic teaching will place these values in a young man's soul. He has to get them by his own observation and lessons.[229]

4) Every good rowing coach, in his own way, imparts to his men the kind of self-discipline required to achieve the ultimate from mind, heart, and body. Which is why most ex-oarsmen will tell you they learned more fundamentally important lessons in the racing shell than in the classroom.[230]

5) One of the first admonitions of a good rowing coach, after fundamentals are over, is "pull your own weight," and the young oarsman does just

---

[227] Ibid., Prologue.
[228] Ibid., 1.
[229] Ibid., 7.
[230] Ibid., 39.

that when he finds out that the boat goes better when he does. There is certainly a social implication here.[231]

6) Where is the spiritual value of rowing? The losing of self entirely to the cooperative efforts of the crew as a whole.[232]

3.12 Organizational Exemplars of Existential Virtual Participation (Touching the Divine)

George Yeoman Pocock is not an Aristotelian or Thomistic philosopher, yet as a craftsman, coach, and sports philosopher, he seems to have an innate grasp of Fran O'ROURKE's explanation of *esse intensivum* and an existential metaphysics of participation. AQUINAS adopts from DIONYSIUS a doctrine of the intensity of plenitude of perfection:

> It is Dionysius' view of participation and pre-eminent presence which leads Aquinas to conceive of esse as the emergent fullness shared by all entitative character. Aquinas' notion on intensive and emergent esse becomes in turn the core and foundation for his existential metaphysics of participation, as Fabro repeatedly emphasizes. Dionysius understands being, above all, as the focus of participation by all things in divine Goodness. All things are preserved in the created fullness of Being.[233]

---

[231] Ibid., 149.

[232] Ibid., 353.

[233] Fran O'ROURKE, *Pseudo-Dionysius and the Metaphysics of Aquinas*, (Notre Dame, Indiana: University of Notre Dame Press, 1992), 156–157. See AQUINAS, *De Veritate*, 29, 3: "Now there are two kinds of quantity: dimensive, which is referred to extension; and virtual, which is referred to intensity; for the excellence (*virtus*) of a thing is its perfection, as the Philosopher teaches: 'Anything is perfect when it attains its proper excellence'; and the virtual quantity of each form is considered according to the degree of its perfection. Both kinds of quantity are differentiated into many species. Under dimensive quantity are included length, width, and depth, and potentially number. Virtual quantity is distinguished into as many classes as there are natures and forms, whose degree of perfection constitutes all the measure of quantity that they have. Now it sometimes happens that what is finite as regard one sort of quantity is infinite as regard another. This is easily

Aquinas indeed himself exploits the idea of virtual intensity to convey the inward nature of things and the varying degrees of their perfection. Intensity expresses the manner of quantity characteristic of metaphysical or spiritual actions, powers, and realities. Furthermore, Aquinas holds that 'virtual' (*virtualis*) signifies an intensity or degree of perfection (*secundum intensionem*): 'the excellence or power-virtus-of a thing is its perfection' (*virtus enim rei est ipsius perfection*), since as Aristotle teaches, anything is perfect when it attains its proper excellence (*virtus*). Thus, the virtual quantity of each form is determined by the measure of its perfection.[234]

In chapter two, we argued from Chester BARNARD that "organizations endure in proportion to the breadth of the morality by which they are governed. This is only to say that foresight, long purposes, high ideals are the basis for the persistence of cooperation." After giving careful attention to the nature of the form of the genus, it is apparent that a Thomistic organizational psychology of foresight, long purposes, high ideals, and persistence of cooperation are grounded on an existential metaphysics of organization. Fran O'ROURKE gives a foundation to this existential metaphysical psychology:

Aquinas explains that the magnitude of *virtus* may be deemed greater or less (*major et minor*) in two ways: in itself. with respect to the things to which it extends, or on the part of the subject by which it is participated. It will be

---

seen if we take dimensive quantity in both cases, for we can conceive a surface which is finite in width but infinite in length. It is also clear if we take one dimensive quantity and another virtual; for if we conceive an infinite white body, its whiteness will not on this account be infinite in intensity, but only (indirectly) in extension; for something whiter might be found. The same is no less evident if both quantities are virtual; for in one and the same subject different virtual quantities can be taken into consideration on the basis of different formalities of the attributes predicated of this subject. Thus, if a thing is called a being, virtual quantity is considered in it with regard to the perfection of existing; and if it is called sentient, this quantity is considered with regard to the perfection of sensing; and so on."

[234] Ibid., 157.

participated variously by different persons or by the same persons at different times. This is intensive greatness, the magnitude which is proper and unique to *virtus*: the inner measure and the density of its presence embraced and embodied concretely in the individual.[235]

BARNARD says that organizations endure in proportion to the breadth of the morality by which they are governed. In terms of a Thomistic psychology of the organizational form, presented in this chapter, we define the function of executive leadership as one of a rational sensing moral character that freely exercises human choice to become as morally virtuous, perfect, and wise as possible in an intense existential participative virtuosity of flourishing excellence. Consequently, the executive and any sharing in this leadership function, as defined by the organization at any operational level, serve as organizational exemplars of existential virtual participation. These exemplar leaders serve as a constant diffusion of the wise and moral character inspired by participation in the organizational "form" of the goodness of perfection. An organizational definition of the diffusion of the essence of leadership is taken from AQUINAS:

> Moreover, the communication of being and goodness arises from goodness. This is evident from the very nature and definition of the good. By nature, the good of each thing is its act and perfection. Now each thing acts in so far as it is in act, and in acting it diffuses being and goodness to other things. Hence it is a sign of a being's perfection that it "can produce its like," as may be seen from the Philosopher in *Meteorologica* IV. Now, the nature of the good comes from its being something appetible. This is the end, which also moves the agent to act. That is why the good is diffusive of itself and of being.[236]

---

[235] Ibid., 160–161. Reference to AQUINAS, *Summa theologiae* I-II, q. 66, a. 1, "If, however, we consider virtue on the part of the subject, it may then be greater or less, either in relation to different times, or in different men."

[236] St. Thomas AQUINAS, *Summa Contra Gentiles* I, C. 37.

Fran O'ROURKE, in his noteworthy grasp of AQUINAS's "existential metaphysics", writes that as with AQUINAS, the greatness of being of spiritual realities resides, according to AUGUSTINE, in their *virtus*: 'When we hear and speak of a great and strong soul, we ought not to think of its size, but of its power (*quantum*).'[237] Speaking of a great and strong soul, we return to our case study of the boys in the boat and two strong souls, i.e., the assistant coach and master craftsman of the art of shell making and Joe Rantz. We have looked at Pocock, the assistant coach whose exemplar existential virtuosity is diffused in his inspiring acts of being and goodness with the crew. It is also the powerful participation in "the goodness and perfection of the form."

The story of this against all odds 1936 Olympic gold medal rowing crew is also the story of one special young man, Joe Rantz. He had been cast aside by his family at an early age, abandoned by his family during the Depression years and left to fend for himself. Joe rowed for the honor of the team, but he also participated to touch the substantial powers of his own soul and regain a shattered self-esteem. He had to learn to trust others and the affirming power of the virtue of team friendship and magnanimity. More than being a member of a championship crew, he learned, despite his years of loneliness, the profoundest meaning of loving friendship early in life.

As AQUINAS comments,

> [Aristotle] teaches that men delight in the fact of being loved, since the very possession of friends seems to be the principal external sign of honor. [...] he draws a conclusion. Since what is essential is more excellent than what is accidental, it follows from premises that being loved is better than being honored inasmuch as friendship is in itself desirable. [...] he shows in what the excellence consists: in loving or being loved. He says it consists rather in loving, for friendship is predicated by way of habit, as has been explained. But a habit terminates at activity; and loving is certainly an activity, while

---

[237] O'ROURKE, *Pseudo-Dionysius and the Metaphysics of Aquinas*, 165–166.

being loved is rather passivity. Hence loving is more proper to friendship than being loved.[238]

But it is the description of Daniel James BROWN interviewing Joe Rantz for the book *Boys in the Boat,* that portrays vividly the meaning of an existential metaphysical participation of a great soul in the loving goodness and perfection of a form. BROWN writes with deep spiritual sensitivity to a person's soul:

His voice was reedy, fragile, and attenuated almost to the breaking point. From time to time he faded into silence. Slowly, though, with cautious prompting from his daughter, he began to spin out some of the threads of his life story. Recalling his childhood and his young adulthood during the Great Depression, he spoke haltingly but resolutely about a series of hardships he had endured and obstacles he had overcome, a tale that, as I sat taking notes, at first surprised and then astonished me.

But it wasn't until he began to talk about his rowing career at the University of Washington that he started from time to time, to cry. He talked about learning the art of rowing, about shells and oars, about tactics and technique. He reminisced about long, cold hours on the water under steel gray skies, about smashing victories and defeats narrowly averted, about traveling to Germany, and marching under Hitler's eyes into the Olympic Stadium in Berlin, and about his crewmates. None of these recollections brought him to tears, though. It was when he tried to talk about "the boat" that his words began to falter, and tears welled up in his bright eyes.

At first, I thought he meant the Husky Clipper, the racing shell in which he had rowed his way to glory. Or did he mean his teammates, the improbable assemblage of young men who had pulled off one of rowing's greatest achievements? Finally, watching Joe struggle for composure over and over, I realized that "the boat" was something more than just the shell or its crew. To Joe, it encompassed but transcended both—it was something mysterious and almost beyond definition. It was a shared experience—a

---

[238] AQUINAS, *Commentary on Aristotle's Nicomachean Ethics,* Book 8, Lecture 8, nn. 1644–1646.

singular thing that had unfolded in a golden sliver of time long gone, when nine good-hearted young men strove together, pulled together as one, gave everything they had for one another, bound together forever by pride and respect and love. Joe was crying, at least in part, for the loss of that vanished moment but much more, for the sheer beauty of it.[239]

In this chapter, we have concisely established a primary metaphysics of organization with special emphasis on the wise person knowing the essential principles (part/whole relations) that generate this or that organization, principles of equality of inequality, the coordination and communication of opposites (principle of contrariety) within the genus, an existential exemplar participation and diffusion of executive leadership. Although this dissertation is on the nature of Thomistic organizational psychology and the functions and diffusion of executive leadership, it has been necessary to establish a metaphysical foundation to develop a Thomistic psychology of leadership in the coming chapters.

We conclude this chapter with closing existential reflections on the principles of the virtual quantity of organization and the executive and other participants in the organizational genus, such as the coach, George Pocock, and the rowing team members, especially Joe Rantz. We describe them as existential exemplars of intense virtual participation. In other words, they participated in the genus from the depth and power of their souls. In order to develop an organizational Thomistic psychology, we must realize that it is about persons in organizations who are called to develop a character of virtuous habits of the soul: a person who understands that being an exemplar of existential virtual leadership does not need to be perfect to inspire others.

Instead, the true executive leader allows people to get inspired by how he/she deals with his/her imperfections. Thomistic organizational psychology is about a continuous focus on excellence rather than success. George LEONARD warns against "bottom-line mentality that puts quick, easy results ahead of long-term dedication to the journey itself."[240] An organization needs thin data to measure short term gains: financial reports, weekly quotas, budget reports measure success

---

[239] BROWN, *Boys in The Boat*, Prologue.

[240] George LEONARD, *Mastery* (New York: Dutton Penguin Books,1991), xi–xii.

or failure rather well. Even more important, the long-term growth of an organization requires thick virtual quantity data. It is the function of executive leadership to judge and measure the intensity of personal and team participation in the organizational genus.

3.13 A Description of Executive Soulful Virtual Leadership

Finally, we conclude this chapter with a complete and excellent description of exemplar executive existential participation taken from a paper of Peter A. REDPATH:

> Experienced leaders know that this or that needs to be done at this or that time, under this or that circumstance or condition, and overcome resistance and induce receptivity when necessary to do what needs to be done when it needs to be done. Beyond experiential knowledge, someone who possesses knowledge through an artistic quality of soul resembles a person with a habit of mathematics who has memorized formulas and knows when they can reasonably be applied to solve this or that at this or that time, under this or that condition or circumstance, reasonable in relation to a tactical plan of operation. People possessed of the philosophy or science of leadership, however, more perfectly possess what they already know by apprehending it in relation to the strategic, or generic, plan and aim articulated in an organizational mission statement that generates the operational principle behind tactical operations in the here and now.
>
> Such people know how to build and preserve organizations and have the qualities of great discoverers, pioneers, and great teachers. Because such people must constantly instill hope, drive out fear, build and restore confidence, energize, and calm emotions, communicate a superior ability to know and unify potentially opposing convictions among free and intelligent agents about the right direction to take within an organizational operation to satisfy the chief organizational aim, such people must, best of all, and through emotional and volitional strength and resolve, be able to

communicate this to themselves and others. As a result, such people can never be absolute skeptics, egalitarians, totalitarians, or anarchists.[241]

Therefore, executive exemplars of existential participation must have the character of discoverer, teacher and capable of instilling hope driving out fear and building and restoring confidence and energize and calming emotions.

---

[241] Peter A. REDPATH, "The Essential Connection between Common Sense and Leadership Excellence," *Studia Gilsoniana*, 3 (2014), 615.

4.

The Sensemaking Soul

The aim of this chapter is to examine the interest especially among emerging psychologies of organizational leadership about the function of spirituality and the soul in the workplace. We describe a paradox of leaders driven by the disruptive forces of digital technology expressing a need for a sense of organizational spiritual meaning and purpose. We give attention to and respond to the issue that leaders find it necessary in the disruptive organizational cadence to acquire more robust sensemaking skills. Therefore, we will explain the Aristotelian-Thomistic approach to common sense making as the exercise of practical reason, premodern induction and craft knowledge principles resting in the soul.

4.1 From Pyramids to the Spiritual Crisis, Soulful Leadership and Organizational Culture

Thus far, as we developed the need for a Thomistic organizational psychology of leadership, we established a certain agreement on the nature of executive leadership between a Thomistic framework of leadership, Chester I. BARNARD, and W. Edwards DEMING. We gave attention to BARNARD's insistence that the executive function requires the capability of creating a diffusion of organizational moral leadership. In Chapter Two, we drew attention to DEMING's focus on the 1980s quality crisis in American industry that he approached as a crisis resulting from a lack of a profound knowledge of an organizational knowledge-based system.

In this chapter, we turn our attention to the crisis of leadership in contemporary organizational psychology. We describe this emerging issue as a crisis of distributed self-leadership, organizational motivational vision and sense making. In previous chapters, we discussed Fogel's postmodern economic cultural movement toward a discovery of a sense of personal and community identity based on a secular sense of spiritual happiness. Daniel PINK, in an acclaimed study, *A Whole New Mind, Moving from Information Age to the Conceptual Age* draws on organizational research from around the world and offers a fresh and challenging look at what it takes to excel in the Conceptual Age. It is the coming age of business, nonprofits, and government where digital technology will favor an executive leadership that encourages organizational creativity, intuition, and a spiritual sense of mission. PINK, in his chapter on the pursuit of organizational meaning in the Conceptual Age, refers to the work of Ian MITROFF, a professor at the University of Southern California's Marshall School of Business and the consultant Elizabeth DENTON's published report *A Spiritual Audit of Corporate America*. After interviewing one hundred executives about spirituality in the workplace, they reached surprising conclusions supportive of the metaphysical spiritual foundation of a Thomistic organizational psychology and the functions of executive leadership:

> Most of the executives defined spirituality in much the same way—not as religion, but as "the basic desire to find purpose and meaning in one's life." Yet, the executives were so understandably concerned that the language of spirit in the workplace would offend their religiously diverse employees that they scrubbed their vocabulary of all such talk. Meanwhile, Mitroff and Denton discovered, the employees were hungering to bring their spiritual values (and thus their whole person rather than one component of themselves) to work but didn't feel comfortable doing so. Read this report and you can almost picture a river of meaning and purpose being damned outside of the corporate headquarters. But here's the kicker: if that spiritual ideal had been released, the companies might have been better off. Mitroff and Denton also found that companies that acknowledged spiritual values and aligned them with company goals outperformed those that did not. In other words, letting spirituality into the workplace didn't distract organizations from their goals. It often helped them reach their goals.

As more companies grasp this idea, we are likely to see a rise in spirit in business—a growing demand from individuals for workplaces that offer meaning as well as money. According to one recent U.S. survey, more than three out of five adults believe a greater sense of spirituality would improve their own workplace. Likewise, 70 percent of respondents to British think tank Roffey Park's annual management survey said they wanted their working lives to be more meaningful. And in the last few years groups such as the Association for Spirit at Work and events such as the annual Spirit in Business Conference have emerged [...]. Rich Karlgaard, the savvy publisher of Forbes, says this is the next cycle of business. First came the quality revolution of the 1990s. Then came what Karlgaard calls "the cheap revolution," which dramatically reduced the cost of goods and allows people around the world to have cell phones and Internet access. "So, what's next?" he asks. "Meaning. Purpose Deep life experience. Use whatever word or phrase you like but know that consumer desire for these qualities is on the rise. Remember your Abraham Maslow and your Viktor Frankl. Bet your business on it."[242]

PINK reports that Ronald INGLEHART, a respected political scientist at the University of Michigan has tracked public opinions in dozens of countries for a

---

[242] Daniel H. PINK, *A Whole New Mind: Information Age to the Conceptual Age* (New York: Riverhead Books, 2005), 214–216. PINK finds support for his thinking on the spiritual organization from the work of Robert William FOGEL's movement of the Fourth Great Awakening mentioned in previous chapters Two and Three, "Spiritual (Immaterial) inequity is now as great a problem as material inequity, perhaps even greater." His words echo FRANKL's a half-century earlier: "People have enough to live, but nothing to live for; they have the means but no meaning" (ibid., 209). PINK contends in the age of High Concept and High Touch; individuals and organizations must examine what they're doing to earn a living and ask themselves three questions: 1. Can someone overseas do it cheaper? 2. Can a computer do it faster? 3. Is what I'm offering in demand in an age of abundance? If your answer to question 1 or 2 is *yes*, or if your answer to question 3 is *no*, you're in deep trouble. Mere survival today depends on being able to do something that overseas knowledge workers can't do cheaper, that powerful computers can't do faster, and that satisfies one of the nonmaterial, transcendent desires of an abundant age.

quarter of a century. Each time he administered his World Values Survey, respondents expressed great concern for spiritual and material matters. For example, 58 percent of Americans think often about meaning and purpose. Substantial, though lower, percentage of Germans, British and Japanese report the same.[243] INGLEHART believes that the advanced world is in the midst of a slow change in its operating principles, a gradual shift from "Materialists values (emphasizing economic and physical security above all) toward 'Postmaterialist' priorities (emphasizing self-expression and the quality of life)."[244]

Meaning, according to PINK, "has become a central aspect of our work and our lives. Pursuing meaning obviously is no simple task. You can't buy a cookbook with the recipe for it—to open a packet, whole-minded ways or individuals, families and businesses to begin the search for meaning: start taking spirituality seriously and start taking happiness seriously."[245] Daniel GOLEMAN, the originator of the emotional intelligence movement, in a 1998 work after a study of executives at fifteen large companies concluded, "Just one cognitive ability distinguished star performers from average: pattern recognition, the 'big picture' thinking that allows leaders to pick out the meaningful and to think strategically far into the future."[246] GOLEMAN found that star performers "relied less on deductive reasoning and more on intuitive, contextual reasoning characteristic of Symphony."[247] PINK's thesis is the following:

> We are entering into an age animated by a different form of thinking and a new approach to life—one that prizes aptitudes that I call 'high concept' and 'high touch'. High concept involves the capacity to detect patterns and opportunities, to create artistic and emotional beauty, to craft a satisfying

---

[243] Ronald INGLEHART, "the Meaning of Life Is on Most People's Minds," *Spirituality & Health*, March/April 2004.

[244] Ronald INGLEHART, *Modernization and Postmodernization: Culture, Economic and Political Change in 43 Societies* (Princeton: University Press, 1997).

[245] PINK, *A Whole New Mind*, 210.

[246] Daniel GOLEMAN, *Working with Emotional Intelligence* (New York: Bantam, 1998), 33.

[247] PINK, *A Whole New Mind*, 138.

narrative, and to conclude seemingly unrelated ideas into something new. High touch involves the ability to empathize with others, to understand the subtleties of human interaction, to find joy in one's self and to elicit it in others and stretch beyond the quotidian in pursuit of purpose and meaning.[248]

4.2 Looking for a New Vision, An Organizational Psychology of the Soul

In the work *A Spiritual Audit of Corporate America: A Hard Look at Spirituality, Religion, and Values in the Workplace* by Ian I. MITROFF and Elizabeth A. DENTON, they study one basic question: what is missing at work. The answer is the soul.

> What is the immense energy or potential that lies at the core of each of us yet remains largely unacknowledged and untapped in our place of work? The simplest definition of the depth and potential of the soul was given over and over again in various participants in our study: The soul is precisely the deepest essence of what it means to be human. The soul is that which ties together and integrates all of the separate and various parts of a person; it is the base material, the underlying platform that makes a person a human being.[249]

The basic ideas and themes of their research and findings are in sharp contrast to the ideas with which current organizations are designed and managed. Their investigation of the emerging culture of, as stated above, the High Concept, High Touch organization are very cohesive with a Thomistic organizational psychology of the soul. MITROFF holds the Harold Quinto Distinguished Professorship at the Marshall School of Business at the University of Southern California in Los Angeles, and DENTON is an independent organizational consultant based in New

---

[248] Ibid., 51–52.

[249] Ian I. MITROFF and Elizabeth A. DENTON, *A Spiritual Audit of Corporate America: A Hard Look at Spirituality, Religion, and Values in the Workplace* (San Francisco: Jossey-Bass, 1999), 5.

York City. She works with executives and teams in both Fortune 100 and entrepreneurial companies to promote vision and values, leadership, and performance effectiveness. Their robust investigation-based qualitative interviews and quantitative surveys focused on the importance of the feeding and care of the soul as critical to the development and sustenance of human beings and the neglect of organizational leadership to give attention to such matters. The issue is succinctly expressed in a sentiment typical of managers and top executives interviewed: "I'm tired of having constantly to park my soul at the door before I go into my organization."[250]

The research construction involved the development of interview questions and mailed surveys that pursued the nature of the spiritual as it relates to the work setting. To ascertain a spiritual sense of meaningful work and personal wholeness, they formulated questions in order that respondents' notions of wholeness could merge from both qualitative responses and mailed surveys based on personal interviews. In a quantitative interview, people were asked to circle numbers with regard to how much and which parts of their personal spiritual and religious concerns they could bring to their organizational life. The results generated a theory based systematic comparison between different types of organizations and helped the investigators find out whether certain organizations, either profit or nonprofit, had an explicitly declared spiritual orientation that allowed people to bring more of their personal spiritual and religious self to work in traditional organizations.[251]

---

[250] Ibid., 4.

[251] Ibid., 32–34. The in-person interviews were designed as much to be conversations as to be structured, systematic explorations of specific topics. With this in mind, questions were used as probes to open up and explore new ideas. Each interview began with a set of questions designed primarily to put the person at ease. They were also intended to capture preliminary information such as where the interviewee was born and went to school, job history, how many people he or she supervised, and so on. Next, the interviewees were asked to indicate the top three things that gave them the most meaning and purpose in their jobs. They chose from a list of items such as being associated with an ethical or good organization, doing interesting work, being of service to others, making money, realizing their full potential and so on. The interviewees were then asked to state their basic values that they believed guided them in making important decisions in their lives. They were also

MITROFF and DENTON, based on their study, came to the conclusive insight of disagreeing with the perilous path that most organizations have undertaken of separating spiritual concerns from the workplace. They write:

> Given that the soul is precisely that aspect of human beings that cannot be confined and compartmentalized without severe repercussions [...] We believe that the workplace is one of the most important settings in which people come together daily to accomplish what they cannot do on their own, that is, to realize their full potential as human beings.[252]

The Massachusetts Institute of Technology Leadership Center in October 2017 published a concept paper on the emerging global crisis in organizational leadership.

> There is broad agreement that the world has become more complex, fast-paced, hazardous, and unpredictable. Economies in crisis, war, nuclear proliferation, global warning, starvation, and disease—the list is long and daunting. For companies, fears might include shrinking revenues,

---

asked how often and under what circumstances they were forced to compromise their basic values in making important decisions at work. Then interviewees were asked to paint a picture of their organization. They rated them on a variety of dimensions such as happy versus sad, ethical versus unethical, autocratic versus democratic, profitable versus non-profitable, caring versus uncaring, worldly versus spiritual, sane versus insane, tolerant versus intolerant of social-moral issues etc. Once these more sensitive issues were broached, then questions were asked that explored the respondent's attitudes toward life and their practice of religion: What meaning does spirituality have for you and how important is it to you? What differences do you perceive between religion and spirituality? Is spirituality a relevant concern and appropriate topic for discussion in the workplace or is it best dealt with outside of work? Respondents were asked about their feelings about spirituality compared to their feelings about the more neutral topic of general philosophical values. They were also asked whether they were aware of any methods that organizations could use to foster fruitful discussions of spirituality without causing people to feel violated or creating dissension.

[252] Ibid., 7.

increasingly competitive markets, or a never-ending race for new product development.

So far, our leadership has been woefully inadequate at solving these problems. The recent past has showcased a leadership stage featuring Greek tragedies filled with leaders who are corrupt, out of touch and unable to act— witness the latest insider trading scandal, the Afghan elections and Wall Street bonuses that make Marie Antoinette's famous, "Let them eat cake" seem like a minor disconnect with the populace."[253]

It is interesting to give attention to the social and moral problem of leadership, as defined by the MIT Sloan School of Management, one of the world's most prestigious schools of leadership and management. Their academic reductionist solution to their crisis of unpredictable global competition and the decline in executive moral rectitude is to call for schools of business and management to develop new styles of distributed leadership.

> While our research is still in its early stages and this list will likely evolve, it is clear that in systems of distributed leadership many more individuals take on the role of leader—whether they have formal positions of authority or not. These leaders engage proactively and collaboratively to create change rather than waiting for direction from above. And they do so not chaotically but in alignment with the shared global purpose that focuses and guides action and with mutual regulation to avoid excess risk.[254]

It is most worthy of note that the MIT Leadership Center ventures as a woeful problem of a struggle between two ideal types of leadership, i.e., command and control leadership exercised individually by those in formal positions in a clearly defined hierarchy and distributed leadership exercised by multiple leaders throughout the organizations—some in formal positions of authority and some

---

[253] Deborah ANCONA and Elaine BACKMAN, "Distributed Leadership, From Pyramids to Networks: The Changing Leadership Landscape," *Leadership Center, Massachusetts Institute of Technology* (October 2017), 1.

[254] Ibid., 4.

not—working collaboratively across organizational level boundaries. It is quite possible that addressing the dialectic of command and control as opposed to distributed style of leadership is a factor worthy of attention in a global shift to a new style of organizational executive leadership. It does seem to ignore the arguments regarding the nature of Thomistic organizational psychology and executive leadership of the previous chapters, especially the metaphysical organizational principles of one and the many, contrariety and equality and inequality. Furthermore, as an effort in a social scientific analysis of the crisis of organizational leadership it stands as a glaring issue compared to the construct of spirituality, religion, and values in the workplace by MITROFF and DENTON:

> This age calls for a new "spirit of management." For us, the concepts of spirituality and soul are not merely add-on elements of a new philosophy or policy of management. Instead, they are the very essence of such a philosophy or policy. No management effort can survive without them. We refuse to accept that whole organizations cannot learn always to foster soul and spirituality in the workplace.[255]

MITROFF and DENTON raise the question that if spirituality defines us and if work plays a large role in our self-definition, why then is there not more systematic study of spirituality in the workplace? "The short answer is that there is a strange alliance of influences from conventional academics to New Age thinkers to guardians of U.S. culture and history which have all put strong barriers in the way of the serious study of spirituality."[256] A cursory online search will present an overwhelming number of works on spirit or soul and a growing number of these books pertain to religion. However, most of the books on spirituality and business are based on personal, anecdotal accounts of a single author's experience with a few organizations. They are not based on the systematic study of the actual experience of a wide range of managers and top experiences. It is not to say such works are not important, but it's not clear how applicable they are to a broad range of executives and organizations. MITROFF and DENTON claim that there are two

---

[255] MITROFF and DENTON, *A Spiritual Audit of Corporate America*, 14.

[256] Ibid., 15.

main obstacles to the development of knowledge of the soul and spirituality in the workplace, namely 1) impediments from the academe, 2) language barriers.

4.3 The Soul, Spirituality, Organizational Leadership, the Academe, and New Agers

In the present-day business world, an MBA is a virtual prerequisite for success. Specially to strive for a position of executive level leadership in a medium to a major corporation, a business degree from one of the top business schools is a virtual necessity. Business schools are populated mainly by academics, not by practitioners. Business academics, as with most academics, must conform to strict standards of research topic and methods. Business studies, hoping to be published in business journals, must deal mainly with the quantifiable aspects of business, e.g., financial analysis, market share, etc. Increasingly, studies are a matter of hypothesis statistical inference testing that includes sophisticated computer and mathematical models to explain the relationship between multiple variables. There are studies dedicated to leadership and a smaller number to ethical issues concerned with ethical variables, but they also are based on well-defined business language, statistical methods and ethical studies which are confined mostly to fringe journals. We discussed in chapter three the difference between thin and thick data and the limitations of grounding studies of organizational leadership primarily on thin data nominalistic analysis that dominate business schools. As MITROFF and DENTON maintain:

> Unfortunately, most academics have been trained to believe that unless something can be measured precisely, it is not a legitimate topic for scientific investigation. An even stronger statement of this belief is the contention that unless something can be measured precisely, it is without meaning. In the extreme, some go as far as to say that unless something can be measured, it cannot even be said to exist.[257]

---

[257] Ibid., 17.

Another problem is that issues of the soul and spirituality get tagged as "soft and fuzzy" or "touchy-feely."

> Traditional academics in schools of business and management concerned about peer acceptance avoid approaching such issues, despite their importance to a psychological ethical understanding of leadership. Thus, we have a situation, when it comes to the study of the soul or spirituality in profit or non-profit organizations, where academic standards do not allow the topic to be approached and at the other extreme so-called New Age scholars who are too loose and lacking in academic social scientific rigor. Furthermore, there is serious mismatch between the language of business and the language of many writers on spirituality. It is perceived by business practitioners as airy, or ethereal, as a plane above the harsh realities of everyday practice.[258]

When studying spirituality and the soul, MITROFF and DENTON found cultural and personal barriers regarding the professional and political appropriateness of conducting inquiries into such a sensitive and private area of research. If you cannot define something, then it is impossible to study it. They discovered that it is possible to get beyond the barriers of defining soul and spirituality by first exploring what soul and spirituality mean to most people. Each person was asked to define spirituality, rather than soul and spirituality. Basically, the interviews endorsed notions of a supreme guiding force and interconnectedness as fundamental components of spirituality. Some did not even try to define the soul directly but merely assumed its existence:

- Spirituality is highly individual and intensely personal. You don't have to be religious to be spiritual.
- Spirituality is the basic belief that there is a supreme power, a being, a force, whatever you call it, that governs the entire universe. There is a purpose for everything and everyone.

---

[258] Ibid., 19.

- Everything is interconnected with everything else. Everything affects and is affected by everything else.

- Spirituality is the feeling of this interconnectedness. Spirituality is being in touch with it.

- Spirituality is also the feeling that no matter how bad things get, they will always work out somehow. There is a guiding plan that governs all lives.

- We are put here basically to do good. One must strive to produce products and services that serve all of humankind.

- Spirituality is inextricably connected with caring, hope, kindness, love, and optimism. Spirituality is the basic faith in the existence of these things.[259]

The main purpose of this spiritual audit was to open and explore new territory, not with people who are primarily academics or spiritual thinkers, but instead with people who are on the firing line in their organizations. We will now examine some of the qualitative results.

What Gives People Meaning in their Work

The hands-down first choice of everyone we interviewed regarding what gave them the most meaning and purpose in their job was "[…] the ability to realize my full potential as a person. In extremely close second place was "[…] being associated with a good organization" or being associated with an ethical organization." The third choice was having "interesting work," while a distant fourth was "making money." Tied for fifth place were "having good colleagues" and "service to humankind."

Parts of themselves that People Can Bring to Work

They were able to express at work their intelligence and creativity significantly more than their feelings, soul, and humor. The overall

---

[259] Ibid., 21–22.

indication is that people are more comfortable expressing their intelligence than their emotions or feelings at work.

It was not surprising to find that the separation that people experienced between their thinking and feeling sides contrasted sharply with what they said was the number one thing that gave meaning in their jobs: the opportunity for each person to realize his or her full potential as a human being.

Basic Values That Govern Most People's Lives

We asked people to list values that govern their lives, most people responded with a common set of basic virtues: integrity, honesty, building and maintaining good relationships, keeping one's word, trustworthiness, being there for one's family and others, and so on. A few listed more metaphysical or spiritual values, such as "being in harmony and in touch with the universe."

How People See Their Organizations

Almost everyone interviewed saw their organization as being caring, ethical and profitable all at the same time. They saw no contradiction in this. Even those interviewees from not-for-profits were in agreement seeing no contradiction between being profitable and ethical.

Emotions at Work

Most of those who were interviewed did not experience strong emotions at work. The feeling of joy was the strongest of any feeling cited. Crying, feeling depressed, or having an epiphany was almost nonexistent. Even joy was usually experienced in rather commonplace ways, for instance, in accomplishing an important task. Less often, joy was experienced in response to others, such as when a coworker or a subordinate accomplished something significant, or at the birth of a child.

Belief in a Higher Power or God and Its Presence at Work

Almost everyone who was interviewed believed in a higher power or God. However, when it came to feeling the presence of that power or God at work, there was a strong and sharp split, with the vast majority of responses clustering at the extreme ends of the spectrum. In other words, an almost equal number of respondents reported having infrequently experienced the presence of a higher power in the workplace as those who reported having strongly experienced the presence of a higher power in the workplace.

What People Pray for at Work

People indicated rarely praying or meditating at work, but when they did it was mainly to prepare themselves for difficult situations and for general guidance in making tough decisions. On occasion they prayed for coworkers who were going through difficult times. Very infrequently people prayed for something good to happen.

View of Religion and Spirituality

Approximately 30 percent of our respondent had a positive view of both religion and spirituality. A very small percentage, roughly 2 percent, had a positive view of religion and a negative view of spirituality. Roughly 60 percent, or the majority of those to whom Mitroff talked, had a positive view of spirituality and a negative view of religion. Finally, 8 percent had a negative view of religion.

Spirituality as a Relevant Topic in the Workplace

Most people felt moderately strongly that spirituality was relevant as a topic in the workplace. When it came to the appropriateness versus the inappropriateness of spirituality, they were in the middle. They also leaned moderately toward the position that spirituality should be dealt with outside work. With regard to general philosophical values, people felt very strongly that it was both relevant and appropriate to discuss them at work.[260]

There were several CEOs and executives interviewed during this study who did see the importance of the discussion of spirituality in the workplace. At the same time, they had extreme disdain for New Age terminology with its gushy, sloppy language and thinking as well as its paraphernalia, such as crystals and beads, but they were not afraid to talk openly about spirituality and the vital role it plays in life and work. Yet most of the CEOs interviewed believed strongly in the need of a type of philosophical spirituality in the workplace. We see the general attitude expressed in the words of one of the CEOs, "I believe not only that spirituality can be discussed in such a manner without dividing people, but also that discussion of it is absolutely key if we are to create and maintain ethical, truly caring organizations."[261]

4.4 Thomistic Psychology of Soul and Leadership and the Postmodern Organizational Quest

The psychologist Daniel GOLEMAN writes about a study of executives at fifteen large companies: "Just one cognitive ability distinguished star performers from the average: pattern recognition, the big picture thinking that allows leaders to pick out the meaningful trends from a welter of information around them and to think strategically far into the future."[262] Increasingly, profit and nonprofit organizational leadership requires creative executives who are able to sense the big picture and respond to a rapidly changing competitive market. Sidney HARMAN is

---

[260] Ibid., 36–43.

[261] Ibid., 48.

[262] GOLEMAN, *Working with Emotional Intelligence*, 33.

an eighty-something multimillionaire CEO of a stereo components company who doesn't find it all that valuable to hire MBAs.

> Instead, I say get me some poets as managers. Poets are our original systems thinkers. They contemplate the world in which we live and feel obliged to interpret and give expressions to it in a way that makes the reader understand how that world turns. Poets, those unheralded systems thinkers, are our true digital thinkers. It is from their midst that I believe we will draw tomorrow's new business leaders.[263]

In contemporary schools of business and management, as we witness with the MIT center of leadership, the economist Robert William FOGEL, MITROFF and DENTON are calling for a new organizational vision. MITROFF and DENTON call for the need of organizations to give attention to the development of an organizational soul and spiritual psychology. On the other hand, the MIT Leadership Center sees that new organizational contexts will be driven by the desire for distributed leadership. Based on MIT's global research, it "envisions the emergence of four organizational contexts, namely Distributed leadership in Hierarchies, Distributed Leadership in Flat Organizations, Distributed Leadership in Nimble Networks and Distributed Leadership across Organizations."[264] The MIT Leadership Center in

---

[263] Sidney HARMAN, *Mind Your Own Business: A Maverick's Guide to Business, Leadership, and Life* (New York: Currency Doubleday, 2003), 10.

[264] ANCONA and BACKMAN, "From Pyramids to Networks: The Changing Leadership Landscape," 2. The Distributed Leadership paper reports five common elements that seem to characterize these systems: 1) Spontaneous Forms of Collaboration: Even in traditional command and control contexts increasingly rapid swarm teams form to solve glitch problems. 2) Multi-directional Influence. There is strong empowerment of product development teams in team selection, budget, and agile involvement cross functional project meetings. 3) Local Entrepreneurship. Self-organized teams brain storming product ideas and gaining venture capital from sources inside the organization. 4) Even in command and control context more middle management and Bottom up input from conception in goals and tactics. 5) Peer Mitigation of Risk. There is clear evidence of shared accountability of organizational survival and mitigation of risk. There are specialized risk assessment groups and risk limitation rules, etc.

their Distributed Leadership paper states that "the research on distributed leadership is still in its infancy. Hopefully, however, these definitions and frameworks will help to begin the process of understanding this new form of leadership that we believe to be so relevant and pivotal at this moment in time."[265]

Then there are the bold extreme calls for new style of executive leadership being forced on global organizations by the impact of the postmodern organizational visionaries like William BERGQUIST in *The Postmodern Organization: Mastering the Art of Irreversible Change*. We quote a significant section from chapter five of this work, *Leadership: Who Moves Us and How*. This passage represents a growing attitude among academic organizational psychologists, like BERGQUIST and ANCONA of MIT, that as postmodern organizations respond to changing technologies, shifting customer needs, artificial intelligence, changing markets, new methods of product design, agile planning, and new revenue sources, a new type of postmodern leadership will emerge. As BERGQUIST predicts, "postmodern leaders must overcome the ghosts of premodern and modern assumptions about leadership, while also retaining many of the valuable lessons learned and taught by premodern and modern assumptions about leadership, while also retaining many of the valuable lessons learned and taught by premodern and modern leaders:"[266]

> As we look back to these earlier eras, we find that leaders in the premodern era tended to be "great men" who were selected for their character and education. Great men not only led organizations, they also influenced history and established societal values. Leaders were either born to greatness or provided with an elitist program of liberal arts and mentorship. They tended to exert authority through a paternalistic concern for the welfare and proper education of those who depended on them. By contrast, the more democratic modern era tends to emphasize structures, processes and procedures that ensure the appropriate expression of leadership and influence. Events—not great men—determine the course of modern history,

---

[265] Ibid., 4.

[266] William BERGQUIST, *The Postmodern Organization: Mastering the Art of Irreversible Change* (San Francisco: Jossey-bass Publisher, 1993), 93.

and values are identified as products of any of the systems and bureaucracy rather than as products of specific individual(s). Those who head modern organizations typically define themselves as mangers rather than leaders. Modern authority is expressed through rules, regulations, roles, and organizational structures.

The postmodern world has called both the premodern and modern notions of leadership into question. The postmodern leader is neither inherently great nor merely a product of a system or bureaucracy. Individual leadership can be effective and influential if applied at the right time, in the right place, in the right manner, and with regard to the right problem or goal. This contingent or situational model of leadership requires careful consideration of both individual and organizational character and style. It also requires a tolerance for ambiguity, recognition of the need for one to learn from his or her mistakes, and a clear sense of personal mission and purpose. It is ultimately spiritual rather than secular in nature.[267]

From the perspective of a Thomistic Organizational psychology of the soul and leadership, we are in substantial disagreement with BERGQUIST and others who look upon a postmodern philosophy of organizational leadership as a proper response to the need for a more non-bureaucratic, more decentralized, more empowering, and distributed leadership. We would, however, agree with BERGQUIST that modern organizational authority has been and continues to be

---

[267] Ibid., 31. Stewart R. CLEGG in *Modern Organizations: Organization Studies in the Postmodern World* (London: Sage Publications, 1995), Professor of Organization Studies and Chair of Management at the University of St. Andrews, describes the postmodern organization: At the base of postmodern phenomena, it will be argued, there would need to be the development of new forms of de-differentiated organization. Such organization might be centered on a concern with flexible specialization. If the postmodern hypothesis is correct, these forms of organization would stand in direct contrast to the centrality of differentiation in the modernist project. Such postmodern organization phenomena may be viewed as possible sources for future isomorphism in organizational practice. They may become a model which will be widely imitated and diffused. There may well be ecological limits to this process of diffusion. Not all organizational niche-space will be favorable or appropriate for postmodern colonization.

expressed in rules, regulations, roles, and organizational structures. Douglas GRIFFIN in *The Emergence of Leadership: Linking Self-Organization and Ethics*, in the tradition of BARNARD, holds that the moral character of a leader is critical to the diffusion of moral goodness in all the activities of the organization. He maintains that modern organizations lost this sense of leadership and the diffusion of moral character under the influence of dogmatic Kantian rationalism:

> Kant, then, presented a notion of ethics as a body of universal imperatives that already exist, just as natural laws do, to be discovered by autonomous individuals, just as natural laws are timeless and universal. It is this notion of universal codes of conduct discovered or formulated by autonomous rational individuals as the basis upon which they are to judge their own and each other's conduct. In this way of thinking, the leader is an autonomous individual, as is everyone else, charged with developing ethical behavior.[268]

GRIFFIN portrays modern organizations as rational Kantian systems of scientific design and industrial engineering efficiency controlled by top-down ethical universal principles. He finds the problem with this Kantian influenced system view is that organizations are not things at all, let alone living things, but rather they are processes of communication and joint action. Since there is an emerging need for more decentralized and participative self-organization, GRIFFIN contends that a new style of participative executive function is required:

> Participation is that of the embodied human beings with each other rather than the modernist concept of the autonomous individual. Experience can be understood not in terms of the individual alone but rather in terms of a world in which the individual plays an active part. Individuals come to an understanding of themselves in the continuity of action, in the world in which they play an active part, and this is a social self-organizing process. Leaders act, and leadership is action. This immediately means that a theory of leadership is also a theory of ethics. Ethical values emerge in interaction

---

[268] Douglas GRIFFIN, *The Emergence of Leadership: Linking Self-Organization and Ethics* (London and New York: Routledge Taylor & Francis Group, 2002), 52.

as a reflection of the emergence of leaders. Large-scale organizational and cultural events emerge in everyday social interaction through participation in local events.[269]

4.5 A Return to the Premodern Thomistic Principles and (Post-Postmodern) Vision of the Organization and Exemplar Liberality

It is obvious from the first three chapters of this thesis that an understanding of organizational leadership from the perspective of a Thomistic psychology is established on a metaphysics of organization and as BARNARD maintains, the executive function of "moral creativeness" is the highest expression of executive responsibility. BARNARD does not speak about the need for a business-organizational ethics as much as a psycho-ethical morale. He asserts that:

> The distinguishing mark of the executive responsibility is that it requires not merely conformance to a complex code of morals but also the creation of moral codes for others. The most generally recognized aspect of his function is called securing, creating, inspiring of "morale in an organization." This is the process of inculcating points of view, fundamental attitudes, loyalties, to the organization or cooperative system, and to the system of objective authority, that will result in subordinating individual interest and the minor dictates of personal codes to the good of the cooperative whole [...]. There is enough experience of the subject it is clear that failure with respect to moral creativeness arises from inadequate attention, lack of persistence in the face of the inertia of human reluctance, and lack of sincerity of purpose.[270]

MITROFF and DENTON claim:

> With few exceptions, most organizations do not acknowledge the concepts of spirituality and soul. If we can assume that they cared in the first place, we

---

[269] Ibid., 213.

[270] BARNARD, *The Functions of the Executive*, 279.

can say that many organizations have lost sight of how to treat those who work for them as whole persons, as people with souls—and that they have lost sight of how to harness the tremendous energy that resides at the core of each of us.[271]

REDPATH writes of the need "to reunite wisdom in a new real postmodernism essentially rooted in a new understanding of the human person. And we need to recover a proper understanding of the nature of philosophy and science, a real modern philosophy; not one falsely-so-called."[272] It is important to note that BERGQUIST, even though he is not a Thomistic organizational psychologist, does seem to agree with REDPATH's call to return to a classical metaphysics of organization to discover a real postmodern Thomistic organizational Psychology. Thus, BERGQUIST holds:

> We must often look to that which is old and that with which we disagree to find the balance and the kernel of truth we need to navigate successfully in our turbulence and confusing postmodern world. We return to the wisdom found in virtually all premodern cultures concerning the façade of progress and the ephemeral nature of planning. While standing on the edge of a postmodern world, we must discover wisdom in the patience and persistence of premodern man. We must return to premodern perspectives regarding the sacred nature of human organizations and once again listen to enlightening stories regarding our own human history and destiny. Only in this way can we successfully tend the complex and irreversible fires of the postmodern world.[273]

A Thomistic organizational psychology responds to the emerging organizational quest for the soul and a spiritual ethos by bringing the issue of executive leadership to a psychology and spirituality of love for the common good and the organizational soul. It is important, as we mentioned in previous chapters,

---

[271] MITROFF and DENTON, *A Spiritual Audit of Corporate America*, 4–5.

[272] REDPATH, *A Not-So-Elementary Christian Metaphysics*, 64.

[273] BERGQUIST, *The Postmodern Organization*, 14.

that we do not restrict our study of organizational psychology to any one type of organization. Furthermore, often we get a better understanding if we examine nonprofits and small to medium size organizations, especially when we examine the executive leadership skills of successful entrepreneurs. One of the best works in the understanding the mind of the successful entrepreneur of small to medium size business enterprises is *Make Up Your Mind: Entrepreneurs Talk About Decision Making* by Ann Graham EHRINGER.

She describes the common themes and recurring patterns in what sixty entrepreneurs said about their strategic decision making. It was originally her PhD dissertation, and, as she emphasizes, it was not a psychological study, "It was a phenomenological one, accepting what was said by the entrepreneurs, rather than probing for what lay underneath their words or what might have been different or more accurate or more real than their stated, shared reflection. Like most of the entrepreneurs in their dealings with other people, I trusted that they told me the truth as they understood it."[274]

In chapter twelve, *Purpose and Personal Principles*, EHRINGER writes, "Their making of decisions was impacted by their personal values. By 'values' the entrepreneurs and I meant 'principles' in which they believed and by which they lived. In a general sense, principles include fairness, integrity and honesty, human dignity, quality, or excellence, potential and growth, and patience, nurturing and encouragement."[275] It is most important to draw attention to EHRINGER's chapter *Purpose and Principles* and her phenomenological research. EHRINGER herself entered into to this research project as a doctoral student in business administration who was also a successful business entrepreneur in her own right.

---

[274] Ann Graham EHRINGER, *Make Up Your Mind: Entrepreneurs Talk About Decision Making* (Santa Monica: Merritt Publishing, 1995), 35. Warren BENNIS, the distinguished professor of Business Administration and Founding Chairman of the Leadership Institute at USC, in his endorsement wrote, "I loved this book. It will turn out to be a classic on entrepreneurs because it lets us into the entrepreneur's world through unfiltered ruminations of entrepreneurs themselves. It's a must read for anyone in making better decisions."

[275] Ibid., 251–252.

She developed a type of structured dialogical conversation with the interviewees; it was a type of open phenomenological method.

> The particular questions I asked depended on where each entrepreneur went with his story and how comfortable he was talking about himself. They are questions any person should ask himself or herself [...]. Sometimes I asked many of these questions, sometimes only a few. I might ask other questions or make comments or follow some direction, evoked by or following the direction of his thought or stimulated by his words.[276]

She describes how frequently during the dialogue their personal values impacted their decisions. "By values the entrepreneurs and I meant principles. They tried to make decisions guided by honor and honesty, and to make them in concert with the best interests of all of the various stakeholders with whom they worked and lived."[277]

We draw attention to the fact that the research was a flowing dialogue of entrepreneurs where the importance of principles frequently occurred. Therefore, we turn to the importance of an understanding of first principles considering a Thomistic metaphysics of organization and a moral psychology. It is REDPATH's *Moral Psychology of St. Thomas* that explains why the issue of principles so naturally appeared during EHRINGER's research. On the urgency of the Aristotelian-Thomistic rediscovery of the most fundamental principles of organizational psychology REDPATH writes:

> As Aristotle and St. Thomas well understood, but Descartes and his enlightened progeny tend to be obviously unaware, metaphysics and ethics are more than subjects of study in which some people in the past and present have had or have an interest. They are chiefly habits of the human soul, habits *generated by an organizational and moral psychology*, out of which essentially grow the widest, deepest, and most psychologically influential

---

[276] Ibid., 34.

[277] Ibid., 252.

principles of organizational behavior and leadership that direct human judgment and choice and cultural and civilizational development.

A chief, glaring weakness confronting the West today is a leadership deficit. For anyone familiar with the classical understanding of metaphysics and ethics contained in the teachings of Aristotle and St. Thomas Aquinas, just why this deficit exists is no mystery. As St. Thomas says, the office of the wise man is essentially twofold: 1) to know order (that is, to be able to recognize organizational principles [part/whole relationships] that exist within things) and 2) to cause order within things. Since no human being can possibly excel at leadership without precisely understanding how things are organized, or how to organize things (the two chief sciences of leadership: metaphysics [speculative wisdom] and ethics [practical wisdom], without some implicit or explicit knowledge of the principles contained within these two classical sciences of organizational psychology, no human being can excel, become the best that he or she can be, at being a good leader. Instead, that person's reasoning inclines to become anarchic.[278]

The interviewee in one of EHRINGER's dialogical inquiry about the nature leadership and intuition responds:

> I don't use the term intuitive because I don't believe it. I think what we call intuition—other than sort of the new age view of it—is the sum of tremendous experience that come in a flash. Intuition is expertise based on experience, but it exhibits itself in a uniformed way. I think all of this stuff about entrepreneurs is a reflection of inner values. In fact, I don't think they say enough about it.[279]

EHRINGER's concept of principles as guidelines for human conduct proven to have enduring permanent value for the organization is somewhat similar to Redpath, i.e., to recognize order and to cause order within things. In her research,

---

[278] REDPATH, *The Moral Psychology of St. Thomas*, 21–22.

[279] EHRINGER, *Make Up Your Mind*, 247.

she detects the principle that entrepreneurs attribute to their success as leaders, i.e., the principles begin to flow naturally from the dialogue.

Given that we are in an age, as REDPATH argues and BERGQUIST to a limited extent agrees, in which there is a need to return to a premodern concept of a metaphysics of organization and a moral psychology, it is interesting what EHRINGER finds in her research:

> Many of these entrepreneurs described feelings of being responsible for some aspect of the common good, and for their communities, as well. They illustrated their common involvement in 'supporting the business community,' 'working in charities,' doing the community stuff,' wanting to teach, establishing a community government that provides a vehicle for negotiating among different needs to arrive at truly harmonious consensus.[280]

The following are examples of this dialogue:

Feelings of Community

This will sound terribly corny, but I truly made this decision with a lot of thought, internally, that I have an opportunity to give some hope to people in ways they'll never get otherwise. I've got an opportunity, now this will sound stupid, but to give people the chance to become middle class when they'll never ever have a middle-class opportunity. I've got the chance to give a lot of people the opportunity to own a house who could never own a house.

I've always given a lot back to the communities, always very deeply involved [...] I was the recipient of the first non-faculty award of merit to something at a local university. Did lots of kind of stuff, speaking and fund raising [...] I'll never forget in the 1960s when we were just starting to cook, and they see me spending a third of my time volunteering with the university. They'd say, "What are you doing that for, where's the payoff?" I said "it's just the way I am, I believe that you keep these things in balance

---

[280] Ibid., 257.

and they'll come back to reward you in the long-run and even if they don't that's fine. The reward is what it is."

I really enjoy helping people, I really get off on it, and it's a kick for me and so to have the opportunity to do it and especially to do it, to help, for your friends.

What I like to do is [...] consult with small businesses that are going in the direction that I've been and to just share with them and help them and perhaps make it a little bit easier for them [...] I would feel good about putting something back that way [...] I'd like to do it on my own terms in a way that feels fulfilling to me. It's like I don't give a lot of time or money to charities unless I feel it's going to where I want it to be going, I'm not giving money to pay for people's salaries [...] but I do to other places where eighty or ninety percent of it goes where it's supposed to go [...] We've got three or four foster children in other countries [...] and I feel like it's making a difference. What we have on our business cards is that we make a difference. That's actually real important to me.

Money

I had no ambition whatsoever to make money, I never thought of it [...] it's certainly nice to have money, but [...] once you reach [...] you make a lot of money, and my money is a report card, once you get past that stage are you going to still play the game? How big a yacht?

Mainly I just wanted to learn. Anytime I wasn't learning I said to myself, 'What am I doing here?' I'm just making money and that's no big deal.[281]

4.5.1 The Exemplar Executive Soulful Leadership and A Vision of Liberality

We see in the above cases entrepreneurs, exemplars of leadership of successful small to medium size organizations, who have a sense of commitment toward giving of their time and resources back to their community. In terms of a Thomistic organizational psychology, it is best described as a psychological moral sense of liberality. St. Thomas teaches:

---

[281] Ibid., 256–257.

According to the Philosopher,[282] it belongs to the liberal man to part with things. Hence liberality is also called open-handedness [*largitas*], because that which is open does not withhold things but parts of them. The term "liberality" seems to allude to this, since when a man quits hold on a thing, he frees it [*liberat*], so to speak, from his keeping and ownership, and shows his mind to be free of attachment thereto. Now those things which are the subject of a man's free handedness toward others are the goods he possesses, which are denoted by the term "money." Therefore, the proper matter of liberality is money.[283]

In the coming chapters, we will turn our attention to the importance of the executive function and the responsibility for the diffusion of a leadership based on a psychology and ethics of virtuous behavior. We will stress in detail that the habit of exemplar leadership requires especially the virtuous habit of moral justice. We will, however, presently, discuss the quest for a proper postmodern organizational vision; therefore, we introduce the issue of justice as it relates to the organizational vision and the function of executive leadership. Justice is defined in Thomistic moral psychology as "the habit enabling one to give each and every person his own right (*jus*) because of a constant and perpetual act of will on the part of the possessor of this habit."[284] There are, however, certain moral habits which deal with operations in relation to another person, yet which do not possess the full nature of the justice which is a cardinal virtue. These are potential parts of justice. These eight habits will be treated in greater detail later because they are germane to organizational leadership and the practice of civility in organizational work, customer relationship, and the external community involvement. They are: 1) liberality, 2) friendliness, 3) veracity, 4) vindication, 5) gratitude, 6) respect for persons, 7) obedience and 8) respect for those in immediate authority over one.[285]

---

[282] That is, Aristotle in Ethic, iv,1.

[283] Aquinas, *Summa theologiae* II-II, q. 117, a. 2.

[284] Vernon J. Bourke, *Ethics: A Textbook in Moral Philosophy* (New York: The MacMillan Company, 1963), 327.

[285] Ibid., 341–342.

Our present concern based on the cases from EHRINGER's study of executive entrepreneurs, as existential exemplars leadership, is the virtue of liberality, as Vernon J. BOURKE explains as part of justice.

> It is the good habit of using and spending material wealth rightly, not only for one's own benefit but for the good of others. The name, liberality, is derived from a Latin word meaning "free," or "freely." This virtue denotes a certain mental freedom from the excessive love of wealth (and from this, liberality has a connection with temperance); it also indicates a freedom in the dispensing of wealth to others; and this externalized operation makes liberality a part of justice.[286]

DEMING was one of the founding fathers of the quality movement of the 1980s, and it was interesting how he would define quality in his four-day seminars. He would teach, "How do you know quality? How do you recognize quality?" He would answer, "I don't know what quality is until I see it." We could say the same thing about leadership. It is easier to give an example of a good leader than to explain a good leader. Or, in all probability, it is perhaps easier to describe a bad leader. MITROFF stated that "the soul is the deepest essence of what it means to be human." If organizational scholars mentioned in this chapter are correct that in the postmodern organizational culture, there is a desire for a greater expression of spirituality and soul in the governance of organizations, then it must begin at the executive levels. Indeed, it must be more than slogans, a policy statement, or a few training sessions in spirituality. The reality and the expression of the soul in an organization is the responsibility of the executive function.

St. Thomas AQUINAS's *Commentary on Aristotle's Nicomachean Ethics* (NE) can be read as a work in moral philosophy, moral psychology, or organizational psychology. REDPATH places AQUINAS's ethics and moral activity against the background of a more completely developed presentation of his profound and inimitable organizational psychology of the person.[287] Therefore, if we take the NE as a foundational text in Thomistic organizational psychology, then we will define

---

[286] Ibid., 349.

[287] REDPATH, *The Moral Psychology of St. Thomas*, 18.

the executive leader as the exemplar of the necessary virtuous habits of organizational leadership and the diffusion of virtuous habits throughout the organization. The executive exemplar is then the virtuous person as defined by AQUINAS:

> The virtuous person correctly passes judgment on individual things that pertain to human activity. In each case that which is really good seems to him to be good. This happens because things seem naturally pleasurable to each habit that are proper to it, that is, agree with it. Those things are agreeable to the habit of virtue that are, in fact, good because the habit of moral virtue is defined by what is in accord with right reason. Thus, the things in accord with right reason, things of themselves good, seem good to it. Here the good man differs very much indeed from others, for he sees what is truly good in individual practical matters, being as it were the norm and measure of all that is to be done because in these cases a thing must be judged good or bad according as it seems to him.[288]

What we learn from the case studies of executive entrepreneur leaders is that their style of leadership establishes the spiritual and moral organizational atmosphere. We could say that their practice of the virtue of liberality is an expression of their soul. Aquinas in his NE gives a phenomenological understanding or feeling of a vital operation:

> But each part of man has a proper operation; for example, the operation of the eye is seeing; and of the hand, touching; and of the feet walking; and so on of the other parts. We conclude, therefore, that some operation proper to man as a whole exists. [...] Now it is evident that each thing has an operation which belongs to it according to its form. But the form of man is his soul, whose act is life, not indeed life as the mere existence of a living thing, but a

---

[288] AQUINAS, *Commentary on Aristotle's Nicomachean Ethics*, Book 3, Lecture 3, n. 494.

special vital operation, for example, understanding or feeling. Hence happiness obviously consists in some vital operation.[289]

There is a sense of a deep-rooted personal understanding and feeling of liberality within the above cases of entrepreneurs. It is a fulfilling sense of happiness because of some vital operation (a spiritual power) to share their good fortune with others. AQUINAS comments on ARISTOTLE's teaching that a person cannot become virtuous by discussing or philosophizing about virtue. Likewise, for virtuous habits to diffuse through an organization the habit of virtuous character must begin as an integral part of the executive function.

> [Aristotle] discredits the false opinion of certain persons who do not perform works of virtues but, by taking refuge in the discussion of virtues think they can become virtuous by philosophizing. Such people, he says, are like the sick who carefully listen to what the doctor has to say but do nothing about carrying out his prescriptions. Thus, philosophy is to the cure of the soul what medicine is to the cure of the body. Hence, as those who listen to the advice of doctors and disregard it will never have a well-regulated body, so those who listen to the warnings of moral philosophers and do not heed them will never have a well-regulated soul.[290]

MITROFF and DENTON conclude their *Spiritual Audit of Corporate America* asking what new sources of knowledge and wisdom an organization needs to draw on in order to move it to a higher ethical plane, what new forms of education are required to develop an organization and its members, especially in non-coercive ways. We suggest that the answer to this question is in the understanding of a Thomistic organizational psychology because it is a psychology based on the rational and sensing faculties of the soul. It is a psychology that is grasped throughout the organization by the diffusion of virtuous habits. It is by means of the experience of the diffusion of virtue that executives, leaders, and workers

---

[289] Ibid. Book 1, Lecture 10, 122–123.
[290] Ibid. Book 2, Lecture 4, 288.

experience a happiness that is more than a paycheck. They begin to experience in their work environment the vital operation of their soul.

4.5.2 Case Study of Organizational Vision and the Diffusion of Executive Organizational Leadership

Robert Bruce SHAW in his work *Extreme Teams* describes companies known for their teamwork and for having a vision of liberality, and they are also some of today's most successful cutting-edge companies, e.g., Pixar, Netflix, Airbnb, Patagonia, Zappos, and Whole Foods. We will quote here from chapter two: *Foster a Shared Obsession: More than a Business, Less than a Cult.* It is clear from this following passage that innovative organizations not only have a moral psychological vision as a business, but they expect employees to be intensely focused on the vision.

> Some believe that corporations, when all is said and done, are legal entities to earn returns for the shareholders. A well-known business pundit argues this view when he says, "Here is the truth: The DNA of a business is to maximize returns to its shareholders. Those with this view argue that the concern that companies show for customers, employees and the environment may be sincere but are always secondary to the need to maximize profits. The problem with this argument is that many successful companies are dedicated beyond making money. Whole Foods says it wants to change the world through nutrition. Pixar strives to touch people through its movies. Zappos sees its highest calling as creating happiness, not only for customers but for the world at large. Airbus wants to create a sense of belonging and community, providing lodging where people feel at home wherever they travel. Those with a cynical bent view these statement as public relations and marketing ploys designed to enhance their brands. But these companies back up their lofty statements with their actions and investments. They fully understand the need to earn a profit—and the consequences if they fail to do so. But they don't focus on profit as their highest calling.

A small story from Zappos illustrates this point. Several years ago, the firm's founder and CEO was attending an all-day out-of-town meeting with individuals from Skechers, a manufacturer of shoes. The group went back to the hotel after the meeting and too many drinks at a local bar. They wanted to order pizza but room service at the hotel was past the 11p.m. deadline. One person in the group suggested that they order out from a pizzeria. Zappos' CEO Tony Hsieh suggested, half in jest, that they call Zappos 800 number for ordering shoes. He said they should, without telling the Zappos call-center employee who they were, ask for help in finding a pizzeria that would deliver to the hotel. Hsieh made a bet that the Zappos call-center employee would help because his firm is dedicated to serving others-regardless of the request. One of the Skechers people took the CEO up on his boast, and made the call, with others in the group listening in on the speakerphone. The Zappos call-center employee was initially confused as to how to respond. But as Hsieh predicted, she then helped locate the desired pizza. Tony Hsieh tells this story to illustrate that his firm's first priority is not selling shoes but, instead, creating happiness through service of others. This statement is more than rhetoric at Zappos. The company, for example, trains team members on how to fully engage callers, with the goal of meeting their needs whenever possible. It wants each caller to Zappos to leave the interaction happier. The company does not use efficiency metrics (number of calls per hour) to reward its call-center employees. Nor does it promote "upselling," where the callers are encouraged to buy more products beyond their initial purchase. Zappos like to publicize that some customers stay on the line with its call-center reps for hours at a time (with a recent call breaking the firm's previous record in lasting 10 hours and 43 minutes). Paying its employees to stay on the phone for hours is hard to justify from a profit perspective—yet that is what Zappos does.

A paradox of cutting-edge firms is that they make more money because money is not what they care most about. In this regard, they don't act like the stereotype of a firm focused only on quarterly earnings. They are not even fixated on growth, even though many of them are among the fastest growing firms in history.[291]

This case study illustrates clearly how organizations decide to focus on a virtuous and moral purpose. It, also, speaks to the executive function that is responsible for the diffusion of the vision into the concrete operations and daily practices of the organization. In the story of Zappos' call-center, we learn that the call center employees respond to the challenging, unexpected, and demanding call with the virtuous habits of friendliness and respect while remaining obedient to the organization vision.

4.6 Thomistic Organizational Psychology, Sensemaking, Induction and First Principles

The nature and methods of organizational sensemaking has become an issue of major inquiry in the fields of organizational psychology and management. In a recognized and respected academic text, *Managing & Organizations: An Introduction to Theory and Practice*, by Stewart R. CLEGG, Martin KORNBERGER and Tyrone S. PITSIS, sensemaking is defined as essential for leadership management of individuals, teams, group innovation and change, and human resources.

What Is Sensemaking?

Top management teams are supposed to set a common frame within which organization members, customers, suppliers, investors, etc., can make common sense of the organization—what it is and what it does. Organization and management theorists term those processes that people share in making a degree of sense together, as sensemaking. We all make sense of everything around us all of the time. One way to think of sensemaking is to compare it with driving, as you drive you interpret and try

---

[291] Robert Bruce SHAW, *Extreme Teams* (New York: American Management Association, 2017), 78–79.

to make sense of other road users' and pedestrians' behaviors, as well as all the traffic signs around you. You are constantly making a sense of a mass of detail, data, and interpretation.[292]

Deborah ANCONA, an organizational psychologist with MIT-Sloan School of Management describes sensemaking as "coming up with a plausible understanding—a map—of a shifting world; testing this map with others through data collection, action, and conversation, and then refining or abandoning; and the refining, or abandoning, the map depending on how credible it is."[293] Her description of sense making is approached with an attitude of extreme relevancy for the education of present day and future MIT leaders, as W. Brian ARTHUR states:

> Sensemaking is most often needed when our understanding of the world becomes unintelligible in some way. This occurs when the environment is changing rapidly, presenting us with surprises for which we are unprepared or confronting us with adaptive rather than technical problems to solve. Adaptive challenges—those that require a response outside our existing repertoire—often present is a gap between an aspiration and an existing capacity—a gap that cannot be closed by existing modes of operating. At such times phenomena have to be forcibly carved out of the undifferentiated

---

[292] Stewart R. CLEGG, Martin KORNBERGER and Tyrone S. PITSIS, *Managing & Organizations: An Introduction to Theory and Practice*, 4th edition (Los Angeles, London, New Delhi, Singapore, Washington: Sage Publication, 2016), 33. See ibid., 35: "Organizations have a considerable interest in their members making common sense. Any organization appears to be only as good as its people, products and services, and if these people are consistently 'on message', making a sense that is common across customers, suppliers, shareholders and employees, then this is a vital factor in assisting organizations to produce consistent products and services."

[293] Deborah ANCONA, "Sensemaking Framing and Acting in the Unknown," in *The Handbook for Teaching Leadership: Knowing, Doing, and Being* (Thousand Oaks: SAGE, 2012), 3.

flux of raw experience and conceptually fixed and labeled so that they can become common currency for communication.[294]

ANCONA uses a gambling analogy from ARTHUR to illustrate the kind of profound uncertainty that we currently face in the education of present and future executive leadership:

> "Imagine you are milling about in a large casino with the top figures of high tech [...]. Over at one table, a game is starting called Multimedia. Over at another is a game called Web Services. There are many such tables. You sit at one.
> "How much to play?" you ask.
> "Three billion," the croupier replies.
> "Who'll be playing? You ask.
> "We won't know until they show up," he replies.
> "What are the rules?"
> "These will emerge as the game unfolds," says the croupier.
> "What are the odds of winning?" you wonder.
> "We can't say," responds the house.
> "Do you still want to play?"[295]

Sensemaking, ANCONA argues, such an environment involves being thrown into an ongoing, unknowable, unpredictable streaming of experience in search of answers to the question, "What's the story?" It means looking for a unifying order, even if we are not sure if one exists:

> Sensemaking provides executive leadership with a better grasp of what is going on in our world and improves the leadership capabilities of visioning, inventing, and relating. Visions and execution capabilities improve because they fit current circumstances. [...] With the focus and energy with a more

---

[294] W. Brian ARTHUR," Increasing returns and the new world of business" *Harvard Business Review* 74 (4), 100–109.

[295] ANCONA, "Sensemaking Framing and Acting in the Unknown," 5.

plausible map of the future, relating, visioning and inventing scenarios become possible. Sensemaking explores a wider system by seeking out many types and sources of data. It combines financial data with trips to the shop floor, listen to employees as well as customers and mix computer research with personal interviews.[296]

The methodology of sensemaking is similar to the method of collecting and analyzing by means of "thick" data as opposed to "thin" data as presented in chapter three. Sensemaking examines new situations without the perspective of stereotypes that are not really present in a situation itself. Organizational sensemaking is similar to the lessons learned from Japanese knowledge management: there is extreme sensitivity to concrete, daily operations and those closest to the front line, to customers, new and emerging technologies, and emerging global market trends.

> Andy Grove, the former CEO and chair of Intel, believed in being 'paranoid.' By that he meant that you always have to be worried about new trends that can destroy or enhance your business, and new competitors that can win in the market. So, he designed Intel to monitor many trends—to do ongoing sensemaking. This involves watching what customers are buying and where they go if they drop Intel, finding out what new research is being done at key universities, continuously sure that this information is accurate and up to date. Why? Because in his industry, it is important to change in markets and technologies early, not when others have already captured a competitive advantage.[297]

Sensemaking educates leaders to put the emerging situation into a new framework to provide organizational members with order. There is the use of images, metaphors, and stories. Again, as previously explained, it is the use of "thick" data to capture key elements of the new situation. From the DEMING quality

---

[296] Ibid., 7; 10–11.

[297] Ibid., 9.

tradition, sensemaking is about the value of learning from small experiments, i.e., if you are not sure a system is working, experiment with something new.

4.7 Why Sensemaking is so Important and the Diffusion of Goodness

The classic article "Organizational Threat Rigidity" by B.M. STAW, L.E. SANDELANDS and J.E. DUTTON explains how threat and fear leads to organizational rigidity.

> Thus, in individuals, teams and organizations, threat results in the consideration of fewer external cues and a reliance on tried and true modes of operating. As a result, threat is often more associated with inertia, protection of the status quo, and sometimes even inaction—the deer in the headlights syndrome. Threat is seen as the time to batten down the hatches, keep outsiders away, and get back to business as usual. Yet, threat conditions are when high levels of sensemaking and change are most needed. Thus, executive leadership and all levels of leadership within an organization need to fight against this organizational fear-based rigidity in order to enable active sensemaking and inventing.[298]

In the face of uncertainty, people look to leadership for direction and reassurance. At the same time, executive leadership realizes that employees need to be treated as capable adults. Sensemaking requires that executive leadership engages in dialogue for knowledge from leaders at the top to employees on the front line. ANCONA gives an example of the impact diffusion of organizational sensemaking from the lower levels of leadership.

> At Best Buy it wasn't top management who began to see what a lack of communication was doing to relationships with employees. She [a mid-level manager] decided to use social media technologies to get employees (there

---

[298] B.M. STAW, L.E. SANDELANDS and J.E. DUTTON "Threat-rigidity effects in organizational behavior: A multilevel analysis," *Administrative Science Quarterly*, 26, 502–524.

are 160,000) to participate in polls, brainstorm new ideas, and attend town hall meetings with management. The result was a greater level of dialogue, more new ideas from increased sales, and a 32 percent drop in turnover.[299]

It is really since the 1980s that organizational psychology, impacted by emerging organizational chaos and learning theory, began to point to the need for the practice of organizational sensemaking. Organizational leadership increasingly influenced by the impact of the eruption of new information technology and shorter competitive time to market product development cycles came to grips with static paradigms of stable mechanical paradigms of organization. The impact of scientific chaos and complexity theory was merged into the principles and methods of executive leadership. Margaret J. WHEATLEY, one of the most influential figures on the impact of scientific chaos on organizational leadership in the late 80s and into the 90s wrote on chaos and the need for a way of sensemaking in organizational leadership:

> But my focus on science is more than a personal interest. Each of us lives and works in organizations designed from Newtonian images of the universe. We manage by separating things into parts, we believe that influence occurs as a direct result of force exerted from one person to another, we engage in complex planning for a world that we keep expecting to be predictable, and we search continually for better methods of objectively perceiving the world.[300]

The basic principle in chaos theory and organizational management fundamental to all-organizational systems is "self-reference." In response to environmental disturbances that signal the need for change, the system changes in a way that remains consistent with itself in the environment.

---

[299] ANCONA, "Sensemaking Framing and Acting in the Unknown," 12.

[300] Margaret J. WHEATLEY, *Leadership, and the New Science: Learning about Organization from an Orderly Universe* (San Francisco: Berrett-Koehler, 1992), 6.

The system is autopoietic, focusing its activities on what is required to maintain its own integrity and self-renewal. An organizational system experiences many changes, fluctuations, and environmental adaptations at the level of individuals and units within the system. There is no central command control that prohibits small, constant changes. The system allows for many levels of autonomy within itself, and for small fluctuations and changes. By tolerating these, it is able to preserve its global stability and integrity in the environment.[301]

Also, as a chaos organizational scientist, WHEATLY explains the nature of organization using a field theory model that she has taken from physics and biology. When she explains her organizational field theory in terms of concrete applications, she seems in search of the Aristotelian-Thomistic framework of REDPATH's inductive reasoning as presented in chapter two and the understanding of organization from the Aristotelian-Thomistic teaching of the generic nature of an organization. For example, WHEATLEY writes the following:

As a generation of managers, we have been focused on many of the ethereal qualities of organization-culture, values, vision, and ethics. Each of these words describes a quality of organizational life that we can observe in our experience yet find elusive to pin down in specifics. Recently, while doing work on customer service for a retail chain, I asked employees to visit several stores. After spending time in many stores, we all compared notes. To a person, we agreed that we could "feel" good customer service just by walking into the store. We tried to get more specific by looking at visual cues, merchandise layouts, facial expressions-but none of that could explain the sure sense we had when we walked into the store that we would be treated well. Something else was going on. Something else was in the air. We could feel it; we just couldn't describe why we felt it… In each of those stores there was a manager who, together with employees, took time to fill the store space with clear messages about how he or she wanted customers to be served. Clarity about service filled every nook and cranny. With such a powerful

---

[301] Ibid., 94.

structuring field, certain types of individual behaviors and events were guaranteed.[302]

---

[302] Ibid., 52–53. See REDPATH, *The Moral Psychology of St. Thomas*, 216: "Essentially, the act of induction involves instantaneously apprehending the chief principle of unity (a one) that exists within a multitude (a many) that harmonizes orders, that multitude into being parts of this or that kind of a whole! Essentially, induction involves being able to grasp the chief principle that essentially causes: 1) organizational harmony, order; 2) some multitude to be unified as harmoniously connected (ordered) so as to generate this or that kind of whole and the acts which that whole naturally inclines to cause (the organization's chief aim: cooperatively to accomplish numerically-one act). For example, within moments of walking into a business organization, school, church, military or medical facility, charitable foundation, political party, or orchestral performance and sensing how it operates, an intelligent person with extensive experience working with one or more of these organizations just mentioned can immediately induce its nature, and determine whether its activities are healthy or unhealthy, strong, or weak. For such a person, doing so requires no extensive process of empirical verification, logical reasoning, or mathematical testing for the simple reason that the inductive skill resides within the high-quality of harmonious cooperation existing between the organization being experienced and the estimative sense faculty, cogitative reason, and virtuously trained intellect of the expert." See also Alberto STRUMIA, *The Sciences and The Fullness of Rationality* (Aurora, Colorado: The Davies, 2009), 145–146, who is both a mathematical physicist and Thomist. He discusses the themes of field, fractals, and complexity in his chapter on *The Emergence of Complexity, The Whole and the Parts*: "Let us take the problem from the point of view of the whole, that we shall also call a complex system, inasmuch as it presents itself to us in a very articulate manner, and one that is difficult to examine in its entirety [...] the complex objects presents properties and behaviors that cannot be explained (deduced) solely through the study of its parts, but which represent something new, that requires the consideration of the whole as an entity that cannot be broken down [...] The whole complex is not divisible in principle into 'simpler' parts since each part has identical properties (univocity), or similar properties (analogy) or at least properties of the same level of complexity of the whole, as a result of which subdivision does not lead to simplification [...] the whole is contained in its parts, an in a certain sense it is replicated in all its parts. This is the case, for example, of fractals and self-similar structures of geometry and physics (at least within certain limits of scale), and self-referential structure in general. In this case, that which is common to the whole and the parts is a kind of

WHEATLEY's use of field theory as a model for organizational leadership has some real promise if it is put within a Thomistic organizational principle of genus and species.

> Genus plus formal difference produce species. And the real species expresses a thing's specific nature, its real definition. Such being the case, no species belonging to any genus can exist apart from, can properly express its definition and nature, without having an essential relation to the chief aim of its genus. And no genus of human activity can exist without having some activity to human happiness.[303]

WHEATLEY, without an Aristotelian-Thomistic understanding of the generic nature of an organization, uses the science of field theory, "especially from biology and morphogenic fields built up through the accumulated behavior of species members:"[304]

> In a field view of organizations, clarity about value or vision is important, but it's only half the task. Creating the field through the dissemination of those ideas is essential. The field must reach all corners of the organization, involve everyone. And be available everywhere. Vision statements move off the walls and into the corridors, seeking out every employee, every recess of the organization. In the past, we may have thought of ourselves as skilled crafters of organizations, assembling the pieces of an organization, exerting our energy on the painstaking creation of links between all those parts. Now we need to imagine ourselves as broadcasters of information, pulsing out messages everywhere. We need all of us out there, stating, clarifying, discussing, modeling, filling all of space with messages we care about. If we

---

property of structure, a form that is actuated both in the whole and in the parts according to its own modality (not always the same) in each one of these."

[303] REDPATH, *A Not-So-Elementary Christian Metaphysics*, 198.

[304] WHEATLEY, *Leadership, and the New Science*, 51.

do that, fields develop-and with them wondrous capacity to bring energy into form.[305]

In chapter three, we discussed in some detail, from the perspective of a Thomistic organizational psychology and metaphysics, the concept of touching the divine by means of constant participation in the organizational genus. We defined the executive function as one of exemplar participation in the organizational whole and in its members as expressions of the virtuous habits of rational and moral excellence. It is, therefore, by means of leadership serving as exemplars of goodness, i.e., "touching the divine," that the loving energy of goodness diffuses throughout the members of the organizational whole and gives a sense of spiritual, moral, and operational excellence. We could say, using the concept of communication taken from Fran O'ROURKE, that the executive function is to energize the organizational whole with the communication of divine goodness:

> Now whereas 'diffusion' is the term used by Aquinas to denote the primacy of finality, he also emphasizes in creation the aspect of divine efficiency which is expressed in the word communication. Now, by causal efficiency is understood an activity whereby one thing enriches another by pouring out its perfection into it, thus sharing its actuality. The agent proceeds outward and gives something of itself. In other words, it pertains to the nature of the good to communicate itself to others. And if the things of nature, in so far as they are perfect, communicate their good to others, it pertains all the more to divine will to communicate its good to others through similitude.[306]

---

[305] Ibid., 55–56.

[306] AQUINAS, *Summa theologiae* I, q. 19, a. 2: "Hence, if natural things, in so far as they are perfect, communicate their good to others, much more does it appertain to the divine will to communicate by likeness its own good to others as much as possible. Thus, then, He wills both Himself to be, and other things to be; but Himself as the end, and other things as ordained to that end; inasmuch as it befits the divine goodness that other things should be partakers therein."

Divine goodness proceeds into things in so far as it communicates itself to them.[307]

4.8 Organizational Sensemaking Principles and Aristotelian-Thomistic Induction

In chapter three, we presented Christian MADSBJERG on sensemaking, especially the meaning of sensemaking and thick data. Given that Thomistic faculty psychology is grounded on a "sense realism" philosophy, since "all ancient Greek philosophy/science depends on a sense realism and a faculty psychology starts with the senses as an essential first principle of organizational psychology and sense making,"[308] as Ancona says,

> Leaders need to engage in sensemaking to understand why their teams are not functioning, why their customers are leaving, and why their operations are falling short on safety and reliability. At a personal level, sensemaking can help in understanding why you have not lived up to your own expectations as a leader, or why you don't seem to be getting along with your own new boss. We teach sensemaking to undergraduates, MBAs, mid-level executives, and top management teams since the ability to understand a changing context is need at every level.[309]

It is important to note that a management school as prestigious as the MIT-Sloan School of Management has identified sensemaking as one of the core capabilities of leadership. It is Karl E. WEICK who introduced sensemaking as the way that we structure the unknown to be able to act in it.[310] Since Thomistic organizational psychology is grounded on Aristotelian-Thomistic faculty psychology and sense realism, it has an important and unique approach to organizational sensemaking. Basically, the approach of Thomistic organizational

---

[307] O'ROURKE, *Pseudo-Dionysius and the Metaphysics of Aquinas*, 245.

[308] REDPATH, *The Moral Psychology of St. Thomas*, 28.

[309] ANCONA, "Sensemaking Framing and Acting in the Unknown," 5–6.

[310] Karl E. WEICK, *Making Sense of the Organization* (Oxford: Blackwell, 2001).

psychology to sensemaking requires a premodern understanding of the executive function of leaders and the importance of the faculty (i.e., power) of induction (inductive reasoning) and organizational first principles.

Understanding the classical nature and method of induction requires at least an elementary grasp of the Aristotelian-Thomistic faculty psychology of perception and abstraction of the universal from the particulars. This is a very important and extensive topic in Aristotelian-Thomistic psychology, but we will concisely summarize the issue of abstraction, universals, and particulars by using the work *Intellect: Mind Over Matter* by ADLER. In chapter three "Is Our Intellect Unique?" he establishes that:[311]

a) Human beings behave in ways that are totally missing from the behavior of other animals. In these respects, we find nothing similar there, even in the slightest degree.

b) In terms of the character of the difference in kind between man and other animals, that difference would be radical if it arose from something that is not present in the constitution of comparable species. Brains and other nervous apparatus are present in both, differing in degree certainly and perhaps also in kind. But if the human mind is unique as compares with the minds of all other animals, and if its uniqueness is the cause of the manifest difference in kind between human behavior and the behavior of other animals, then we are justified in regarding the difference rooted in a property of human nature not present in any other species.

c) While thought is present in both man and higher animals, animal thought is perceptual thought; only human thought is conceptual. While motivating appetites or desires are present in both man and other animals, only man has an intellectual appetite, a will that is able to make free choices.

d) Other animals live entirely in the present. Only human individuals are time-binders, connecting the perceived present with the remembered past and the imaginable future. Only man is a historical animal with a historical tradition and a historical development. In the case of other species, the life

---

[311] Mortimer J. ADLER, *Intellect*, 24-40.

of succeeding generations remains the same as long as no genetic change occurs.

e) To say that human artistry is creative, not instinctive, is to say that it consists of acts voluntarily done, involving both thought and choice on the part of the individual artist.

f) There is much evidence that animals in the wild do communicate with one another by cries or sounds of various sorts and by bodily gestures, including facial grimaces. But all these animal expressions function as signals, communicating emotional states, desires, or purposes. None is a designative sign functioning, as a word in human language, to name something.

g) Why do we find these differences between the linguistic training of chimpanzees and the learning of a language by human beings? Because the mind of the chimpanzee, like the minds of all other animals, consists solely of sensory powers and so cannot rise above the level of sense perception.

h) At the risk of belaboring this point unduly, I wish to take a moment to be precise as possible about the difference between perceptual and conceptual thought. Two things must be said about concepts. The first is that concepts are (1) acquired dispositions to recognize perceived objects as being of this or that kind and at the same time (2) to understand what this or that kind of object is like, with the result (3) that the individual having formed a concept is able to perceive a number of sensible particulars as being of the same kind and to discriminate between them and other sensible particulars that are different in kind. The second thing that must be said about concepts is that they are acquired dispositions to understand what certain types of objects are like, both when they are not actually perceived and also when they are not perceptible.[312]

i) The crucial aspect of human behavior is our use of general terms—all of the common nouns in our vocabulary that name kinds or classes of things, some of which have perceptible instances and some of which do not. Everything perceptible, memorable, and imaginable is a particular individual thing, an attribute of that thing, or an occurrent event. We can,

---

[312] Ibid., 25–35.

for example, perceive visible figures that are triangles of a particular shape and size; we can also imagine or remember particular triangles. But we cannot by means of our sensitive powers think of triangularity in general, triangularity not particularized by shape, size, or color. Yet we use the word "triangle" and all other general terms in our vocabulary with understanding of the universals—the kinds or classes of things—to which our general terms refer.[313]

j)   The argument then reaches its conclusion as follows. Our concepts are universal in their signification of objects that are kinds or classes of things rather than individuals that are particular instances of these classes or kinds. Since they have universality, they cannot exist physically or be embodied in matter. But concepts do exist in our minds. They are there as acts of our intellectual power. Hence that power must be an immaterial power, not one embodied in a material organ such as the brain. The action of the brain, therefore, cannot be the sufficient condition of conceptual thought, though it may still be a necessary condition thereof, insofar as the exercise of our power of conceptual thought depends on the exercise of our powers of perception, memory, and imagination, which are corporeal powers embodied in our sense organs and brain.

k)   Our cognitive sensory powers do not and cannot apprehend universals. Their cognitive reach does not go beyond particulars. Hence, we would not be able to apprehend universals if we did not have another and quite distinct cognitive power—the power of intellect.[314]

l)   Philosophers who call themselves nominalists deny the existence of universal objects of thought. In doing so, they are in effect denying the existence of intellect as radically distinct from the senses. They try to explain our significant use of general terms or common names without permitting their significance to be construed as referring to anything except particulars—never to anything that is universal.[315]

---

[313] Ibid., 39.

[314] Ibid., 50–51.

[315] Ibid., 40

It has been necessary to present these statements basically to identify that the unique approach of a Thomistic organizational psychology to sensemaking rests on the issue of the difference between perceptual and conceptual thought. It is necessary to grasp this essential principle if we are to appreciate the Aristotelian-Thomistic teaching of sensory induction and first principles as necessary for organizational sensemaking. Therefore, the main lesson we must take from ADLER is that Thomistic organizational psychology looks at the nature of organizational sensemaking as a study of organizational conceptual thought in the attempt, as the father of sensemaking WEICK states, "To structure the unknown so as to be able to act in it."[316] We argue that sensemaking is a conceptual act of the intellect, rather than a study "by means of sense perception modeling, such as an information processing approach to social perception."[317] Even as we move out of the industrial age of organizational pyramids into digital organizational networks, we argue that a Thomistic rational sensemaking psychology grounded on classical sense realism, inductive reasoning and principles allows an organization to develop a sensemaking tradition, where "Sensemaking tradition organizations are learning organizations that learn to draw on past wells of sense making to ensure their continuity with the past and to guide their progress into the future."[318] WEICK maintains that:

> People do know best that to which they are committed, but not because they knew it and then became committed. It is just the opposite. Action leads the sensemaking process; it does not follow it. People need to be less casual about action since whatever they do has the potential to bind them and focus their sensemaking. In action, repetitive action, and idiosyncratic action all have direct effects on what people know and how well they know it. Action is

---

[316] Quoted in ANCONA, "Sensemaking Framing and Acting in the Unknown," 3.

[317] James L. BOWDITCH, Anthony F. BUONO and Marcus M. STEWART, *A Primer on Organizational Behavior* (Hoboken: Wiley, 2008), 48.

[318] CLEGG, KORNBERGER PITSIS, *Managing & Organizations*, 46.

intelligence, and until it is deployed, meaning and sense will be underdeveloped.[319]

Organizational rational sensemaking focuses upon the idea that the reality of everyday organizational life must be seen as an ongoing accomplishment which takes particular shape and form of the situations in which they find themselves. It is BARNARD who even back in the 30s had an intuition in his work for a need of an activity sensemaking in formal organizations.

> An organization comes into being when (1) there are persons able to communicate with each other (2) who are willing to contribute action (3) to accomplish a common purpose [...]. The vitality of organizations lies in the willingness of individuals to contribute forces to the cooperative system. The willingness requires the belief that the purpose can be carried out, a faith that diminishes to the vanishing point as it appears that it is not in fact in process of being attained. Hence, when effectiveness ceases, willingness to contribute disappears. The continuance of willingness also depends upon the satisfactions that are secured by individual contributors in the process of carrying out the purpose. If the satisfactions do not exceed the sacrifices required, willingness disappears, and the condition is one of organization inefficiency. If the satisfactions exceed the sacrifices, willingness persists, and the condition is one of efficiency of organization.[320]

This quote from BARNARD is extremely important in terms of organizational psychology, worker sensemaking and participation in organizational efficiency to achieve excellence. Let us take the example of the Washington State rowing team in chapter three. If the athletes were to follow obediently the extremely arduous demands of the coach and continue to lose in competition, then the team would begin to think that the way he is coaching them does not make sense. In other

---

[319] Karl E. WEICK, "Sensemaking in Organizations: Small Structure with Large Consequences," in J. Keith MURNIGHAN (Ed.), *Social Psychology: Advances in Theory and Research* (Cliffs: Prentice Hall, 1993), 33.

[320] BARNARD, *The Functions of the Executive*, 82.

words, it does not make sense if the satisfactions are not worth the sacrifices: activities not making sense translates into organizational inefficiencies.

In terms of exemplar executive leadership, REDPATH states:

> Leadership, in short, is chiefly communications activity: an ability to communicate (in a way that need not be verbal or totally rational) specific superiority, exceeding other organizational parts in organizational strength, through which a leader is able to convey to, and elicit from, those led (other parts of an organization) receptivity to taking directions essentially related to the chief aim of an organization as an organization.[321]

If we follow WEICK's line of thought that action leads the sensemaking process rather than following it, we see a certain amount of agreement between the Thomistic metaphysics of organizational leadership insofar as actions lead to sensemaking. REDPATH holds that the art or science of anything as a generic whole cannot exist apart from its species. For example, "Every species of art or science studies some species of organization and the chief aims of that organization, and some species of human production or performance related to such species of organization and its specific aims."[322] Therefore, it is a fundamental principle of Thomistic organizational sensemaking that we discover the rational sense of organizational activities by asking continuously the basic question: What are the activities and causative principles of the past, the present and coming into the future that make sense in terms of motivating the organizational whole to excellence?

4.9 Return to Aristotelian-Thomistic Induction and Principles of Organizational Craft Knowledge

ARISTOTLE holds that all our scientific understanding about some given subject domain is a certain sort of explanatory demonstration. One of the necessary

---

[321] REDPATH, "The Essential Connection between Common Sense and Leadership Excellence," 614.

[322] REDPATH, *The Moral Psychology of St. Thomas*, 45

requirements is that the study—or we could say organizational sensemaking—must begin with first principles proper to the scientific domain being studied. As Marc GASSER-WINGATE explains, first principles from which demonstrations begin as "explanatory primitives" cannot be demonstrated.[323] For ARISTOTLE, we learn first principles by induction which is a form of cognition that begins with perception and proceeds through a series of increasingly sophisticated states in which various universal concepts come to be formed in our souls.

The question, therefore, arises how do we learn first principles by induction? "Aristotle does not put forth some sort of inductive inference all aspiring scientists should follow."[324] Instead, he offers a high level-level psychological account of our learning of first principles that describes how various concepts arise in our souls, and which cognitive states are involved in the acquisition. ARISTOTLE sees PLATO's position that the ability to grasp first principles from innate states resulting from a form of Platonic recollection as absurd. ARISTOTLE says that perception is a capacity that gives rise to certain states in a perceiving subject, and these states are meant to constitute the basic form of knowledge from which our knowledge of first principles is derived.

It is necessary to make the point that we have the capacity of perception to discover first principles, but the capacity only gives rise to the cognitive movement to universals. We are not talking about an intuitive type of knowledge as found in a non-Aristotelian-Thomistic sense psychology, as the organizational psychologist Roy ROWAN writes:

Defining Intuition

What is this mystical power, magical facility, this guardian angel that is smarter than we are and can take care of us, provided it is allowed to function? The athlete speaks of mind and movement coalescing or, less poetically, of eye-hand coordination. The Zen Buddhist describes the sound of one hand clapping. The businessman talks about gut feeling. Their

---

[323] Marc GASSER-WINGATE, "Aristotle on Induction and First Principles," *Philosophers Imprint* 16 (4), February 2016, 2.

[324] Ibid.

vocabularies differ, but their inner messages have the same submerged origin.

Intuition is knowledge gained without rational thought. And since it comes from some stratum of awareness just below the conscious level, it is slippery and elusive, to say the least [...]. So where does the first glimmer of a new concept, new product, new market, or new solution to a problem come from? Elusive as it is, we do know certain characteristics of this inner impression or hunch. It concerns relationships, involves simultaneous perception of a whole system, and can draw a conclusion—not necessarily correct—without proceeding through logical intermediary steps. That's why intuition comes with that queasy feeling of almost but not quite knowing.[325]

The approach of ROWAN's psychological definition of intuition as a type of mystical event is, as ADLER would suggest, a nominalist perception and the inability to understand the cognitional relationship between sensing of and the forming of universals.[326] We will confront the same problem in the coming chapters of organizational psychological nominalism when we confront issues of leadership, decision making and risk taking.

Sensemaking as inductive is a process from sense perception to memory. From repeated memories of the same thing comes experience. As a result, the whole universal comes to rest in the soul, the one apart from the many, that which is one and the same in all things comes as a principle of art or understanding. AQUINAS states:

---

[325] Roy ROWAN, "What Is It" in Weston H. AGOR (Ed.), *Intuition in Organizations: Leading and Managing Productively* (London: Sage, 1989) 84–85.

[326] See St. Thomas AQUINAS, *Commentary on Aristotle's Posterior Analytics*, Lecture 29: "For sensing is properly and per se of the singular, but yet there is somehow even a sensing of the universal. For sense knows Callias not only so far from as he is Callias, but also as he is this man. As a result of such an attainment pre-existing in the sense, the intellective soul can consider man in both. But if it were in the very nature of things that sense could apprehend only that which pertains to particularity, and along with this could in no wise apprehend the nature in the particular, it would not be possible for universal knowledge to be caused in us from sense-apprehension."

Then, he [Aristotle] shows, in view of the foregoing, how the knowledge of first principles comes about in us; and he concludes from the foregoing that from sensing comes remembrance in those animals in which a sensible impression remains, as has been stated above. But from remembrance many times repeated in regard to the same item but in diverse singulars arises experience, because experience seems to be nothing else than to take something from many things retained in the memory.[327]

Organizational Leadership Sensemaking Implication:

In organizational executive leadership knowing from experience the principles required for decision making are critical and come from years of experience. An executive must know the principles that pertain to decision making as it pertains to leadership and sensemaking in a given organizational subject domain.

AQUINAS states:

However, experience requires some reasoning about the particulars, in that one is compared to another: and this is peculiar to reason. Thus, when one recalls that such an herb cured several men of fever, there is said to be experience that such an herb cures fevers. But reason does not stop at the experience gathered from particulars, but from many particulars in which it has been experienced, it takes one common item which is consolidated in the mind and considers it without considering any of the singulars. This common item reason takes as a principle of art and science. For example, as long as a doctor considered that this herb cured Socrates of fever, and Plato and many other individual men, it is experience; but when his considerations arise to the fact that such a species of herb heals a fever absolutely, this is taken as a rule of the art of medicine.[328]

Organizational Leadership Sensemaking Implication:

---

[327] Ibid., Lecture 20.
[328] Ibid.

Deming taught that organizational leadership requires profound knowledge. In the above passage, Aquinas gives an explanation of the nature of the profound knowledge required for executive leadership. It is the ability to make decisions and rule because the executive leader learns from experience. This learning from experience means that universal principles of action and rules of decision making are "resting in the mind" of the executive leader.

AQUINAS states:

> This, then, is what he means when he says that just as from memory is formed experience, so from experience or even from the universal resting in the mind (which, namely, is taken as if it is so in all cases, just as experience is taken as being so in certain cases. —This universal is said to be resting in the mind, inasmuch as it is considered outside the singulars, which undergo change. Furthermore, he says that it is one outside the many, not according to an autonomous existence but according to the consideration of the intellect which considers a nature, say of man, without referring to Socrates and Plato. But even though it is one outside the many according to the intellect's consideration, nevertheless in the sphere of existents it exists in all singulars one and the same: not numerically, however, as though the humanity of all men were numerically one, but according to the notion of the species. For just as this white is similar to that white in whiteness, not as though there were one numerical whiteness existing in the two, so too Socrates is similar to Plato in humanity, but not as though there were numerically one humanity existing in the two) the principle of art and science is formed in the mind.[329]

Organizational Leadership Sensemaking Implication:

Organizational leadership is not so much about a science of leadership, as it is the art of leadership, especially executive soulful leadership. Since it is an art, the leader must be a continuous learner redefining and applying principles. As we learned in the case study on Southwest airlines, Herb Kelleher maintained that

---

[329] Ibid.

organizational strategy is a continuous process of defining and redefining organizional principles.

AQUINAS states:

And he distinguishes between art and science, just as he did in *Ethics* VI, where it is stated that art is right reason in regard to things to be made. And so, he says here that if from experience a universal in regard, to generation is taken, i.e., in regard to anything that can be made, say in regard to healing or husbandry, this pertains to art. Science, however, as it is stated in the same place, is concerned with necessary things; hence if the universal bears on things which are always in the same way, it pertains to science; for example, if it bears on numbers or figures. And this process which has been described is verified in regard to the principle of all sciences and arts. Hence, he concludes that there do not pre-exist, any habits of principles in the sense of being determinate and complete, neither do they come to exist anew from other better-known pre-existing principles in the way that a scientific habit is generated in us from previously known principles; rather the habits of principles come to exist in us from pre-existing sense.[330]

Organizational Leadership Sensemaking Implication:

As a rule, organizations, especially business, are, under the stress of competition. The ability to compete, strive for excellence and victory requires the principles that build character and, as we will present in the next chapter, necessary to face difficult challenges. It is a character of efficiency and effectiveness grounded on principles of artful skill and right moral behavior that are most required.

And he gives as an example a battle which starts after the soldiers have been beaten and put to flight. For when one of the soldiers shall have, taken a stand, i.e., begun to take a battle position and not flee, another takes his stand next to him, and then another, until enough are gathered to form the

---

[330] Ibid.

beginning of a battle. So, too, from the sense and memory of one particular and then of another and another, something is finally reached which is the principle of art and science, as has been stated.[331]

But someone could believe that sense alone or the mere remembrance of singulars is sufficient to cause intellectual knowledge of principles, as some of the ancients supposed, who did not discriminate between sense and intellect. Therefore, to exclude this the philosopher adds that along with sense it is necessary to presuppose such a nature of mind as cannot only suffer this (i.e., be susceptible of universal knowledge, which indeed comes to pass in virtue of the possible intellect) but can also cause this in virtue of the agent intellect which makes things intelligible in act by abstraction of universals from singulars.[332]

In regard to the development of a Thomistic organizational psychology, there are three important concepts in the above passage on the topic of induction. *First,* to grasp the full impact of a Thomistic psychology of induction it is initially necessary to approach the topic from within a framework of the Aristotelian-Thomistic explanation of the difference and dynamic relationship between universal concepts and particular sense perception, as we described in detail from ADLER. This is an issue of paramount importance because it differentiates a Thomistic organizational psychology from theoretical methods of organizational psychology grounded on a nominalistic mindset.

Second, these passages will also become important in future chapters, when we consider the dynamics of executive decision making and risk-taking, e.g., from sensing comes remembrance in those animals in which sensible impression remains, as has been stated above. But from remembrance many times repeated in regard to the same item but in diverse singulars arise experience, because experience seems to be nothing else than to take something from many things retained in the memory.

Third, important concept, especially in terms of the contemporary concern in organizational psychology for sensemaking, is ". . . and he gives as an example a

---

[331] Ibid.
[332] Ibid.

battle which starts after soldiers have been beaten and put to flight. "For when one of the soldiers has taken a stand, i.e., begun to take a battle position and not flee another takes his stand next to him, and then another, until enough are gathered to form the beginning of a battle. So, too, from the sense memory of one particular and then of another and another, something is finally reached which is the principle of art and science, as has been stated." This is an important metaphor that seems to suggest the progress from perception to first principle resembles a rooting in which soldiers make successive stands.

GASSER-WINGATE makes an Aristotelian argument of a progressive, inductive root position in our soul. It is the same sort of process that leads us to grasp higher and higher principles, since induction is the process responsible for our first grasp of a universal. Therefore, we grasp first principles through repeated inductions of this sort rather than relying on a single inductive step. The important point GASSER-WINGATE makes in developing craft knowledge is that grasping universals does not simply consist in an ability to form general judgments or identify some group of individuals as members of a certain class.

In terms of a psychology of induction, AQUINAS, commenting on ARISTOTLE, describes four stages of inductive reasoning to first principle, namely perception, memory, experience, and the unnamed stage beyond experience in which the subject grasps the whole universal. GASSER-WINGATE develops his explanation in the article "Aristotle on Induction and First Principles." He introduces an Aristotelian concept of induction that is most applicable to the development of a Thomistic organizational psychology of induction and its application to sensemaking and principles. He states that "objects of perception, for Aristotle, are particular things in particular places at particular times."[333] He points out that at the perceptual stage the perceiving subject will have some relation to the universal instantiated by the things he/she perceives.

The process of inductive reasoning also consists in recognizing the explanatory relation between the universals. His argument, therefore, is the following:[334] We come to know demonstrative first principles (and come to know them in a (theoretically sensitive manner) by induction if induction is understood in a

---

[333] Ibid., 11.

[334] See GASSER-WINGATE, "Aristotle on Induction and First Principles," 13–15.

certain way-roughly, as a cognitive progress from a range of particular truths to some universal explanation why all these truths hold. The philosopher adds that along with sense the nature of the mind is to be susceptible to universal knowledge in virtue of the possible intellect and causes this in virtue of agent intellect.

In terms of a psychology of induction, AQUINAS, commenting on ARISTOTLE, describes four stages of inductive reasoning to first principle, namely perception, memory, experience, and the unnamed stage beyond experience in which the subject grasps the whole universal. GASSER-WINGATE develops his explanation in the article "Aristotle on Induction and First Principles." He introduces an Aristotelian concept of induction that is most applicable to the development of a Thomistic organizational psychology of induction and its application to sensemaking and principles. He states that "objects of perception, for Aristotle, are particular things in particular places at particular times."[335] He points out that at the perceptual stage the perceiving subject will have some relation to the universal instantiated by the things he/she perceives.

Consequently, part of what makes the inductive development possible is our capacity to achieve a form of experience on the basis of repeated perceptions of some nature retained in memories. In his *Metaphysics*, Aristotle describes experience in some detail. He says that a person of experience is able to:

> have a judgment that when Callias was ill of this disease this did him good, and similarly in the case of Socrates and in many individual cases, is a matter of experience; but to judge that it has done good to all persons of a certain constitution, marked off in one class, when they were ill of this disease, e.g. to phlegmatic or bilious people when burning with fevers—this is a matter of art.[336]

GASSER-WINGATE continues to develop experiences in relation to craft. An experienced doctor, then, remembers the particular treatments which cured particular patients with particular diseases. On the basis of past cases, he/she is able to determine which treatment will be effective given some particular patient with

[335] Ibid., 11.
[336] ARISTOTLE, *Metaphysics*, book 1 (981a7-12).

some particular disease. The experienced doctor doesn't pick a treatment by recognizing that Callias belongs to the type 'phlegmatic human being' noting that an instance of being affected with by malarial fever would be a good treatment. Reasoning of this sort is only available to a physician capable of identifying the explanation for symptoms of some given type independently of any particular case presented- and as Aristotle goes to explain such an ability is proper to the person who knows the craft of medicine. Therefore, experience does require more than memory, since the experienced person has internalized some of the connections between his/her memories and is able to predict future outcomes on the basis of new perceptions of a certain type.

A physician possessing, the craft of medicine differs from an experienced doctor in two significant ways: first, the physician can identify the explanation for some successful treatment, while the experienced doctor acts without the explanatory knowledge, and second, the physician can recognize the effects of some type of disease in some type of patient, while the experienced doctor merely treats symptoms on a particular, case by case basis. So even if an ability to make judgments about types of individuals "marked off in one class" is a criterion for craft-knowledge, it is really our grasp of explanations which makes us wiser and allows us to "know in a stronger sense." The main mark of craft induction is explanatory knowledge."[337]

4.10 Thomistic organizational executive leadership and the diffusion of Organizational Common Sensemaking

ANCONA defines sensemaking as "the activity that enables us to turn the ongoing complexity of the world into a situation that is comprehended explicitly in words and that serve as a springboard into action."[338] Furthermore, she states: "In the realm of business sensemaking can mean learning about shifting markets, customer migration, or new technologies. It can mean learning about culture, politics, and structure of a new venture or about a problem that you haven't seen

---

[337] See GASSER-WINGATE, "Aristotle on Induction and First Principles," 11–14.

[338] ANCONA, "Sensemaking Framing and Acting in the Unknown,".

before."[339] She proclaims that sensemaking is common sense. Sensemaking consists of "five major tasks: observe, question, act, reassess and communicate."[340] Leaders communicate in these tasks simultaneously, as each element of sensemaking informs the others. With all due respect to the theory and methodology of MIT's sensemaking in action key tasks, we must ask from the perspective of a Thomistic organizational psychology is their model of organizational analysis and scenario construction about common sense or is it really different than the traditional organizational idea of a "think tank." When it comes to the craft of sensemaking Thomistic organizational psychology is grounded on a metaphysics of common sensemaking.

In July 2014, Peter A. REDPATH at the Inaugural Congress, Renewing the West by Renewing Common Sense gave a presentation to an audience of academic scholars and attendees from government, nonprofit and business organizations that possessed an interest in common sense leadership and leadership. This keynote and seminal presentation has since been published in the Studia Gilsoniana (2014) under the title The Essential Connection between Common Sense Philosophy and Leadership Excellence. We turn to this paper to establish a Thomistic organizational concept of common sense that differs from the MIT concept and approach to sensemaking from a common-sense realist approach to common sense and leadership and organizational sensemaking. We present REDPATH teaching on common sense and leadership excellence in terms of core principles that relate to the issue of sensemaking and the Aristotelian-Thomistic teaching of craft knowledge and induction.

a) An art or science grows out of a human habit to which a subject known relates. That the subject known helps generate and activate within a natural human knowing faculty. Every art, science or philosophical activity grows out of the experiential relationship between the specific habit of an artist, scientist, or philosopher and a known material or subject that activates the habit.

---

[339] Ibid., 1.

[340] MIT Leadership Center, "Making a Difference by Making Sense," *Brochure* *www.mineducacion.gov.co/cvn/1665/articles-112257_archivo_pdf2.pd*

b) According to St. Thomas, all philosophy, science starts in sense wonder essentially involving a complicated psychological state of fear, intellectual confidence about the unity of the truth and the essential reliability of our senses and intellectual faculties, personal hope to achieve intellectual, volitional, and emotional satisfaction through resolving the wonder and putting fear to rest.

c) For Aristotle science is not chiefly a system, and it does not solely consist in a scientific demonstration. Scientific demonstration culminates scientific understanding like a crescendo culminates a symphonic musical performance. Science is chiefly a generic habit of knowing (of right judging about definitions, concepts, images, and sensible and non-sensible natures [operational organizations]). Science chiefly exists in the scientist's distinctive and comprehensive (that is, generic) habit of sensing, abstracting, imagining, conceiving, and judging; but chiefly in judging in relation to the way a scientist is inclined by habit to abstract and relate concepts and images in a unique act of judging, reasoning, and drawing conclusions (species of the scientist's generic habit). This is a comprehensive understanding (a scientific explanation) that, as history of philosophical experience has taught us, to be completely sure of being scientific, culminates in demonstration and a process of verification that demonstrative knowledge is possessed through testing what a scientist considers to be demonstrative knowledge in the form of a confirmed hypothesis (somewhat like editing the final draft of a book for typographical errors). Strictly speaking, considered in and of itself, a demonstrative syllogism or system of demonstrative syllogisms is no philosophical, no scientific explanation. Like Aristotle says, art and science, philosophy, presuppose experience, or much memory habitually related to judging that some multitude is essentially related as parts to a whole (that is, as species [organizational parts] to a genus, or organizational whole.

d) Strictly considered, experience, art, philosophy, and science are not bodies of generically new knowledge, added to something a leader already knows. They are more or less perfect, or maturely developed habits, ways of possessing knowledge a leader already has about some operational, organizational whole a leader leads.[341]

Based on our explanation of induction and principles of a common-sense science of leadership, the position of Thomistic organizational psychology is that organizational sensemaking is much more than leaders, as portrayed the MIT Center of Leadership, in terms of "leaders develop a persuasive story and align their organization to achieve effectiveness."[342] In this dissertation, we have been constructing a Thomistic organizational psychology of executive leadership and the diffusion and participation in the executive function of leadership throughout the organizational whole. In chapter three, we established a principle of an equality of inequality within an organizational whole structure of leadership. We have, also, established this principle with an existential definition that exemplars of existential participation must have the character of discoverer, teacher and capable of instilling hope, driving out fear, building and restoring confidence and energizing and calming emotions.

Given the definition of the executive function as one of exemplar of participation in the organizational genus, it follows that it is the role of the executive leader to motivate, inspire as the organizational exemplar of leadership common sensemaking. As the exemplar, he/she must be driven by a sense of wonder about the excellence of the organization. More insights into the Thomistic teaching on induction are required in order to place induction and first principles in the context of the executive leadership function and the organizational whole. AQUINAS explains the difference between *quia* and *propter quid*:

> Demonstration is a syllogism causing scientific knowledge and proceeds from the causes both first and immediate of a thing. Now this is to be understood as referring to demonstration *propter quid*. But there is a difference between knowing that a thing is so and why it is so. Therefore, since demonstration is a syllogism causing scientific knowledge, as has been

---

[341] REDPATH, "The Essential Connection between Common Sense and Leadership Excellence," *Studia Gilsoniana,* 3 (2014) 605–608.

[342] MIT Leadership Center, "Making a Difference by Making Sense" *brochure.*

said, it is necessary that a demonstration *quia* which makes one know that a thing is so should differ from the demonstration *propter quid* which makes one know why.[343]

An Aristotelian-Thomistic theory of demonstration is required for scientific knowledge. Aquinas states that "the scientific knower, if he is to know perfectly, must know the cause of the thing known [...]. But if he were to know the cause by itself, he would not yet know the effect actually—which would be to know it absolutely—but only virtually, which is the same as knowing in a qualified sense."[344] In other words, when it comes to organizational craft knowledge and causative, common sense principles,

> we know it in something else in which it exists either as a part in a whole (as we are said to know a wall through knowing the house), or as an accident in its subject (as in knowing Coriscus we are said to know who is coming toward us), or as an effect in its cause (as in the example given earlier, we know the conclusion in the principles), or indeed in any fashion similar to these.[345]

In regard, to the function of the executive exemplar leader, in terms of causative principles essential to virtual intensity (excellence) of the whole organization, he/she must have a *propter quid* understanding of principles. In contemporary organizational language, we could use GASSER-WINGATE's terminology of theoretically sensitive, i.e., the Chief Executive Officer and the diffusion of this higher level of leadership must possess theoretical-sensitive knowledge of the organizational principles.

However, throughout the whole organization there should be a *quia* comprehension of causative principles. In simple terms, the chief executive must have a *propter quid* craft knowledge of principles and those of executive levels and other levels of management. Of course, we are speaking here of organizational

---

[343] AQUINAS, *Commentary on Aristotle's Posterior Analytics*, Lecture 23.
[344] Ibid., Lecture 4.
[345] Ibid.

principles of leadership, and we do share agreement with the MIT Leadership Center belief that sensemaking is a necessary capability of leadership, especially at executive and senior levels of organizational leadership. For example, if it is a software development company there will be parts (divisions) of the scientific organization, where software engineers will have only a *quia* craft knowledge of the causative principles of design and writing good code. Yet, the executive and higher levels of organizational leadership must have *propter quid* craft knowledge that engineers are adhering to proper code writing operational principles.

ANCONA, the MIT organizational psychologist, states:

> At an organizational level, leaders need to engage in sensemaking to understand why their teams are not functioning, why their customers are leaving, and why their operations are falling short on safety and reliability. At a personal level, sensemaking can help in understanding why you have not lived up to your own expectations as leader, or why you don't seem to be getting along with your boss.[346]

A Thomistic organizational psychology agrees with the belief that leadership sensemaking is an essential element of the executive function. We, also, hold that it is necessary for any role of organizational leadership. BOWDITCH and BUONO present the various constructs and leadership traits and in their synthesis, conclude that the two major characteristics of a leader are the following:

> Direction: a leader's ability to provide direction to his or her subordinates and organization. This dimension is composed of vision (the ability to create and project beneficial images), concept (ability to provide the best explanation of key events, and focus (capacity to focus on important goals). Drive to Execute: the leader's ability to motivate others. This category includes ego drive (self-definition of oneself as significant), competition (the

---

[346] ANCONA, "Sensemaking Framing and Acting in the Unknown," 4.

desire to win), achiever (energy), courage (relishes challenge), being an activator (proactive).[347]

In the coming chapters, we will continue the thesis of vision, particularly the organizational spiritual vision as presented in this chapter. PINK based his vision of the High Concept, High Touch on organizational research from around the world that offers a fresh and challenging look at what it takes to excel in the Conceptual Age. It is the coming age of business, nonprofits, and government where digital technology will favor an executive leadership that encourages organizational creativity, intuition, and a spiritual sense of mission. It is important to note that BERGQUIST predicts that, as explained previously, there is a need for a post-postmodern psychology of the organization.

If organizations are to be grounded on a High Concept, High Touch psychology, then it is a Thomistic organizational psychology based on a common-sense psychology of the executive function and diffusion of leadership that offers the best way. PINK did not say that contemporary organizations must become High Perception, High Conception organizations. We have argued that meaning and sensemaking is not a matter of perception i.e. organizational concepts do not come from perception, rather they come from rational sensing induction and guiding first principles, i.e., a Thomistic faculty psychology. We could say that inductive first principle High Concept, High Touch is not a matter of MIT's model of "observe, question, reassess, define, and communicate," rather it is wonder, inquiry, abstraction from sense particulars to craft knowledge, discovery of causative principles, and diffusion of craft knowledge throughout the organizational whole.

In this chapter, we have brought attention to a major issue in contemporary empirical studies in organizational psychology, i.e., the quest for the organizational soul. We see this new pursuit of the High Concept (Meaning) High Touch (sensemaking organization). Besides the authorities proposing this organizational viewpoint, there are, also, voices of highly influential executives for a greater and more committed organizational sense of a social-moral vision and soulfulness. For

---

[347] James L. BOWDITCH and Anthony F. BUONO, *A Primer on Organizational Behavior* (Hoboken: Wiley, 2008), 215

example, we hear this call to a vision of social purpose by Laurence FINK, the world's largest investor, who sends his missives to executive timed to the Global Davos Conference:

> Finance: Wall Street titan demands good deeds
>
> He plans to hold companies accountable for not just their financial performance but also their contribution to society. Laurence Fink, the founder and chief executive of investment firm Black Rock, wrote this week to more than 1,000 CEOs of global companies and declared that his firm, which manages more than $6 trillion in investments, will invest only in companies that "do more than makes profits." They must make a positive impact on society. Given that Fink has "the clout to make this kind of demand," the letter could prove to be a "watershed moment of Wall Street."[348]

Finally, we have examined the growing importance in empirical organizational psychology of leadership on the nature of sensemaking. Organizational sensemaking is extremely necessary "as cultural values change, new technologies and media, new forms of organization and altering employment patterns and new thinking in management contribute to the transformation of the workplace and changing realities of work."[349]

We, though, argue, in this chapter, for a premodern method of common sensemaking because it is by means of classical induction within the organizational whole and the grasping causative first principles embodied in the organizational culture that a common sensemaking is the best approach to executive direction and the drive to communicate, execute and motivate excellence. Without common sensemaking and guiding first principles, organizations become encapsulated in a rhetoric use of buzzwords such as *flexibility, market/customer orientation, flattening structures, managerial excellence, productivity, quality, retraining, participation,* and *creativity.* Within the all-pervasive discourse of "restructuring"

---

[348] Andrew Ross SORKIN, "Wall Street Titan Demands Good "Deeds, Andrew Ross Sorkin," *The Week* (January 26, 2018), 31.

[349] MIT Leadership Center, "Making a Difference by Making Sense" brochure.

employees continue to experience less and less meaning and satisfaction in their work—i.e., less soul.

Armand MAURER, one of the truly great Thomistic philosophers of the modern era, teaches this concept:

> Intellectual beings by nature, they grasp intuitively a multitude of truths in the unity of a single idea. In this respect they resemble God, who simply by knowing his essence, knows all things. Human reason, on the other hand, as the most imperfect of all intellects, must grasp unity in multiplicity rather than multiplicity in unity. Human knowledge begins in the senses which present reason with a vast variety of data; but in this multiplicity, it sees unity and thus gathers simple truths from it. At the end of its reasoning, therefore, the human mind approaches the angelic intellect in gathering up a multitude of truths in the unity of simple principles or ideas.
>
> Natural philosophy, he tells us [Aquinas], uses a method most in harmony with our natural way of knowing as rational beings. For this reason, its method is properly called rational. To begin with, this science deals with the changing sensible world, which is our first and most congenial object of knowledge: the one that our reason is best adapted to understand. It stays closest to this world in its changing and sensible character, and in the multiplicity of data it presents to us.[350]

One of the advantages of EHRINGER's study *Make Up Your Mind* is her existential phenomenological method of researching and constructing very descriptive profiles of entrepreneur executives as analyst, decision makers and strategist under conditions of stress and high risk taking. We will conclude this chapter by looking at one these entrepreneurs and his philosophy organizational guiding principles:

Brief Case Study: So, You Need Guiding Principles

A Successful Executive Entrepreneur

---

[350] Armand MAURER (Ed.), St. Thomas AQUINAS, *The Division and Methods of the Sciences* (Toronto: The Pontifical Institute of Mediaeval Studies,1968), xxxii-xxxiii.

I suspect that what I and most entrepreneurs do is make ourselves frantically busy [...] but [that works] to the detriment of our families. At home at night, in the shower in the morning, on the golf course on the weekend, sitting on the beach-while supposedly relaxing you're thinking about work.

I do most of [my abstract] thinking in the so-called off-hours. So, the reality is as an entrepreneur I work all the time. Personal time has become planning time. In spite of my good formal academic training, I've never developed a formal training or planning operation within my company.

Personal values are by far the biggest influence on my decisions. While money's important, it's more important to do a job well and have it reflect well on me. I think [this] is my personal insecurity more than anything else. But it's the driving factor. People who don't articulate a few core principles and stick with them [...] go by the wayside. You either find them out or get rid of them, or they aren't comfortable, and they disappear.

I've said to everybody, "Don't. ever make the short-term decision. Make your decisions based on something that you can live with a year from now—or two."[351]

My philosophy is that there aren't many single answers to things. There are an awful lot of areas where you can go either way and it probably isn't going to be the end of the world. I think my philosophy on the successful entrepreneur is that you need a couple of very basic principles that set you in a certain direction. You will be a much more successful leader if you stick with those than if you get yourself heavily involved in every little detailed decision.

I've always thought that Ronald Reagan was a successful president. He wasn't the brightest man that was ever the president of the United States, maybe one of the least bright. But, on an issue like taxes, he made up his mind that lower tax rates are better for people in general. When Reagan sat in a meeting-or, on a much smaller scale, when you are president of your own company-competing forces will come in with their arguments. And if your people are good, they will have very good arguments, so you need

---

[351] EHRINGER, *Make Up Your Mind*, 302–303.

guiding principles. Reagan was a successful president because he had a guiding principle. He wouldn't get confused with all the arguments. He'd simply say, when it was all said and done, does that mean more taxes? In business, we must do the same thing. My guiding principle was that I was going to be number one in my market. I picked a business that was very small, that required very little capital to get in, and that could quickly become a dominant force in the business.[352]

Comments: We will call the interviewee in EHRINGER's study "Mr. Smith." Mr. Smith had served in the Army. Even though he liked the military organization and especially the team aspect, he left military service for a business career. He started his business career as a management trainee, while, simultaneously earned an MBA and went to work for a large financing corporation. He noticed that he was facing in the corporate world the same issue that he faced in the military, "If I wanted to get where I wanted to be within the corporation—a high level management job—I was going to have to start moving. He discovered that the advantage in a large corporation is the getting to know people and possible deals that they talk about.

At the age of 38, he and two other contacts had the idea to start a real estate auction company. With new partners and knowledge of the real estate and financing market, they were able to start a highly successful entrepreneurial enterprise.

What is most interesting about Mr. Smith is that from his risk taking and self-directed, experiential learning of a specific subject matter (real estate auction business), *he came to the awareness as an executive leader of the absolute necessity of guiding principles, especially in moments of critical decision making and common sense making. So much so that he does not care to have employees on his team who cannot live by guiding principles i.e. there must be a diffusion of the guiding principle throughout the organizational whole.* From the perspective of Thomistic organizational psychology standpoint of "craft knowledge," it is said that by means of induction, he has come to know the *first propter quid principles necessary for organizational excellence.*[353]

---

[352] Ibid., 295.

[353] Ibid a summary of a case history interview and comments, 289-1295

5.

The Estimative Soul

The aim of this chapter is to explain one of the most indispensable concepts for an understanding and practice of organizational exemplar soulful leadership, i.e. the power and acts of the estimative soul. We bring focus to the critical importance of the estimative soul at all levels of organizational leadership. We explain the important development of the estimative sense powers and acts of the soul in confluence with practical reason, the habit of prudence and mastery of the emotions. It is this confluence of soulful faculties from the research of Peter A. Redpath that allows a formative Thomistic definition of estimative intelligence. It is the understanding of estimative intelligence that relates critically to the selection and development of organizational soulful leadership. Also, by means of definitions and case study applications we describe the nature of estimative intelligence under tense, highly threatening and chaotic situations. Also, we present a Thomistic faculty-behavioral-psychology that describes the nature of rational emotional behavior that drives out fear and stimulates hope in arduous individual and team organizational activities.

5.1 The Hierarchical-Heterarchical Organizational Tension

In chapter two, we examined the nature of dysfunctional executive leadership in terms of the small dark soul of leadership, meaning the reality of dysfunctional "toxic leadership" behavior. It was argued that, because it is grounded on a metaphysical-moral concept of leadership as opposed to an empirical organizational psychology grounded on a moral-value-neutral philosophy of leadership, a Thomistic organizational psychology is most suited to confront the issue of toxic, egocentric behavior.

In chapter three, we introduced the Thomistic understanding of a proper common sense, embedded habits of leadership, diffusion of leadership habits throughout an organizational whole, and the necessity of the function of a wise "enlightened" executive sensing power of the soul. Chapter three, however, is crucial because, therein, we developed a metaphysics of organization and its implication for the function of executive leadership. Based on a metaphysics of the generic nature of the organization, because it is grounded on a metaphysical-moral-concept of leadership as opposed to an empirical organizational psychology grounded on a moral-value neutral philosophy of leadership with a description of existential, executive, virtual leadership.

In chapters three and four we start to develop the metaphysics of organization and moral psychology of Aquinas from the Thomist Peter A. REDPATH. In a recent review of REDPATH, *The Moral Psychology of St. Thomas Aquinas: An Introduction to Ragamuffin Ethics*, Brian WELTER concisely and accurately describes REDPATH's Thomistic vision that we have applied to the executive function and diffusion of organization leadership.

> Western civilization lost its understanding of the nature of philosophy as an organizational psychology." By this he [Redpath] specifically means the lost "understanding of the nature of metaphysics, ethics, and science *as habits of leadership excellence of the human soul.*" Hierarchy plays a central role in Redpath's vision, starting from the "chief end" of creation, an end "that unites and harmonizes some multitude into being parts of the whole." Ultimately, for St. Thomas, "the genus called 'creation' is the generating principle of all other genera and species.[354]

It is in chapter four that we presented two of the major contemporary issues of organizational science and psychology, i.e., the emerging visions of the

---

[354] Brian WELTER, "Book Review: Peter A. Redpath, The Moral Psychology of St. Thomas Aquinas: An Introduction to Ragamuffin Ethics," *Studia Gilsoniana* 6(4), October-December 2017, 634–635.

organization and the importance of the discipline of leadership and sensemaking. We point out that the emerging change of organizational vision is fundamentally a change in the structure of the postindustrial organization. For example, the issue of the structural coordination in post bureaucratic organizations is addressed in depth by Katherine C. KELLOGG, Wanda J. ORLIKOWSKI, and JoAnne YATES, "Life in the Trading Zone: Structuring Coordination Across Boundaries in Post Bureaucratic Organizations."

> The emerging organizational form is comprised of flat organizational structures with distributed accountability, decentralized decision making, and multiple evaluative principles. In these emerging heterarchical organizations, workers with different functional skills and occupations work on short term projects that represent collaborative efforts. Consequently, there are shifting centers of expertise, accountability, relationships, roles, boundaries, work process, composition, performance criteria and watchword executive attitude and authority.[355]

---

[355] Katherine C. KELLOGG, Wanda J. ORLIKOWSKI, and JoAnne YATES, "Life in the Trading Zone: Structuring Coordination Across Boundaries in Post Bureaucratic Organizations," *Organization Science* (January-February 2006), 23.

Table 1: Distinguishing Features of Hierarchical and Heterarchical Organization

Organizational Dimension	Hierarchical Organization	Heterarchical Organization
Form of organizing	Permanent Hierarchy	Temporary work Team
Decision authority	Centralized	Decentralized
Accountability	Fixed, top-down	Shifting, distributed
Relations	Vertical, dependent	Horizontal,
Division of labor and roles	Stable, specialized	interdependent
Boundaries	Clearly specified,	Dynamic, blurred
Work process	persistent	Fuzzy and permeable
Composition	Routinized,	Improvised, flexible,
Performance criteria	standardized, rule-based	participative
Watchword	Homogeneous	Heterogeneous
	Established singular	Emergent, multiple
	Stability, inertia	Speed, adaptability

Furthermore, in chapter four, we also brought attention to the research of PINK, MITROFF and DENTON about the growing desire for organizations to appreciate and focus to a certain extent on the spiritual and moral needs of employees impacted by the demands of a corporate existence. MIT Sloan School of Management, aware of the organizational structural changes and psychology of leadership, has seen the need to define leadership proficiency in organizational sensemaking as essential in the emerging clash between hierarchical and heterarchical organization, as seen in the above Table 1 of distinguishing features. In chapter three, we establish, based on REDPATH's Aristotelian-Thomistic metaphysics of organization, that there is always within the generic nature of any organization, based on the principle of the equality of inequality, a need for the function of executive leadership. Therefore, an organization will always have a core structure of a command and control function. From the perspective of a Thomistic organizational psychology, it is really a matter of the nature and responsibility of executive leadership to establish a psychological-moral manner of leadership compatible, if necessary, with a heterarchical organizational culture, or in many emerging cutting-edge organizations where a hybrid hierarchical-heterarchical structure seems to evolve.

Having established some fundamental concepts and principles on the nature and need of a Thomistic organizational psychology, we continue in this chapter to develop a Thomistic organizational faculty-behavioral-psychology as best suited to respond to the hierarchical-heterarchical tension. Furthermore, we will continue to advance the argument that the solution to the hierarchical-heterarchical dialectic is a rediscovery of a premodern metaphysics of organization and an Aristotelian-Thomistic faculty psychosomatic behavioral psychology of executive character and the diffusion of leadership.

5.1.1 *Why Thomistic Organizational Behavioral Psychology and the Hierarchical- Heterarchical Tension*

We are proposing a Thomistic behavioral psychology of the function of executive leadership and the diffusion of leadership throughout the organization. We have chosen in this dissertation to address the issue of the executive function of leadership because, as established in chapter three, the approach to the issue of organization leadership is grounded on a metaphysical organizational principle of equality of inequality. Consequently, it follows that a philosophy and psychology of leadership must come from the executive level of the organization. The evidence from multiple studies in organizational science and leadership seems clearly, at the risk of simplistic reductionism, to focus on two issues: 1) where the modern bureaucratic organization was rigid, the post bureaucratic organization is flexible, and 2) where the modern bureaucratic organization is structured on stable "directed-order," the post bureaucratic organization is structured on a "flexible emergent order."[356] It is the IBM Systems Action Research division that conducted research in the area of national and organizational strategy. Some of the work was funded by the U.S. government through DARPA (Defense Advanced Research Project Agency) interested in new approaches to supporting policy making. It is action research, defined as grounding organizational theory in contextual exploration, emphasizing participation and embracing change, and it resulted in the following *Cynefin* framework for sense-making.

The Cynefin framework

The name *Cynefin* is a Welsh word whose literal translation into English as habitat or place fails to do it justice. It is more properly understood as the place of our multiple affiliations, the sense that we all, individually and collectively, have many roots, cultural, religious, geographic, tribal, and so forth. We can never be fully aware of the nature of those affiliations, but they profoundly influence what we are. The name seeks to remind us that all human interactions are strongly influenced and frequently determined by the patterns of our multiple experiences, both through the direct influence of personal experience and through collective experience expressed as stories

The Cynefin framework originated in the practice of knowledge management as a means of distinguishing between formal and informal communities, and as a means of talking about the interaction of both with structured processes and uncertain conditions. It has now outgrown its application in knowledge management, having been in use by our group for several years in consultancy and action research in knowledge management, strategy, management, training, cultural change, policymaking, product development, market creation, and branding. We are now beginning to apply it to the areas of leadership, customer relationship management, and supply chain management.[357]

---

[356] C.F. KURTZ and D.J. SNOWDEN, "The new dynamics of strategy: Sense-making in a complex and complicated world," *IBM Systems Journal* 42(3), 2003, 465.

[357] Ibid., 467.

What is most pertinent to a Thomistic organizational psychology is the appreciation that the *Cynefin* framework is constructed on an Aristotelian concept of causation. In their method of science, order and epiphenomena, the researchers state:

> Aristotle defined four types of cause: the material (what you are made of, your muscles and organs), the efficient (how you came to be, the fact that your parents gave birth to you), the formal (your type, your species), and the final (your function, your life itself, your place in the universe). He believed that to understand an event or entity, one had to consider all of these factors in the particular, the mysterious as well as the ordered. As others have pointed out, the focus of Western thinking post Kant on efficient cause only is to the detriment of knowledge.[358]

KURTZ and SNOWDEN contend in the age of hierarchical-heterarchical tension, organizational science has turned to a new awareness of complexity science and the dynamics of contrary states of "directed order" and "emergent order." They maintained that KANT separated things we can know empirically from things that are the province of God, and thereby helped to section of all but efficient causes to epiphenomena that could be safely ignored. Fueled by the positivism of COMTE and the advances in physics and biology a social science (sociology) developed it held that it was theoretically possible to discover laws like those of physics which could explain the behavior of people in societies. Because of the Kantian-Comte impact on the science of society they describe the growth of a management science incapable of understanding, let alone responding, to the issue of organizational chaos and emerging organization:

> The development of management science, from stopwatch carrying Taylorists to business process reengineering, was rooted in the belief that systems were ordered; it was just a matter of time and resources before the relationships between cause and effect could be discovered. The case study approach of many M.B.A. programs and the desire for precise recommend-

---

[358] Ibid., 463.

dations from policy teams and external consultants perpetuate the underlying assumption of universal order. Good leadership is linked to certain competences that (it is claimed) can be mapped and identified, and then replicated. The desire for order can even lead people to accept completely abhorrent working conditions and political structures simply to avoid "chaos" (a tendency exploited by dictators from Pisistratus to Hitler and beyond). All of these approaches and perceptions do not accept that there are situations in which the lack of order is not a matter of poor investigation, inadequate resources, or lack of understanding, but is a priori the case—and not necessarily a bad thing, either.[359]

Cynefin is a sophisticated framework based on many years of action research and implementation with various organizational clients since the 80s. It is based on the science of complex systems and chaos theory as applied to organizations. Complexity science and chaos theory deal with the phenomena in nature and social organizations, i.e., as the genus (organizational whole) redefines itself for adaptation.

> In order to exist, organisations must be able to reproduce their specific organisational dynamics and at the same time to evolve and shape themselves in a vital structural coupling with the ever-changing dynamics of their environments. We refer to this crucial survival process of the interlocked adjustment of internal chaotic dynamics to the chaotic dynamics of the environment as: organisational autopoiesis. [...] Organisational autopoiesis displays many of the key characteristics required of nonlinear dynamic systems. One of these key characteristics is the lack of linear cause-effect relationships.[360]

---

[359] Ibid., 463–464.

[360] Vladimir DIMITROV and Lloyd FELL, "Autopoiesis in Organizations," http://www.biosong.org/Dimtrov.pdf. According to the authors, the main characteristics of organizational autopoiesis are the following: 1) sensitivity to initial conditions: when in chaotic dynamics small, seemingly insignificant decisions can cause large effects; it is called extreme sensitivity to initial conditions, also known as the "butterfly effect." 2) Ibid., 1-4 :

This framework has major implications for executive leadership and various levels of organizational leadership because, as a rule, decisions are not made in the same set of circumstances under which previous decisions have been made, either by the same organization or by more organizations.

What happens in the IBM *Cynefin* framework is the dependence on organizational complexity and chaos theory points to the incapability of traditional modern organizations use of a Kantian style of efficient causality sensemaking in a complex and complicated world. Also, the research method deployed in the *Cynefin*, and its continual field applications and modification of techniques in

---

Strange attractors: In its everyday manifestation, chaotic organizational dynamics are attracted by "islands" of relative stability (called strange attractors) within the sea of chaos. These islands of dynamic stability represent specific kinds of settled organizational activity (for instance, activity toward technological innovation, market share expansion, introduction of new markets, new products etc.). The strange attractor represents the outward manifestation of organizational autopoiesis. 3) Non-linear Dynamic: In nonlinear chaotic systems, one cannot pass through the same coordinates twice. In organizational management, it means that a) Decisions that have led to beneficial results in the past will not necessarily lead to beneficial results in the future, b) A constant innovation process is necessary in order to remain successful. 4) Fractal Structure: In their chaotic domain, organizations should sustain a fractal structure. For instance, several layers of similar structural patterns and configurations should be observed at the overall organizational level, at sub-organizational levels, at group levels and at the individual. What is essential is that it does not become simpler when one goes from a higher to a lower level. The whole of the organizational structure consists of whole of sub-organizational structures. The fractal structure is vital for realization of the reproductive mechanism embedded in the process of organizational autopoiesis. 5) Edge of Chaos: When in a critical stage, organizational behavior is thrown into an out-of-equilibrium zone, a special zone between order and disorder, where emergence of new qualitative states may take place, and transformation of the organization may occur. 6) Self-organization: The turbulence of non-linear dynamic produces vortices (like whirlpools in troubled waters or tornados in a fierce sky). Each vortex is impregnated with energy, out of which a self-organizing (sucking) force may emerge. The self-organizing force of the vortex cannot appear, unless the participating stream-either masses of running water or turbulent air (flows of irritating ideas in the human brain, burning emotions in the human heart, etc.) are both: (i) permanently in motion (i.e., out of equilibrium), and (ii) interacting intensively with each other.

organizational consultancies, is based on the principles and methods of complexity and chaos theory. Organizational complexity science deals with three strands of concepts applied to organizational dynamics: 1) chaos theory unfolding and enfolded future, 2) chaos theory as a formative teleology and 3) dissipative structure theory: constructing an unknowable future.[361] The *Cynefin* framework is fundamentally based on the assumption that chaos has a continuous impact on an organization that requires an organizational formative teleological sensemaking leadership, as we see expressed in the *Cynefin* position paper on the dynamics of sense-making in a complex and complicated world:

> Complexity science. A new awareness of the ancient counterpart to order began over a century ago with Poincaré and several others and has surged in recent decades. In fact, there is a fascinating kind of order in which no director or designer is in control, but which emerges through the interaction of many entities. Emergent order has been found in many natural phenomena: bird-flocking behavior can be simulated on a computer through three simple rules; termites produce elegant nests through the operation of simple behaviors triggered by chemical traces; each snowflake is a unique pattern arising from the interactions of water particles during freezing. The patterns that form are not controlled by a directing intelligence; they are self-organizing. The new science of complexity spawned by these findings is interdisciplinary, touching fields from mathematics to evolution to economics to meteorology to telecommuni-

---

[361] Ralph D. STACEY, Douglas GRIFFIN and Patricia SHAW, *Complexity and Management: Fad or Radical Challenge to Systems Management* (London and New York: Routledge, Taylor & Francis Group, 2000), 85. See ibid., 27: "Organizational formative teleology is subordinated in the sense that the identity of the organism, its final form or mature state, is pre-determined and the system moves toward it. The final form is already contained in the formative self-organizing process of interaction itself. The parts are only functional or causal parts inasmuch as they form the whole and the whole must therefore in a sense be given before one can decide what is a part and what is not. In this sense Formative teleology is subordinate to the formative casualty of self-organization; subordinate in the sense that it is 'contained' in the formative process."

cations. In the domain of emergent order, the goal "to predict (and thereby control) the behavior of systems not yet studied (but similar to those that have been studied) under conditions not yet extant and in time periods not yet experienced" is difficult if not impossible to achieve—but other goals are achievable.[362]

Executive leadership, living in the age of complexity and chaos, attention to existing on the edge of chaos and the dynamics of self-organization is critical. It means that

> One step further the organization falls into deep chaos in which it may be overwhelmed with change. One step back and he organization is in the region of order. However, being in order, the organization is not able to adapt sufficiently to remain viable. It is just on the frontier between these two regions at the edge of chaos where a delicate, dynamic balance between random chaos and rigid order can emerge. This state is impregnated with the seeds of innovative transformations.[363]

There is an important distinction between the *Cynefin* framework of organizational dynamics and a Thomistic framework. *Cynefin* action study looks upon organizations as structures, where a Thomistic metaphysics looks upon organizations in terms of a genus, i.e., the generic nature of an organizational

---

[362] KURTZ and SNOWDEN, "The new dynamics of strategy," 464.

[363] DIMITROV and Lloyd FELL, "Autopoiesis in Organizations." Sally J GOERNER, in "Chaos and the Evolving Universe," *World Futures General Evolution Studies* (8), 1988, provides an excellent description of the phenomena of complexity and self-organization: "In a recursive, completely interwoven world, whatever one does propagates outward returns, recycles and comes back in a completely unpredictable form. We can never fully know to what results our action leads. We take action; the action can have a very potent shaping effect. Then we relax the drive to control and allow the process to unfold—the process learns, shapes, and changes itself through all its inseparable components, not under the direction of one of them only. Together with overall change in the process, we also change, almost unnoticeably, without any strain."

whole. The IBM *Cynefin* grounded on a complexity-chaos meta theory of order and un-order built a four-quadrant cross boundary construct model of four organizational domains: the ordered domain of known causes and effects, the ordered domain of knowable causes and effects, the un-ordered domain of complex relationships and the un-ordered domain of chaos. An in-depth explanation of these domains and the practical application and methodology is beyond the purpose of this thesis, except to mention it is a complexity-chaos construct that applies to an organization where it is defined in terms of its capability of maintaining a system equilibrium and self-organizing creativity in adapting to complex and chaotic environments. It is a construct that is designed to apply to a wide range of organizations, e.g., from a manufacturing to a software entrepreneurial organization, or a profit to nonprofit, or government to religious institutions.

The advantage of the *Cynefin* construct it is that it studies organizations as dynamic systems from the perspective of leadership.

> People have a high capacity for awareness of largescale patterns because of their ability to communicate abstract concepts through language, and, more recently, because of the social and technological infrastructure that enables them to respond immediately to events half a world away.[364]

Their basic methodology is to use various tactics to draw focused attention, e.g., narrative stories surrounding issues, oral histories, collected anecdotes, published reports, historical documents, as people construct composite fables to express issues to sensitive subjects, interview people to analyze the history of the organization by going backward. It is basically, as presented in the previous chapter, a method of inductive sensemaking. It is not, however, a method of Thomistic inductive methodology that is dedicated to the revealing of organizational first principles. The *Cynefin* complexity method is focused on an organizational whole from the perspective of the essential opposition in the organization whole between the dynamic opposition of the desired order and emergent order. In terms of executive leadership, it means that the organization

---

[364] KURTZ and SNOWDEN, "The new dynamics of strategy," 465.

must function as a learning organization continuously aware of the implication of internal and external randomness, i.e., the executive balance desired order and emergent order (randomness).

5.1.2 Emergent Order, Open Systems, and the Learning Organization

It is a Thomistic metaphysics of organization and a psychology of leadership that is most equipped to address the issue of organizational opposition of desired order and emergent order which is really a matter of the quest for perfection within an organizational whole. It is the quantum physicist Valerio SCARANI who, in *The Universe Would not be Perfect Without Randomness: A Quantum Physicist's Reading of Aquinas*, discusses fortune and chance (emergent order) in the *Summa Contra Gentiles*, "It would be contrary to [...] the perfection of things, if there would be no chance events."[365] Aquinas accommodates both an all-powerful God and free human beings. According to SCARANI, along with Aquinas's general observation that all the beings we perceive are limited in their being, he strikes a surprisingly modern insight that not only human free will but the whole of creation, including its material aspect, possess relative autonomy from God. This autonomy is to be the foundation for his discussion of fortune and chance.[366] In terms of an organizational whole, there is always the opposition of desired order and emergent order. SCARANI rephrases Aquinas in his own words:

1) If nothing rare would happen, we would conclude to necessity. Thus "fortune and chance" are the manifestation of contingency, which is God's respect of the autonomy of created beings.

2) The second argument combines finality and finiteness: all beings act for an end, but finite beings may fail with regard to the intended end, thus bringing about unintended effects.

---

[365] AQUINAS, *Summa Contra Gentiles* III, C. 74.

[366] Valerio SCARANI, "The Universe Would Not Be Perfect Without Randomness: A Quantum Physicist's Reading of Aquinas," *Proceedings of the Conference Quantum* (Vienna, 19–22 June 2014), 168–169.

3) The third argument is different: it is the classic *concursus causarum*. Since God does not determine everything and each being has its own autonomy it is possible that an initially independent causal chains collide to produce an unexpected effect. The example of Aquinas is more than clear: "For example, the discovery of a debtor, by a man who has gone to market to sell something, happens because the debtor also went to the market."

4) In yet another chance of perspective, the finite beings are no longer considered as agents, but as beings, whose properties are not all necessary. The actual text, a scholastic demonstration, sounds very convoluted to us; so, let me try my own example. A given woman is a human being, is tall, is dressed in blue, and is a physicist. "While being human" is obviously essential, the other features look accidental and uncorrelated among them—but who knows, maybe there is a deep common cause for all the features of this woman? Aquinas argues that against such a higher causality: it is proper of finite beings to have indeed many accidental features.

5) The fifth argument has some flavor of the second and the third: the power of a finite cause is necessarily finite and therefore cannot extend to all things that can happen.[367]

---

[367] Ibid., 171–172. See AQUINAS, *Summa Contra Gentiles* III, C. 74: "[1] It is obvious from what we have shown that divine providence reaches out to singulars that are generable and corruptible. [2] Except for the fact of their contingency, and the fact that many of them come about by chance and fortune, it does not seem that providence is inapplicable to them. For it is only on this basis that they differ from incorruptible things, and the universal natures of corruptible things, to which providence does apply, as people say. But contingency is not incompatible with providence, nor are chance or fortune or voluntary action, as we have shown. Therefore, nothing prohibits providence from also applying to these things, just as it does to incorruptible and universal things. [3] Again, if God does not exercise providence over these singulars, this is either because He does not know them, or because He is not able to do so, or because He does not wish to take care of them. Now, it cannot be said that God does not know singulars; we showed above that God does possess knowledge of them. Nor can it be said that God is unable to take care of them, for His power is infinite, as we proved above. Nor, indeed, are these singulars incapable of being governed,

From reflections on primarily the *Summa Contra Gentiles* SCARANI explores, as a quantum physicist, the question of contingency and concludes his paper with this statement:

---

since we see them governed by the use of reason in the case of men, and by means of natural instinct in the case of bees and many brute animals that are governed by some sort of natural instinct. Nor, in fact, can it be said that God does not wish to govern them, since His will is universally concerned with every good thing, and the good of things that are governed lies chiefly in the order of governance. Therefore, it cannot be said that God takes no care of these singulars. [4] Besides, all secondary causes, by the fact of being causes, attain the divine likeness, as is evident from what we said above. Now, we find one thing in common among causes that produce something: they take care of their products. Thus, animals naturally nourish their young. So, God takes care of the things of which He is the cause. Now, He is the cause even of these particular things, as is obvious from our previous statements." So, He does take care of them. [5] Moreover, we showed above that God does not act in regard to created things by a necessity of His nature, but through His will and intellect. Now, things done by intellect and will are subject to the care of a provident agent, for that is what such care seems to consist in: the fact that certain things are managed through understanding. And so, the things that result from His action are subject to divine providence. But we showed before that God works through all secondary causes, and that all their products may be traced back to God as their cause; so, it must be that the things that are done among singulars are His works. Therefore, these singulars, and also their motions and operations, come under the scope of divine providence. [6] Furthermore, foolish is the providence of a person who does not take care of the things needed by the things for which he does care. But it is obvious that, if all particular things vanished, their universals could not endure. So, if God be only concerned with universals, and if He be entirely negligent of these singulars, then His providence will be foolish and imperfect. [7] However, suppose someone says that God takes care of these singulars to the extent of preserving them in being, but not in regard to anything else; this is utterly impossible. In fact, all other events that occur in connection with singulars are related to their preservation or corruption. So, if God takes care of singulars as far as their preservation is concerned, He takes care of every contingent event connected with them."

Message in an Old Bottle

In these notes from the window, I tried to grasp Aquinas' effort of rationalization. It's a message in a bottle from a cultural world that is no longer ours: in particular it would be grossly anachronistic to read Aquinas as a precursor of quantum physics. But we are allowed to read the message and derive some inspiration for our times.

Aquinas' study is very far from a naïve god-of-the-gaps argument, which would run: "there are things I cannot predict, the only possible explanation is to invoke the intervention of God or some other spirit." Chance and fortune are neither God's doing nor the devil's: they are the manifestation of the fitness of created beings, and of the autonomy that God's providence gave them. Since this autonomy is a sign of God's respect for his creation, chance and fortune are to be considered positive realities.[368]

In chapter three, we argued, based on the principle of the virtual quantity of the organizational whole, led and inspired by executive leadership and the diffusion of said leadership, that an organization must continuously strive for the perfection of the genus. We are giving attention to the issue of AQUINAS's teaching on perfection and randomness. On the topic of organizational leadership and the dynamics of desired order and emergent order, we will also examine AQUINAS's position that divine providence does not exclude contingency from things. AQUINAS is of importance because it is argued that a Thomistic organizational behavioral psychology of executive leadership is most suited to understand and respond to the opposition of desired and emergent order and the dynamics of variation in an organizational whole as "open systems."

It has been shown that the operation of providence, whereby God works in things, does not exclude secondary causes, but, rather, is fulfilled by them, as far as they act by God's power. Now certain effects are called necessary or contingent in regard to proximate causes, but not in regard to remote causes [...]. So, since there are many things among proximate causes that may be

---

[368] Ibid., 173.

defective, but not all effects subject to providence will be necessary, but a good many are contingent.[369]

In this passage, it does seem that AQUINAS is also compatible with the science of systems and the nature of variation and causation within an organizational system. As mentioned previously, DEMING in the 1980s introduced the quality movement to American profit and non-profit organizations. Much of DEMING's extraordinary success as a consultant to Japanese and American industry was his insistence on executive leadership understanding of the science of variation and the control of variation in the output of products, goods, and services. For Deming, the function of executive leadership is to lead by means of profound knowledge. Deming's profound knowledge is comprised of four parts: 1) Appreciation for a system, 2) knowledge about variation, 3) theory of knowledge, and 4) psychology."[370] For DEMING, leadership requires knowledge about variation: "Life is variation and there will always be, between people, in output, in service, in product. What is the variation trying to tell us about a process, and about the people that work it?"[371] In organizational systems science, variation is inevitable change in the output or result of a system or process because all systems vary over time. Two types of variation are (1) common cause, which is inherent in a system, (2) special cause which is caused by special events in the system indicating the system is moving from a state of statistical control above or below control limits. Without an understanding and focus on variation two costly mistakes are made in attempts to maintain the harmony of the system:

Mistake 1. To react to an outcome as if it came from a special cause, when it actually came from common causes of variation.

Mistake 2. To treat an outcome as if it came from common causes of variation, when actually it came from a special cause.[372]

---

[369] AQUINAS, *Summa Contra Gentiles* III, C. 72.

[370] DEMING, *The New Economics*, 98.

[371] Ibid., 93.

[372] Ibid., 99.

Alberto STRUMIA writes in *The Sciences and the Fullness of Rationality*, as a Thomistic mathematical physicist, about interdisciplinary investigations comparing Aristotelian-Thomistic logic and metaphysics with the recent problems involving the theory of complexity, formal ontology, and the problems of foundations. He confronts the major issue facing modern science (natural and social) as one of foundations.

> Today the problem of foundations is the principal problem of the sciences, considered as a form of knowledge. Here I am not speaking of the ethical problems linked to the technical and practical applications of science. This is another discussion, and an extremely important one, but it would bring us far from our topic. Furthermore, it cannot be addressed on steady ground until we have resolved the problems of rationality and of science as theory. The sciences are the fields today that show us the need for foundations. These foundations guarantee the sciences the very possibility of existing and of progressing as sciences. Historically, one would have spoken of the "metaphysical basis" of science; today rather one prefers to speak of a "theory of foundations". However, the problem is essentially the same.[373]

STRUMIA is a mathematical physicist who explores the need for an Aristotelian-Thomistic meta science. Basically, his philosophy of modern science is that with a science without a metaphysical foundation "everyone can say 'whatever he wants' about 'anything' and maintain he is right."[374] In science, he writes:

> Knowledge is reduced to facts whose value is merely instrumental, technical—and therefore it seems impossible to provide a foundation for science itself as a demonstrative form of knowledge for everyone; instead it

---

[373] Alberto STRUMIA, *The Sciences and The Fullness of Rationality*, trans. By Philip LARREY and Peter WAYMEL (Aurora: The Davies, 2009), 6–7.

[374] Ibid., 2.

seems we can only create technical instruments that become pure instruments of power.[375]

In his thesis on the need for fullness of rationality and science, he examines changes in the conceptions of science, concerning aspects of the epistemological reflections of the 20th century, reflections on science and truth, reflections on the problem of the foundations of mathematics, and most important for purposes of our present discussion, he addresses the emergence of complexity: whole and the parts. In chapter seven, "The Emergence of Complexity the Whole and the Parts," he treats the same issue, as a Thomistic mathematical physicist and meta-scientist, of the one and the many and also equality and inequality within a genus.

If we take the problem from the point of view of the whole as a complex structure, as does STRUMIA:[376]

1) The complex object presents properties and behaviors that cannot be explained (deduced) solely through the study of its component parts, but which represent something new that requires the consideration of the whole, an entity that cannot be broken down.

2) Today the term "information" is often used, which recalls the Aristotelian term "form." We must not be hasty to view them as identical, even if the term "form" has, in fact, entered into current epistemological language. In the Aristotelian context, one would say that the whole possesses a form that makes it one, with new properties not present in the various parts. Such is the case in all complex structures of physics (non-linear systems), and above all chemistry (molecules) and biology of living creatures.

If, again with STRUMIA, we take the problem from the point of view of the part, we must consider the dynamics of open systems:[377]

---

[375] Ibid.
[376] Ibid., 144–146.
[377] Ibid., 152–153.

1) If the question of the whole and parts, from the point of view of the whole, deals with the structure of the systems considered (of whatever nature they may be: physical, biological, etc.) and we take the part, considered as a system, now the main aspect to study no longer regard the internal structure, but its relations with the exterior, the rest of the whole, the environment. A system in relation with the exterior is called (in the language of science) an "open system." Its behavior in relation with environment is its dynamics [...] the only future for mathematics and logic is that of renouncing the myth of "closed" formal systems such as the axiomatic systems and returning to work on an open logical system in analogy to open physical systems (dissipative structures), the object of the theory of complexity.

2) The introduction of new axioms in the course of work is what characterizes the concept of an "open" logical system. It is clear, furthermore, that the introduction of new axioms cannot be arbitrary, and that the invention cannot be reduced to a question of simple creativity, to a merely psychological question

3) There remains, therefore, only one possibility: that the formal method is not the only method of Mathematics (or logic). In such case the introduction of new axioms will be linked to a specific logical method: the analytical method, [...] In this sense, logical systems are no longer limited to the use of the pure axiomatic method but will include in themselves, as a fundamental ingredient for the introduction of new axioms, the analytical method typical of pre-modern classical logic and its characteristic inferential procedures (induction, abduction, abstraction, analogy).

In the previous chapter, we put forth a method of common sensemaking, induction and establishing first principles as method of observation, a collection of thick data, and testing. We now add to the method of classical induction some of the IBM *Cynefin* inductive methods that give a more complete definition to inductive gathering of thick data, i.e., narrative stories surrounding issues, oral histories, collected anecdotes, published reports, historical documents, as people construct composite fables to express issues to sensitive subjects, interview people to analyze the history of the organization by going backward. A Thomistic organizational psychology of soulful leadership is not interested in logical axioms; rather it searches for first principles of leadership within the organizational whole that amplifies the perfection of the organizational whole. It is these first principles by means of a diffusion of leadership, character, knowledge sharing, and dialogue that individual and team participation increases in virtual intensity.

In this chapter, we have added to the argument from the IBM study, the physicist Valerio SCARANI, and the mathematical physicist Alberto STRUMIA because we argue that a Thomistic organizational psychology is not a study on the psychological traits of a leader. It is psychology of the functions of executive leadership, but it is a psychology grounded on an Aristotelian-Thomistic metaphysics of organization. In terms of contemporary organizational psychology, it is based on a meta-psychology of organization that makes it most compatible with the movement toward hierarchical-heterarchical organizations because it is an organizational psychology most suited for the basic tension in an organization of desired order and emerging order.

5.2 Emergent Organizational Leadership Behavior, Estimative Intelligence and Attention

Thus far, we have argued that the framework of a Thomistic organizational behavioral psychology is the most suitable for the global forces of change and the implications facing modern organizations. A Thomistic framework looks upon the contemporary organization as in two basic contraries within the emerging organization, i.e., 1) hierarchical-heterarchical tension and 2) the issue of desired order and emerging order. Again, we return to the research of IBM systems division that has identified five forces that are generally predicted to emerge and create pivotal change in society, business, work, and new styles of leadership in profit and non-profit organizations. To give more definition to this forecast we list the five forces:

1) Exponential pattern of technological change: Disruptions through break- throughs and rapid adoption of new technology will lead to respond by faster and more adaptation to rapid reinvention. The workforce will drive this force through their behaviors and preferences, but it will also bring job loss and skill obsolescence. This will lead to continuous worker adaptation to new models of work and organization.

2) Social and organizational reconfiguration: As the workforce exerts more control over how work is accomplished, their increased autonomy and decision-making authority will make the workplace more power-balanced and less authoritative, and structure more through social networks and less through hierarchy. Work relationships will be more project-based and less exclusively employment-based, and the notion of workers will join or engage with the organization based on aligned purposes rather than filling a job. Organizations will tap more diverse avenues for sourcing and engaging talent that extend beyond traditional employment.

3) A truly connected world: information will be more abundant, richer, and more available to everyone. Work will be accomplished from anywhere, creating a truly global talent ecosystem. New media will enable increasingly seamless global and real-time communication, creating much faster ideation and product development, go-to-market strategies that are more divers, and shorter product/strategy durations. Organizational reputation becomes a pivotal currency and work markets and can be enhanced or destroyed in real time.

4) All inclusive, more diverse talent market: Multiple generations will increasingly participate as workers, today's minority segments will become majorities, older individuals will work longer, and work will be seamlessly distributed around the globe through 24/7 operations. Organizations that win will develop new employment contracts and hone new leadership styles and worker engagement approaches to address the varied cultural preferences in policies, practices, work design, rewards, and benefits.

5) Human and machine collaborations: Analytics, algorithms, and automation will become increasingly adept at enhancing productivity and human decisions. Big data will be used to access knowledge, gain insights, and uncover deeper connections. An increasing array of tasks and work will be automated, increasing the pace of discovery and reducing the half-life of knowledge. Organizations will evolve from considering "people versus machines" to optimally designing tasks that people and computers successfully share[378]

The interface of humans and artificial intelligence will lead to harder, faster, and smarter work, especially making faster and smarter market/sales, customer services and operational decisions. Reading this list of forces on hierarchical-heterarchical structure of present and future organizations obviously will place heavy demands on the function of executive leadership and the work force, e.g., adaptation to rapid reinvention, autonomy and decision making authority, less authoritative structures, more through social networks and less through hierarchy, seamless global and real time communication, much faster idea and product development, and an evolving embryonic relationship between worker and machine. We will call these the human, strategic and structural demands of the Hierarchical-Heterarchical Organizational Contrariety (H-HOC). We believe that the H-HOC will require new styles of executive, team, and administrative leadership.

Furthermore, based on Alberto STRUMIA, the H-HOC will require a science of complexity that deploys a premodern classical methodology of induction abduction, abstraction and especially analogy. Given the intellectual and emotional challenges of the H-HOC organizational milieu, it is highly questionable that the leadership education of schools of business, management, finance, and engineering are adequate for the task. Again, H-HOC will require a return to a premodern organizational psychology. As REDPATH writes:

---

[378] Barbara ELSBERG, Teresa ROCHE, Susan LOVERGAN, "Emergent Leadership. Executive Summary, Five Forces of Change, Emerging Trends in Leadership Development," CHREATE, June 2016, 3.

Loss of an understanding of the nature of philosophical metaphysics and ethics as essential means for inculcating with maximum *intensity principles of leadership within the psychological makeup of leaders is, in fact, a chief cause of the present civilization decline, anarchy of the West.* Centuries ago, Western civilization lost its understanding of the nature of philosophy as an organizational psychology. With that loss, the West also lost its understanding of the natures of metaphysics, ethics, and science *as habits of leadership excellence of the human soul:* acts of organizational excellence that human beings generate, cause, through acquired habits existing within innately possessed power of the human soul.[379]

In business school, students in their marketing courses are introduced to the basic marketing mix of the four P's: a product, price, place, and promotion. To have a market there must be a product, good or service, sold at the proper price, with the proper distribution channel and properly promoted. This mix applies to any organization of any size and it applies to profit or non-profit organizations. The four P's are known as the internal factors of the marketing mix because they are under the control of organizational leadership. There are also the external environmental factors that impact the strategic implementation of the market mix that are not under organizational executive control, i.e., social, cultural, legal, political, environmental, and technological resources. In terms of the external factors it is the function of executive leadership to scan continuously the environment for threat and opportunities that may impact the organization in a positive or negative way. Since the 80s a more sophisticated method of SWOT impact analysis of internal/external environmental forces has developed, note environmental is used loosely as a set of forces outside the organization. As is common knowledge, SWOT is an environment competitive matrix analysis of an organization's strengths, weaknesses, opportunities, and threat in terms of four competitive elements, i.e., organizational strengths, weakness, opportunities, and threats.

---

[379] REDPATH, *The Moral Psychology of St. Thomas*, 22.

Table 2: SWOT Analysis

Strengths	Weaknesses	Opportunities	Threats
What does your organization do better than your competitors?	What does your organization need to improve?	What market trends lead to increased sales?	What are the advantages that competitors have over your organization?

- Strengths: Internal attributes and resources that support a successful outcome.
- Weaknesses: Internal attributes and resources that work against a successful outcome.
- Opportunities: External factors that the entity can capitalize on or use to its advantage.
- Threats: External factors that could jeopardize the entity's success[380]

The SWOT methodology is a tool used by profit and non-profit organizations for strategic planning. We mention it here not just as a tool for the purpose of strategic planning, rather we would describe it as a component of the premodern inductive method of gathering varied thick quantitative and qualitative data for the purpose of knowledge of first principles in highly evolving organizational environments constantly impacted by the five forces identified in the above IBM study. In terms of a Thomistic organizational psychology of executive leadership, it means that the attitude of executive attention to SWOT-like forces and the estimate impact on the equilibrium of desired order and emergent organizational order is critical. Consequently, two types of leadership behavior are required, i.e. the habit of estimative behavior and the habit of attention. Before we define the habit of organizational estimative behavior and the habit of attention, we will begin

---

[380] SWOT, ANALYSIS STRENGTHS WEAKNESSES OPPORTUNITIES AND THREATS ANALYSIS, searchcio.techtarget.com

with case studies. We use behavioral case studies because we examine these two habits as overt acts of behavior in organizational sensemaking situations.

5.3 Organizational Leadership and Faculty-Behavioral-Psychology

Before beginning these case studies, we are using these cases to present issues that will allow in the coming chapter to develop a more explicit Thomistic organizational behavioral psychology of leadership. In chapter one, we did explain that a Thomistic organizational psychology of leadership is differentiated from empirical approaches to organizational psychology of leadership because, by definition of the subject matter, it requires attention to metaphysical, spiritual, and moral principles of executive leadership and the diffusion of the character of leadership throughout the organization. In the coming case studies, we will begin to move toward establishing a psychology of leadership grounded on a Thomistic teleological behavioral psychology. The support for this effort is basically found in REDPATH's understanding of the moral psychology of St. Thomas Aquinas, particularly faculty psychology. He writes:

> As I finally got around to writing this book, *The Moral Psychology of St. Thomas Aquinas: A Introduction to Ragamuffin Ethics*, I became increasingly aware that a chief reason St. Thomas's teaching serves as effective apologetic for defending universal moral principles is because his moral psychology is essentially rooted in behavioral psychology, immersed in the natural human desire to understand the nature of organizations and organizational leadership and to educate human beings to become organizational leaders.[381]

REDPATH, we suggest, concisely expresses the nature of his Thomistic behavioral psychology in chapter twelve, "The Intellectual Virtue" where he

---

[381] Peter A. REDPATH, "Why nothing short of the moral psychology of estimative intelligence can hope to educate present and future leaders to promote global peace," *Third Annual Aquinas Leadership International World Congress*, Huntington, New York, 8 July 2016.

explains the nature of right reason in practical science. He explains that in all moral virtue and art, a man with right reason keeps his eye on a mark, and an object. It is important to note in terms of REDPATH's construct of a Thomistic behavioral psychology that he writes, "a man with right reason keeps his eye on a mark, and object."[382] From the perspective of a Thomistic behavioral psychology, AQUINAS discusses intention in his *Summa theologiae*:

> Intention, as the very word denotes, signifies, "to tend to something." Now both the action of the mover and the movement of the thing moved, tend to something. But that the movement of the thing moved tends to anything is due to the action of the mover. Consequently, intention belongs first and principally to that which moves to the end: hence we say that an architect or anyone who is in authority, by his command moves others to that which he intends. Now the will moves all the other powers of the soul to the end. Wherefore it is evident that intention, properly speaking, is an act of will.[383]

Intention is not used in the same way as cognitive folk psychology where intentionality is based on mental states of the mind, such as beliefs, desires, or conceptual cognitive maps. In a Thomistic behavioral psychology the person is moved to a formal object that stimulates the agent to act.

Based on REDPATH's *Moral Psychology*, there are ten essential teachings for a Thomistic faculty-behavioral-psychology of contingent beings operative in contingent situations:[384]

1) St. Thomas tells us that Aristotle describes the basic specific divisions of the human soul into: a) rational absolutely considered (*simpliciter*) whose formal objects are necessary beings, whose principles are unchangeable and invariable, that exist and act in one fixed way, and b) rational relationally considered (*secundum quid*) by participating by reason

---

[382] REDPATH, *The Moral Psychology of St. Thomas*, 339.

[383] AQUINAS, *Summa theologiae* I-II, q. 12, a. 1:

[384] REDPATH, *The Moral Psychology of St. Thomas*, 341–342; 123; 130; 154–155.

perfected by moral virtue, whose formal objects are contingent beings, whose principles are somewhat contingent, variable.

2) St. Thomas justifies this division by saying that different parts of the soul should correspond (be proportionate) to different formal objects (proportionately in intensive quantity, qualitative receptivity, and capacity) that essentially stimulate them to act. The qualitative, intensive quantum, receptivity and capacity of the faculty must be qualitatively proportionate in qualitative power fit receptivity to the intensive quantum activity of the agent that activates it.

3) Knowledge, he says, exists in parts of the soul according as they have some greatness of likeness (a proportion of likeness) to the thing known. According to its peculiar nature, each faculty of the soul is qualitatively proportioned, proportioned in receptive capacity, natural ability, to know formal object that stimulate it to act.

4) Aristotle calls "scientific" that part of the rational soul whose formal object, external stimulus, is necessary beings: beings that exist and act in only one way. He calls "estimative" that part of the rational soul whose formal object is contingent beings. He maintains that estimating, deliberating, refer to the same formal object, what is changeable, contingent. Because no one deliberates about what acts, exists, in only one way, he says that deliberation is an inquiry not yet concluded, like argumentation.

5) We can understand contingent beings in two ways: abstractly and concretely. Abstractly, we understand contingent natures according to fixed part/whole relationships in terms of their organizational parts being capable of generating generic acts. Concretely considered, we understand contingent natures according to the way they operate, exist, in contingent situations.

6) Practical sciences like prudence and art proceed concretely, consider things as they concretely exist. They consider composite wholes as generating, causing, specific acts in individual circumstances. They do this through the use of particular reason, the estimative sense, which initially collates, mnemonically specifies some multitude into a quasi-nominalistic, sensory, experiential, some multitude into a temporal, generic relation:

For example, that whenever, in the past, some person has been sick with this disease, when given this medication, this person's health has been improved, or totally restored. Thus understood, contingent beings and operational universals can be formal object of speculative and operational universals can be formal objects.

7) While prudence helps us rationally to focus, fix on, the right means to achieve a right end (the right reasoning to do so), the cardinal moral virtues of justice, courage, and temperance keep us appetitively focused on the right ends to pursue (right desires that satisfy real needs).

8) St. Thomas defines what, today, we generally call an "emotion" (but what he calls a "passion") as psychosomatic change reaction: 1) caused within the sense appetite of a human being located within particular, cogitative, reason by the presence in a human of an image, 2) which draws a faculty toward or pushes away from union with or separation from a formal object (external stimulus), 3) apprehends as sensibly agreeable as it is in itself (that is, as co-natural or not co-natural [proportionate] in qualitative strength of power to the faculty it activates). Aquinas maintains that, to some extent, emotional reaction always: 1) starts with some physical modification of an organ or an image; 2) involves bodily changes, including influence on the heart and blood flow; 3) contains a sense image and has a cognitive, conceptual component; and 4) seeks to terminate in rest in pleasure union with, or separation from, its cause.

9) Thomas divides the sensory appetite into two emotions; parts: 1) the higher passions (irascible appetite), whose formal object is some sense good (or evil) considered as helpful with which to unite (or helpful to avoid); and 2) lower passions (concupiscible appetite), whose formal object is sense good or evil considered as pleasurable, but necessarily helpful or harmful to avoid or not avoid.

10) In the passions of the concupiscible appetite (for example, the passions of pleasure and pain), St. Thomas claims that only a contrariety of terms (not of relations) exists between the opposites (one of which is perfect [pleasure] and attracts us; the other of which is imperfect [pain] and repels us). By nature, all-natural inclination of the concupiscible appetite is to

move forward toward pleasure and away from pain. Since every passion is a movement of the sense appetite as a result of sense knowledge, in agreement with Aristotle, St. Thomas maintains that pleasure is a passion, a psychic movement, "instantaneously" and essentially constituting a being as existing according to its nature. St. Thomas says that, by calling pleasure "a movement of the soul," or "a psychic movement," he is designating pleasure's genus. In calling pleasure "a state of existing constituting a thing in agreement with its nature," he is assigning the cause of pleasure presence of its "co-natural good," the good suitable to its nature. By saying that this state happens "all at once," he means this state is not a process. He means it is the terminus of a process that happens in an instant.

We have presented these teachings of a Thomistic faculty-behavioral-psychology because we are turning to case studies of behavioral agents in "contingent situations" of organizational "extreme emergent" disorder. Thus far, in this thesis we have been making the argument that a Thomistic organizational behavioral psychology based on a premodern metaphysics of organization and moral psychology is the most appropriate for the evolving psychology of executive and diffusion of leadership for H-HOC organizations, i.e., profit, nonprofit, government, religion, national, global, and volunteer.

The above ten Thomistic behavioral teachings will be developed in the following case studies, as we examine concrete situations of extreme emergent disorder. The situations presented in the case studies call for organizational leadership at all levels of the organization to develop a habit of character capable of responding readily to the contingent situations of an emergent critical order. We are presenting situations that call for leaders under pressure to estimate and respond to emerging threats and opportunities impacting on an organizational whole. In other words, leaders are known for their character under behavioral decision making and emotional stress. We are introducing behavioral psychology in this chapter. We will apply a Thomistic teleological behavioral framework by comparing the implications of the above behavioral propositions of REDPATH with the teleological behaviorist, Howard RACHLIN.

The teleological behavioral psychology of RACHLIN rejects a psychological science of efficient causes using internal mechanisms to explain overt behavior and opts for another psychological science, based on Aristotelian final causes, using external objects and goals to explain behavior. Efficient-cause psychology is designed to answer the question of how a particular act is emitted; final-cause psychology is designed to answer the question of why a particular act is emitted. Physiological psychology, and modern cognitive psychology, and some parts of behaviorism including Skinnerian's behaviorism are efficient cause psychologies; final cause psychology, a development of limited stimuli-response and operant behavior Skinnerian behaviorism is called teleological behaviorism. Each of these two conceptions of causality in psychology implies a different view of mental terms.

In contrast, HOWARD RACHLIN, who has a solid understanding of Aristotelian causation, nature of substances and sense perception, claims that his efforts are "less than an interpretation of Aristotle's actual views than a reconstruction of those views for the purpose of modern behaviorism."[385] He supports his arguments resorting to at least two contemporary Aristotelian philosophers, H. RANDALL, who maintains that "For Aristotle life or psyche is the behavior of the organism as a whole in its environment. Aristotle is thus as a thoroughgoing behaviorist";[386] and J.R. KANTOR, who "considers behaviorism the modern movement closest to Aristotle's 'naturalistic' psychology."[387]

As we continue in the application of a Thomistic organizational teleological behavioral psychology, like RACHLIN, we are involved less with an interpretation of Aquinas's rational and moral psychology as much as a reconstruction of his views for the purpose of developing views of soulful leadership for organizations. Therefore, much of this effort will rely heavily on St. Thomas AQUINAS's

---

[385] Howard RACHLIN, "Teleological Behaviorism," *American Psychologist* 7(1), November 1192, 1371.

[386] Quoted from H. RANDALL, *Aristotle* (New York: Columbia University Press, 1960), 66.

[387] RANDALL is referring to J.R. KANTOR, *The Scientific Evolution of Psychology*, Volume 1 (Chicago: Principia Press,1963), 161.

Commentary on ARISTOTLE's *Nicomachean Ethics*.[388] Even though, neither ARISTOTLE nor AQUINAS wrote on organizational psychology, as the topic is pursued in modern psychology, this work reads also as a work in moral and organizational psychology, especially as a behavioral psychology of organizational leadership. It is most fitting because, as mentioned in chapter two, founded on the views of BARNARD executive leadership is one of moral rectitude. It is necessary that organizational and moral psychology are part of the same genus of the organizational psychology of the function of executive exemplar leadership and the organizational diffusion of leadership.

AQUINAS begins his *Commentary* by saying, "It is the business of the wise man to know order. The reason for this is that wisdom is the most powerful perfection of reason."[389] Therefore, how do we know a truly wise leader? How do we know whether someone has a character worthy of the executive function? How would we recognize someone with the potential for leadership? Aristotelian-Thomistic behavioral psychology of leadership would answer that it is someone who knows the nature of organizational order. AQUINAS, then, continues:

> Even if the sensitive powers know some things absolutely, nevertheless, to know the order of one thing to another is exclusively the work of the intellect or reason. Now a twofold order is found in things. One kind is that of parts of a totality, that is, a group among themselves, as the parts of a house, is mutually ordered to each other. The second order is that of things to an end. This order is of greater importance than the first.[390]

It is this second order that is most important to the organization, "as the order of the parts of an army among themselves exists because of the order of the whole army to the commander."[391] It is here that we begin to recognize evidence of a Thomistic teleological behavioral organizational psychology. Behavior moving to an end, organizations moving to an end and leadership commanding and

---

[388] AQUINAS, *Commentary on Aristotle's Nicomachean Ethics*, Book 1, Lecture 1.

[389] Ibid.

[390] Ibid.

[391] Ibid.

controlling to an end is the basic first principle of a Thomistic teleological psychology of leadership. Likewise, RACHLIN holds the following:

> The mind is behavior on a higher level of abstraction. The mind [psyche] stands to behavior as a more abstract pattern (such as a dance) stands to its own particular elements (the steps of a dance). For Aristotle, the more abstract pattern is what he called the final cause of its particular components; that is, the mind is a final cause of behavior. Final causes answer the question: Why did this or that occur? Why did you take that step? Answer: Because I was doing that dance (Our more familiar efficient causes are answers to the question: How did this or that occur?). A science of final causes is called teleological science.[392]

Therefore, an organizational leader must understand the science of order, as AQUINAS explains.

> Now order is related to reason in a fourfold way. There is one order that reason does not establish but only beholds, such is the order of things in nature. There is a second order that reason establishes in its own act of consideration, for example, when it arranges its concepts among themselves, and the signs of concept as well, because words express the meanings of the concepts. There is a third order that reason in deliberating establishes in the operations of the will. There is a fourth order that reason in planning establishes in the external things which it causes, such as a chest and a house.[393]

We, consequently, take the position that St. Thomas's *Commentary* may also be read as a text on the nature of behavioral organizational psychology of leadership.

Before beginning our case studies on the order of things and estimative behavior, we will explain somewhat the meaning of estimative human power and

---

[392] Howard RACHLIN, *The Escape of The Mind* (Oxford, New York: University Press, 2014), 15.

[393] AQUINAS, *Commentary on Aristotle's Nicomachean Ethics*, Book 1, Lecture 1.

its importance to a behavioral psychology. Based on the above propositions for a Thomistic behavioral psychology, it is put forth that for ARISTOTLE and AQUINAS the conception of behavioral actions and passions are categories of movements. In teaching number 8, we mentioned that in an Aristotelian-Thomistic behavioral psychology passions (what today are called emotions) and actions are stimulated by an external object. It is the perceived form of the object that stimulates the internal estimative sense to move toward or away from the perceived object. We will in the next chapter discuss in greater depth the dynamic of behavioral perception and the rational sensing agent, habit and the unity of virtue and leadership.

For purposes of the following case studies, we will provide a brief explanation from REDPATH and an Aristotelian description of passion and movement. These two descriptions of estimation and movement are necessary in understanding the dynamics of behavior in situations of emergent order, particularly extreme emergent order. REDPATH writes on the behavioral power of cogitative reason and the estimative sense.

> Furthermore, for the apprehension of forms like danger and difficulty, which external sense qualities cannot convey, St. Thomas says an "estimative" power (which he sometimes calls "particular" or "cogitative" reason) is appointed. He claims that the *sense memory exists to preserve these forms* […] Knowing the past, the time that we sensed something, is an act of sense memory, not of the imagination. […] A physical sense quality activates the sense faculties of other animals. *The way man and other animals receive and preserve these sense qualities, however, radically differs.* Other animals perceive forms of sense good and evil only by some natural instinct. Man perceives them through relating ideas. Hence, the power in other animals St. Thomas calls "estimative," in man he calls "cogitative." Because *the way the faculty works is by discovering some sort of relation between individual ideas and human self-preservation*, he also calls it "particular reason." For it relates ideas in an individual way just as the intellectual reason relates them universally.[394]

---

[394] REDPATH, *The Moral Psychology of St. Thomas*, 100.

RACHLIN presents an Aristotelian teleological behavioral account of action, passion, movement, and decision making. For him, ARISTOTLE conceives actions and passions as two categories of movements. The process of action is as follows:

In the world, an object consisting a certain substance in a certain form transmits its form through the air or another medium (making an impression much as a signet ring makes an impression of its form on wax) one or more of a person's sense organs. The form of the object combines in the person's imagination with other forms from memory. The combined images are reflected upon by thought and the person engages in thoughtful (i.e., rational) behavior.

Aristotle's mechanism for action may be understood as a kind of decision theory with Imagination and Memory standing for representation while "rational thought" stands for the decision mechanism. When Aristotle developed the laws of deductive logic, he believed that he was merely describing rational thought.

Aristotle believed that animals other than humans are not capable of rational thought. However, because all animals (including humans) have sensitive souls, all are capable of different kind of movement-passions. Aristotle's concept of passions differed from modern notions in the sense that passions, for him, are movements—they cannot boil up inside. For him, a man cannot just feel passionate, he has to be passionate. Nevertheless, Aristotle's concept of passions is like the modern concept in the sense that he thought passionate movement requires rational control.

Again, an object in the world transfers its form through a medium to a sense organ and into a person's body. When the form of an object enters the body, it interacts with the soul. Aristotle conceived of the soul as a kind of organization; therefore, we can say that the form of the object comes into contact with the body's organization (not the more complex organization of the rational soul possessed only by humans, but a subcategory of that organization, the sensible soul, possessed by all animals).

At the point the form of the object can be in harmony with the form of the soul or out of harmony with the form of the soul (much as a square peg with a round hole): If its form is in harmony with an animal's soul, the object causes pleasure. Pleasure in turn implies the existence of a desire to move toward the object, and desire implies the occurrence of the movement itself. If, on the other hand, the form of the object is out of harmony with the animal's soul, the object causes pain; pain implies the existence of a desire to move away from the object, and the desire implies the occurrence of the movement itself.

As ARISTOTLE conceived it, all human behavior is some mixture of action and passion.[395]

5.4 Thomistic Organizational Behavioral Psychology of Passion, Estimation and Movement in Contingent Organizational Situations

We will discuss in the next chapter in more detail the Thomistic behavioral psychology of passion (emotions), habits of virtue and leadership. However, we will open the examination of passion and movement as it applies to our present consideration of organizational behavior in situations of desired and emergent order. We are giving particular attention to the fact that, as RACHLIN describes, the form of the object can be in harmony with the form of the soul or out of harmony with the form of the soul, but if the object implies the existence of a desire to move away from the object, and the desire implies movement itself. When we observe an agent from the perspective of Aristotelian-Thomistic behavioral psychology in its decision-making process in a contingent situation, we look at an event as comprised of two categories, i.e., of action (according to Aristotle governed by the rational aspect of the soul) and passion (a psychic movement of the sense appetite). In the following cases, we are primarily concerned with organizational members, when in the process of performing operational functions, they find themselves in a collapse of desired order and in a situation of emergent order turned to terrifying chaos. In these two cases, it is really a matter of life-threatening chaos, where the emergent order calls for acts of high virtuous behavior. The two selected cases deal with contingent situations but also situations of violent emotional activation. The

---

Howard RACHLIN, *Judgment, Decision and Choice: A Cognitive/Behavioral Synthesis* (New York: W.H. Freeman and Company, 1989), 230–232.

understanding of the nature of violent emotional response in situations is taken from ADLER. He writes:

> I have repeatedly referred to bodily emotions and sensual desires. I have used the word "bodily" to signify that, properly understood, emotion is a passion that the body suffers, and we consciously experience when a complex set of bodily reactions occurs: changes in respiration and pulse, changes in epidermal electricity, increases of blood sugar and adrenaline in the blood due to reaction on the part of glands of the internal secretion, papillary or contraction. In short, an emotion is widespread, violent bodily communication that is consciously experienced and accompanied by strong impulses to act in a certain way.
>
> When the emotion is thus defined and understood, there would appear to be only two violent bodily emotions that we experience: anger and fear. The sexual passion that occurs when sexual desires are consummated may be a third, but it is seldom a violent or as widespread a bodily commotion as anger or fear.[396]

ADLER's concept of the violent emotions is most important in the application of an organizational psychology of executive leadership. It was DEMING, as he introduced Total Quality Management to profit and non-profit organizations in the 70s and 80s in his famous Four-day management seminars and in his pivotal work of the quality movement *Out of the Crisis* who insisted on the responsibility of executive leadership to eradicate management by fear. Throughout this work he gives clear and vivid examples of the destructive impact of management by fear on the organizational dedication to quality and excellence of performance. For example, he writes:

> Drive out fear. No one can put in his best performance unless he feels secure. "Se" comes from the Latin, meaning without, cure means fear or care. Secure means without fear, not afraid to express ideas, not afraid to ask questions.

---

[396] ADLER, *Intellect*, 170.

Fear takes on many faces. A common denominator of fear in any form, anywhere, is loss from impaired performance and padded figures.

Some actual expressions of fear follow.

I am afraid that I may lose my job because the company will go out of business.

I have a feeling that Dave (higher up) may move to another company. If he does, what will happen to me?

I could do my job better if I understood what happens next. If I did what is best for the company, long term.

I'd have to shut down production for a while for repairs and overhaul. My daily report on production would take a nosedive, and I'd be out of a job.

I'd like to understand better the reasons for some of the company's procedures, but I don't dare ask about them.

I am afraid that I may not always have an answer when my boss asks something.

My boss believes in fear. How can he manage his people if they don't hold him in awe? Management is punitive.

I am afraid to admit a mistake.[397]

5.4.1 Case One: The Order of Things, Estimative Behavior, Violent Emotions, and the Inept Police Officer

A recent tragic incident occurred on Feb. 14, 2018 at Marjory Stoneman Douglas High School in Parkland, Florida. Four armed officers and years of experience did nothing to stop Nicholas Cruz from massacring 17 people at a high school. Four sheriff's deputies hid behind cars instead of storming Marjory Stoneman Douglas High School in Parkland Florida, during the school shooting. News release records revealed the Broward County Sheriff's Office had received at least 18 calls about the troubled teen shooter over the past decade.

Sources from Coral Springs, Fla., Police Department [told news agencies] that when its officers arrived on the scene Wednesday, they were shocked to

---

[397] DEMING, *Out of Crisis*, 59–61.

find three Broward County Sheriff's deputies behind their cars with weapons drawn. The school's armed resource officer, Broward County Sheriff's Deputy Scot Peterson, was also outside. He resigned on Thursday after his failure to act was publicly revealed. The Coral Springs police officers entered the building to engage the shooter on their own, before other Broward County deputies arrived, two of whom joined the police inside, the sources said. It was unclear whether the shooter was still inside at the time […]. Coral Springs City Manager Mike Goodrum confronted Broward County Sheriff Scott Israel during a vigil for victims the next day, saying students could have been dying in the school while the deputies held back. News of the deputies' apparent inaction came after the sheriff's office released records showing how many times it had received alarming records about Cruz, 19, over the years- including two that specifically warned he was a potential school shooter. The records show that a neighbor called in February 2016 to report that Cruz "planned to shoot up the school" and had posted photos to Instagram of himself posing with guns. The information was passed on to Peterson, but it was not clear what, if anything, he did with it. Another person phoned the sheriff's office in November last year to say the teen was stockpiling guns and knives and warn that "he could be a school shooter in the making," the records show. But the caller was told to contact the Palm Beach Sheriff's Office instead because Cruz had moved out of Broward, according to the records. In September 2016, a peer counselor told Peterson that Cruz had tried to kill himself by drinking gasoline, was cutting himself, possessed hate symbols and expressed a desire to buy a gun "for hunting." This time, Peterson did make a report, but a mental-health worker determined Cruz didn't meet the state's criteria for involuntary commitment to a psychiatric facility, the records show. Cruz stayed at the school for another five months before he was transferred out.[398]

---

[398] Ruth BROWN, "Four sheriffs' deputies hid during Florida school shooting," *New York Post,* February 23, 2018, https://nypost.com/2018/02/23/four-sheriffs-deputies-hid-during-florida-school-shooting/.

Encountering extreme emergent order, a police officer must have an estimative sense of what is the next right thing to do, the right way, for the right motive. It is in a situation of extreme high contingencies ARISTOTLE and AQUINAS taught that an individual must call upon special powers of the soul to do the next right thing, the right way and for the right motive. By estimative intelligence we are referring to the integrated functioning of according to AQUINAS the four interior senses as explained by REDPATH.

How to properly distinguish the four interior senses

1) Common or differentiating, sense; 2) imagination; 3) estimative sense (called "particular" or "cogitative" reason in human beings); and 4) sense memory

Because a thing's nature does not fail in providing a substance with the necessary powers to exercise its proper act in a maturely-developed way, ST. THOMAS maintains that human nature must provide man's sensitive soul with as many faculties and actions needed for a human being to live the life of a *perfect* animal (that is, an animal that has all the sense faculties possessed by the highest species of the genus animal). He adds that, because a faculty of the soul is the proximate principle of the soul's operation, if one sense power cannot generate the needed acts, diverse powers must exist to help generate them. [...]

Furthermore, for apprehension of forms like danger and difficulty, which the external sense qualities cannot convey, ST. THOMAS says an "estimative" power (which he sometimes calls "particular or cogitative" reason) is appointed. He claims that the *sense memory exists to preserve these forms.* As a sign of the difference between imagination and sense memory, ST. THOMAS points to the fact that we find animals strongly stimulated to remember by something harmful or otherwise. He adds that knowing the past, the time that we sensed something, is an act of sense memory, not of imagination. [...] Regarding external sensible qualities received and preserved through the external sense faculties, St. Thomas asserts that no difference exists between man and other high animals. A physical sense quality activates the sense faculties of other animals. *The way man and other animals receive and preserve these sensible qualities, however, radically differs.* [...]

Other animals perceive forms of sense good and evil only by some natural instinct. Man perceives them through relating ideas. Hence, the power that in other animals St. Thomas calls "estimative," in man he calls "cogitative." *Because the way this faculty works is by discovering some sort of relation between individual ideas and human self-preservation,* he also calls it "particular reason." For it relates ideas in an individual way just as the intellectual reason relates them universally in an individual way just as the intellectual reason relates them universally. *According to St. Thomas, physicians during his time assigned an organ, the middle part of the head to this faculty of cogitative reason.*[399]

The officer arrives and fear kicks in, and then his habit of estimative intelligence must kick in. For an organization to exist in a complex and complicated environment where the desired order (command and control order) and common-sense making breaks down, then emergent order estimative intelligence must take over, i.e., the execution of the doable deed or you could say the order of doing the next right thing, the right way, for the right motive.

Deputy Scott Peterson was the armed school officer who arrived within four minutes of the shooting, but he did not enter the building. He was severely criticized by the media for not entering the building and seen as a cowardly police officer. He defended his character by saying the initial call was about the sound of firecrackers, then he hesitated uncertain of the exact location of the shoots. Most important, he claimed that he was following standard policy and waiting for backup support. In other words, he followed the "rule book." AQUINAS would expect an officer of the law in a contingent situation of the community being attacked to arrive at the scene of battle and do more than follow a rule book. He would expect an officer of the law who has vowed to protect and serve, to estimate, master his violent emotions and exercise the virtue of fortitude (courage).

---

[399] REDPATH, *The Moral Psychology of St. Thomas*, 97, 100.

In Book Three, Lecture 16, we clearly see that *Aristotle's Nicomachean Ethics* and *Aquinas's Commentary* is also a synthesis of behavioral and a moral philosophy. The book is a behavioral enumeration of the types citizen behavior required for civic order. It is also clearly, what we would call today, an organizational behavioral psychology. Aquinas would expect the police officer to act as a police officer in a perilous situation and exercise the virtue of fortitude as a member of a service, like military service. Officer Scott Peterson in this case of the mass shooting in a high school is expected to be more than an officer of policy and daring; the virtue of fortitude requires an officer of bravery. Aquinas explains the difference between bravery and daring in Book Three, Lecture XVIII.

> He says first although fortitude is concerned with both daring and fear, it is not concerned with each in the same manner. But praise of this virtue consists rather in this, that a person behaves well with respect to terrifying things. One who is not disturbed by frightening evils but conducts himself as he ought in regard to them is more commended for bravery than one conducts himself well in regard to daring. The reason is that fear is a threat to a man from someone stronger rising up against him. But daring originates from the fact that a man thinks that the one he attacks is not too powerful to overcome. It is more difficult to stand against a stronger man than to rise up against an equal or weaker one.[400]

AQUINAS gives special attention to civic fortitude and the highest civic fortitude belongs to those who undergo dangers for the sake of honor as opposed those who face danger for fear of punishment or rulers who face dangers because of pressing compulsions.[401] Furthermore, he says real fortitude is a moral virtue because a person has the rational and the sense knowledge of doing the next right thing for the right reason and for the right motive. Citizens, as AQUINAS observes, "can undergo dangers to avoid penalties and disgrace, which according to civil laws are inflicted on the cowardly and to acquire honors by which the same laws, are

---

[400] AQUINAS, *Commentary on Aristotle's Nicomachean Ethics*, Book 3, Lecture 18, n. 583.

[401] Ibid., Lecture 16, n. 561.

inflicted, but real virtue comes about by a person with the voluntary moral habit of fortitude"[402] (courageous for the sake of the harmony of the organizational whole). The citizens of Parkland, Florida expected that officer Scott Peterson, who served as the officer assigned to protect the students of Marjory Stoneman Douglas High School, would arrive at the scene of the shooting, and courageously charge into the school and protect the students. Instead, he remained outside waiting for the arrival of more support. Although at the same time, there were teachers inside the school who stood bravely unarmed in the path of the shooter offering their lives to protect students. Yet, Peterson, joined by three more officers, remained outside the building with guns drawn behind a vehicle waiting for backup. AQUINAS would portray these officers as ignominious officers compared to the teachers who exercised civic fortitude to protect the students. AQUINAS would describe the police officers as soldier who are do not respond to the perilous emergent order of the community.

> In "Soldiers turn," he compares the fortitude of the soldier and the citizen. He says that soldiers fight bravely so long as they do not see danger threatening. But when the danger exceeds the skill they have in arms and when they lack numbers and adequate military preparations, they become cowardly. Then they are the first to run away; they were daring for other reasons when they thought the danger was not imminent. Therefore, when they first see the danger, they take to their heels. But those who possess the fortitude of the citizen- refusing to leave the danger-lose their lives, as happened in a certain place where the citizen remained after the soldiers had fled. The reason is that citizens think it disgraceful to run away and choose to die rather than save themselves by flight. But soldiers expose themselves to dangers because, from the beginning, they think themselves more powerful, they take to flight fearing death more than ignominious escape. It is not so with the brave man who fears disgrace more than death.[403]

---

[402] Ibid. 562.

[403] Ibid. 570

What we witness at the mass killing in Parkland, Florida was described in an editorial as

> This most peaceful and orderly of places has been devastated by the most violent and chaotic of acts. And amid the horse trails, bike paths and gated communities of a city that prides itself on "country elegance," the response to a shooting last week that killed 17 people at Marjory Stoneman Douglas High School has been a raw, growing, and furious burst of activism and demand for change.[404]

Parkland Florida, until the massacre, was known as one of the placid, non-criminal activities and desire ordered communities in the state of Florida. The school officer Scott Peterson was close to retirement and he had served in this community of mostly parking and speed violations. Peterson was not an officer like an officer in a dangerous on the edge of emergent chaos city such as Baltimore. AQUINAS holds that in particular cases soldiers will turn cowardly because they lack experience and teaches that "no one fears to do what he believes he has learned to do well."[405] Consequently, we might ask the question, if Officer Peterson was really trained and had the knowledge to respond to the shooting situation, or did

---

[404] Kevin SULLIVAN, Tim CRAIG, and William WAN, "'People are angry': Pain turns political in Parkland after school shooting," *The Washington Post*, February 17, 2018, https://www.washingtonpost.com/ national/people-are-angry-pain-turns-political-in-parkland-after-school-shootings/2018/02/17/2b06e8ce-136f-11e8-8ea1-c1d91fcec3fe_story.html

[405] AQUINAS, *Commentary on Aristotle's Nicomachean Ethics*, Book 3, Lecture 18, "'In particular cases' he treats the fortitude of the soldier. He explains this question in a twofold manner. First, he shows what leads soldiers to fight bravely. Next, he compares the fortitude of the soldier and the citizen, at 'Soldiers turn cowards' he says that in individual cases experience seems to be a kind of fortitude. In any undertaking on who has knowledge from experience works boldly and without fear, as Vegetius says in his book on military affairs: 'No one fears to do what he believes he has learned to do well'. For this reason, Socrates thought fortitude was knowledge which is acquired by experience. He even thought of all the virtues are kinds of knowledge."

he hear the rapid sound of a loud assault weapon and estimate that the danger exceeded his skill and weapon power and did not move into the school.

We could also look at this case from the perspective that law enforcement must face the issue H-HOC of desired order and emergent order. Meaning that, law enforcement organizations must move from responsive crime investigation and local law enforcement organization to crime prevention and intelligence communication network, and flexible tactical units as a blending of a desired state order and increasing attention to emergent order law enforcement.

The traditional officer that walked the beat and knew the desired order of his neighborhood is gone. If the school had police officers who were members of the administrative staff, they would have known about the shooter who had been expelled from the school. The proper security at points of entry would have known this person by sight.

A Thomistic organizational psychology contends that it is necessary to understand the contrariety of desired order and emergent order in present day law enforcement. It is more than just banning firearms; it is a question of structuring security based on estimative intelligence and human agents educated to do the next right thing, the right way and for the right motive.

Also needed re-examine the issue of school random violence and the ability to plan for the complexity of the blending of desired order by means of greater inter agency communication and emergent order by identification of possible threats to the local communities. It is quite simply the executive responsibility of chief of police to emphasize that first responder police officers must be officers of moral fortitude who are capable of making the needed estimative judgments and executing the necessary movements required by dangerous contingent situations.

Most of all, any organizational executive, especially an executive leader responsible for the protection of a community, should hold unreservedly to AQUINAS's teaching on organizational training: No one fears to do what he believes he has learned to do well.

Therefore, from the perspective of a Thomistic behavioral psychology of the executive level of Parkland, Florida sheriff's department must ask if this was the right officer, with the right training, with the right character to be assigned to such a critical civic responsibility. In a contemporary policing environment in a heavily armed population, the executive leadership must constantly engage in some type of SWOT analysis of the organizations ability to identify, investigate, and remove from the community individuals with a high profile of a possible mass killer.

Therefore, leadership must constantly examine the organizational whole for the intelligence strengths and weaknesses in terms of human, communication, and technological resources. Following REDPATH, we could say that the peace and security of a community requires the executive leadership of a police department to possess the appropriate "habits of particular reason and an estimative sense rightly to apprehend real ends, real deeds and the prudentially-grasped enabling means to secure them."[406] In other words, in a complex and complicated environment of local policing the executive leadership requires officers with a character of proven estimative intelligence, especially in situations of violent emergent order. It is, therefore, this character of estimative intelligence that must diffuse throughout the leadership and officers of the department.

5.5 Chaos, Violent Emotions, Estimative Intelligence, the Collapse of Team Sensemaking and First Principles

In the following case study, we continue to unfold estimative intelligence as the habit of particular reason and an estimative sense rightly applied to apprehend real ends, real deeds, and the prudentially grasped means to secure them. In the coming chapter, the importance of the habit of prudence to an organizational behavioral psychology will be developed in depth. For purpose of this case, since we are examining the nature of team leadership in a contingent situation as part of an organizational whole, we will use the definition of a prudent man (or woman) from AQUINAS. In case two, we are focusing our attention on a team crew leader, at the same time the team leader is placed in a situation that suggests glaring failures in executive planning in preparation for violent emergent order. First it is necessary to understand the importance of the virtuous habit of prudence according to AQUINAS:

---

[406] REDPATH, "Why nothing short of the moral psychology of estimative intelligence…"

[Aristotle] shows what the subject of prudence is. He says that since there are two parts of the rational soul—one of which is called scientific and the other estimative or conjectural (*opinativum*)—it is clear that prudence is a virtue of the second of these, viz., the conjectural. Opinion indeed deals with contingent things, as prudence does. Nevertheless, although prudence resides in this part of the reason as in a subject—because of this it is called an intellectual virtue—it is not connected with reason alone, as art or science, but it requires rectitude of the appetitive faculty. A sign of this is that a habit in the reason alone can be forgotten (for example, art and science), unless the habit is a natural one like understanding. Prudence, however, is not forgotten by disuse, but it is destroyed by the cessation of right desire which, while remaining, is continually engaged with the things belonging to prudence, so that oblivion cannot come along unawares.[407]

Thus far, we have given attention to the function of leadership at the executive levels with the understanding that organizational psychology of leadership must start at the top of the organization. The function of executives is to serve as existential exemplars of a rational and moral leadership. It is not a leadership of rules, policy or even values. It is a leadership of a virtuous character of rational and moral excellence that by means of a cultural diffusion rests in the souls of leaders, supervisors, team leaders and teams and workers.

In case study 2, we will examine the issue of leadership as it exists at a team level of an organization. There are different types of teams in organizations ranging from permanent working crews to temporary ad hoc teams. Of course, today in the H-HOC teams and with emerging decentralized nature of authority increasing autonomy is given to teams. In case study 2, our attention is focused on a working crew with a supervisor in the field who has a tremendous amount of responsibility for his workers who must work as a coordinated crew in dangerous and often death-defying situations. They are situations that call for a very experienced crew leader with proven estimative intelligence and simultaneous mastery of violent emotions in a chaotic emerging situation.

---

[407] AQUINAS, *Commentary on Aristotle's Nicomachean Ethics*, Book 6, Lecture 4.

5.5.1 Case 2: The Mann Gulch Disaster

Mann Gulch is a well-known case study and appears in organizational and management science textbooks; it is written by Karl E. WEICK who is acclaimed as the originator of the organizational sensemaking movement, previously discussed.

It is WEICK who has serious reservations about the enthusiasm of mainstream texts on knowledge management. He sees organizational learning as an activity often a threat to organizational knowledge. For Weick organizing involves ordering and controlling that means decreasing the variety of ideas whereas learning disorganizes existing knowledge and increases variety. Learning means changing knowledge and therefore it means questioning those in power.[408]

Improvisation is a concept of learning that WEICK uses to deal productively with the tension between learning and organizing.

Actors and jazz musicians improvise, and so do employees; rather than sending people to seminars where they learn things they cannot apply back in the organization, learning on the job (improvisation) encourages people to play around with everyday patterns and to change not radically but in situ. Improvisation is always in play based on the interplay between the past, present and the future; by carefully listening and changing past rhythms, something new emerges. Also, errors play an important role within improvisation. To enable learning and development, errors are tolerated and used as starting new emerges. Also, errors play an important role within improvisation. To enable learning and development, errors are tolerated and used as starting points for future improvisation. Finally, improvisational learning is a team event, not a one-person show. It relies on the feedback of

---

[408] CLEGG, KORNBERGER PITSIS, *Managing & Organizations*, 352; source: K. E. WEICK and F. WESTLEY, "Organizational Learning: affirming an oxymoron," in S.R. CLEGG, C. HARDY and W.R. NORD (Eds.), *Managing Organizations Review* (London: Sage, 1999), 190–208.

others, their feelings (rather than their rational capacities alone), and their contributions to change.[409]

As we suggested, in the previous appraisal WEICK's concept of sensemaking we contended that organizational sensemaking is best understood by means of a premodern concept of induction and first principles. In case 2 we will continue the line of argumentation that the phenomena of desired order and emerging order tension in a hierarchical-heterarchical organization is best addressed by a Thomistic behavioral psychology of estimative intelligence and leadership in contingent situations.

5.5.2 The Collapse of Sensemaking and First Principles

WEICK wrote this case study about the death of 13 men in the Mann Gulch fire disaster, made famous in Norman Maclean's book *Young Men and Fire*. He analyzed the case as the interactive disintegration of the structure and the sensemaking in a minimal organization. He examined four potential sources of resilience that make groups less vulnerable to forestall disintegration, including improvisation, virtual role systems, and the attitude of wisdom and norm of respectful interaction. We will consider some of WEICK's analysis, but we, also, will analyze the case form the viewpoint of a Thomistic behavioral organizational psychology of estimative intelligence, first principles and group rational sensing and moral integration. Basically, WEICK was concerned about two issues: 1) Why do organizations unravel? And 2) How can organizations be more resilient?

---

[409] Ibid., 353. See MINTZBERG, AHLSTRAND and LAMPEL, *Strategy Safari*, 177–178: "Researchers sympathetic to the learning approach found that when significant strategic redirection did take place, it rarely originated from a formal planning effort, indeed often not even in the offices of the senior management. Instead strategies could be traced to a variety of little actions and decisions made by all sorts of different people) sometimes accidentally or serendipitously with no thought of their strategic consequences). Taken over time these small changes often produced major shifts in direction. In other words, informed individuals anywhere in an organization can contribute to the strategy process."

THE INCIDENT

As Maclean puts it, at its heart, the Mann Gulch disaster is a story of a race. The smokejumpers in the race (excluding the foreman Wag Dodge and Ranger Jim Harrison) were ages 17-28 unmarried, seven of them were forestry students and 12 of them had seen military service. They were a highly select group and often described themselves as professional adventurers.

A lightning storm passed over the Mann Gulch area at 4 pm on August 4, 1949 and is believed to have set a small fire. The next day, August 5, 1949, the temperature was 97 degrees and the fire danger was rating 74 out of a possible 100 which means "explosive potential." When the fire was spotted by a forest ranger, the smokejumpers were dispatched to fight it. Sixteen of them flew out of Missoula, Montana at 2:30 pm in a C-47 transport. Wind conditions that day were turbulent and one of smoke jumpers got sick on the airplane, didn't jump, returned to the base with the plane, and resigned from the smokejumpers as soon as he landed. His repressions had caught up with him, as Maclean writes: "The smokejumpers and their cargo were dropped on the south side of Mann Gulch at 4:10 from 2000 feet rather than the normal 1200 feet, due to the turbulence. The parachute that was connected to the radio failed to open.

The crew met ranger Jim Harrison who had been fighting the fire alone for four hours collected their supplies and ate supper. About 5:10, they started to move along the south side of the gulch to surround the fire. Dodge and Harrison however, having scouted ahead, were worried that the thick forest near which they had landed might be a "death trap." They told the second in command to take the crew across to the north side of the gulch and march them toward the river along the side of the hill. While Hellman did this, Dodge and Harrison ate a quick meal. Dodge rejoined the crew at 5:00pm and took his position at the head of the line moving toward the river. He could see flames flapping back and forth on the south slope as he looked to his left.

At this point the reader hits the most chilling sentence in the entire book. "Then Dodge saw it." What he saw was that the fire had crossed the gulch just 200 yards ahead and was moving toward them. Dodge turned the crew around and had them angle up the 76-percent hill toward the ridge at the top. They were soon moving bunch grass that was two and a half feet tall and were quickly losing ground to the 30-foot high flames that were soon moving toward them at 610 feet per minute. Dodge yelled at the crew to drop their tools, and then, to everyone's astonishment, he lit a fire in front of them and ordered them to lie down in the area it had burned. No one did, and they ran for the ridge. Two people, Sallee and Rumsey, made it through a crevice in the ridge unburned. Hellman made it over the ridge burned horribly and died at noon the next day. Doge lived by lying down in the ashes of his escape fire, and one other person, Joseph Sylvia, lived for a short while and then died. The hands-on Harrison's watch melted at 5:56 which has been treated as the time 3 people died.

After the fire passed, Dodge found Sallie and Rumsey, and stayed to care for Hellman while Sallie and Dodge hiked out for help. They walked into the Merriweather ranger station at 8:50pm and rescue parties immediately set out to recover the dead and dying. All the dead were found in the area of 100 yards. It took 450 men, five more days to get the 4,500-acre Mann Gulch fire under control. At the time the crew jumped on the fire, it was classified as a Class C fire, meaning its scope was between 10 and 99 acres.

The Forest Service inquiry held after the fire, judged by many to be inadequate, concluded that "there is no evidence of disregard by those responsible for the jumper crew of the elements of risk which they expected to take into account in placing jumper crews on fires." The board also felt that in placing the men would have been saved had they ". . . heeded Dodge's efforts to get them to go into the escape fire area with him." Several parents brought suit against the Forest Service, claiming that people should not have been jumped in the first place, but these claims were dismissed by the Ninth Circuit U.S. Court of Appeals, where Warren E. Burger argued the Forest Service case.

Since Mann Gulch, there have been no deaths by burning among Forest Service firefighters, and people are now equipped with back up radios, better physical conditioning, the tactic of building an escape fire, knowledge that fires in timber west of the Continental Divide burn differently than do fires in grass east of the Divide, and the insistence that crew safety take precedence over fire suppression.[410]

WEICK, as an organizational psychologist, was primarily focused on the question of

> In a fluid world, wise people know that they don't fully understand what is happening right now, because they have never seen precisely this event before. Extreme confidence and caution can destroy what organizations most need in changing times namely, curiosity, openness, and complex sensing.[411]

The question is important because in the movement to hierarchical-heterarchical organizations work is increasingly done in small temporary teams, crews and outfits were mistakes are costly. Like BARNARD's definition of a formal organization as a system of consciously coordinated activities or forces of two or more persons,[412] WEICK explains that "if a role system collapses among people for whom trust, honesty, and self-respect are underdeveloped, then they are on their own. And fear swamps their resourcefulness."[413] The Mann Gulch crew was a temporary team brought together for an ad hoc task under a crew leader with experience, although each member of the team had a certain skill set that qualified them as capable to fight a gulch fire. The crew had a supervisor, a strategy planned at the top, little formalized behavior and the person in charge using his estimative sense to prudentially grasp the situation, i.e., do the next right thing, the right for

---

[410] Karl E. WEICK, "The Collapse of Sensemaking in Organizations: The Mann Gulch Disaster," *Administrative Science Quarterly*, 38 (1993), 628–629.

[411] Ibid 641

[412] BARNARD, *The Functions of the Executive*, 42.

[413] Weick, "The collapse of Sensemaking in Organizations, 643

the right motives—to fight the fire and survive the combat. It was a situation of an emergent order on the edge of chaos and violent emotions. It was an ad hoc, somewhat of a desired order organization with rules and roles that enable a team to co-ordinate effectively and efficiently to complete the necessary task. In the crew at Mann Gulch there were at least three roles: the leaders, second in command, and crewmember. As WEICK explains, there were behavioral rules:[414]

1) The person in the lead sizes up the situation, makes decisions, yells orders, picks trails, sets the pace, an identifies escape routes.
2) The second in command brings up the rear of the crew as it hikes, repeats orders, sees that the orders are understood, helps the individuals coordinate their actions and tends to be closer to the crew and more a friend with them than the leader.
3) And finally, the crew clears a fire line around the fire, cleans up after the fire, and maintains trails. Thus, the crew at Mann Gulch is an organization by virtue of a role structure and interlocking routines.

WEICK reflects, as an organizational psychologist, that members of especially organizations with minimal order like the Mann Gulch crew are highly susceptible to loss of meaning, especially in the midst of incomprehensible events. He believes that people have a need to act as if events cohere in time and space and change unfolds in an orderly coherent manner. Based on the deep need to believe in the orderly organization of the universe, when the rational sense of this order is violently disrupted, as in the Mann Gulch disaster, he hypothesizes that a cosmology episode occurs when people suddenly and deeply feel that the universe is no longer a rational orderly system. What makes such an episode, so shattering is that both the sense of what is occurring and the means to rebuild that sense collapse together. A cosmology sense is the opposite of the déjà vu; rather it is this: "I've never been here before, I comprehend what order means, and I'm losing the race with the advancing fire." WEICK theorizes:

---

[414] Ibid., 633.

This is what the smokejumpers may have felt increasingly as the afternoon wore on and they lost what little organizational structure they had to start with. As they lost structure, they became more anxious and found it harder to make sense of what was happening, until they finally were unable to make any sense whatsoever of the one thing that would have saved their lives, an escape to the fire.[415]

From the perspective of a Thomistic behavioral psychological analysis, we have a situation similar to case 1, where there is perilous emerging disorder evolving into chaos. In such a situation, it is wise to realize ADLER's attention to the violent emotions of fear and anger. It is important to realize that in situations of threatening emerging disorder proportionate to the bodily sense of threat the violent emotions challenge rational control of the estimative sense and particular reason, i.e., estimative intelligence. Thus, as WEICK points out, as the day and the fire progressed, the crew members did less and less of what made sense.

> The crew expects a 10:00 fire but grows uneasy when the fire does not act like one. [...] Dodge and Harrison are eating supper, and the crew then wonders if the fire is serious as they hike to the river. [...] People are unclear who is in charge of the crew. [...] The flames on the south side of the gulch look intense. David Navon is taking pictures; crew members conclude it is not that serious, even though their senses tell them otherwise. [...] Crewmembers know they are moving close toward the river where they will be safe from the fire, and start angling upslope, but not running straight for the top. Why? (Dodge is the only one who sees the fire jump the gulch ahead of them.) [...] As the fire gain on them, Dodge says, "Drop your tools," but if the people in the crew do that, then who are they? Firefighters? With no tools? [...] The foreman (Dodge) lights a fire that seems to be right in the middle of the only escape route people can see. [...] The foreman points to the fire that he has started and yells, "Join me," whatever that means. "To hell with that, I'm getting out of here." [...] Each individual faces the

---

[415] Ibid., 633–634.

dilemma, I must be my own boss yet follow orders unhesitatingly, but I can't comprehend what the orders mean.[416]

The fire is no longer a 10:00 fire. The noise created by the wind, flames and exploding trees is deafening. The crewmembers are strung in a line with fellow firefighters who are relative strangers. They have never fought a fire previously as an integrated experienced and tested team. When the temperature rises, crew members can no longer communicate about their sense knowledge. It is hard to make team sense when each member seems to perceive something different. Consequently, it leads WEICK to state this general principle:

> The crew's stubborn belief that it faced a 10:00 fire is a powerful reminder that positive illusions can kill people. But the more general point is that organizations can be good at decision making and still falter. They falter because of deficient sensemaking. The world of decision making is about strategic rationality. It is built from clear questions and clear answers that attempt to remove ignorance. The world of sense making is about contextual rationality. It is about vague questions, muddy answers, and negotiated agreements that attempt to reduce confusion.[417]

5.5.3 Thomistic Organizational Faculty-Behavioral-Psychology and Common Sensemaking

In chapter four, we reasoned that a more proper understanding of organizational sensemaking is better approached as a method of common sensemaking. Common sensemaking of an organizational virtual quantity is achieved by means of an organizational sense making that leads to first principles. These first principles serve as causative principles of organizational of self-preservation and perfection. According to a Thomistic psychology of executive leadership and the diffusion of executive exemplar leadership character throughout the organization, it is a matter of the speculative and practical

---

[416] Ibid., 635.

[417] Ibid., 636.

understanding of first principles by all levels of organization leadership from the chief executive officer to a crew supervisor. A situation like the Mann Gulch situation is a situation where crewmembers driven by the most violent of emotions fear and anger are unable to focus, listen and obey the common-sense solution of the crew foreman.

AQUINAS says a person is virtuous who makes the effort to discover and apply first principles.[418] Consequently, we should expect that one of the characteristics of organizational leadership is the capability to discover and apply first causative principles, as the principles apply to his/her craft. Mann Gulch started with the assumption of the crewmembers that they were going to combat a 10-level fire. Although this crew had never previously worked as a team, they were experienced smokejumper fire fighters. They had confronted danger before, but it was the first time as a disintegrated organization that all previous patterns of either familiar desired order or manageable emergent order disappeared. Their sense of an ordered environment was replaced by the violent emotional sense of cosmic chaos, i.e., emptied of order and rationality. In this state of chaos, it is Dodge the crew leader who, in WEICK's terminology, is the Bricoleur that improvises under treacherous condition.[419]

---

[418] See AQUINAS, *Commentary on Aristotle's Nicomachean Ethics*, Book 2, Lecture 4: "If it should be asked how this is possible, since nothing can move itself from potency to act, we must answer that the perfection of moral virtue, which we are treating, consists in reason's control of the appetite. Now, the first principles of reason, no less in moral than in speculative matters, have been given by nature. Therefore, just as by means of previously known principles a man makes himself actually understand by personal effort of discovery, so also by acting according to the principles of practical reason a man makes himself actually virtuous."

[419] See Morris JANOWITZ, "Changing Pattern of Organizational Authority," *Military Establishment Authority Science Quarterly*, 1959, 481–639: "The collapse of role systems need not result in disaster if people develop skills in improvisation and bricolage. Bricoleurs remain creative under pressure, precisely because they routinely act in chaotic conditions and pull order out of them. Thus, when situations unravel, this is simply normal natural trouble for bricoleurs, and they proceed with whatever materials are at hand knowing these materials intimately, then they are able, usually in the company of other similarly skilled people, to form the materials or insights into novel combinations."

In situations of organizational emergent order or a chaotic and violent emotional situation common sensemaking of the situation at hand is required. Another way of stating the issue is that situations of organizational critical disorder call for, as WEICK describes, a Bricoleur who remains the creative problem solver under pressure and is able to improvise.

Furthermore, from the perspective of Thomistic behavioral psychology the Bricoleur is the agent of estimative intelligence who despite the violent emotional tension remains able to engage in rational thought prudentially grasps and applies first principles to the situation at hand.

A tactic used to fight a prairie fire was first mentioned in James Fenimore Cooper's 1827 novel, *The Prairie*. WEICK points out that there is no evidence that the foreman Dodge had read the book. Dodge's experience had been in timbered country where such a tactic wouldn't work. In a timber environment the escape fire is too slow and consumes too much oxygen. The fire Dodge built could not last long enough for the crew to move around and dodge the fire. There was just enough room to lie down on the ground.

WEICK describes emergent creativity as "figuring out what you already know in order to go beyond what you currently think."[420] We could say, in terms of a Thomistic faculty psychology, that Dodge under threatening conditions makes decisions and problem solving by means of analogy. Dodge was a hands-on experienced woodsman, besides being smokejumper and a fire fighter. He was very experienced in various methods of adaptation, problem solving and improvisation in the woods. He was the improvising Bricoleur who is someone able to create order out of whatever materials were at hand. As WEICK points out he would have known basic principles about the subject matter of starting a backup fire you:

> Dodge would have known at least two things about fire. He would have known the famous fire triangle [i.e., first principles]—you must have oxygen, flammable material, and temperature above the point of ignition to create a fire. A shortage of any one of these would prevent a fire. In his escape, the escape fire removed flammable material. And since Dodge had been with the Forest Service longer than anyone else on the crew, he would also have

---

[420] WEICK, "The Collapse of Sensemaking in Organizations," 639.

known more fully their four guidelines at the time for dealing with fire emergencies. These included: 1) start a backfire if you can, (2) get to the top of the ridge where the fuel is thinner, (3) turn into the fire and try to work through it, and (4) don't allow the fire to pick the spot where it hits you. Dodge's invention, if we stretch a bit, fits all four. It is backfire, though not in the conventional sense of a fire built to stop a fire. The escape fire is lit near the top of a ridge. Dodge turns into the main fire and works through it by burning a hole in it, and he chooses where the fire hits him. The crewmembers who tried to outrun the fire moved toward the ridge but not facing the fire, they allowed it to pick the spot where it hit them.[421]

What is vividly clear from this situation is the required character of a leader in an emergent situation. First, we must realize the extremely difficult behavioral challenge facing Dodge with a team that has never worked together in chaotic life-threatening conditions. For example, confronting the conditions of the Mann Gulch disaster would require a team of more than individual experience, rather it would call for a team with a sense of oneness, (i.e., a team thinking and moving as an integrated genus.)

If contemporary organizations are serious about the increasing importance of decentralized teams in the hierarchical-heterarchical organizational contrariety (H-HOC), then teams with major goals and task responsibilities must be understood as a genus and not just as tactical units with traits of coordinated, effective, and efficient activities. This was the major problem in the Mann Gulch disaster. It did not act as a generic unit.

Instead of behaving like a genus capable of fighting a fire (a fire-fighting unit) in an emergent situation on the edge of chaos, it lost its organizational unity. Dodge was able to improvise because, for a start, he had the capability to think in terms of analogy. He is an outdoor woodsman who had learned the principle of improvising with the conditions of materials at hand and performing fighter fighting in various conditions. He is able to transfer the principle of survival of combating the woods and fire from one situation to another.

---

[421] Ibid.

We call it the "generic transfer of an organizational principle of analogy." Dodge is an experienced leader who from the time the crewmembers arrive at the site, he is constantly estimating the risk factors of the fire as touching his senses and his particular reason is activated. AQUINAS describes particular reason as the following:

> Contingent things can be understood in two ways: in one way according to their universal concepts (*rationes*) in the other way as they are in the concrete. Accordingly, the universal concepts of contingent things are immutable. In this way demonstrations are given about contingent things, and the knowledge of them belongs to the demonstrative sciences. Natural science is concerned not only with necessary and incorruptible things but also with corruptible and contingent things. Hence it is evident that contingent things considered in this way belong to the same part of the intellective soul (called scientific by the philosopher) as necessary things, and the reasons presented proceed with this understanding. In the other way contingent things can be taken as they are in the real order. Thus, understood they are variable and do not fall under the intellect except by means of the sensitive powers. So, among the parts of the sensitive soul we place a power called particular reason or the sensory power of judgment, which collates particular impressions. It is in this sense that the Philosopher here understands contingent things, for thus they are objects of counsel and operation. For this reason, he says that necessary and contingent things, like speculative universals and operable things, belong to different parts of the rational soul.[422]

Dodge's behavior as a leader is to be in a constant state of estimative behavior attempting to prudentially grasp the strategy and tactics to escape the fire. It is Dodge who must serve as the executive leader of the crew firefighting genus, i.e. organizational whole. It is his task to decide what is the most doable deed to execute

---

[422] AQUINAS, *Commentary on Aristotle's Nicomachean Ethics*, Book 6, Lecture 1.

in order to escape.[423] Once Doyle has engaged in particular reason and has a prudent grasp of the doable deed in terms of tactics and materials; he is prepared to execute the plan because the rational thought of his practical intellect moves him effectively because from his varied experiences as a crewmember and foreman, by his inductive reasoning capacity and receptivity to first principles he knows both universal (famous fire triangle) and practical principles (four survival guidelines).

We often say when we speak about the nature of leadership that we want a person who is practical. Simultaneously, we assume that the practical person has learned from experience. It is interesting how we will use metaphors in companies when we are looking for leaders, e.g., "we want a person who gets down to the concrete, we want people with good grades, but they must have street smarts. We want leaders who can get the job done." On the other hand, we will use metaphors of estimation, e.g., "We want people who can see the big picture." Wayne Dodge is not only focused on the situation at hand, he begins to focus intensely via his estimative sense. He estimates the risk and danger of the particularities of the situation perceiving by means of his external and internal senses. Simultaneously, he must estimate not only a strategy for fighting the fire, but as he senses it is not a level-10 fire he must think in terms of an escape strategy.

Any efficient and effective leader in contingent situations must think analogically as a leader in emergent to chaotic disorder in the organization of the

---

[423] See REDPATH, *The Moral Psychology of St. Thomas*, 349–350: "Prudence is about giving good advice regarding organizing plans of action (strategies and tactics) related to changeable matters worthy of deliberation: concrete actions to take in variable situations. Furthermore, Aristotle maintains that prudence and art cannot be identical because they are different intellectual acts having generically different formal objects, qualitatively different kinds of doable deeds. Prudence studies the genus of action, chiefly aims at terminating choice in a well-done deed, while art studies the genus of making, and chiefly aims at terminating choice in a well-made product, producing some organized whole (like a house or a bridge). Aristotle and St. Thomas maintain that knowledge of contingent beings cannot possess truth's certainty in affirming truth and rejecting falsehood and cannot perfect the intellect as speculative knowing can. However, it can perfect the intellect as commanding, controlling, prescribing the useful, doable deed, and directing human acts to satisfy ends. As Aristotle says, art is a habit concerned with making something through reason. Hence, every productive habit directed by reason is art."

genus. In the Mann Gulch disaster, Dodge must move to a new emerging final cause, i.e., to escape. Here we learn the most important issue of emergent leadership, when there is no desired order of efficiently and effectively defeating the fire, the purpose, the emerging form of the genus (team as an organizational whole) is to escape. Doyle could not come up with a plan, unless he is able to estimate the situation and then from memory and imagination begin to see an escape route. He must draw upon the universal principles about the nature of fire and the practical guideline principles and by analogy from previous experience apply his knowledge to the Mann Gulch escalating fire. It is impossible to lead in such an emergent situation without the ability to estimate, draw upon embodied first principles and set a plan for the doable deed. Without estimative intelligence and first principles, a person cannot lead in emergent order situations.

As argued in the previous IBM policy paper, the major issue for organizational executive leadership is the contrariety of the harmony between desired order and emergent order. Therefore, it calls upon an executive leadership based on a Thomistic concept of estimative intelligence which is the foundation of leadership and practical reasoning, i.e., "doing the next right thing, for the next right reason, the right way." Yes, leaders must be practical; however, we must be careful in the use of the meaning of being practical. A person cannot be practical without right reason. Being practical is not just being efficient. The leader must exercise his/her full rational powers and execute the plan for the right motive. Dodge builds the escape route for the right end; he wills to lead his crew to safety as the good leader, and here we have the full meaning of the practical leader. AQUINAS describes the meaning of being practical as follows:

> Every worker acts for the sake of something belonging to a thing, i.e., which has some use, as the use of a house is habitation. This then is the end of the worker, viz., something made and not a thing done. Therefore, it is not something done, since in immanent actions the good action itself is the end, for example, rightly desiring or justly becoming angry. As the practical mind is for the sake of this end, either a thing made or an action, so also the appetitive faculty is for the sake of some particular end.[424]

---

[424] AQUINAS, *Commentary on Aristotle's Nicomachean Ethics*, Book 6, Lecture 2.

According to a Thomistic organization behavioral psychology of leadership, a leader must see the big picture and touch concrete activities, situations, and operations, and this is achieved when the leader uses his/her full rational powers, i.e. rational and sense knowledge. AQUINAS writes:

> [Aristotle] infers from the premises that knowledge of the truth is the work of each part of the intellect, namely, the practical and the speculative or scientific and the estimative (*ratiocinative*). Then he deduces lastly that those habits by which the truth—the good of the intellective part—is manifested, are virtues of both divisions of the intellect.[425]

In the Mann Gulch disaster, the team is experiencing the violent emotion of fear and senses the collapse of order. The crew came with a clear purpose and belief to put out a small fire quickly and they encountered a big calamitous one. It is a team called to a low-level threat task that suddenly turns into a catastrophic fire. The crew members sense of being a part of a genus (organizational whole) collapses because their sense of order has turned to chaos. Since they have lost the sense of being part of the harmonious order of a genus, each member, in a way, must become their own genus. Furthermore, when the foreman yells out the command, "do what I am doing," they trust their individual athletic ability and attempt to outrun the fire up the hill. They would have lived if they had trusted Wayne Dodge because he knows the necessary universal and practical principles. Even though the concept of the "escape hole" applied to brush fires by analogy, he applies the tactic to a timber fire. It was a team without the experience of fighting major fires. They had been thrust into a situation of not only emergent disorder, but emergent disorder equates to emergent genus in chaos and it equates to the destruction of the generic nature required for survival. When the sense of the crew members as being a part of a common sensemaking genus collapses, it becomes everybody for themselves.

It is similar in a business organization when the estimative intelligence of employees begins to realize that the executive levels of an organization is unable to lead the organizational whole in times of crisis. There is initially a collective sense

---

[425] Ibid.

of demotivation. Wendelin KUPERS has a scholarly comprehension of the emotional causes, processes, and effects of demotivation of organizational demotivation.[426] Employees sense the collapse of the organizational generic nature, with cultural changes, new technologies and media that transform work patterns, ongoing downsizing, delayering strategies, outsourcing certain functions, and increasing job insecurity. When employees experience "genus collapse" they look for their escape route. In the generic collapsing organization most often, it is the most productive, intelligent, and respected employees with the most impressive resumes and are recognized throughout the industry who are the first to escape. Or, employees, in the state of violent emotions, facing "genus collapse" cease to focus on a level of organizational excellence (virtual quantity), and look for a safe corporate, non-risk niche.

In these two cases we have applied ADLER's concept of the "violent emotions" of anger and fear because in stressful, threatening competitive or highly career threatening task performance situations these are the emotions most physiologically experienced. Indeed, it is the experience of the "violent emotions" that leads to the impulsive movements of an unhealthy estimative sense. By far, the strongest indication of the collapse of an organizational genus is when there is in an organizational atmosphere of growing fear and brooding despair. As we saw in the Mann Gulch situation, the supervisor, as a leader, tempers his fear and focuses his rational thought and estimative sense on a doable escape route.

We maintained (in chapter three) that the primary function of executive leadership is "to constantly instill hope, drive out fear, build and restore confidence, energize, and calm emotions." The virtues of hope and courage (confidence) and the prudential grasp of the situation [prudence] must be expressed at any level of leadership, especially in the age of the hierarchical-heterarchical organizational tension, where the eruption of fear and anger lays dormant as emergent disorder can easily lead to chaos. Put simply, the function of executive leadership is to express the character of being known for making

---

[426] Wendelin KUPERS, "A Phenomenology of embodied passion and the demotivational realities of organizations," St. Gallen Switzerland: Institute for Leadership and H-R Management, 2001. Retrieved from http://www.mngt.waikato.ac.nz/ejrot/cmsconference/2001/Papers/Passion%20for%20Organising/Kupers.pdf

decisions that lead to "doing the next right thing, the right way, for the right motive," most importantly as organizational desired order is threatened.

5.6 The Contending Genus and Teleological Behavior, Instilling Organizational Hope and Driving Out Fear

Before discussing the challenge of leadership to constantly drive out fear and instill hope, we must begin to turn our attention presently and in the coming chapter to the nature of a Thomistic organizational psychology and an organizational Thomistic teleological behavior and a faculty psychology. We open this behavioral application in the present chapter because it is necessary to appreciate the dynamics of the violent emotions of fear, anger, and leadership, as it relates to the desired order-emergent order contrariety and the collapse of organizational harmony. AQUINAS has a rather extensive and somewhat complicated organizational psychology of the virtuous habits of behavior, particularly as it relates to emotions and the movements of the sense appetite.[427]

In terms of an Aristotelian-Thomistic behavioral psychology, emotions are movements of the sense appetites. As mentioned in the core principles of a Thomistic behavioral psychology, St. Thomas defines what, today, we generally call an emotion (but what he calls a passion) is a psychosomatic change reaction. When discussing emotions in the framework of a Thomistic behavioral psychology, we will use the word passions rather than emotions. The reason for the use of Aristotelian-Thomistic concept of passion is that it is much more expression of the feeling of movement which draws a faculty toward or pushes it away from union

---

[427] REDPATH, *The Moral Psychology of St. Thomas*, 63: "Total qualitative completeness in ability, power, to possess act makes something perfect; and completeness in ability to possess perfection make something good. And the limits of ability to have, to possess, to resist or receive having completeness in act is determined by the principle of virtual quantity, which is precisely what St. Thomas understands by a "form. "Forms are limited principles of receptivity and resistance to act, and chiefly to the act of existence. In a way, forms are limited principles of receptivity and resistance to act, and chiefly to the act of existence."

with or separation from a formal object (external stimulus).[428] As we continue to apply a Thomistic faculty-behavioral-psychology, we will sometimes use the behaviorist language of discriminative stimulus to describe a faculty drawn toward or pushed away from a formal object. We will, also, use the word passion because the word emotion in contemporary psychology is associated with the concept of emotional intelligence and because of the influence of the theory of emotional intelligence in regard to organizational leadership. In the final chapter, we argue that the Thomistic concept of particular reason and emotional mastery is a more fitting concept for understanding the nature of organizational leadership than emotional intelligence.

5.6.1 The Nature of Teleological Behavioral Psychology and Organizational Action

We must, therefore, give a concise presentation of the Thomistic behavioral psychology of the passions and hopeful, fearful, and calming action. An Aristotelian-Thomistic behaviorist approaches the understanding of behavior based fundamentally on the observation of actions and passion. We start with an Aristotelian-Thomistic definition of action:

> I am talking about human operations of those springing from man's will following the order of reason. But if some operations are found in man that are not subject to the will and reason, they are not properly called human but natural, as clearly appears in operations of the vegetative soul. These in no way fall under the consideration of moral philosophy. As the subject of natural philosophy is motion, or mobile being, so the subject of moral philosophy is human action ordered to an end, or even man, as he is an agent voluntarily acting for end.[429]

---

[428] Ibid., 126.

[429] AQUINAS, *Commentary on Aristotle's Nicomachean Ethics*, Book 1, Lecture 1.

AQUINAS presents the study of human action, what we would call today a science of teleological behavior, since it is human action ordered to an end. The teleological behavioral study is of the person who voluntarily acts for an end. AQUINAS expands into what we call today an organizational teleological behavioral psychology:

It must be understood that, because man is by nature a social animal needing many things to live which he cannot get for himself if alone, he naturally is a part of a group that furnishes him to live well. He needs this help for two reasons. First to have what is necessary for life, without which he cannot live the present life; and for this, man is helped by his domestic group of which he is apart. For every man is indebted to his parents for his generation and his nourishment and instruction. Likewise, individuals, who are members of a family, help one another to procure the necessities of life.[430]

He uses military organization as an example, and then divides his study into three parts:

It must be known moreover that the whole which the political group or the family constitutes has only a unity of order, for it is something absolutely one. A part for this whole, therefore, can have an operation that is not the operation of the whole as a soldier in an army has an activity that does not belong to the whole army. However, the whole does have an operation that is proper to its parts to the whole—for example, an assault of the entire army and likewise, the movement of the entire army. Likewise, the movement of the boat is a combined operation of the crew among the boat [...]. Thus, moral philosophy is divided into three parts. The first of these, which is called individual (monastic) ethics, considers an individual's operations as ordered to an end. The second, called domestic ethics, consider the operations of the domestic group. The third, called political science considers the operations of the civic group.[431]

---

[430] Ibid.

[431] Ibid.

It is easily missed when reading AQUINAS that moral philosophy is about the science of human action as ordered to an end. Even more so, the modern-day reader would miss that it also is a science of organizational behavior. AQUINAS and ARISTOTLE teach that man is by nature a social animal, but it is necessary to realize that this man is a social animal whose actions are ordered to an end. As a result, we are also organizational by nature. Aquinas explains that "like the movement of a boat and the combined operation of the crew it is a kind of whole with a unity of order."[432] This moral philosophy as a science which considers an organizational whole and the unity of its parts is divided into three parts, i.e., the individual, the domestic and the political. It is, consequently, necessary to grasp that a moral philosophy and organizational psychology are part of the genus of the science of organization, i.e., social order, as REDPATH describes:

> *Loss of an understanding of the nature of philosophical metaphysics and ethics as essential means for inculcating with maximum intensity principles of leadership within the psychological makeup of leaders is, in fact, a chief cause of the present civilizational decline, anarchy, of the West.* Centuries ago, Western civilization lost its understanding of the nature of philosophy as an organizational psychology. With that loss, the West also lost its understanding of the natures of metaphysics, ethics, and science as habits of leadership excellence of the human soul: acts of organizational excellence that human beings generate, cause, through acquired habits existing within innately possessed powers of the human soul [....] An organizational psychology of the human person (facultative self-understanding) generates rudimentary principles of moral awareness out of which grows cultural awareness; and out of principles of cultural awareness (habits of the soul) are generated all other human virtue (leadership qualities of soul), including the virtue of prudential leadership that proximately causes principles that generate habits of art, philosophy, and science (philosophy and science being actually identical).[433]

---

[432] Ibid.

[433] REDPATH, *The Moral Psychology of St. Thomas*, 22-23.

5.6.2 *Powers of Rational Thought, Behavioral Action and Passions*

In terms of behavior, AQUINAS's mechanism for action can be understood as a kind of decision theory with the sensitive powers allowing a living being to interact with and respond to the outside world:

- Locomotion (self-movement)
- Five external sense-hearing, sight, smell, touch, and taste
- Four internal senses-memory, imagination, common sense, and estimative sense
- Eleven passions (emotions)
- Concupiscible appetite is attraction to pleasure (whether trying to an easily obtainable good, or avoiding an easily obtainable good, or avoiding and easily avoidable evil).
- Irascible appetite is something responding to/ desiring a difficult good or avoiding a difficult evil.

Stimuli arouse the sense powers inside or outside of the person. In the approach of a teleological behavioral psychology, we refer to stimuli as discriminative stimuli, i.e., the external senses correlate with behavior. In the next chapter, effort will be given to a more complete explanation of Thomistic faculty-behavioral-psychology. Presently we are focused on RACHLIN's school of Teleological Behaviorism. Teleological Behaviorism (TB) is quite different than the Skinnerian school of stimuli, response and operant behavior based on classification of behavior in terms of classical and instrumental conditioning.

Table 3: Skinnerian Radical Behavioral Model 4 Basic Kinds

	Stimulus Presented	Stimulus Removed
Pleasant Stimulus	*Positive reinforcement*	*Omission*
Noxious Stimulus	*Punishment*	*Escape (negative reinforcement)*

The consequences of a specific act classify instrumental conditioning. For example, if a specific act is followed by the presentation of a pleasant stimulus (a reward), the instrumental conditioning is classified as positive-reinforcement conditioning.[434]

RACHLIN's Teleological Behavior differs from Skinnerian behavior in major ways:

> It is a behavioral method that observes actions and passions, according to Aristotle, as governed by the rational aspects of the soul unique to humans. The process of actions is as follows:
>
> In the world, an object, consisting of a certain substance in a certain form, transmits its form through the air or another medium (making am impression much as a signet ring makes an impression of its form on wax) to one or more of a person's sense organs. The form of the object combines in the person's imagination with other forms from memory. The combined images are reflected upon by thought and the person engages in thoughtful (i.e., rational) behavior (See Figure 1).

Figure 1

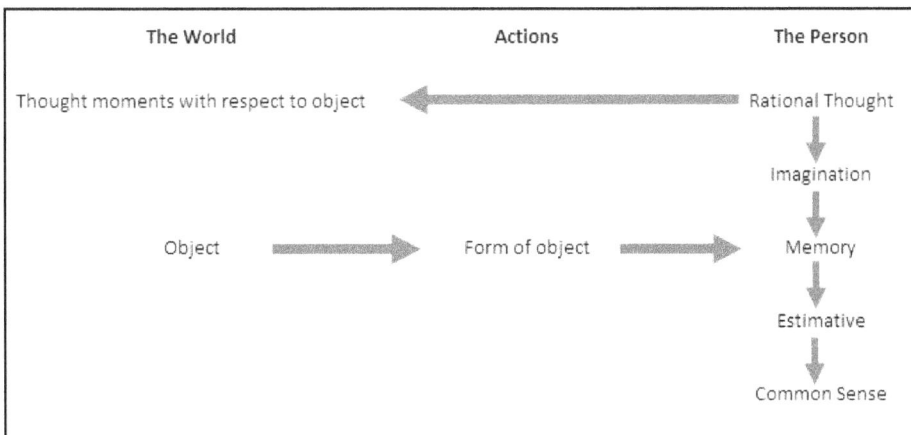

---

[434] Howard RACHLIN, *Introduction to Modern Behaviorism* (San Francisco: W.H. Freeman, 1970), 79.

Aristotle believed that animals other than humans are not capable of rational thought. However, because all animals (including humans) have sensitive souls, all are capable of a different kind of movement-passions. Aristotle's concept of passions differed from modern notions in the sense that passions, for him, are movements- they cannot boil up inside. For him a man cannot just feel passionate, he has to be passionate.

Again, an object in the world transfers its form through a medium to a sense organ and into a person's body. When the form of an object enters the body, it interacts with the soul. Aristotle conceived of the soul as a kind of organization; therefore, we can say that the form of the object comes into contact with the body's organization not the more complex organization of the rational soul possessed only by humans, but a subcategory of that organization, possessed by all animals.

At that point the form of the object can be in harmony with the form of the soul or out of harmony with the form of the soul (much as a square peg is in harmony with a square hole and a round peg with a round hole). If its form is in harmony with an animal's soul, the object causes pleasure. Pleasure is in turn implies the existence of a desire to move toward the object, and the desire implies the occurrence of the movement itself. If, on the other hand, the form of the object is out of harmony with the animal's soul, the object causes pain; pain implies the existence of a desire to move away from the object, and the desire implies the occurrence of the movement itself (see Figure 2).[435]

Figure 2

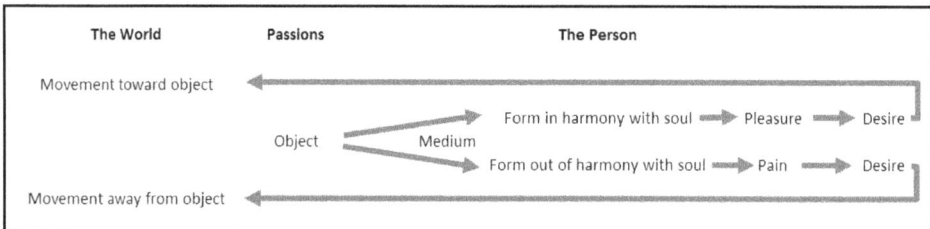

The World	Passions	The Person		
Movement toward object				
	Object	Medium	Form in harmony with soul → Pleasure → Desire	
			Form out of harmony with soul → Pain → Desire	
Movement away from object				

---

[435] RACHLIN, *Judgment, Decision and Choice*, 230–232.

It seems to hold that the mind must be inside the body and controlling it, as a driver controls the motion of a car. The reason for the confusion is that for modern science a cause is usually what ARISTOTLE called efficient cause: "For Aristotle, the mind is not an efficient cause but a final cause of bodily movement."[436] Radical Skinnerian efficient causality behaviorism uses a narrow classification of environment or behavior, i.e., the belief that complex processes, whether mental or behavioral, may be explained in terms of small units and rules for their combination. However, Teleological Behaviorism uses a broad classification of environment or behavior. The belief that stimuli or responses broadly classified may be lawfully described without reference to smaller units, as follows:[437]

Teleological Behaviorism accepts mental states as objects of scientific study but, once and for all rejects introspection as a path to scientific truth. From the viewpoint of TB, introspective reports are parts of patterns of overt behavior that can be explained, like any other such patterns, in terms of contingencies of reinforcement. And this includes such apparent introspective certainties as "I know my own head," "I know what I like," and, "I think therefore I am." TB does not deny that we know things, that we may be certain of things, that we have sensations or that we think. However, TB does deny that such events occur inside the organism and are available to the organism alone. TB asserts that those events occur in patterns of the organism's overt behavior and are available to anyone who can observe those patterns over extended periods of time.[438]

What we are applying, and will continue in the coming chapter, is a Thomistic faculty behaviorism that involves the interaction of rational thought, actions, and passions. Behavior we could, also, refer to it as rational behavioral psychology which is different than cognitive behavioral psychology. Mainly, the cognitive psychologists differ in that their aim is to use their observations to discover the

---

[436] RANDALL, *Aristotle*, 124.

[437] RACHLIN, *Introduction to Modern Behaviorism*, terminology glossary.

[438] Howard RACHLIN, "About Teleological Behaviorism," *The Behavior Analyst*, 2013, 36, 209–210.

internal (computer-like) mechanism underlying behavior; rational behavioral psychologists attempt to explain behavior in its own terms.[439] If we agree that Thomistic behavioral psychology holds that the intellect desires the truth of things, i.e., to receive things in themselves, this means that we are able by rational thought to know that we know, think about our thinking, consequently the proper operation of the intellect is to know, and the proper operation is to know the truth. Therefore, the intellect (rational thought) has three proper operations: abstraction, judgment, and reasoning.

AQUINAS divided the passions (emotions into two categories based on attraction to the good and aversion to the good). REDPATH uses a terminology to describe the sense appetite that fits into a more behavioral psychology.

> He refers to the passions as the propelling passions (emotions) and the contending passions (emotions). The propelling emotions are reactions to object which are perceived simply as fitting or unfitting in relation to sense desire. The mark of a contending passion (emotion) is much like the mark of a contender in boxing. There is a definite order of movement to the passions: 1) love and hatred, 2) desire and aversion, 3) hope and despair, 4) fear and daring, 5) anger and 6) pleasure (+) and pain (-).[440]

Table 4: The Eleven Passions (Emotions)

Propelling (Concupiscible)		Contending (Irascible)	
Simple Good +	Simple Evil -	Difficult Good	Difficult Evil -
Love	*Hatred*	*Hope*	*Courage*
Desire	*Aversion*	*Despair*	*Fear*
Joy	*Sadness*		*Anger*

---

[439] RACHLIN, *The Escape of The Mind*, 58.

[440] Peter A. REDPATH, *The Moral Wisdom of St. Thomas* (Lanham: University Press of America, 1983), 61–62: "An emotion is a reaction caused within either the propelling or contending sense appetite by the suspicion that something pleasant or unpleasant, useful or useless, safe or harmful and accompanied by physiological change."

From the perspective of a Thomistic organizational psychology of leadership we have moved in this chapter to an Aristotelian-Thomistic behavioral psychology. In the coming chapter, in more detail, we will defend why and how this behavioral application is most compatible with a Thomistic psychology of soulful leadership. Even more important, we will suggest that it is best, in the age of contemporary psychology, to refer to traditional rational psychology as a faculty-behavioral-psychology. The main purpose, however, in this chapter is an examination of the hierarchical-heterarchical tension of desired order and emergent order from the perspective of function of executive leadership and the diffusion of a character of leadership throughout the organization. We selected two case studies of situations in critical emergent status calling for emotional mastery and right decision making, where order turned into chaos. In case 2, the Mann Gulch disaster was a situation of the collapse of a sense of the organizational genus. We observed the critical phenomena of members of an organization experiencing a sense genus collapse. When this collapse of genus occurs, an atmosphere of a lack of hope and fear diffuses throughout an organization. It is at the point of an emerging genus collapse that employees driven by the passions of despair and fear begin to look for an "escape route" form the genus. Indeed, in the Mann Gulch case 2, whatever chance the smokejumpers might have had to survive is not seen by the crew as an integrated team. Their only chance of survival was to think and feel like the members of a genus. It is difficult because a genus is based on leaders and members with a respect for principles, and leaders who understand the importance of contrariety and blending units and teams into one functional genus.

5.6.3 Organizational Collapse of Harmony and Contending Passions

In an organizational whole (genus), there is always the tension of desired order and emergent order. It is a simple principle, but it is most important. If I ask a CEO "how is business," he might say, "it has been good for three months, but right now something strange is going on. I hope it does not last for long." It is the contrariety tension. AQUINAS teaches, "Hence, the object of the irascible power is said to be the difficult (*arduum*), because the irascible power tends toward overcoming contraries and winning out over them."[441] The irascible tension calms down by the guidance of the rational soul. A leader must be aware of the irascible tension in self and others in order to lead.

When the irascible tension is high and driven by the violent passions of fear and anger which so easily blend together, *three behavioral patterns will kick in*, and fear means:

1) Forget everything and run,
2) False evidence appears as real, or
3) Face everything and recover the rational powers of my soul.

Number 2 is very important because executive leadership in a high state of irascible tension will usually spend much time and money collecting unnecessary and false evidence (information, data) that only increases the tension in the long run. It is particular reason and mastery of the contending (irascible) passions that allows an agent to pay attention with an appropriate level of tension to solve the problem at hand, i.e., option 3. Take option 1 and the agent looks for an escape route from the tension. It is the case study of the Mann Gulch Disaster, which establishes the principle of the leader and "controlling irascible tension." Another way of putting the principle is that: *Really competent leaders can give maximum attention with minimum tension and really incompetent leaders give minimum attention and maximum tension.*

Organizational harmony will collapse in an environment of continuously high irascible tension because estimative attention decreases. We are putting this forth as a Thomistic organizational behavioral principle of leadership in irascible situations of emergent to chaotic dynamics under the potential of generic collapse. The basic behavioral contrariety-tension is, "all the passions of the irascible power take their origin from passions of the concupiscible power and terminate in the latter."[442] The irascible tension of contrariety (the *arduum*) is, as AQUINAS describes, the phenomena.

---

[441] AQUINAS, *Summa theologiae* I, q. 81 a. 2.
[442] Ibid.

This is clear also from the fact that the irascible is, as it were, the champion and defender of the concupiscible when it rises up against what hinders the acquisition of the suitable things which the concupiscible desires, or against what inflicts harm, from which the concupiscible lies.[443]

AQUINAS teaches the irascible tension principle: "the soul resists opposing things [...] the irascible power tends toward overcoming contraries and winning out over them."[444] Of course, the tension is only resolved by focus on rational

---

[443] Ibid.

[444] Ibid.: "The sensitive appetite is one generic power and is called sensuality; but it is divided into two powers, which are species of the sensitive appetite—the irascible and the concupiscible. In order to make this clear, we must observe that in natural corruptible things there is needed an inclination not only to the acquisition of what is suitable and to the avoiding of what is harmful, but also to resistance against corruptive and contrary agencies which are a hindrance to the acquisition of what is suitable and are productive of harm. For example, fire has a natural inclination, not only to rise from a lower position, which is unsuitable to it, toward a higher position which is suitable, but also to resist whatever destroys or hinders its action. Therefore, since the sensitive appetite is an inclination following sensitive apprehension, as natural appetite is an inclination following the natural form, there must needs be in the sensitive part two appetitive powers—one through which the soul is simply inclined to seek what is suitable, according to the senses, and to fly from what is hurtful, and this is called the concupiscible: and another, whereby an animal resists these attacks that hinder what is suitable, and inflict harm, and this is called the irascible. We say that its object is something arduous because its tendency is to overcome and rise above obstacles. Now these two are not to be reduced to one principle: for sometimes the soul busies itself with unpleasant things, against the inclination of the concupiscible appetite, in order that, following the impulse of the irascible appetite, it may fight against obstacles. Wherefore also the passions of the irascible appetite counteract the passions of the concupiscible appetite: since the concupiscence, on being aroused, diminishes anger; and anger being roused, diminishes concupiscence in many cases. This is clear also from the fact that the irascible is, as it were, the champion and defender of the concupiscible when it rises up against what hinders the acquisition of the suitable things which the concupiscible desires, or against what inflicts harm, from which the concupiscible flies. And for this reason, all the passions of the irascible appetite rise from the passions of the concupiscible appetite and terminate in them; for instance, anger rises

thought and principles of action. However, first an estimative leader must master the emotions before he/she is able to focus in rational thought.

5.6.4. Virtuous Leader and Mastery of the Irascible Passions

Both ARISTOTLE and AQUINAS teach that a person is not virtuous unless the person is moved to develop moral character. A person must decide that he/she wishes to act as a virtuous person which requires control of the appetites. We could call it a "mastery of the passions." A person, according to AQUINAS, becomes a virtuous leader by the personal effort of understanding, discovery and by acting according to the principles of practical reason that he/she becomes actually virtuous. All the emotions are caused by love since love is the passion that draws us to the good (whether it is present or absent). Consequently, love is the principle and first passion that makes the other passions possible. As a result, al the passions are organized under the genus of the concupiscible because the purpose of the passions is to draw the soul to the pleasure that is in harmony with the soul. However, in the genus (organizational whole) of passion the irascible passions rank as the highest because of their utilitarian importance.

Since organizations exist in the contrariety of the desired and emerging order tension and depending on the nature and developmental stage of the organization, understanding the behavioral dynamics and mastery of irascible passions is a critical element of leadership.

Redpath explains the behavioral dynamic principles of the contending passions of hope and fear:[445]

1) There exists two opposites (contraries): a) perfect pleasure that attracts us, b) imperfect pleasure that repels us.

2) By nature, all animals have a natural inclination of the concupiscible appetite to move toward pleasure and away from pain (see Figure 2).

---

from sadness, and having wrought vengeance, terminates in joy. For this reason, also, the quarrels of animals are about things concupiscible—namely, food and sex, as the Philosopher says."

[445] REDPATH, *The Moral Psychology of St. Thomas*, 130–131.

3) Passions in the irascible appetite are complicated because species of opposition exist. The passions of hope and fear, simultaneously, can have contrary terms (such as safe and dangerous) and have opposite relational movements toward the same object (like moving toward and away from the fear-generating subject). A hopeful person might, for instance, attack something painful or dangerous and, if the thing in question was a real danger to personal health or safety, get a pleasure of a qualitatively greater kind in doing so.

4) The objects of the concupiscible (propelling) appetite attract us in simple and straightforward way (as pleasurable goods), while the object of the irascible appetite attract us chiefly as useful goods, but, secondarily as pleasurable or painful goods.

5) The passion of love is in the concupiscible (propelling) appetite and is the first principle of all other passions. Love is present wherever a human passion is present, and pleasure is present when love is satisfied.

6) Nevertheless, hope, not love, is the chief passion of the irascible appetite, the first principle of all the irascible passions, all of which contain love and hope as essential parts of the composites, constitutional make up.

7) The passions of the concupiscible appetite essentially relate to anything imaginable, while the passions of the irascible appetite focus only on doable deeds. The formal object of the concupiscible appetite is anything we presently can imagine to be likable/loveable or unlikable/unlovable, while the formal object of the irascible appetite is anything, we can imagine to be future, possible, and difficult.

We have taken the position that organizations are in a constant state of desired order and emergent order. Depending upon the nature of internal and external emergent factors, the organizational response can be one of best-case scenario hope or courage, or worst-case despair and fear. For example, it is a best-case opportunity for growth, expansion or and amplification of the virtual intensity (perfection) of the organization. Or, it is a worse case internal or external factor that threatens virtual intensity of the organizational whole. Therefore, it is the responsibility to remain vigilant to the positive or negative impact of emergent disorder. It is not only the executive level that must remain attentive to the implications of internal and external emergent disorder, but every level of leadership and every individual member of the organization.

Again, we emphasize in this study of organizational leadership that the impact of emergent disorder exists in any organization, e.g., profit, government, nonprofit, religions, education, volunteer and even the family and neighborhood organizations. As organizations experience the stress of the emergent order the organization and members enter into the state of contending tension. When agents are in the state of contending tension, as a rule, often the first behavioral response will come from fear and/or anger because the desired order is disrupted. AQUINAS teaches, "Fear is startled at things unwanted and sudden, which endanger things beloved, and takes forethought for their safety."[446]

---

[446] AQUINAS, *Summa theologiae* I–II, q. 42 a. 5: "Augustine says (*Confess.* ii, 6): 'Fear is startled at things unwonted and sudden, which endanger things beloved, and takes forethought for their safety'. I answer that, As stated about, the object of fear is an imminent evil, which can be repelled, but with difficulty. Now this is due to one of two causes: to the greatness of the evil, or to the weakness of him that fears; while unwontedness and suddenness conduce to both of these causes. First, it helps an imminent evil to seem greater. Because all material things, whether good or evil, the more we consider them, the smaller they seem. Consequently, just as sorrow for a present evil is mitigated in course of time, as Cicero states (*De Quaest. Tusc.* iii, 30); so, too, fear of a future evil is diminished by thinking about it beforehand. Secondly, unwontedness and suddenness increase the weakness of him that fears, in so far as they deprive him of the remedies with which he might otherwise provide himself to forestall the coming evil, were it not for the evil taking him by surprise. Reply to Objection 1: The object of hope is a good that is possible to obtain. Consequently, whatever increases a man's power, is of a nature to increase hope, and, for the same reason, to diminish fear, since fear is about an evil which cannot be easily repelled. Since, therefore, experience increases a man's power of action, therefore, as it increases hope, so does it diminish fear. Reply to Objection 2: Those who are quick-tempered do not hide their anger; wherefore the harm they do others is not so sudden, as not to be foreseen. On the other hand, those who are gentle, or cunning hide their anger; wherefore the harm which may be impending from them, cannot be foreseen, but takes one by surprise. For this reason, the Philosopher says that such men are feared more than others. Reply to Objection 3: Bodily good or evil, considered in itself, seems greater at first. The reason for this is that a thing is more obvious when seen in juxtaposition with its contrary. Hence, when a man passes

When organizations are in states of contending tension, they must have leaders who are experienced in the mastery of the emotions and their competence in the practice of estimative intelligence. It is such leadership that is capable of practicing this principle: *Really competent leaders that can give maximum attention with minimum tension as opposed to really incompetent leaders who can give minimum attention and maximum tension.* The state of tension has a behavioral impact of fear because, as AQUINAS explains, fear is an expectation.

> Hence philosophers, in giving a definition of fear say that it is an expectation of evil. Expectation is here taken generally for any movement, of the appetitive faculty toward some future things although expectation properly speaking is directed only to the good, as is hope.[447]

The initial task of the contending leader, no matter the fear of emergent disorder, is to calm the tense fearful and angry passions by focusing on hope. However, in order to focus on hope fear must be minimalized and utilized. The basic responsibility of leadership is to approach emergent disorder by means of strategy and tactics. Initially, it is necessary to estimate the risk factors involved in addressing an emergent threat or possibility. If it is a threat, then two estimations must be made: 1) Have we faced a risk like this before? 2) Do we have the resources of human power, technology, economic, etc., to attack the issue? In facing organizational emergent issues, it calls for the exercise of particular reason to focus on the "doable deed." Meaning, the initial inquiry seeks to answer the question are we capable of doing the next right thing, the right way for the right motive.

In doubtful matters AQUINAS maintains we deliberate about our abilities and other issues that can affect performance, getting the job done. AQUINAS does not

---

unexpectedly from penury to wealth, he thinks more of his wealth on account of his previous poverty: while, on the other hand, the rich man who suddenly becomes poor, finds poverty all the more disagreeable. For this reason, sudden evil is feared more, because it seems more to be evil. However, it may happen through some accident that the greatness of some evil is hidden; for instance, if the foe hides himself in ambush: and then it is true that evil inspires greater fear through being much thought about."

[447] AQUINAS, *Commentary on Aristotle's Nicomachean Ethics*, Book 14, Lecture 14.

develop a structured cognitive behavioral method for seeking deliberation counseling. He, instead, gives sound behavioral principles: 1) fear makes men of counsel (face everything and recover the rational powers of my soul); 2) we take counsel on great matters, because we distrust ourselves;[448] 3) counsel essentially involves the work of the estimative sense (particular reason: things seem to him greater or smaller than they are); 4) fear incites to counsel more than hope does (false evidence appearing as real).

Here, we will introduce an important principle of teleological behaviorism that we will continue to enhance in the coming chapter. A teleological behaviorist sees aims and purposes as patterns of movements. Furthermore, all mental terms sensations—perception, imagination, thought, belief, knowledge and so forth—

---

[448] AQUINAS, *Summa theologiae* I–II, q. 44 a. 2: "A man of counsel may be taken in two ways. First, from his being willing or anxious to take counsel. And thus, fear makes men of counsel. Because, as the Philosopher says, 'we take counsel on great matters, because therein we distrust ourselves'. Now things which make us afraid, are not simply evil, but have a certain magnitude, both because they seem difficult to repel, and because they are apprehended as near to us, as stated above. Wherefore men seek for counsel especially when they are afraid. Secondly, a man of counsel means one who is apt for giving good counsel: and in this sense, neither fear nor any passion makes men of counsel. Because when a man is affected by a passion, things seem to him greater or smaller than they really are thus, to a lover, what he loves seems better; to him that fears, what he fears seems more dreadful. Consequently, owing to the want of right judgment, every passion, considered in itself, hinders the faculty of giving good counsel. The stronger a passion is, the greater the hindrance is it to the man who is swayed by it. Consequently, when fear is intense, man does indeed wish to take counsel, but his thoughts are so disturbed, that he can find no counsel. If, however, the fear be slight, so as to make a man wish to take counsel, without gravely disturbing the reason; it may even make it easier for him to take good counsel, by reason of his ensuing carefulness. Hope also makes man a good counsellor: because, as the Philosopher says, 'no man takes counsel in matters he despairs of', nor about impossible things, as he says in *Ethic.* iii, 3. But fear incites to counsel more than hope does. Because hope is of good things, as being possible of attainment; whereas fear is of evil things, as being difficult to repel, so that fear regard the aspect of difficulty more than hope does. And it is in matters of difficulty, especially when we distrust ourselves, that we take counsel, as stated above."

refer to patterns in overt behavior (movement toward some future things), as RACHLIN states:

> Any superiority of a person's perception of his mind over another person's perception of his mind lies in the quantity of his observations of his own behavior (he is always there when he is behaving), not in their quality. There is nothing inherently superior in a first-person perspective on the mind over a third person perspective. In fact, because your behavior is more clearly seen by an observer than by you, a third person perspective may be more accurate.[449]

5.7 Organizational Leadership, Extreme Teams, and the Contending Behavioral Zone (CBZ)

We are defining a concept of the Contending Behavioral Zone (CBZ). We are using the terminology to express an individual, team, interdepartmental group, etc., a formal or informal organized effort to achieve a task. The task requires over time the behavioral coordination and cooperation of human resources, technology, financial resources, etc., to achieve a difficult and arduous end. Participants in the CBZ could be members of a business organization, volunteer organization or it could be a family planning a summer vacation, etc. Basically, when individuals participate in a CBZ, they are dedicated to a task that requires an intense actualization of rational thought and emotional mastery of the contending passions. We prefer to use the terminology of contending passions because it is more clearly expresses the existential dynamics of the members of the CBZ. More accurately, participating members of a CBZ are engaged as an organizational whole by means of rational thought (particular reason) and mastery of the contending passions to an end in terms of a final cause that moves the CBZ. It is the final cause, i.e., the purpose for the existence of the CBZ that also serves as the formal object of the CBZ. It is a highly flexible organizational concept that could apply to various divisions, departments, and units of an organization.

---

[449] RACHLIN, *The Escape of The Mind*, 181.

One of the most obvious factors in this emerging hierarchical-heterarchical paradigm shift is the importance of highly effective, autonomous, and decentralized teams. It could be said from the perspective of a Thomistic metaphysics of organization (as explained in chapter three) that the emerging concept of the critical importance of team leadership and diffusion of executive authority to team levels means teams begin to function as a subordinate organizational genus. In our behavioral construct of the dynamics of a CBZ, we, therefore, focus our attention on team dynamics, leadership, and amplification of organizational excellence. However, we will first describe in the following Table 5 the important differences in an organizational structure between work groups and teams. A work group can enter into a CBZ because, as stated, CBZ belongs to a behavioral psychology that serves as the underlying faculty powers of rational thought and emotional mastery, especially for team leadership and development.

Table 5: Standard Organizational Description: Work Groups and Teams: Similarities and Differences[450]

	Work Groups	Teams
Accountability	*Individual accountability*	*Individual and team accountability*
Orientation	*Fulfill narrowly defined duties*	*Focus on broader, external needs (e.g. customer service)*
Leadership Work Assignments	*Assigned to single person* *Individually based goals and objectives assigned*	*Shared leadership* *Collective work products, team understands organizational strategy and creates goals and*

---

[450] BOWDITCH, BUONO and STEWART, *A Primer on Organizational Behavior*, 161.

		objectives with that context
Meetings	*Organizational controlled, Focused on efficiency*	*Team controlled, focused on open-ended discussion and problem solving*
Decision Making	*Social pressures impede divergent thinking, Group members screen/filter outside information*	*Divergent thinking is encouraged, information from outside the team is sought*

As we see in Table 5, an organizational team focuses on broader organizational needs essential to organizational performance and executes assignments based on goals and methods within the context of organizational strategy. The leaders must design the team operation grounded on an Aristotelian-Thomistic concept of organizational causation. A development of this causation, as opposed to a modern linear cause-effect causation is beyond the intention and scope of this thesis.[451]

A team leader assigned to an organization "of a team doable deed" is engaged in an action of practical intellect, i.e., "the appetitive faculty is for the sake of some particular end."[452] As the leader and team begin to focus on the types of causation to achieve the particular end, they begin to experience the behavioral focus and energy of being a team moving to a final cause as members of a CBZ. Accordingly, the focus of attention is first on clarifying the purpose of the team, i.e., the final cause. It is the final cause that is concerned with the contribution the team will

---

[451] The construct is developed in McVey, "Thomistic Scientific Leadership and Common-Sense Triad of Organizational Harmony," 579, where it is proposed that the Deming theory of organizational management is based on Aristotle's teaching of practical intellects and four interactive types of planning and execution formal, material, efficient and final causation.

[452] Aquinas, *Commentary on Aristotle's Nicomachean Ethics*, Book 6, Lecture 2.

make to the amplification of the virtual quantity (perfection) of the organization. It then becomes a matter of the plan, the formal cause, to achieve the end. The plan must include the method and the technology (efficient causality), and the materials (material causality) needed to achieve the final cause, the doable deed.

An organizational team achieves success by means of an interactive network of members who share common and diversified talents and passionate expressions of behavior in the continuous movement toward the final object, i.e., the successful completion of the doable deed. Additionally, as argued in chapter three, the team is also a subordinate genus driven by an organizational metaphysics and psychology of excellence. Organizational teams are classified as of four types based on the research of SHAW as of teams based on results and/or relationships (see Table 6).

Table 6: Team Results[453]

Team Relationships are…	Inferior	Superior
Close/personal	*Comfortable Teams:* Members get along well but don't have the drive or toughness needed to deliver results.	*Extreme Teams:* Members work as a cohesive group to deliver extraordinary results.
Distant/Formal	*Indifferent Teams:* The team's performance is mediocre at best. Member relationships are distant or even antagonistic.	*Stressed Teams:* The team delivers results but at a cost-members feel vulnerable, isolated and at risk.

---

[453] SHAW, *Extreme Teams*, 199.

SHAW gives careful attention to the practices of cutting-edge teams. These are teams that are recognized for their organizational functional excellence. We use this concept of a cutting-edge extreme team because to practice as an extreme team requires an intense CBZ. Shaw finds that there are two common challenges to build an extreme team: 1) where no team currently exists; 2) transform a present team to the status of extreme team.

Shaw recommends 4 Rs of Transformation to Extreme Team Status:[454]

Right Purpose: Extreme teams take purpose to a higher level of intensity and dedication. Therefore, the team must attract people who are obsessed with the team's work and reason for being. People in cutting-edge teams view their work as a calling beyond making money as their reason for working. The purpose of the team must tap into the passions of the members.

Right People: Leaders and the team must hire people who have the qualities needed by the group for success. The mistake is to focus on the technical or functional skill. The early team members are critical because they set the tone for future hiring. Screening for the right behavioral characteristics is critical.

Right Priorities: The leader needs to clarify the team's vital priorities and success metrics. These priorities and measurement should be few in number and clearly communicated to the team. Everyone must know the goal and the plan of how to achieve it. For example, Airbnb is an example of a firm that is rigorous in clarifying what needs to be done each year to move the company forward. The firm's annual goals are summarized on a single page of paper (The Sheet), which is communicated throughout the organization.

Right Practices: Leader and the members must define, at the simplest level, the few essential beliefs and behaviors that will define what is expected of team members. The team must agree upon measurements of performance for individuals and team. There is a focus on creating a sense of community and belonging.

---

[454] Ibid., 24–25.

In SHAW's work on cutting-edge companies and teams two powerful causative organizational principles are apparent: 1) Fostering a shared obsession. He claims that cutting-edge organizations and their teams have a cult-like quality, seeing themselves as unique and destined to improve the world. These teams and companies also have a deep faith in their ability to overcome adversity. It is the issue of a spiritual vision that we presented in chapter three. 2) They possess the capacity of taking comfort in discomfort. Extreme organizations and their teams are biased in favor of conflict.

> These teams believe that fighting over the right issues, regardless of the discomfort it causes, results in better outcomes. Equally important is the ability of these teams to take on big challenges and the risks associated with innovation. Contrast this approach to what is found in conventional organizational teams where people view conflict as something to be avoided or a sign of failure.[455]

CBZ teams have the outstanding characteristics of being able to work together over long periods of time under extreme degrees of tension and conflict.

> Traditional firms and teams can suffer from "terminal niceness"-creating what Jack Ma of Alibaba calls "a little white rabbit culture."

> Cutting-edge firms and extreme teams, in contrast, realize that tension and conflict are essential to achieving their goals.

> Their skill is creating environments where people are comfortable with being uncomfortable. In so doing, they increase the likelihood that conflicts are surfaced and resolved in a productive manner.[456]

We can see from these two causative principles on the nature of cutting-edge organizations that extreme teams must exist in a continuous state of being in a CBZ

---

[455] Ibid., 25.
[456] Ibid., 190–191.

(contending behavioral zone). If we want to truly express the nature of an extreme team, we could say that a compelling vision and the passions of love, hope and fear motivate extreme teams into action to bring the vision into operational expression. The concept of "being in a zone" means that there exists in the leader and the team a sense pleasure and goodness well worth the struggle in pursuing a formal/final cause.[457] There is a sense of joy received from the vision. We are using AQUINAS's meaning of vision:

> But if one considers the matter carefully, the operation of the intellect which is vision, must needs rank before delight. For delight consists in a certain repose of the will. Now that the will finds rest in anything, can only be on account of the goodness of that thing in which it reposes. If therefore the will reposes in an operation, the will's repose is caused by the goodness of the operation. Nor does the will seek good for the sake of repose; for thus the very act of the will would be the end, because the operation is its good: but it seeks to be at rest in the question, because the operation is good. Consequently, it is evident that the operation in which the will reposes ranks before the resting of the will therein.[458]

BENNIS, the acclaimed scholar, and author on leadership writing in the 1980s, said that the crisis of leadership resulted from a lack of executive vision: "What's

---

[457] AQUINAS, *Summa theologiae* I, q. 5 a. 4: "Since goodness is that which all things desire, and since this has the aspect of an end, it is clear that goodness implies the aspect of an end. Nevertheless, the idea of goodness presupposes the idea of an efficient cause, and also of a formal cause. For we see that what is first in causing, is the last caused. Fire e.g. heats first of all before it reproduces the form of fire; though the heat in the fire follows from its substantial form. Now in causing, goodness and the end first, both of which move the agent to act; secondly, the action of the agent moving to the form; thirdly, comes the form. Hence, in that which is caused the converse ought to take place, so that there should be first, the form whereby it is being; secondly, we consider in its effective power, whereby it is perfect in being, for a thing is perfect when it can reproduce it's like, as the Philosopher says; thirdly, there follows the formality of goodness which is the basic principle of its perfection."

[458] Ibid., I-II, q. 4 a. 2.

going on is that the people in charge, particularly in business and government, have imposed change rather than inspiring it."[459] He adds that change is the metaphysics of our age, and it is time for us to control events rather than being controlled by them:

> Positive change requires trust, clarity, and participation. As this juncture, all three seem as distant as Jupiter. But we have reached Jupiter, and so perhaps we can finally reach ourselves. Only people with virtue and vision can lead us out of this bog and back to the high ground.

> First, such people must gain our trust. Second, they must express their vision clearly so that we all not only understand but concur. Third, they must persuade us to participate. That seems simple enough, and tidy, but in practice it seldom happens that way. Indeed, any fundamental alteration in the ways we live is apt to be messy and rancorous—especially today, when we are naturally rancorous.[460]

5.8 Executive Organizational CBZ Leadership and Moving to the Vision

From the perspective of an Aristotelian-Thomistic behavioral organizational teleology, the chief function of executive leadership is to keep the organization moving toward the organizational aim. REDPATH states:

> Since every acting form is a species (a more or less perfect *having* of a generic, organizational whole, unity), we have to judge the goodness of all finite forms, or organizations, in relation to their more perfect or less perfect participation in the goodness of their respective organizational aim (their *bonum ex genera* [generic, or organizational, good]), not their *malum ex genera* (organizational defect) in as much as this good exists within each and every part of the organization (in other words, we have to consider the intensive quantum, or qualitative, *greatness of having* of the organizational

---

[459] BENNIS *Why Leaders Can't Lead*, 26.

[460] Ibid., 27–28.

whole that a part contains to the extent that it has been able to absorb into its nature, as much as possible, the chief organizational aim).[461]

In chapter Three, we discussed in depth the importance of organizational vision. We will conclude this chapter by relating the issue of the organizational vision and extreme organizational team development in the context of team leadership in the contending behavioral zone. We will give a concise example of a CBZ. We will take the example of a high school student who, throughout his high school years, had a passionate desire to become a medical doctor. He was, in other words, stimulated by a pleasurable image and propelling passion of becoming a doctor. He has a love for the profession of medicine. The aspiring young doctor begins initially to imagine himself as a doctor. He desires an end, i.e., to become a doctor and in order to move to the end he must imagine himself as a doctor. It is a good and pleasing stimulus that moves the propelling and contending passions and powers of the soul.

The desiring medical doctor must begin by means of a teleological imagination of becoming a physician. A behavioral teleological conception of imagination follows from the teleological conception of sensation, as AQUINAS commenting on ARISTOTLE states, "Imagination is a sort of movement: that just as the sensing subject is moved by sensible objects, so, in imagining, one is moved by certain appearances called phantasms."[462]

In terms of a teleological behavioral psychology, imagination can have an effect as powerful as sensation. RACHLIN explains:

> Imaging is acting and not dreaming. Vividness of imagination is not vividness of the interior image but of overt behavior. Suppose two people are asked to imagine a lion present in a room. One closes her eyes and says, "Yes, I see it, a mane and a tail, that's right, it's walking around," and so on. The other runs screaming for the door. The first person is not really imagining the lion, but just striking a pose (as bad actors do) or imagining a picture of a lion. The second person is really imagining the lion. The location, intensity,

---

[461] REDPATH, *The Moral Psychology of St. Thomas*, 120.

[462] St. Thomas AQUINAS, *Commentary on Aristotle's De anima* 3, Lecture 6.

orientation, or even the existence of an image in her head would be irrelevant to the process. A good imagination is not just an aid or a tool in good acting. Rather, good acting is good imagining.[463]

We could say that the young man in high school has a sense of what it is that physicians do, and he begins to imagine performing the overt behavior of a physician. As a result, he has established a vision of a purpose-driven future which is, as we learned above from AQUINAS, essential to the formation of the will to become a physician. As AQUINAS states, "But if one considers the matter carefully, the operation of the intellect which is vision, must needs rank before delight. For delight consists in a certain repose of the will."[464] This vision is extremely important because it serves to activate the passions and powers of the soul for the career challenge of the high school student. In order to achieve this vision, it will require the focused faculties of his soul to achieve his final purpose. We can, also, describe this vision in terms of a teleological behavioral psychology that RACHLIN defines as the meta-discriminative stimuli.

> Sounds and sights correlated with behavior are, in the behaviorist's language, called discriminative stimuli. For the behaving person they serve as signals for valuable behavioral patterns. A red traffic light is a discriminative stimulus for stopping the car because, in the red light's presence, it is safer to stop than go. The actor who acts one way while on the stage and another way off the stage is responding in complex ways to two complex sets of discriminative stimuli. Good actors are able to turn on and off entire personalities (that is, behavioral patterns) in different situations as one or another situation presents itself. The art takes a great deal of skill. Good acting is imagining. Actors often complain that their real personalities become lost among the roles they play. That is, the off-stage discriminative stimuli fail to control the actor's behavior as they should—resulting in the neglect of family and friends—and the actor feels "alive" only on the stage. The same might happen to a businessperson. The set of discriminative

---

[463] RACHLIN, *The Escape of The Mind*, 23.

[464] AQUINAS, *Summa theologiae* I-II, q. 4 a. 2.

stimuli controlling her behavior at work comes to overlap in harmful ways with the set of discriminative stimuli controlling her behavior at home. We often fail to make the subtle behavioral adjustments constituting discrimination among complex, overlapping everyday-life situations. In such cases we discover, in our environments, still more complex and abstract sets of rules (moral rules) they may guide our behavior both in business and among families and friends—both on stage and off, as it were. We call these *rules meta-discriminative stimuli*.[465]

Our young aspiring physician must sense and imagine himself as a future physician. However, a meta-discriminative stimulus is more than an operant response to a stimulus; rather, the meta-discriminative stimulus is the vision that must rest in the will.[466] As the teleological behaviorist RACHLIN states, we need to discover, in our environments, still more complex and abstract sets of rules (moral rules) may guide our behavior. In terms of an Aristotelian-Thomistic behavioral psychology, it is the vision that rests in the intellect as the end that moves the aspiring young student and the rational appetite of the will. Consequently, as AQUINAS states:

> Now the object of the will is good and the end in general, and each power is directed to some suitable good proper to it, as sight is directed to the perception of color, and the intellect to the knowledge of truth. Therefore, the will as agent moves all the powers of the soul to their respective acts except the natural powers of the vegetative part, which are not subject to our will.[467]

The vision as the meta-discriminative stimuli serves as a set of integrated abstract rules that will guide the aspiring physician through high school, as a college premedical student, medical school, and residency. The life of the hopeful

---

[465] RACHLIN, *The Escape of The Mind*, 181.

[466] AQUINAS, *Summa theologiae* I-II, q. 4 a. 2.

[467] Ibid., I, q. 82 a. 4.

doctor in study, social life, friendship, etc., must become organized around the vision. The behaviorist Edwin B. HOLT writes:

> There is at any moment of life some course of action (behavior) which enlists all the capacities of the organism: This is phrased voluntaristically as "some interest or aim to which a man devotes all his powers," to which his whole being is consecrated. This matter of the unthwarted lifelong progress of behavior integration is of profound importance, for it is the transition from behavior to conduct, and to moral conduct. The more integrated behavior is harmonious and consistent behavior toward a larger and more comprehensive situation, toward a bigger section of the universe; it is lucidity and breadth of purpose.[468]

The physician aspirant, as he moves along his career path, will continue to organize all the overt behavioral activities and extended patterns of his aspirant life around a more rational and passionate vision of becoming a physician. In this behavioral movement the immediate stimulus of the intellect, will and passions are intensified by a much more organized and integrated meta-discriminative stimulus, i.e., "a harmonious and consistent behavior toward a larger and more comprehensive situation." Unfortunately, in contemporary philosophical and psychological studies, behaviorism is most often associated with Skinnerian Stimuli-Response and Operant Conditioning, and it has been replaced for the greater part by cognitive psychology or a mild form of cognitive behavioral psychology. In the next chapter, we will examine schools of behavioral psychology that are compatible with what we are calling a Thomistic faculty-behavioral-psychology. Specifically, we will explore the behaviorist William Baum's theory of molar behaviorism and continue with the work of RACHLIN and HOLT.

We, presently, draw more attention to HOLT because, we argue, even though he is not an Aristotelian-Thomistic behaviorist, his thoughts seem compatible with the Thomistic behavioral perspective expressed by REDPATH. For example, HOLT, somewhat similar to RACHLIN's concept of the meta-discriminative stimuli, which

---

[468] Edwin B. HOLT, *The Freudian Wish, and Its Place in Ethics* (New York: Henry Holt, 1915), 199.

he describes as "some interest or aim to which a man devotes all his powers." Above REDPATH stated, "we have to consider the intensive quantum, or qualitative, goodness of having of the organizational whole that a part contains to the extent that it has been able to absorb into its nature, so much as possible, the chief organizational aim."[469] The concept of aim as being different from a vision is extremely important because an aim involves practical reason, and the practical intellect targets to operational behavior. We might say that the practical intellect aims to an end that requires an operational plan. AQUINAS holds that the practical intellect has a beginning in a universal consideration. For example, the physician aspirant has a vision of becoming a doctor, i.e., he has a universal consideration. The vision, therefore, starts with the practical intellect and must terminate in an end. The universal reason does not move without the particular, i.e., the aim, the plan, the method for becoming a physician.[470] It will take many years of hard work and dedication for the aspiring physician to graduate from medical school and complete his residency. Besides having a motivating vision and a dedicated organized aim, his career goal will require a mastery of the passions, or we could call it emotional mastery. As he moves toward completion of the vision, i.e., the meta-discriminative stimuli, he will spend a number of years living in the Contending Behavioral Zone (CBZ). We have used this example of dedication and pursuit of a medical career to explain a behavioral process of pursuing a pleasing desirable and good purpose of becoming a physician over time, while mastering the passions of hope, fear, and courage over an arduous extended period of time and character development. We put forth a similar behavioral process as it applies in organizational team motivation: 1) vision as a meta-discriminative stimulus, 2) behavior and imagination, 3) from vision to the concrete behavioral organizational aim, 4) continuous mastery of passions and existing in the CBZ over extended periods of time.

---

[469] REDPATH, *The Moral Psychology of St. Thomas*, 120.

[470] See AQUINAS, *Commentary on Aristotle's Nicomachean Ethics*, Book 6, Lecture 2.

5.9 CBZ Fearless Extreme Team Focus on Perfection "Being the Best at What Matters the Most"

Cary D. LOHRENZ has written, *Fearless Leadership: High Performance Lessons from the Flight Deck*[471] that is about much more than leadership. Carey's story is about looking life straight in the eyes and saying bring the challenges, victories, hard times, and the absolute joy of meaningful accomplishments. LOHRENZ is the first female F-14 Tomcat fighter pilot in the US Navy who has flown missions worldwide as a combat ready pilot. Her knowledge and experience in leading high-performance teams has made her a highly sought-after business consultant and leadership speaker. She has delivered her training to such companies as AT&T, Black & McDonald, Cisco, Comcast, Covidien, Kimberly-Clark, New York Life, Lincoln Financial, Prudential, Safeway, Sanofi, Southern California Edison, State Farm Insurance, Say Ray Boats, Walmart, etc. She graduated from the University of Wisconsin, where she was a varsity rower, also training at the pre-Olympic level. After graduation she attended the Navy's Aviation Officer Candidate School before starting flight training and her naval career. She has an MBA in Strategic Leadership.

We have selected her work as a case study because she gives an excellent phenomenological description of teamwork and leadership of teams functioning in organizational wholes as contending behavioral zones of the stimulus of a pleasing yet arduous task, and the existential dynamics of hope, courage, and fear. She writes:

> The cockpit of an F-14 is one of the most demanding environments on earth, and it's where I learned some of my most unforgettable lessons not just flying, but also in life and leadership. My journey to that cockpit—one that began when I decided to pursue a seemingly impossible dream that involved many challenges and trails—gave me indispensable insights as well. And my path after leaving the military, paved largely with my work among business leaders, from Fortune 500 executives to middle managers, has helped me

---

[471] Cary D. LOHRENZ, *Fearless Leadership: High Performance Lessons from the Flight Deck* (Austin: Greenleaf, 2014)

further distill those lessons, share them with others, and then watch as leaders and their teams flourish.

In the years since I left the Navy and began working as a leadership consultant, I've been struck again and again by the parallels between the world of naval aviation and the world of business. In both, leaders must perform highly complex and high-pressure tasks in a constantly changing environment. People are counting on you to make the right moves. Mistakes can result in huge financial losses or damage to your career. But no parallel asserted itself more strongly than this one: High-performing teams require fearless leaders. [...] The ability to work though fear kept me alive as I operated under dangerous conditions and in life-or-death situations on the flight deck of that aircraft carrier, and it's what keeps any leader relevant, respected, and moving forward. If you're able to shape the fear into something useful, you'll be unstoppable. Letting fear be your copilot is a fundamental element of the art of leading well.[472]

LOHRENZ understands as an exemplar of organizational leadership that organizational and team success begins with a bold and doable vision. Using an extreme team building teleological behavioral psychology, she teaches leaders that "You and your team have to be able to see yourself accomplishing that dream without losing your way or getting distracted. The right vision can make that possible."[473] She also understands that the vision must become a concrete aim: "If you want your vision to be effective, you have to paint a full vivid picture of the desired end. The more realistic and vibrant your conception of where you want to be, the more it will keep your team and you on track toward the goal."[474] It is interesting that she stresses that a major problem in building a high-performance team—we would add keeping a leader and the team in the CBZ—is the focal point, i.e., the concrete aim. She argues that the ability to concentrate, to focus and to ignore distractions is the biggest predictor of a leader and his/her team's success.

---

[472] Ibid., 13–14.
[473] Ibid., 109.
[474] Ibid., 123.

In the hierarchical-heterarchical tension organizational culture, many leaders find it challenging to cope with the increasing pace and unpredictability of change, LOHRENZ introduces a concept of the "focus on three" that she takes from the leadership style of the late Steve Jobs.

> When Steve Jobs made his return to Apple in 1997, the company was nearly bankrupt—it had sixty days of cash left—and was producing dozens of different types of products and peripherals. He shut down 1,040 projects and focused on four major categories: Consumer, Pro, Desktop and Portable. Then he assembled his top one hundred teammates and brainstormed products, ideas, and what Apple should be doing next. They whittled the list down to a top ten, and then slashed that list further. He was famous (or infamous) for saying, "We can only do three!"[475]

The organizational leadership principle, here, is a vision must become a clear, vivid and a doable concrete aim that leads to, as LOHRENZ says, that "You are laser focused on three things."[476] Like LOHRENZ, EHRINGER, in her extensive research on successful entrepreneurs and executive leaders of small to medium size business organizations, finds a similar fascination with the leadership behavior of focus. Here are examples of her interviews on executive leadership focus:

Focus

Focus, or being focused, was another decision tool of the *self at work*. For many entrepreneurs, focus was both a by-product and an objective of their decision-making processes.

One of the main things that I had to do was to decide what is it that I want to do in business… It's very hard to do more than one of them… so I really make it a very strict point to focus on what we do… it's kind of like a seed that I plant, and I'll just keep it in front of me for a while and see how it develops and how I feel about it and what direction does it go on. If it just

---

[475] Ibid., 123.
[476] Ibid., 123.

kind of sits there… then that's telling me that… right now is not the time to do it, perhaps sometime in the future but not right now… (would be a) change of focus.

When you're doing your own internal decision-making, you tend to eliminate a lot of factors and focus on a few, there are a whole bunch of things dancing around in the background, but you focus on a few. […]

My objective… the objective of this company is [our work], and it's nice to make money at it, but our focus isn't the bottom-line, our focus is what we do.

You know in addition to all the other things, like doing it, I think I've been successful because I've been very focused on making money.[477]

It is interesting to note that REDPATH frequently uses the concept of "is it doable?" or "is it a doable deed?" as a first principle of a dynamic behavioral psychology. He particularly relates the issue of "doable deeds" to the irascible appetite, or we could say the issue of team leadership in the CBZ focus (see above, behavioral teachings 7 and 8). It is not just a matter of having a chief organizational aim; rather, it must be a chief organizational "doable aim."

The vision must be expressed as a clear and vivid meta-discriminative stimulus that, as LOHRENZ suggests, moves organizational high performing teams to, as CALLOWAY says, *Be the best at What Matters the Most.* She gives examples of aspirational and inspirational organizational visional statements:

BMW: "The Ultimate Driving Machine."

Google: "Organize the world's information and make it universally accessible and useful."

Think Nike: "Just do it."

Navy: The F-14 Tomcat community has the legendary "Anytime Baby!" slogan. It was embroidered in bold letters on the patch next to a spunky, gun-

---

[477] EHRINGER, *Make Up Your Mind*, 111–112.

slinging tomcat mascot and prominently displayed by F-14 pilots. The phrase was originally thrown out as a challenge to the US Air Force's F-15 to go one-on-one against the F-14 in a dogfight. The F-14 prevailed. "Anytime Baby!" lived on as powerful, unifying statement of what F-14 pilots and their aircraft were capable of.[478]

In this Navy F-14 slogan, we have an excellent example of an organizational meta-discriminative stimulus. We can describe the function of a meta-discriminative vision in terms of HOLT's integration of and dedication of behavioral powers, as a course of action (behavior) which enlists all the capacities of the organism: this is phrased voluntaristically as some interest or aim to which a man devotes all his powers, to which the whole being is consecrated. It is the challenge of leadership to engage the organization in a behavioral participation in the soul power of the vision. HOLT was not an Aristotelian-Thomistic behaviorist, but he maintains that behaviorism is the integration of the soul.

> In those happy individuals in whom the daily integration of behavior is successfully accomplished the soul is a unit and a moral unit. In others in whom the integration has been frustrated the soul is not a unit, but a collection of warring factions seated in one distracted body. Such a creature has not one soul, but many, and misses of morals and of freedom by exactly as much as it has missed of unity, that is of the progressive integration of behavior. [...] With such a doctrine of the soul as this, behaviorism can rest unperturbed while the sad procession of Spirits, Ghost Souls, 'transcendental' Egos, and what not, passes by and vanishes in its own vapor. For all these are countless monads, and they have no windows. In fine, for behaviorism there is one unbroken, conduct, moral conduct, and the unified soul.[479]

It is important to emphatically distinguish an organizational vision from a wish because if there is one incompetent act of an executive or team leader it is to

---

[478] LOHRENZ, *Fearless Leadership*, 129.
[479] HOLT, *The Freudian Wish*, 201.

confuse a wish statement with a vision statement. Therefore, when it comes to the matter of organizational behavior, we should give attention to AQUINAS's definition of the "wish." He states primarily that a wish is not a choice. A wish might look like a choice because it belongs to the power of the rational appetite, the will, but it refers to an absolute good. A choice is an act of some power; choice is an action toward an end.[480] When a true and effective leader puts forth a vision it is a choice, the leader takes a stand in the competitive battle similar to the stand on first principles discussed in chapter four with AQUINAS' metaphor of "a stand in battle."

When a leader puts forth a vision statement, it must be expressed as a "doable deed"; otherwise, the leader is perceived as incompetent and a mere political organizational disguise of leadership. The team members immediately sense that he/she is not the leader who will successfully lead them into the arduous and competitive CBZ. The leader takes a courageous stand and lays his vision on the table before the team.

The vision or better still the vision as a concrete doable aim is a choice, and as AQUINAS points out, "Choice is not concerned with impossible things."[481] The vision, as LOHRENZ holds, is really a prediction of successful completion of the organizational mission to *Be the Best at What Matters the Most*. LOHRENZ understands the difference between an organizational political wish and an organizational concrete doable vision statement. She writes regarding poor vision:

> Want to know what doesn't work? Vision statements that are saddled with boring corporate-speak gobbledygook. Let me share an example. I'll preface this by saying that I love Volvo's super-safe vehicles and its great record of superior engineering. But here is the company's vision statement: "By creating value for our customers, we create value for our shareholders. We use our expertise to create transport-related products and services of superior quality, safety, and environmental care for demanding customers in selected segments. We work with energy, passion, and respect for the individual." What the heck does that even mean? That wouldn't fire me up

---

[480] AQUINAS, *Commentary on Aristotle's Nicomachean Ethics*, Book 3, Lecture 5.
[481] Ibid.

to get out of bed on a frosty morning in Sweden! There's too much jargon, and it's neither aspirational nor inspirational.[482]

The vision statement, according to LOHRENZ, must be simple, memorable, and repeatable, i.e., a concrete doable aim that moves a team to high performance. She gives the example of Bill McCarthy, vice president of sales at Cisco who understands the vision statement as an engaging, motivating, and behavioral reinforcement of the concrete aim, the meta-discriminative stimuli. She explains:

> He goes to extraordinary lengths to not only define the vision—where he wants the team to go—but also consistently share it with them over and over and over, in every possible forum for his teammates. What are their goals? He understands that in today's noisy working environment, too many people tend to forget what their leaders shared with them yesterday unless it actually matters to them—unless they can internalize the vision.[483]

When Bill is asked the major organizational behavioral question, how do you reinforce the vision? He responds:

> You can almost think of it like a campaign. That's how much work it will take—like you're running for office as you establish that vision, that platform. You remind people, here's what we are working on, here is what we are trying to accomplish, and you use the common language, the terminology to get people aligned to that vision. You then lay out strategy that engages your team and gets the personal interest of the people you are talking to, and you share with them what the future could look like.[484]

There is one sure way that an organizational executive or team leader appears weak and ineffective, and it is by leading by wishful motivation, such as "I wish I had better people," "if everybody could have wonderful dreams about our future,"

---

[482] LOHRENZ, *Fearless Leadership*, 129.

[483] Ibid., 131.

[484] Ibid., 132.

"bring your wish list to the next meeting and we will see what we can do," etc. AQUINAS, in his analysis of wish and choice makes clear that "if a person should say that he chooses something impossible he will appear foolish."[485]

We conclude this discussion on the nature of extreme teams, or in LOHRENZ's definition high performance teams, emphasizing that hope is the chief passion of the irascible appetite, and the first principle of all the irascible passions. It is the rational and passionate belief in the organizational vision that guides an extreme team to act courageously and with daring in the face of arduous tasks and unexpected threatening events to accomplish a most rewarding and pleasurable vision of excellence and team perfection.

Throughout these chapters we have been stressing various themes that in the modern world the nature of organizational management and executive leadership has been changing, going from a hierarchical leadership authority machine structure era to a heterarchical visionary leadership diffusion era.[486] It is worthy of note that the Global Center for Digital Business Information Study, *Redefining Leadership for a Digital Age*, in a survey of 1,042 executives and in-depth interviews with nineteen digital leaders between October 2016 and January 2017 identified competencies and behaviors of the Agile Leaders of the Digital Age. They discovered a remarkable similar profile consistent across industries, organizations, and geographies. The core competencies and behaviors were: 1) Humble, 2) Adaptable, 3) Visionary, 4) Engaged. Thus far, we have, from a Thomistic organizational psychology, identified these four leadership characteristics.

---

[485] AQUINAS, *Commentary on Aristotle's Nicomachean Ethics*, Book 3, Lecture 5.

[486] See John William WARD, "The Ideal of Individualism and the Reality of the Organization," *The Business Establishment*, ed. Earl F. Cheit (New York: Wiley, 1964): "A well-designed machine is an instance of total organization, that is, a series of interrelated means contrived to achieve a single point. The machine consists always of parts that have no meaning and no function separate from the organized entity to which they contribute. A machine consists of a coherent bringing together of all parts toward the highest possible efficiency of the functioning whole, or interrelationships marshaled wholly toward given results. In the ideal machine, there are no extraneous parts, no extraneous movement: all is set, part for part, motion for motion, toward the functioning whole. The machine is, then, a perfect instance of total rationalization of a field of action and of total organization. This is perhaps even more quickly evident in that larger machine, the assembly line."

Furthermore, we have argued that it is a Thomistic organizational behavioral psychology that is constructed on the proper first principles of a faculty-behavioral-psychology of visionary leadership for the modern era, or as has been suggested as post- postmodern visionary leadership.

The importance of vision is at the core is the driving formal and final object of the organizational whole. BENNIS perhaps puts it best: If it is really a vision, you'll never forget it. In their book on leadership, BENNIS and NAMUS devote much attention to vision. Here are various ideas which are highly compatible with a Thomistic organizational behavioral psychology, especially the insistence in image and vision:[487]

1) To choose a direction, a leader must first have developed a mental image of a possible and desirable future state of the organization. This image which we call a vision may be as vague as a dream or as precise as a goal or mission statement. The critical point is that a vision articulates a view of realization in some important ways that now exist.

2) A vision is a target that beckons. Note also that a vision always refers to a future state, a condition that does not presently exist and never existed before. With a vision, the leader provides the all-important bridge from the present to the future of the organization.

3) By focusing attention on a vision, the leader operates on the emotional and spiritual resources of the organization, on its values, commitment, and aspirations. The manager, by contrast, operates on the physical resources of the organization, on the capital, human skills, raw materials, and technology.

4) If there is a spark of genius in the leadership function at all, it must lie in this transcending ability, a kind of magic, to assemble-out of the variety of images, signals, forecast and alternatives- a clearly articulated vision of the future that is at once simple, easily understood, clearly desirable and energizing.

---

[487] Gleaned from W. BENNIS and B. NAMUS, *Leaders: The Strategies for Taking Charge* (New York: Harper & Row, 1985), 89, 90, 92,103.

6.

The Enlightened Big Soul

The aim of this chapter is to describe the magnanimous soulful exemplar, Big Soul. It is the Big Soul executive leader who is the opposite of the Dark Soul executive leader. The magnanimous leader is truly humble, yet he/she is dedicated to executing great deeds. It is the Big Soul exemplar that inspires emulation from the followers who are inspired by the virtue of his/her magnanimity. We stress that the magnanimous big soul exemplar is unlike the ego centered dark soul leader who rules by power and authoritarian policies. The Big Soul exemplar stays close to the rational, moral, and spiritual everyday issues of his/her people and their organizational insights and decisions. The magnanimous exemplar is known for his/her virtuous heft which we elucidate as moral virtuous behavior. We also conclude in this chapter explaining the importance of a faculty- behavioral concept of observable molar behavior, as it relates to the organizational understanding and observation of moral virtue in workplace contending behavioral episodes over time.

6.1 A Rational Moral Teleological Faculty-Behavioral-Psychology

In *Masquerade of the Dream Walkers*, REDPATH writes of ROUSSEAU's rejection of philosophical reason as the measure of truth.

> Like all philosophers of subjectivity, Rousseau is a Transcendental Sophist. His thought is a synthesis of poetry and sophistry. At every stage of education, his criterion of truth is inspiration (the measure of poetic truth) and strength (the measure of sophistic truth). In this way, truth's measure is

enthusiastic revelation, strong feeling. Hence, he says that, as Emile's educational guide, when he hears the Savoyard Vicar speaking about conscience, he thinks he is "hearing the divine Orpheus sing."[488]

Again, we return to one of the recurring proposals of this thesis that in the movement of organizations to hierarchical-heterarchical structures a Thomistic faculty-behavioral-psychology is the most appropriate modern organizational psychology. In chapter four, we looked at research that people want to work for organizations where they feel a sense of soul. They want to work in a place that has a sense of spiritual and ethical meaning. They want to feel that working for this type of an organization gives them a sense of happiness and human flourishing.

Recently, the message for the meaningful organization seems to be taking hold with one large global organization, LinkedIn. Fred KOFMAN is the vice president of the philosophy of leadership at LinkedIn. Indeed, the title in itself is most important because we could never have imagined in a traditional business organization until recently having a vice president of philosophy. KOFMAN goes about the world conducting workshops for large corporations on Transcendental Leadership, speaks on TED and YouTube. There is much about the need for a profound understanding of the importance of spirituality and ethics as driving forces of success in digital age organizations. There is a problem for Thomistic psychologists because KOFMAN seems to find his definition of the Transcendent Leader basically in ROUSSEAU's rejection of philosophical rational truth with the replacement of inspiration. For example, he describes the foundation of Transcendental Leadership in the following Rousseauian manner:

> Transcendental leadership dissolves the hardest organizational problems in a liquid mix of significance, nobility, virtue, and solidarity. [...] Transcendental leadership demands that we have the ability to look deeply inward—beginning with recognizing our inevitable mortality—and the self-discipline to embody the principles that inspire others to passionate commitment. [...] I ask you to inspire others through a common purpose, a

---

[488] Peter A. REDPATH, Masquerade of the Dream Walkers: Prophetic Theology from the Cartesians to Hegel (Amsterdam-Atlanta: Rodopi, 1998), 94.

strong set of ethical principles, a community of like-minded people, a feeling of unconditional empowerment, and a passionate drive to achieve.[489]

The problem with Rousseauian Transcendental Leadership is that it is not grounded on philosophical rational moral truth, especially the rational and moral concept of a wise leader, as ARISTOTLE and AQUINAS teach:

> He [Aristotle] teaches that the magnanimous person must be worthy of great things. One who thinks himself worthy of great things contrary to truth, i.e., of which he is not really worthy, is foolish. It is characteristic of a wise man to keep everything in proper order. But the virtuous man is neither unwise nor foolish because virtue operates according to right reason [...]. Consequently, it is clear that the magnanimous man is the person just described, i.e., one worthy of great things who thinks himself worthy.[490]

The major issue with a Rousseauian organizational psychology of transcendental leadership is that if rational and moral truth is rejected as the foundation for the definition of leadership, then leadership is basically defined by an inspiring will. Furthermore, the Rousseauian would say it is a Transcendental Leadership grounded on a conscious organizational collective willing. Yet according to a Thomistic psychology, it is not truly a matter of willing so much as it is a matter of "Rousseauian willfulness," because it is impossible to separate rational thought and the will, since the will is an appetite of the intellect. In other words, unless a vision, purpose, aim or principle rest in harmony with the soul as founded on rational and moral truth, we only strive with willful inspirational energy. It is the psychiatrist Leslie H. FARBER who in his existential psychology of will addresses the issue of the crisis of "the Age of the Disordered Will." He writes:

---

[489] Fred KOFMAN, *The Meaning Revolution: The Power of Transcendent Leadership* (New York: Currency, 2018),18, 20.

[490] AQUINAS, *Commentary on Aristotle's Nicomachean Ethics*, Book Four, Lecture 3, n. 737

There are, need I say, many feasible and relevant objects for the conscious utilitarian will. Much of our education has been accomplished under its dominion. Our day-to-day existence simply could not be gotten without this will. Our burgeoning technology—that may destroy us all— owes everything to this realm of will. But I would call this the Age of the Disordered Will, and I would do so because it seems to me that increasingly we apply the will of the second realm to those portions of life that only will not comply, but that become distorted—or even vanish—under such coercion.

Let me give a few examples: I can will knowledge, but not wisdom; going to bed, but not sleeping; eating, but not hunger; meekness, but not humility; scrupulosity, but not love; commiseration, but not sympathy; congratulations, but not admiration; religiosity, but not faith; reading, but not understanding. I would emphasize that the consequence of willing what cannot be willed is that we fall into the distress we call anxiety. And since anxiety, too, opposes such willing, should we, in our anxiety about anxiety, now try to will away that anxiety, our fate is still more anxiety. Within this impasse, meaning, reason, imagination, discrimination fail, so that the will is deprived of its supporting and tempering faculties. Under these reduced circumstances a man is, in a sense, all will. Or nothing but will. His disability is willfulness, meaning the state of being "governed by will without yielding to reason," which is Webster's definition.

Day in, day out, every citizen is instructed by the public media that there is no portion of his life that is not wholly within his control or, in my vocabulary, wholly subject to his will. If life is difficult for you, an evening of television watching will teach you how to dispel your miseries through aspirin, deodorant, mouthwash, dance lessons, laxatives, vitamins, hair lotions, and edifying panel programs. And more professional sources can provide tranquilizers, stimulants, psychoanalysis, sleeping pills, or instruction in sexual technique—all the elixirs and panaceas that have offered us for a better life. Nor do I mean to suggest we all live like hayseeds at a country fair, at the mercy of a snake oil salesman who happens to pass through town. After all, whoever really believed in the conjugal possibilities of Lavoris? The problem is less rational and at the same time more pathetic than that. The underlying presupposition for both the bombardiers and the bombarded is that, in varying degree, everything and nothing is possible for our will.[491]

FARBER was somewhat influenced by what he called ADLER's "Aristotelian-Scholastic understanding of the will" as an appetite related to a rational and moral ordering toward an end perceived as the pleasing, desirable and good. He writes, "I understand will to be the category through which we examine that portion of our life which is the mover of our life in a direction or toward an objective in time."[492] This movement of direction over time can occur in an instant raising of a hand or an extended behavior over time. He then divides the will into two realms. These realms of will are somewhat similar to the concept of chapter five of the Contending Behavioral Zone. We could say that FARBER is talking about will as divided into two types of will behavioral zones (movements toward a formal object). In realm (zone) one, the will moves in a direction which is a purpose. It is what we have previously described as the doable deed. He uses a metaphor to explain his concept of the realms of will (wills contending zone):

> I suggest imagining a sports activity—tennis, for example. When our game is most fluid and effortless, we cannot really be said to be planning our shots and strategies; if we are thinking about the game, we are not aware of thinking; though will is involved in our shots maneuvers, we cannot be said to be aware of will itself. We are, so to speak, of a piece—mind and body seamlessly and unselfconsciously joined in a totality. Will is so wedded to our faculties, our perception, our motor possibilities that it may be said to be unconscious in this first realm.
>
> Now let us assume that because of our opponent or ourselves, our game goes badly, requiring us to assess our failure. "It is the forehand that's at fault," we say. "Too slow and too much top spin." Will, clearly has become conscious, for now we will ourselves to stroke the ball differently and are

---

[491] Leslie H. FARBER, *The Ways of the Will* (New York: Basic Books, 2000), 79.
[492] Ibid., 77.

conscious of our willing. [...] The second realm is the utilitarian will, in that we do this to get that. We grasp the racket so that its face is more perpendicular, and as the serve arrives, rush to it and hit more energetically—all this willing in order to achieve a more effective forehand shot.[493]

From standpoint of an Aristotelian-Thomistic Behavioral Psychology, it is proposed if FARBER's first and second realms of will are seen as one genus then we are talking about a psychology of willing similar to the contending behavioral zone (irascible passions) of chapter five. In the first and second realm of will the object is to win the game of tennis. The will is moved in the first and second realm by the desire to win at tennis. AQUINAS maintains that the intellectual soul inclines to seek what is suitable, not the realm of the will in and of itself. The sensitive appetite of the soul needs to be divided in two:

1) an appetite through which the intellectual soul inclines to seek what is suitable, according to the senses and intellect, and to flee from what is hurtful (St. Thomas calls this the "concupiscible" appetite); and

2) another appetite whereby a human being resists attacks that hinder getting what is suitable, humanly good, and harms a human being (St. Thomas calls this the "irascible" appetite). [...] because its tendency is to overcome and rise above difficulties that hurt a human being, the proper object of the irascible appetite is something difficult, dangerous.[494]

FARBER was a practicing psychiatrist who developed his theory of the Disordered Will as the underpinning theory for his method of psychotherapy, especially for the treatment of anxiety and depression. It does appear that FARBER viewed the disordered will syndrome as individuals attempting to will a pleasurable, happy, and flourishing existence, but unable and/or unwilling to exist over extended periods of time in the tension of contrariety of the concupiscible and irascible behavioral zones. As we previously put forth, it is by means of the proper

---

[493] Ibid., 76–77.

[494] REDPATH, *The Moral Psychology of St. Thomas*, 104.

formal object, i.e., vision, aim, doable deed, the meta discriminative stimulus and the mastery of the passions that individuals achieve the difficult, demanding and finally rewarding end. We cannot achieve this in life if we only understand realm one willing. We cannot understand the ability to will unless we understand the unity of will, intellect, concupiscible (propelling) and irascible (contending) appetite as a confluence of powers toward union with a formal object.

6.1.1 Practical Soul Executive Leadership, Rational Moral Action and Practical Behavior

We began this dissertation with a presentation of the thinking of BARNARD on the functions of the executive. BARNARD was selected as one of the initial contributors to the discipline of organizational management as a system. Even more important, he was the prophetic voice in his work of 1938 that held one of the primary responsibilities of executive leadership is the moral intensity of an organization.

> Organizations endure, however, in proportion to the breadth of the morality by which they are governed. This is only to say that foresight, long purposes, high ideals, are the basis for the persistence of cooperation.
>
> The endurance of the organization depends on the quality of leadership; and that quality derives from the breadth of the morality upon which it rests. High responsibility there must be even in the lowest, the most immoral organizations; but if the morality to which the responsibility is low, the organizations are short lived. A low morality will not sustain leadership long, its influence quickly vanishes, it cannot produce its own succession.[495]

Regarding the nature of organizational leadership, we continue to argue it is best to return to BARNARD's prophetic voice on organizational moral rectitude (goodness). Along with the return to a BARNARD's philosophy of moral organizational order, we argued that there is a need for a return to a premodern Aristotelian-Thomistic faculty psychology of the soul.

---

[495] BARNARD, *The Functions of the Executive*, 282–283.

Following the BARNARD 1938 school of organizational leadership it is interesting to read the popular consultant organizational psychologist, KOFMAN, the vice president of executive development and leadership philosopher at LinkedIn. He did his PhD in economics and taught managerial accounting and control systems at MIT. He discovered that the tools of economics do not motivate employees and material incentives account for perhaps 15 percent of employee motivation. He maintains that the other 85 percent is driven by our need to belong, especially by the conviction what we do day in and day out matters. One of his most fundamental principles on executive leadership is the following:

> If you hope to be an inspiring leader, the first thing you must understand is that such leadership has nothing to do with formal authority; it has everything to do with moral authority. Hearts and minds cannot be bought or forced; they can only be deserved and earned. They are given only to worthy missions and trustworthy leaders. This applies not only to organizations but also to many domains of human activity.[496]

We are applying a Thomistic organizational psychology of leadership, more precisely we have focused on the function of organizational executive leadership. We find it necessary to define the executive leadership based on the fact that we are giving attention to leadership of an organizational whole (genus). It is the primary function of the executive level to define a philosophy and psychology of leadership character that diffuses throughout the organization becoming operational in terms of leadership behavior at all levels. There are two primary functions of executive leadership. First, the leader is known as a rational and moral exemplar of virtuous behavior. We are here agreeing with KOFMAN that in the hierarchical-heterarchical organizations formal authority becomes the rational moral authority of the executive exemplar's virtuous behavior. AQUINAS, as he discusses the nature of organizational rational-moral authority and virtue, teaches:

> [...] what is perfect being in any order of reality must be considered a measure in that order, because all other things are judged more or less

---

[496] KOFMAN, *The Meaning Revolution*, 9.

perfect according as they approach or recede from what is most perfect. Consequently, since virtue is the proper perfection of man and the virtuous man is perfect in the human species this should be taken as the measure in all man's affairs.[497]

Second, the executive exemplar is the chief executive visionary of the organization. A visionary organizational leadership practice is like an infusion of behavior. The vison is the active ingredient which is injected into the employees. It causes them to jump up and down with great energy. The vision is acted out in overt behavior. It is acted out in everyday organizational life in the art and drama of leading and following. The vision is understood as a deep rational, moral, and operational script that comes to life with conviction every day. This script comes from the visionary leader's practical and realistic understanding of the organizational subject matter as an art and inductive science. It is his task to take the vision beyond words not so much by means of a formal plan and program, but by means of everyday practical sense-making and leader-worker behavior.

This rational-moral vision explanation of Michael NOVAK in *Business as a Calling: Work and the Examined Life* is perhaps one of the finest modern classic works on a rational-moral understanding of executive business leadership. He writes on the Virtue of Practical Realism:

> I have never met a businessman who did not pride himself on being realistic. Even the romantic ones among them (entrepreneurs tend to have broad romantic streaks) are willing to bet their fortunes on being in closer touch with reality than others.
>
> Many of the most innovative have worked their way up from the skunk works and back rooms, where they have paid their dues by getting their hands dirty and facing day-to-day frustrations. In fact, it is often their strong sense of how the world really works, from the bottom up, that gives them confidence that their ideas—no matter how unrealistic others may think them—are in touch with reality, and that it is others who are living by illusions.

---

[497] AQUINAS, *Commentary on Aristotle's Nicomachean Ethics*, Book 9, Lecture 4.

In academic circles today, realism is regarded as outmoded. There is only opinion: yours, mine, and those of billions of others. There are only "perceptions."

Who knows whose perceptions are "true"?

Business is oriented to action. (Even patents are not given for ideas alone but for "ideas reduced to practice.") Action require goals. Getting to goals requires strategies. Strategies require tactics. Each must suit the available personnel and other resources. The need for practical realism at every step is obvious.[498]

NOVAK is correct with his claim that businesspeople pride themselves on being realistic. However, it is not only businesspeople who pride themselves on being a realist. A successful executive leader of any type of organization would take pride on being a realist. For example, if a candidate for a position as the executive director of a nonprofit was submitting a resume of his/her qualifications for the position, the candidate presents him/herself as a realist. Any person aspiring to executive leadership or really any level of leadership must prove that he/she is a realist. Being an organizational realist means being oriented to action. "Action requires goals. Getting to goals requires strategies. Strategies require tactics," as Novak explains in business "the need for practical realism at every step is obvious."[499] The concept of a practical realist is extremely important, and this concept of a leader being a practical realist is likely a description worthy of any successful leader. In NOVAK's study on business as a high moral calling, he is obviously influenced by an Aristotelian-Thomistic moral psychology of leadership. We see this thinking as he writes on practical wisdom:

Aristotle identified "practical wisdom" (*phronesis*) as the capacity to order all the parts of the self and all the components of action in a realistic and effective way. The person of practical wisdom is like an archer, Aristotle said. In action, there are an infinite number of ways to get things wrong; but to

---

[498] Michael NOVAK, *Business as a Calling: Work, and the Examined Life* (New York: The Free Press, 1996). 128–130.

[499] Ibid., 130.

act in the right way, at the right time, with the right emphasis, with regard to the right persons, and with exact appreciation for all the relevant circumstances, is to "hit the mark exactly," like an arrow thudding into a bull's-eye.[500]

In the 1980s DEMING drastically changed the focus of American organizational leadership from cost effective efficiency and maximization of profit to quality and customer satisfaction. He taught that the greatest financial loss for any business is the loss of a customer because of poor quality. When customers do not get what they paid for, they go elsewhere. Quality, DEMING argued, is being focused on customer satisfaction. He preached:

A good question for anybody in business to ask is *what business are we in?* To do well what we are doing—i.e., to turn out a good product, or good service, whatever it be? Yes, of course, but this is not enough. We must keep asking *what product or service would help our customers more?* We must think more about the future. What will we be making 5 years from now? 10 years from now?[501]

Just as DEMING begins his treatise on quality talking about the basic executive function is to turn out a good product or a good service, in AQUINAS we begin with the basic principle that the executive function is responsibility for the moral rectitude of the organizational whole. It means that organization leadership and all the workers are responsible for doing good, and in order to do good, leaders and employees must be good. AQUINAS holds that all beings desire good insofar as they tend to good. NOVAK recognized the need for leadership to return to the Aristotelian-Thomistic concept of goodness.

Indeed, the Greeks spoke of goodness under a word, *kalos*, that works as well for beauty as for loveliness. *Kalos* signifies a kind of grace in action. Goodness is to get everything right, to pay a proper reverence to every aspect

---

[500] Ibid., 105.

[501] DEMING, *The New Economics*, 10.

of things. A good action hits the mark in all respects. When an action is in some way deficient, from one point of view or another, its goodness is marred. Sound business practices depend heavily on *kalos*.

Sadly, the role of *kalos* in the moral life has been lost in the modern tradition after Kant speaks of morals largely in terms of "duty," "ought," "thou shalt" and "thou shalt not." In sharp contrast, when Aristotle needed a metaphor for goodness in action, he turned to athletics rather than to law or command or duty, as in his example of the archer's "hitting the mark." To him, a good action represented not so much a law obeyed as an instance of beauty in act.[502]

The responsibility of executive leadership is not to institute an ethical system of formal authority. Also, organizational ethics is not a condensed training program in organizational ethics. For example, BOWDITCH, BUONO and STEWART present six simple questions about ethical behavior:

1) Is it right? (based on the deontological theory of moral rights)
2) Is it fair? (based on the deontological theory of justices)
3) Who gets hurt? (based on the utilitarian notion of greatest good for the greatest number of people)
4) Would you be comfortable if the details of your decisions were reported on the front page of your local newspaper? (based on the universal principle of disclosure)
5) What would you tell your child to do? (based on the ontological principle of reversibility)
6) How does it smell? (based on the gut principle that ethical theory or not, we usually have a sense of whether something feels "good")[503]

The authors suggest that the underlying goal of these questions is to develop the ability to recognize ethical issues in organizational life, moving away from the type of moral blindness that typifies many business decisions. The problem with

---

[502] NOVAK, *Business as a Calling*, 106.

[503] BOWDITCH, BUONO and STEWART, *A Primer on Organizational Behavior*, 106.

these questions is that they are based on a simplification of principles from an applied framework of the Center for Business Ethics at Bentley College. These questions are an ethics of formal decision-making guidelines. In a formal authoritarian organizational structure, they give a sense of protection. Yes, we have trained our people in ethical decision making, and we hold them responsible for making the right decisions. These types of questions have nothing to do with the development of character by means of an organizational moral psychology and a culture of rational moral habituation grounded on a rational moral psychology. If we use the thinking of NOVAK, we could say that this type of instrument lacks *kalos*, meaning it will never lead to graceful, harmonious, and everyday leaders and workers practicing rational-moral habituated behavior.

The problem with business and management ethical systems is that an organizational whole requires an executive leadership that understands rational moral psychology. Quite simply, this means, as we have argued, that leaders and employees are at their best as learning, productive and contributing persons when they exist in an organization that knows the power of the soul. Also, it is the understanding of the faculties of the soul and the diffusion of virtuous behavior from-top-to-middle-to-bottom and from bottom-to-middle-to-top of the organization. A Thomistic organizational rational moral psychology is not about ethical policy and systems; rather, it is about the existential, dynamic, and everyday habits of virtuous behavior.

6.1.2 *The Faculties of the Soul, Moral Psychology and Practical Leadership Behavior*

In chapter four, we referred to PINK's theory of the need for a whole new organizational mind, since we are moving from an information age to a conceptual age. We have expanded PINK's insight into the evolving organizational conceptual psychology to the hierarchical-heterarchical hybrid structure. It is a structure engaged in the tension of the desired order and emerging order of the information-disruptive digital age. We see that it is not so much of a need for a conceptual (cognitive) psychology; rather, it is a need to return to a premodern Aristotelian-Thomistic psychology of the soul, i.e., the faculties of the soul. PINK claimed that the new organizational psychology must be one of "High Concept and High Touch." High concept is the ability to create artistic and emotional beauty, to detect patterns and opportunities, to combine unrelated ideas. "High Touch" is to understand the subtleties of human interaction, to find joy in one's self and others, to stretch beyond the quotidian in the pursuit of purpose.

In response to PINK's concern, we suggest that a psychology based on the faculties of the soul is such a high concept-high touch organizational psychology. It is by means of the faculties of the soul that allows leadership to touch true, good, beautiful, and inspirational big plans, and it is powers of sense knowledge that activates (moves) high touch leadership by means of the soul's cogitative reason and sense memory that abstract the particular decisions from the day to day sense experiences to turn the plan into doable deeds and a rational aim. Recently, REDPATH has written on this high concept intellect, high touch sensing soul that we are attempting to express, as follows:

> While St. Thomas considers human reason to be a faculty of an immortal human soul, remarkably, St, Thomas maintains the specific difference of a human being resides in the genus "animal," not in the genus "spirit." Strictly speaking, according to St. Thomas, human beings are not incarnate spirits. We do not belong to the genus "spirit." We are not differentiated in our genus by being on the lowest level of intellectual spirit, being the dumbest of angels. Essentially, we belong to the highest rank within the genus animal (the qualitative maximum [leaders, rulers] in and of the animal genus, which is specifically divided into rational and irrational. St. Thomas locates our human, specific difference in an otherness, an animal rationality, existing within the sensitive or animal part of the intellectual soul.
>
> In the case of the human soul, St. Thomas understands the soul's relation to an animal body to consist in essentially connecting through human sense faculties (and chiefly what he calls "particular," or "cogitative" reason) of an animal body, an immortal intellectual soul, and the activities of the whole person to sense reality. He maintains that doing so enables the animal genus to become perfectly itself. The "sensitive soul," not a disembodied, or abstract, rationally (the generic part of the human nature), causes animal

rationality (a reason in touch with sense reality and proximate cause of rationality—and philosophically—doable human deeds).

In so doing, what had been reason acting abstractly, syllogistically, and previously considered as abstract principles, overflows into the sensory and appetitive part of the soul, and, through the activity of particular reason into the whole material creation. In so doing, human reason and its principles of rationality exit in a concrete, uniquely-animal, command-and-control way (as a kind of appetitive, sensory, reasoning establishing personal relations throughout the material world). It is within reason existing as such a command and control principle of the sense faculties and emotions in the animal part of the human soul that St. Thomas precisely locates deliberative choice, common sense, the moral virtue of prudence, and our specific, human difference.[504]

As we have established, the approach of a Thomistic psychology of organizational leadership is behavioral. However, it most important to state that it is a behavioral psychology grounded on the faculties of the soul. Therefore, it is the human soul that is the principle of human intellectual operation. The intellectual soul is the chief form and unifying cause of all parts of the body that causes the body to live. In other words, the whole soul is in the whole body in each of its parts.[505] It is for this reason that "a person knows how the act of knowing is his own unique action."[506] It is the human soul that is the conductor of self-preservation and a coherent life. Of course, it is not only the human soul, but it is also the animal soul that exits with this conductor of self-preservation of soul and its estimative sense of what is harmful or threatening to life (the movement of the soul). We see the same philosophical/scientific awareness of the powers of the soul in HOLT, one of the earliest and founders of behavioral psychology, who also has an appreciation for the study of behavior within the context of generic wholes. He writes:

---

[504] Peter A. REDPATH, "An American Perspective on Christian Philosophy of St. Thomas Aquinas: Midwife to Birth of a New and Improved Global Civilization of Freedom!" 6–7, as yet unpublished presentation to be delivered.

[505] See AQUINAS, *Summa theologiae* I, q. 76 a. 1.

[506] REDPATH, *The Moral Psychology of St. Thomas*, 77.

To study the behavior of the bee is of course to ask the question, "What is the bee doing?" This is a plain scientific question. It is doing of course a great many things; now it is visual organ is stimulated and it goes for a moment to rub antennae with another bee of its own hive; and so forth. But this is not an answer. We ask, "What is the bee doing?" And we are told, "now its visual organ is stimulated, and it darts toward a flower; now its olfactory organ is stimulated, and it goes for a moment to rub antennae with another bee of its own hive; and so forth." With a little persistence we could probably get a materialistic biologist to answer, "Why, the bee isn't doing anything." Whereas an unbiased observer can see plainly enough that "The bee is laying by honey in its home."

My point is that often too materialistically minded biologist is so fearful of meeting a certain bogy the 'psychic,' that he hastens to analyze every case of behavior into its component reflexes without venturing to observe it as a whole. In this way he fails to note the recession of the stimulus and the infallibly objective reference of behavior. He does not see that in any case of behavior no immediate sense stimulus whatsoever will figure in a straightforward and exact description of what the creature is doing: and 'What?' is the first question which science puts to the phenomenon […] to describe the what the bee does in terms of sensory stimuli, but also in much of the bee's conduct it would not be possible to point out any physical object on which the bee's activities turn or toward which they are directed. It lays up a store of honey in its home. If we suppose that here the parental hive is the physical object around which the bee's activities center, we soon find ourselves wrong, for when the swarm migrates the bees know the old hive no more but continues its busy life of hoarding in some other locality. The fact is that the specific object on which the bee's activities are focused, and of which they are a function, its 'home,' is a very complex situation, neither hive, loyalty, coworkers, nor yet flowers and honey, but a situation of which all of these are the related components. In short, we cannot do justice to the case of the bee, unless we admit that he is the citizen of a state, and that this phrase, instead of being a somewhat fanciful metaphor or analogy, is the literal description of what the bee demonstrably is and does.

Many biologists shy at such a description. [...] They will not describe the bee's behavior as a whole, will not observe what mere reflexes when cooperating in one organism can accomplish, because they fear, at bottom, to encounter the subjective or the psychic. They ought not to be afraid of this, for all that they have to do is describe in the most objective manner what the bee is doing.[507]

HOLT was of a functional-purpose school of behavioral psychology. He preferred to study the development of behavior as functional-purposeful adaptation to an environment. The importance of this above passage is that it touches upon what AVICENNA called the estimative sense[508] in animals and AQUINAS wisely incorporated into his explanation of the human soul and the internal senses, as the cogitative sense.[509] This long passage from HOLT is important because he touches upon one of the most important sense powers of the soul, the estimative power (also commonly, the estimative sense). It is a power of knowledge whose characteristic act is concrete evaluation or estimation. AQUINAS reasoned that there is a similar estimative power in the human soul that he defines as the cogitative power. It does seem that HOLT in establishing his school of purposive functional behavioral psychology is really adopting unaware the Aristotelian-Thomistic teaching of the relationship of the soul's estimative power and behavior, as seems clear in AQUINAS:

---

[507] HOLT, *The Freudian Wish*, 77–80.

[508] PEKKA KÄRKKÄINEN, *Internal Senses*. https://doi.org/10.1007/978-1-4020-9729-4_246

[509] AQUINAS, as is seen in his Summa theologiae (1,78,4, sed contra) applied Avicenna's estimative sense insight to elaborate on human nature as man possessing an estimative intelligence (particular or cogitative reason) capable of estimating with an animal intelligence danger, threat, risk. We have been contending based on the research of Peter A. Redpath that a confluence of practical reason, the habit of prudence and the cogitative sense (estimative soul) allows for the development of the practical concept of "estimative intelligence."

Again, we must observe that if an animal were moved by pleasing and disagreeable things only as affecting the sense, there would be no need to suppose that an animal has a power besides the apprehension of those forms which the senses perceive, and in which the animal takes pleasure, or from which it shrinks with horror. But the animal needs to seek or to avoid certain things, not only because they are pleasing or otherwise to the senses, but also on account of other advantages and uses, or disadvantages: just as the sheep runs away when it sees a wolf, not on account of its color or shape, but as a natural enemy: and again, a bird gathers together straws, not because they are pleasant to the sense, but because they are useful for building its nest. Animals, therefore, need to perceive such intentions, which the exterior sense does not perceive. And some distinct principle is necessary for this; since the perception of sensible forms comes by an immutation caused by the sensible, which is not the case with the perception of those intentions.[510]

It is this faculty of cogitative reason that, REDPATH rightly explains, locates deliberative choice, common sense, the moral virtue of prudence, and our specific, human difference. Also, it is of highest importance to the application of a Thomistic Organizational Behavioral Psychology. Indeed, we argue it seems impossible to understand an organizational psychology of executive leadership and rational-moral behavior without an understanding of cogitative reason, what AQUINAS calls particular reason:

Now, we must observe that as to sensible forms there is no difference between man and other animals; for they are similarly immuted by the extrinsic sensible. But there is a difference as to the above intentions: for other animals perceive these intentions only by some natural instinct, while man perceives them by means of coalition of ideas. Therefore, the power by which in other animals is called the natural estimative, in man is called the "cogitative," which by some sort of collation discovers these intentions. Wherefore it is also called the "particular reason," to which medical men assign a certain particular organ, namely, the middle part of the head: for it

---

[510] AQUINAS, *Summa theologiae* I, q. 78 a. 4.

compares individual intentions, just as the intellectual reason compares universal intentions. As to the memorative power, man has not only memory, as other animals have in the sudden recollection of the past; but also "reminiscence" by syllogistically, as it were, seeking for a recollection of the past by the application of individual intentions. Avicenna, however, assigns between the estimative and the imaginative, a fifth power, which combines and divides imaginary forms: as when from the imaginary form of gold, and imaginary form of a mountain, we compose the one form of a golden mountain, which we have never seen. But this operation is not to be found in animals other than man, in whom the imaginative power suffices thereto. To man also does Averroes attribute this action […]. So, there is no need to assign more than four interior powers of the sensitive part—namely, the common sense, the imagination, and the estimative and memorative powers.[511]

Without an understanding of the faculties of the internal senses, i.e., common sense, imagination, estimative and memorative powers it is not possible to construct a practical and realistic organizational behavioral psychology. AQUINAS teaches that, because a faculty of the soul is the proximate principle of the soul's operation, if one sense power cannot generate the needed acts, diverse powers must exist to help generate therm. Therefore, to know and to do many things, according to AQUINAS, requires man to possess a "proper" and "common sense" faculty. A proper sense stimulates a sense faculty to act by distinguishing one sensible stimuli from another, e.g., differentiating white from black, or green. Let us take an example of proper sense stimulation of the sense of sight by the color red identified by the proper faculty as red, as an animal or human sensitive soul must have the ability to sense all the qualities that the other senses sense of the color read. We could say it is a type of gestalt like internal sensing. The proper sense only knows the sensible quality form that stimulates it. An animal in the highest animal form of life apprehends a thing at the moment and must also apprehend the thing when it is absent. As AQUINAS explains, the bird is not directly stimulated by straw yet is still moved to gather the straw and build a nest. In order to have this instinctual

---

[511] Ibid., q. 74 a. 4.

movement, the bird, or the bee in HOLT's example of purposive behavior must have the faculty of common sense. In order to apply a Thomistic Organizational Behavioral Psychology of the function of executive leadership, we must emphasize the importance of the Aristotelian-Thomistic development in the animal genus of the estimative sense to particular reason and the importance of what REDPATH calls "estimative intelligence."[512]

VERNON J. BOURKE in his selections from the writings of AQUINAS concisely describes the dynamics of the internal senses and what we describe Thomistic psychology as high concept (rational soul) and high touch (sensitive soul) in focused confluence of powers. We summarize and interpret BOURKE, on the confluences of the internal senses as follows: An animal is moved toward a present thing and absent thing.

Therefore, an animal must not only take in the species when it is stimulated but when it is absent. Thus, it must take in and retain.

It is also for animal behavior to seek after, to flee from, things not only because they are agreeable or disagreeable in the sensory process but on account of other advantages and disadvantages and utilities, or on account of their harmful aspects. For example, a sheep, seeing a wolf approaching, runs away as if from a natural enemy and not because of the unsuitable coloring or shape.

It is necessary for the animal to preserve meaningful purpose by means other than sense pleasure. Therefore, there must be the faculty of common-sense perception of meaningful purpose. The imagination is a sort of treasure house of memories of forms taken in by sensation and is directed to the retention or preservation of these forms. The estimative power is directed to the apprehension of the meanings that are taken in by sensation. The memorative power, which is also a sort of treasure house for meanings, is for their retention.

---

[512] REDPATH, *The Moral Psychology of St. Thomas*, 97–100. Cf. AQUINAS, *Summa theologiae* I, q. 77 a. 3: "Nevertheless, we must observe that things which are accidental do not change the species. For since to be colored is accidental to an animal, its species is not changed by a difference of color, but by a difference in that which belongs to the nature of an animal, that is to say, by a difference in the sensitive soul, which is sometimes rational, and sometimes otherwise."

Note, as far as sensible forms are concerned, there is no difference between man and other animals; they are stimulated in quite the same way by external meanings as mentioned above. With man it is called the cogitative sense and always remains a sense because it continues to know the particular, individual, singular features of reality. Animals perceive intentions by some natural instinct, while man does so by some sort of inference.

In the area of memorative power, man has not only memory, for the sudden recall of past items, just like the rest of the animals, but he also has reminiscence, something like a memory for searching out, in a syllogistic way, things of the past in terms of individual meanings. As AQUINAS states in Question 74 that there is a fifth power midway between the estimative and the imaginative powers. For AQUINAS, the cogitative sense comes to participate in the life of reason, as AQUINAS states in Summa theologiae Question, 1, q 78, a.4: Reply to Objection 4: Although the operation of the intellect has its origin in the senses: yet, in the thing apprehended through the senses, the intellect knows many things which the senses cannot perceive. In like manner does the estimative power, though in a less perfect manner. Reply to Objection 5: The cogitative and memorative powers in man owe their excellence not to that which is proper to the sensitive part; but to a certain affinity and proximity to the universal reason, which, so to speak, overflows into them. Therefore, they are not distinct powers, but the same, yet more perfect than in other animals.

The cogitative always remains a sense and continues to know the particular, individual, singular features of reality and directed by universal reason, the cogitative power grows into particular reason. It remains particular because its objects never rise from their concrete individuality to the level of universality. It is because of particular reason, therefore, that we can describe Thomistic psychology as high concept (rational soul) and high touch (sensitive soul) in focused confluence of powers.

The rational moral agent must focus his/her sense knowledge of all apposite circumstances governing his/her behavior. It means the agent must view his/her action as a whole unit, or as we will discuss shortly an organizational behavioral event, e.g. the bee gathering honey, the bird gathering straw.

The cogitative process requires imagination to be pictured in advance because a rational sensing moral agent must think this: If I act at this time and place, with these people present, with these means, in this way, for this particular purpose-the action will be of this character, and it will probably have these consequences. In a way, the act is enacted, tried out, in imagination, while it is being considered. Shortly, we shall consider it is the prudent person, organizational leader who looks ahead in this way, especially when engaged in problem solving, strategy, goal and tactic making behavior.[513]

6.2 Practical Reason, Estimative Intelligence and Leadership and Behavioral Locus of Control

We turn to the study *Redefining Leadership for a Digital Age* of chapter four to the international survey of executive expectations of leadership abilities in a digital age. One of the major characteristics of leadership the executives deemed necessary was adaptability. It is assumed in an organization in the digital age that change is constant, disruptive, and unexpected. It requires executive directors, executive level senior vice presidents and down the line to team leaders who are able to rationally change their minds based on new information. The capability of adapting to change has become a major asset in the age of digital emerging leadership. It is the age of making smarter, harder, faster decisions. The executive summary of the *Redefining Leadership* study states:

> Being adaptable is key to the success of both the organization and the Agile Leader. At an organizational level, it means being ready to innovate and react to opportunities and threats as they appear. At an individual level, it means being open to new ideas, to changing an opinion when convinced of the need, and to successfully communicate that revised opinion to relevant stakeholders, like peers, teams, and customers. Changing your mind, which to some is regarded as a sign or weakness or lack of conviction, should be regarded as a strength when faced with changing information. Agile Leaders

---

[513] Vernon J. BOURKE, *The Pocket Aquinas* (New York: Washington Square Press, Inc.,1960) 122-124

are not afraid to commit to a new course of action when the situation warrants it.[514]

Decision making has been a major concern of empirical organizational psychology since its conception about the relationship between a person's ability to lead and the capacity of intuitive reasoning, especially in terms of problem solving, decision making, and strategic-tactical thinking. For example, it is Weston H. AGOR who has dedicated his scholarship to the nature of management decision making, *The Logic of Intuitive Decision Making: A Research Based Approach for Top Management*.[515] AGOR, like most empirical psychologists and management scientists who study the nature of intuitive decision making, never really defines the meaning of intuitive decision making. He simply says that it as a "way of knowing [...] recognizing the possibilities in any situation."[516] He continues suggesting that "it is best for us to think of intuition as being a highly rational decision-making skill-one that is logical for managers to use."[517] He continues his argument that "if we could accept the fact that intuition is an extension of the logical, we would be more comfortable with it."[518] AGOR as a materialistic empirical management scientist wants to hold, "just because modern science is not presently capable of explaining step-by-step how intuition works does not mean that it is not a rational brain skill."[519] Basically, the problem AGOR makes is that he is attempting to define intuition in terms of an introspective study of the brain and logic; most important, it is not a matter of brain logic. Of course, for a Thomist the issue is a matter of a faculty psychology and the rational and sensitive soul, particular reason, and the passions. We can state the issue more simply that it is not possible to

---

[514] Michael R. WADE, Andrew TARLING and Rainer NEUBAUER, "Redefining Leadership for a Digital Age, IMD Business School,"
www.imd.org/globalassets/dbt/docs/Global-leadership, 11

[515] Weston H. AGOR, *The Logic of Intuitive Decision Making: A Research Based Approach for Top Management* (New York: Quorum Books, 1986).

[516] Ibid., 5.

[517] Ibid. 7.

[518] Ibid., 5.

[519] Ibid.

understand organizational decision making without an understanding of estimative intelligence. However, if we must place particular reason within an understanding of the human intellect, will and sense appetites then we can call it the individual's behavioral locus of control, i.e., how a person controls and organizes rational-moral behavior. The individual's locus of control and organization of behavior is defined by Redpath thus:

> In two ways, St. Thomas says, the irascible [contending] and concupiscible [propelling] appetites are inclined to *listen to reason*, obey the higher part of the intellectual soul: the intellect, or reason, and the will.

> 1) They obey the intellectual reason in their own acts because *in human beings the faculty of particular reason replaces the estimative power that in irrational animals is the proximate principle that moves the sensitive appetite.* For example, as St. Thomas has already said, a sheep, judging the wolf as a natural enemy, is actually afraid. But, St. Thomas adds, *universal* reason naturally guides and moves particular reason. [...]
> 2) Following the lead of Aristotle, St. Thomas claims that the sense appetites obey the will as to their execution. The will is the proximate principle, mover, of the appetites. *In brute animals movement follows immediately upon judgment made by the estimative faculty that something is dangerous.* For example, St. Thomas observes, because it has no superior appetite (that is, a will) to oppose it, fearing the wolf, the sheep, *immediately* flees. It does not take time to stop to compose a syllogism about whether or not to run. On the contrary, a man, at times, awaits the command of his superior (that is, more *universal*) appetite, the will, before fleeing danger. He does not naturally incline immediately to follow the dictates of his estimative sense.[520]

---

[520] REDPATH, *The Moral Psychology of St. Thomas*, 105, 106.

6.2.1 The Practical Reason, Prudence, and the Good Decision Maker

Like ARISTOTLE, AQUINAS divides the intellect (reason) into speculative and practical. The good speculative intellect "consists simply in the true and false, in such a way that the absolutely true is its good and the absolutely false is its evil."[521] But knowledge of the contingent is useful according as it gives direction to the human operation of what is contingent, and practical science is concerned with the contingent as in the area of the particular. The speculative only deals with the contingent according to universal reason.[522]

As BOURKE explains,[523] the human intellect needs to be perfected by carefully repeated acts of right reasoning. When geometry or algebra are first studied, a person must slowly reason with difficulty and practice to conclusions. Right reasoning skill consists of the basic, natural tendency of the intellect, plus habits gained from continued use of the intellect. Such habits perfect the intellect so that the thinker can reach universal conclusions, first principles and causes in a better way than he/she could at the beginning of the study. It is with study that the intellect acquires greater speed, facility, and accuracy in thinking. Also, intellectual reasoning leads to practical and particular conclusions. Scientific habits of mind are only indirectly useful to the process of reasoning to singular conclusions. For example, an economist may know a great deal about the science of microeconomics and at the same time is unable to manage the cash flow and revenue stream of a small business. Practical thinking requires the development of a habit in the human intellect.

It is not easy to decide one way of acting which is best for a person in a given rational moral decision-making situation. There are, as a rule, complications that arise with decisions regarding the variety of formal kinds of action, from the rational and moral exigencies of the decision-making situation that call for mastery of the passions (or commonly today known as emotional intelligence) which make up the context of any rational moral decision-making action. The rational-moral

---

[521] AQUINAS, *Commentary on Aristotle's Nicomachean Ethics*, Book 6, Lecture 2.
[522] Ibid., Lecture 3.
[523] BOURKE, *Ethics*, 235.

good decision maker in the face of propelling and contending exigencies learns that successive problems and decisions of the same nature are easier to decide. The metaphysical explanation of such improvement is much the same as in the case of the student of geometry. The habit of right reasoning is acquired. This habit which perfects the practical intellect so that it can solve a concrete problem more quickly, more easily and more accurately, is named *prudence*.

The most important issue from the above statements on practical reason for a behavioral organizational psychology is that the rational-moral good decision maker in the face of propelling (concupiscible) and contending (irascible) exigencies learns that successive problems and decisions of the same nature are easier to decide. It is important because the rational-moral decision making, and mastery of the passions develops, and so must estimative intelligence develop, as it over time learns from the experience of problem solving. Of course, when we are problem solving, we are moved by the passions of the contending sense appetite that masters by the power of particular reason.[524]

It is here that we must include the pivotal intellectual habit of prudence that enables the intellect to know the universal rules of good human action (behavior). Neither moral science nor ethics solve the individual problems of human or organizational life. The practical science prepares the way for the use of prudence, but prudence must have developed by a rational-moral sensing agent. It is by repeated and continuous behavioral application to individual rational-moral problems that the behavioral habit of prudence is developed. In turn, it is the habit of prudence that seeks to focus, measure, and target the passions and powers of the soul in union with a formal object, thereby amplifying the agent's estimative intelligence for participation in the contending behavioral zone of organizational rational-moral decision making and problem solving.

BOURKE uses a metaphor to describe the confluence between the practical intellect, particular reason, and the virtue of prudence at it relates to problem solving in the genus of contending passions (violent emotions). We will call it a case of an agent estimative intelligence and the contending passions.

---

[524] Ibid., 231–238.

Prudence is not a moral science. It is a habit enabling the intellect to know the universal rules of good human action. Neither ethics nor moral theology solves the individual problems of human life. The practical sciences prepare the way for the use of prudence, but prudence must be acquired by each moral agent making repeated and continued application of whatever moral science he has, to his own individual moral differences.

To understand this point, let us think of a boxer who has a smart manager. The manager tells his fighter about the weaknesses of his opponent. A general plan is outlined throughout the early rounds, tire him out, and refuse to be into close fighting. Then, in the last rounds, he is to take the initiative and knock out the opponent. This is all theory and few such plans work out as preconceived. The opponent may have much the same instructions. The crowd may boo both of them stalling. The referee may warn them that he will stop the fight and stop payment of the purses, if they refuse to mix it up. Now, the experienced fighter will know how to adapt his plan to such unforeseen developments. He may notice that his opponent is not using his left hand much; it may be broken. His experience (which is also a practical habit gained from repeatedly facing similar situations) enables him to take advantage of the new circumstance and decide quickly on a change of plans. Notice that the manager cannot do all of his thinking for his fighter. The actual fighting must be done by the boxer and each blow must be quickly adapted to the individual circumstance, as well as to the end, which is victory. This means the fighter must do his own practical thinking. He needs a sort of prudence to outwit his opponent. He does not acquire this prudence simply by listening to his manager. He gets it from his own experience in the ring, if he is smart enough to remember it and profit by it.[525]

Like the fighter, the rational-moral agent needs experience to do well. Prudence is the habit which coordinates moral theory, moral experience, and particular knowledge of a novel rational-moral situation. Prudence may be defined

---

[525] Ibid., 236.

as the intellectual habit enabling the agent to reason to the right conclusion to his/her rational moral problem.

The management scientist Paul C. NUTT wrote a classic work *Making Tough Decisions: Tactics Improving Managerial Decision Making.*[526] In the 1980s and 90s, it was one of the recognized empirical texts on the study of decision making. In the first part of the work he gave attention to the nature of problem solving as primarily the challenge for individual and team decision makers to methods for uncovering core problems, assessing future conditions, testing, and learning. Fundamentally, problem solving involved three major tasks: 1) identify the real problem, 2) the methodology for solving the problem, 3) clear expectations of alternative solutions. He used a variety of quantitative statistical methods, decision trees and value metrics, and cost-benefit analysis for making decisions. The first part of his book on individual and team identification of problem solving had several group dynamic techniques for problem clarification. The second part of his work was by far so statistically oriented that few organizations found it to be practical for the everyday decision making and problem solving. If we approach organizational problem solving and decision making from the Thomistic perspective of estimative intelligence and the virtue of prudence, then we arrive at a less esoteric and more valuable everyday method of solving rational moral problems and making prudent organizational decisions.

First, we must clarify the meaning of the rational moral psychology of an organization as an integral part of the organizational behavioral psychology. These are not two separate disciplines because in an organization, as we mentioned in early chapter two adhering to the thoughts of BARNARD, DEMING and DRUCKER, the moral goodness of the organization is a fundamental executive responsibility. We are using moral rectitude in the sense of a diffusion of moral goodness throughout the organizational whole (genus). Organizations are comprised of behavioral activities, events, and operations. In organizations from the viewpoint of human resources workers are hired and promoted because of their skill sets which are operational, e.g., a bank teller, machine operator, salesperson, medical doctor, lawyer. They must have skills, and they are expected to execute those skills

---

[526] Paul C. NUTT, *Making Tough Decisions: Tactics for Improving Managerial Decision Making* (San Francisco, Oxford: Josey-Bass, 1990).

with a certain level of proficiency. If a company is to strive for excellence or the maximum of reasonable perfection (virtual quantity), then more is required than proficient skills. Josef PIEPER writes:

> Human activity has two basic forms: doing (agree) and making (facere). Artifacts technical and artistic are the "works" of making. We ourselves are the "works of doing." And prudence is the perfection of the ability to do, whereas "art" (in St. Thomas' sense) is perfection of the ability to make. "Art" is the "right reason" of making (*recta ratio factbilium*); prudence is the "right reason" of doing (*recta ratio agibilium*).
>
> The man who does good follows the lines of an architectural plan which has not been conceived by himself and which he does not understand as a whole, nor in all of its parts. This architectural plan is revealed to man from moment to moment. In each case he sees only a tiny segment of it, as through a narrow crack. Never, so long as he is in the state "of being-on-the-way," will the concrete architectural plan of his own self become visible to him in its rounded and final shape.
>
> Paul Claudel defines conscience—which, as we have said, is in a certain sense equivalent to prudence itself—as "the patient beacon which does not delineate the future, but only the Immediate.[527]

The executive and his senior vice presidents of the executive level must serve as exemplars of virtue in the organizational works of making (skills) and works of performing their skills with a moral commitment to not just performing the skill well but being a virtuous performer. As NOVAK expressed above, an exemplar leader represents an organizational tradition of *kalos* which signifies a kind of grace in action: goodness is to get everything right, to pay a proper reverence to every aspect of things. A good action hits the mark in all respects as performer.

EHRINGER characterizes the analytical mind, feelings, and morals of entrepreneurs as executive leaders. She categorizes her thematic phenomenological method into recurring themes regard the decision-making and

---

[527] Josef PIEPER, *The Four Cardinal Virtues* (South Bend: University of Notre Dame Press, 1952), 29–30.

problem-solving style of the entrepreneurs. One of the themes she identifies, is attention to goodness and decision-making as essential in creating a successful business. Often in the interviews the interviewees referred to making good decisions. It seems obvious that they are referring to something deeper than a skill set. One of the main reasons for using EHRINGER's research is that she seems to hit the crux of executive levels of exemplar leadership. It is the ability to be a good decision-maker.

Her research is of a strong descriptive phenomenological type that holds closely to the language of the successful entrepreneurs who have developed their skills as good decision makers from varied experiences and the development, as defined in chapter five on inductive craft knowledge, of first principles. It is noted that these entrepreneurs have acquired their craft knowledge from experience gained in decision making in everyday behavior in an organizational contending behavioral zone genus. She writes:

> At its best, this process embodies flexibility informed by principle and an attitude of openness to opportunity that serves principle.
>
> The patterns of decision-making these entrepreneurs describe combine analysis and emotion. Each pattern uses one and then the other element to arrive at a decision. The stories in this book suggest that each of us *has an instinctive, habitual pattern of inclining toward either analysis or emotion when faced with a decision.* To be effective, we must validate or negate that inclination by attending to the other—by using analysis supported by feelings or heeding emotion confirmed by data.
>
> These elements—analysis and emotion—are connected through the interweaving, and further validation or negation, of intuition. *Intuition is not emotion, nor is it feeling, nor is it mysticism. It is our tacit knowledge of the matter at hand, our unconscious knowledge.* It is a product of our experience and specific expertise and, therefore, favors the experienced and the expert. It is our most important decision-making tool.
>
> Tools of the self at work include thinking, reading, writing, focus, creativity, and introspection. Tools of working with other include consensus-building, listening, planning, strategy, and negotiation.

Decisions are also influenced by other people and events and experience. Again, our skill—particularly our ability to learn to listen—and our awareness, strongly determine whether the influence of others will be effective and valuable to us.

The greatest influence on decision-makers is their personal principles. These define us a human being, determine our purposes and drive us toward the decisions that achieve our purposes.

Making good decisions comes from an awareness of all these forces—from an awareness of mind and our process, patterns, and purposes. Only with this most personal knowledge can we put to good effect the other aspects and general rules of making good decisions.

The key to good decision-making is knowing ourselves and how we think. As decision makers, we need to know what we want—and how we want to reflect back on a well-lived life—and to be guided by that knowledge.

Other Steps to Good Decisions

What else do these sixty entrepreneurs say about good decision making? They stress flexibility and fluidity and an appreciation for variability, as well as an understanding of their discursive and unstructured merging of analysis and emotional decision processes. They would recommend real world training in the *attitudes, experiences and skills of flexibility, fluidity, and variability, since those are so uncommonly found in the literature in academic programs.*

Necessary, too, for good decision-making as these entrepreneurs described it, is clarification that intuition—or their tacit knowledge—is a tool of the experienced and expert, and, wherever it might be acquired, it is applicable to only relevant issues. It is a decision tool best acquired or developed through intensive or extended experience in some area of knowledge and then applied to that same or a similar area of knowledge.[528]

If there is an academic organizational philosophy that is compatible with a Thomistic Organizational Behavioral Psychology, it is the Visionary

---

[528] EHRINGER, *Make Up Your Mind*, 306–307; emphasis added.

Entrepreneurial Learning School of Strategy Making as an emergent process.[529] It is an approach to executive leadership very similar to EHRINGER's findings on entrepreneurial decision, strategy making and executive leadership, as we see in her following comments on entrepreneurial education.

On the proper education of an entrepreneur ends with a curricular recommendation or two for the proper education of the entrepreneur, most directed at improving entrepreneurship programs. This led EHRINGER to ask, what might these entrepreneurs add? Based on her research, we could summarize the results thus:[530]

1) They would begin by recommending grounding in ethical principles, preferably through an evolving, step by step learning of the kind that teaches the student entrepreneur how to fish.

2) They would recommend concentrations in how to be conscious, to be aware, to feel, to be thoughtful, to seek perspective, to consider diverse options and welcome diverse opinions, how to focus on others and relate to others.

3) How to manage and how to lead, and how to live a balanced life-with emphasis on the attitudes of each, rather than the tasks.

4) Big curriculum! They might say it is probably most accessible in a good classical, liberal arts program, rather than in a business school.

5) Most important, learn firsthand through concentrated experience in an industry that interest them, through concentrate experience in an industry that interest him/her, that focused expertise which is the basis of the intuition that he/she will need to inform his/her decision making.

EHRINGER's phenomenological research is not a quantitative study. Yet, from the standpoint of a Thomistic metaphysics of organizational wisdom and an organizational psychology, we are most interested in the interpretation behind the words. The first reflection is metaphysical because it stands out as a clear Aristotelian-Thomistic metaphysical wisdom motif.

---

[529] MINTZBERG, AHLSTRAND and LAMPEL, *Strategy Safari*, 123–147.

[530] Ibid., 308.

Now the reason for undertaking this investigation is that all men think that the science which is called wisdom deals with the primary causes and principles of things. Hence, as we have said before, the man of experience is considered to be wiser than one who has any of the senses; the artist wiser than the man of experience; the master planner wiser than the manual laborer and speculative knowledge wiser than practical knowledge. It is quite evident then, that wisdom is a science of certain causes and principles.[531]

6.2.2 Right Reason and a Moral Order Thomistic Hermeneutics

Let us probe behind the words of the entrepreneurs from a Thomistic philosophical analysis that "An instinctive pattern of inclining toward analysis and emotion when faced with a decision […] Intuition is not emotion, nor is it feeling, not is it mysticism […] tacit knowledge of the knowledge at hand." In terms of a Thomistic faculty psychology we are speaking about estimative intelligence and the confluence of powers between the sensitive and rational soul. We observe in these entrepreneurial reflections that they stress the extreme importance of learning from their experiences. Of course, from a Thomistic philosophical/psychological hermeneutics we interpret their acquired skill as good decision makers as the result of a craft knowledge. It is the craft knowledge that is gained by means of inductive reasoning and the discovery of first principles, as the Aristotelian-Thomistic teachings explain.

The entrepreneurs have sensed that good decision-making is also a matter of sensing a rational moral foundation of principles that guide their executive leadership decision-making: "we need new paradigms for decision-making and new principles for judgment-such as the old fundamental ones, those of the Golden Rule that many of them described as the basis of their own decision-making." The executive entrepreneurs asked, "how to manage and how to lead, and how to live a balanced life—with emphasis on the attitudes of each, rather than the tasks." It is a question addressed by ARISTOTLE and AQUINAS: "As the Philosopher [Aristotle] says […] it is the business of the wise man to order. The reason for this is that

---

[531] AQUINAS, *Commentary on Aristotle's Metaphysics*, Book 1, Lecture 1.

wisdom is the most powerful perfection of reason whose characteristic is to know order."[532]

We are able to live a balanced life because we have the capacity to know what we should do; choose the appropriate means to do it; and then use these means. It is function of reason and will to order free actions toward an end. A wise person is able to live a balanced life (an ordered life) because he/she is capable of both speculative and practical reasoning. With speculative reasoning, we are able to think and make rational-moral sense about the intellectual implications of the world about us. A person cannot just think about life because life is about action; it is about how we must behave as rational-moral persons. When we begin to think about how to act, we are using practical reasoning.

It is the same power of the intellect whether we are engaged in speculative or practical reason. When we know things, we use speculative reason before we can reasonably decide what to do about these things. When we decide what to do about things, we use practical reason. If the will is not ordered by reason, it is only driven by the senses. The first thing, according to Thomistic moral psychology, is that the will is ordered by reason. If we understand Thomistic moral psychology, then it is clear why the entrepreneur successful executive leader decision making is a process that "embodies flexibility informed by principle and an attitude of openness to opportunity that serves principle."[533]

The words of the structured interviews of the entrepreneurs are testimony to the Thomistic cognitive teaching that we learn things by perceiving them with our senses and interpreting and understanding what has been sensed by means of the innate power of the intellect. Obviously, it appears that the successful entrepreneurial executive matures as a good decision maker because he/she trust their first practical principles acquired from experience. A human agent must first have sense experience and then some inductive comprehension of what he/she has experienced. These achieved concepts and the consequent judgments are not innate. Therefore, one's knowledge of fist principles is acquired.

---

[532] AQUINAS, *Commentary on Aristotle's Nicomachean Ethics*, Book 1, Lecture 1.

[533] EHRINGER, *Make Up Your Mind*, 306.

6.2.3 The Executive Exemplar Leadership, Decision-Making, and Behavioral Habits of Synderesis and Prudence

We began our application of a Thomistic psychological understanding of the executive function of leadership by establishing a crossover trading zone of ideas on principles of leadership with BARNARD, especially his insistence on the moral character required of the executive position and the responsibility for the diffusion of a moral character as expressed in all levels of leadership, supervisory and worker rational-moral behavior. BARNARD held that individuals most suited for leadership are those who exemplify a behavioral pattern of moral responsibility. He writes:

> Responsibility is the power of a particular moral code to control the conduct of the individual in the presence of strong contrary desires or impulses. For instance, two men may have substantially identical codes as respects a given field of activity, but the code will be dominant as respects the conduct of one man under adverse immediate conditions, while it will not be dominant as respects the other under the same or similar conditions. With reference to that code, the first man is said to be responsible, or to possess responsibility, or to have the capacity of responsibility; the second man not.[534]

BARNARD, both as a practicing executive and organizational scientist, was an organizational purposive behaviorist. As a purposive organizational behaviorist, it is his conviction that the proper rational moral purpose is the unifying principle of leadership behavior. It is this purpose as it is expressed in verbal and non-verbal organizational behavior that is the executive challenge. Therefore, it requires leaders with the necessary moral character to exemplify the appropriate rational moral behavior. It is not only a matter of understanding general organizational policy. BARNARD says that executives and leaders must have, what he calls, a character of creative morality, and it is the highest exemplification of responsible executive leadership.

---

[534] BARNARD, *The Functions of the Executive*, 263.

In fact, probably most executive decisions appear in the guise of technical decisions, and their moral aspects are not consciously appreciated. An executive may make any important decisions without reference to any sense of personal interest or of morality. But where creative morality is concerned, the sense of personal responsibility—of sincerity and honesty, in other words—is acutely emphasized. Probably few persons are able to do such work objectively. Indeed, few can do it except on the basis of personal conviction-not conviction that they are obligated as officials to do it, but conviction that what they do for the good of organization they personally believe to be right.[535]

It is necessary in these two passages from BARNARD on executive moral responsibility and in executive decision making to realize that technical and moral issues are of the same decision-making genus. It is for BARNARD a rational moral principle that operational, technical, strategic and personnel decision making are not just a matter of cost benefit analysis but are also moral issues pertaining to the organizational whole. We could say from the position of Thomistic behavioral organizational psychology that BARNARD expects executives and leaders at organizational executive levels to exemplify the behavior of a virtuous person. Aquinas says that "the virtuous person correctly passes judgment on individual things that pertain to human activity [...] the habit of moral virtue is defined by what is in accord with right reason."[536] Then in the same place AQUINAS explains why it makes sense that only the virtuous person is capable of serving as the organizational executive exemplar known for making rational and moral decisions.

Here the good man differs very much indeed from others, for he sees what is truly good in individual, practicable matters, being as it were the norm and measure of all that is to be done because in these cases a thing must be judged good or bad according as it seems to him.[537]

---

[535] Ibid., 281.

[536] AQUINAS, *Commentary on Aristotle's Nicomachean Ethics*, Book 3, Lecture 10.

[537] Ibid.

The essential qualification for an executive level leader is the ability to be a highly competent decision maker. It is not that BARNARD is a reductionist on this matter, but if the characteristic of being a highly competent decision maker is lacking then a person could not qualify for executive leadership. BARNARD states, "In short, a characteristic of the services of executives is that they represent a specialization of the process of making organizational decisions—and this is the essence of their functions."[538]

It is the phenomena of executive level decision-making that effects to various degrees the strategic planning of an organization down to the operational everyday technical/moral decisions and problem solving in the pursuit of the organizational end. But, as stated from AQUINAS, it is the virtuous person's decision-making behavior that serves as the exemplar of rational moral decision making by individuals, groups, and teams. BARNARD held that the exemplar decision maker must have a special sense of creative morality. We could say that he insisted that the executive exemplar leaders have a keen sense of the good in their decision making. It was more than just a general concept of good, i.e., speculative principle. What is needed is the ability to form a first practical judgment.

It is a practical proposition that relates the good to concrete organizational decision-making behavior and the consequent action. Thomistic moral psychology requires that the intellect exercise a special effort to the implication of a first principle of rational moral decision making: "The good should be done; the evil should not be done."[539] The soul intensifies its power so that it is keen to see the truth of this first practical principle.

---

[538] BARNARD, *The Functions of the Executive*, 189.

[539] AQUINAS, *Summa theologiae* I-II, q. 94 a. 2: "Now as 'being' is the first thing that falls under the apprehension simply, so 'good' is the first thing that falls under the apprehension of the practical reason, which is directed to action: since every agent acts for an end under the aspect of good. Consequently, the first principle of practical reason is one founded on the notion of good, viz. that 'good is that which all things seek after'. Hence this is the first precept of law, that 'good is to be done and pursued, and evil is to be avoided'. All other precepts of the natural law are based upon this: so that whatever the practical reason naturally apprehends as man's good (or evil) belongs to the precepts of the natural law as something to be done or avoided."

Strengthening quality of the intellect is also an innate *habitus* of first principles, and in Thomistic terminology this *habitus* of first practical principle is called *synderesis*. It is the intellectual *habitus* which makes it possible to acquire such knowledge from experience. *Synderesis* is a *habitus*, whereas conscience is an act of judgment. *Synderesis* is the habit that retains and focuses on universal knowledge of first principles of practical reasoning. Conscience is not concerned with the universal, but with a particular application of practical reasoning and organizational rational-moral decision making.

An executive level leader must have a keen sense of rational moral judgment involved in organizational decision making. We are arguing in this dissertation that the executive serves as an exemplar of virtuous behavior within the organizational culture. The exemplar is known for making wise practical judgments. Like BARNARD, we have pointed out that organizational decision making most often, at higher to lower levels of decision making, is an issue of technical and moral nature. It is for this reason that we refer to all organizational decision making to various degrees as being of a rational moral nature. Execution and implementation of leadership decisions require acts of conscience and judgment of choice to be right and good, both must be in accord with right reason. The habit of reasoning rightly about proposed moral actions or engaging in the process of organizational decision making is called *prudence.*

A prudent decision maker must not only judge moral actions rightly, but he/she must also choose and do right actions. There are three acts that are basically proper to the virtue of prudence deliberation, right judgment, and right perception of action. BARNARD was not an Aristotelian-Thomistic student, but in returning to his work of 1938 he called for a new type of behavioral knowledge not found in schools of business, engineering, and the social sciences. For example, he wrote:

> The moral factors upon which the vitality of organization depends are treated mostly as subjects for glowing generalities in inspirational addresses and there is woeful lack of appreciation of the interrelationships between character and ability.
>
> There is no science of organization or of cooperative systems; and the development of the sciences called social has clearly lagged far behind those

physical and mathematical. One reason for this appears to be a false emphasis upon intellectual and mental processes both as factors in human relations and as matters of study.

In the common-sense, every day, practical knowledge necessary to the practice of the arts, there is much that is not susceptible of verbal statement—it is a matter of know-how. It may be called behavioral knowledge. It is necessary to doing things in concrete situations. It is nowhere more indispensable than in the executive arts. It is acquired by persistent habitual experience and is often called intuitive.[540]

At the beginning of this dissertation, we went to some length to explain that there is a compatible trading zone of concepts, principles, and methods of investigation between various schools of behavioral psychology, which we will develop in more detail shortly, and a Thomistic organizational behavioral psychology construct. BARNARD in 1938 called for a new organizational behavioral knowledge, and we argue that such a behavioral knowledge is discovered in a Thomistic faculty-behavioral-psychology, especially a behavioral knowledge of the functions of executive leadership.

In the last sentence of the above passage, BARNARD claims that one learns the executive arts by persistent habitual experience and what is often called intuitive. BARNARD refers to habitual experience and intuition as the foundation of this necessary behavioral knowledge. We find the concept of habitual experience in of itself and intuition unable to serve as the foundational construct of an organizational behavioral knowledge. In this work, we propose that the proper construction of an organizational behavioral knowledge, as desired by BARNARD and required by the emerging hierarchical-heterarchical organization, is a Thomistic faculty-behavioral-psychology. It is a psychology that is constructed on a foundation of metaphysics of organization of one and the many, genus and species, virtual quantity, and a faculty psychology.

A faculty psychology is necessary because the concept of experience and intuition cannot explain organizational behavior, especially the executive art of leadership. A Thomistic faculty-behavioral-psychology seeks the foundation of

---

[540] BARNARD, *The Functions of the Executive*, 290–291.

rational moral executive leadership in the exercise of particular reason and the habit of prudence in deciding and doing the next right thing for the good of individuals and the organizational whole. In other words, we are stating that the foundation of the executive practice is the Thomistic concept of "estimative intelligence."

We must also add that experience as experience does not a leader make, let alone an executive exemplar. We learned in chapter four that exemplar leaders must have a sense of inductive reasoning. They must learn from the experience of a given subject matter the first principles that pertain to the particular craft knowledge or a similar domain. Not having the ability to learn first principles from experience using inductive reasoning should automatically exclude a person from leadership at any organizational level.

Even though BARNARD does not approach his concept of organizational behavioral psychology as a premodern Aristotelian-Thomistic behavioral knowledge reconstruction, he does seem in his work to have a Thomistic metaphysical sense of the organization as a genus of contrariety of forces. He refers to this contrariety as the limiting and complementary factors of the organization. It is the dynamics of controlling these forces in the organizational whole that are the continuing decision-making underpinnings of effective strategic action. He takes this concept of problem-solving decision-making factors from the economist John R. COMMONS:

> But the limiting and complementary factors are continually changing places. What was the limiting factor becoming complimentary, when once it is under control; then another factor is the limiting one. This limiting factor, in the operation of an automobile, at one time may be the electric spark; at another the gasoline, at another the man at the wheel. This is the meaning of efficiency—the control of the changeable factors at the right time, right place, right amount, and the right form in order to enlarge the total output by the expected operation of complementary factors.[541]

---

[541] Ibid., 204, and John R. COMMONS, *Institutional Economics: Its Place in Political Economy* (London and New York: Macmillan, 1934), 629.

It is this last sentence for BARNARD that refers to the meaning of effective organizational decision making, and what he calls the leadership exercise of control "at the right time, right place, right amount and right form" so that the organizational purpose is properly redefined and accomplished. Again, he quotes Professor COMMONS:

> But out of the complex happenings, man selects the limiting factors for his purposes. If he can control these, then the other factors work out the effects intended. The "cause" is volitional control of the limiting or strategic factors. [...] The "effects" are the operations of complementary factors.[542]

BARNARD, as we observe in this following passage from chapter eight, "The nature of Executive Responsibility," always returns to the issue of limiting and complementary factors as issues pertaining to concrete expressions of the organizational moral authority factor and a faith in executive exemplar leadership:

> The limitations imposed by the physical and biological constitution of human beings, the uncertainties of the outcome of cooperation, the difficulties of common understanding of purpose, the delicacy of the systems of communication essential to organization, the dispersive tendencies of individuals, the necessity of individual assent to establish the authority for coordination, the great role of persuasion in securing adherence to the organization and submission to its requirements, the complexity and instability of motives, the never-ending burden of decision-all these elements of organization, in which the moral factor finds its concrete expression, spell the necessity of leadership, the power of individuals to inspire cooperative personal decision by creating faith: faith in common understanding, faith in the probability of success, faith in the ultimate satisfaction of personal motives, faith in the integrity of objective authority, faith in the superiority of common purpose as a personal aim of those who partake in it.[543]

---

[542] Ibid., 205, and COMMONS, *Institutional Economics*, 632.

[543] BARNARD, *The Functions of the Executive*, 259.

Since executive leadership decision making is a continuous process of controlling limiting and complementary organizational factors, or as we have maintained in previous chapters the balancing of emergent and desired organizational order, we can see executive decision-making is of the utmost importance to the success of all levels of organizational leadership, but it is perhaps the most determining factor of the nature of executive levels of leadership. The decision making, in terms of the related strategic factor, that defines the behavior of the executive leader. The question that faces the executive continuously is "to do or not to do this!" Strategic planning is not a process that it is done once a year. A strategic plan is a visionary decision to move the organization toward an end, a purpose. It is a plan of action, but all organizational decisions relate to action either to do or not to do. There is always the element of the plan as the executive vision that is by means of an intense organizational strategic team decision making formed into practical goals and tactics. It is here that we draw attention to the fact that since the 60s in the scientific literature on organizational strategy there is scholarly consensus on ten schools of how organizational strategy should be formed:

1) design school strategy formation as a process of conception,
2) the planning school strategy formation as a formal process,
3) the positioning school strategy formation as a visionary process,
4) the entrepreneurial school strategy formation as a visionary process,
5) the cognitive school strategy formation as a mental process,
6) the learning school strategy formation as an emergent process,
7) the power school strategy formation as a process of negotiation,
8) the cultural school strategy formation as a collective process,
9) the environmental school strategy formation as a reactive process,
10) the configuration school strategy formation as a process of transformation.[544]

We do not need to examine these schools in detail because we are not concerned with a study on strategic planning. We do, nevertheless, list them to

---

[544] MINTZBERG, AHLSTRAND and LAMPEL, *Strategy Safari*, 5.

point out that the schools of entrepreneurial visionary process and the learning schools of emergent process are most compatible with a Thomistic faculty-behavioral-psychology of the executive exemplar leader and the diffusion of the virtuous habit of leadership throughout the organization. It is the entrepreneurial decision-making strategic school that holds boldly to the requirement of the executive leader as the visionary leader.[545]

The entrepreneurial-visionary school of executive leadership maintains that a firm grasp of "estimative intelligence," mastery of the irascible (contending) passions is absolutely essential, and exemplar virtuous behavior is the essence of the executive function. As Peter F. DRUCKER wrote, "Entrepreneurship requires that the few available good people be deployed on opportunities rather than frittered away on solving problems."[546] DRUCKER also firmly believed that the success of all organizations in the information society would depend upon entrepreneurial-visionary leadership claiming that central to the business enterprise is the entrepreneurial act of economic risk taking. In the visionary organization the focus is on opportunities, problems are secondary. What is an entrepreneur? EHRINGER asks the question and concludes after her extensive study of entrepreneurial thinking that:

> The word "entrepreneurial" seems to be a high-tech rubber band, capable of being wrapped around virtually any phenomenon which has an aura of cleverness, creativity, newness, or apparent riskiness. Its definitions and extensions are almost endless.[547]

Before describing the advantages of an entrepreneurial visionary psychology of organizational exemplar executive leadership, it is necessary to make a necessary distinction between two types of entrepreneurial behavior. In order to establish this distinction, we must return to chapter two, where we discussed the nature of organizational leadership and pathological behavior, i.e., the dark soul of executive

---

[545] Ibid.

[546] Peter F. DRUCKER, "Entrepreneurship in Business Enterprise," *Journal of Business Policy* (1,1, 1970), 10.

[547] EHRINGER, *Make Up Your Mind*, 354.

leadership. We referred to Manfred Kets DE VRIES who refers to the "dark side of leadership" as the Darth Vader aspect of leadership which grows out of personality traits such as narcissism, self-deceit, and abuse of power that leaders are unwilling to face and acknowledge their weaknesses. Consequently, ever aware of the "dark soul" of the executive entrepreneurial visionary, we approach this type leader as of two types we will call: 1) the prudent visionary exemplar executive leader, and 2) the other is the shrewd, crafty visionary exemplar executive leader.

First, we have the visionary executive leader, who is known as a prudent person. In Book Six of Aristotle's *Nicomachean Ethics* (in which he considers the intellectual virtues), we learn that the prudent person is known by the power of the habit to give good advice about proper and useful goods (i.e., about things good and useful for the benefit of the total life of man).

> Therefore, if a man who is capable of giving good advice for a particular incident is presumed prudent in some matter, it follows that he will be absolutely prudent who gives counsel about things touching the whole of life.[548]

We must give careful attention to the fact that AQUINAS teaches that the prudent person is not just practical. The prudent person is known for giving good advice in particular matters, but he/she is known as being prudent about giving good counsel in matters touching the whole of life. This is extremely important because shortly we argue that an exemplar leader must be known by other members of the organization for his/her virtuous behavior as an authentic and coherent observable overt lifestyle not just in matters of organizational leadership.

Second, AQUINAS warns that there is a difference between a prudent and a shrewd person. He holds that two things are needed in a work of virtue, i.e., the right intention and means.

> This is done by prudence, which gives good advice, judges, and orders the means to the end. In his way, both prudence and moral virtue concur in a

---

[548] Ibid.

virtuous operation: prudence perfecting the part rational by essence, and moral virtue perfecting the appetitive part, rational by participation.[549]

Then AQUINAS makes a critical observation that there are persons who seem to give good advice, judge well and lay out the appropriate means, but there is something other than prudence at work. He defines it as "an operative principle called shrewdness, as it were a certain ingenuity or skillfulness. This is of such a nature that, by means of it, man can do the things ordered to an end—either good or bad."[550] The concern of ARISTOTLE and AQUINAS is that there is always a need for caution with a shrewd person, particularly with a shrewd executive leader. AQUINAS warns about the shrewd doer of the deed: "When the intention is good ingenuity of this sort deserves praise, but when the intention is bad, it is called craftiness, which implies evil as prudence implies good."[551] For AQUINAS, there is nothing wrong with a prudent person being shrewd; the problem is the crafty and shrewd person. It is the crafty and shrewd person who always leans toward the dark soul of dysfunctional executive leadership.

FOWERS is a leading scholar in the field of philosophical psychology who represents in empirical psychology a resurgence of Aristotelian Virtue Psychology. One of FOWERS's major concerns is that psychologists prefer an instrumental perspective. In psychology's concern for a value-free neutral discipline, it dictates that values and goals should be left to individuals. Instrumentalism is a rational moral position that defines an individual's relationship with the world and with each other in means-ends terms, suggesting that strategically pursuing desired objects and experiences is the central business of life. Instrumental theories of social exchange and cognitive theories characterize individuals as self-interested actors who seek to maximize their outcomes and instrumental means dominate the discipline of empirical organizational psychology and ethics.

In contrast to instrumentalism, virtue ethics claims that the best kind of life is characterized by the overall integrity and harmony of the individual's aims

---

[549] Ibid.

[550] Ibid.

[551] Ibid.

and actions. This harmony is evident in the ways in which such a life is organized around internal goods that one pursues by being the kind of person who embodies those ends.[552]

FOWERS, also, draws attention to the strength of the instrumental impulse in attempts to understand the important issue of practical intelligence. He focuses on the research of the cognitive psychologist Robert J. STERNBERG who is one of the most recognized researchers into the nature of practical intelligence.[553] In his comments on STERNBERG, we see that based on instrumental psychology the understanding of the executive leader as an exemplar of practical wisdom and virtuous behavior is impossible. FOWERS indicates at best we can hope for a shrewd to crafty leader.

A further indication of the strength of the instrumental impulse in psychological theorizing emerges in Sternberg and associates concept of practical intelligence, a concept of wisdom. These authors defined practical intelligence as the ability to find a more optimal fit between the individual and the demands of the environment [...]. Sternberg differentiated practical

---

[552] FOWERS, *Virtue and Psychology*, 61.

[553] Robert J. STERNBERG, "Implicit theories of intelligence and creativity and wisdom," *Journal of Personality and Social Psychology*, 1985 49, 607–627; Robert J. STERNBERG, *Wisdom and its relations to intelligence and creativity*, in Robert J. STERNBERG (Ed.), *Wisdom: Its Nature, Origins, and Development* (Cambridge: Cambridge University Press, 1990), 142–159; Robert J. STERNBERG et al., *Practical Intelligence in Everyday Life* (Cambridge: Cambridge University Press, 2000). A good part of STERNBERG's assumptions on practical intelligence are taken from his research on successful intelligence where he distinguishes between academic and practical intelligence. It is triarchic theory of successful intelligence. Success depends on a balance of analytical, creative, and practical abilities to adapt, shape, and select environments. It is important to note from a Thomistic perspective of the practical intellect and particular reason that there is no real discussion of emotional mastery (irascible passions), except for few pages on an EQ inventory. But most critical is that there is no treatment of the relationship between practical everyday intelligence and decision making. Also, the greater part of this work is more of a study of the nature of "tacit knowledge."

intelligence from wisdom by defining practical intelligence as the ability to solve practical problems in which one's own interests and seek the common good. Sternberg and his colleagues portrayed practical intelligence as a kind of cleverness, shrewdness, or effectiveness as a kind of cleverness in problem solving that is quite detached from the moral dimension of life. Practical intelligence is about problem solving, not about pursuing worthwhile aims, or expressing good character.

Interestingly, Sternberg saw wisdom as a special case of practical intelligence, which inverts the classical view that cleverness is subordinate to wisdom. In a classical vision, wisdom is the superior attainment, and the practical intelligence he described is a deficient form of practical reasoning, one that neglects questions of character and the centrality of what is good. Practical intelligence may be very useful, but it can serve any end, egocentric or cooperative, beneficial, or destructive.[554]

A practical, realistic, and effective organizational psychology of leadership is most oriented to a behavioral psychology. Primarily, organizational executives and various levels of leadership find it most effective to think in terms of action, activities, processes, and behaviors. It is a wise executive leader who has a policy of recruiting and hiring good people, but this executive must have some sense of rational, moral, and technical goodness. It is the prudent exemplar leader who has the necessary developed habit of *synderesis*. As we see from FOWERS analysis of an instrumental psychology of practical intelligence, an executive decision maker is required to have an innate rational sense of moral principles and relate these principles to concrete, everyday decision making and the selection of potential organizational leaders.

As BOURKE points out, the habit of *synderesis* and practical syllogistic superior reasoning is a necessary qualification for executive and all levels of organizational leadership. For example:[555]

---

[554] FOWERS, *Virtue and Psychology*, 113.

[555] BOURKE, *Ethics*, 224–229.

Major: It is wrong for salespeople to lie to customers (judgment of *synderesis*)

Minor: This delivery date we promised the customer is not possible (judgment of superior reason)

Conclusion: It is a lie; I cannot tell this to the customer (judgment of conscience)

One of the major responsibilities of any practical and prudent exemplar executive is the recruitment of employees who have the capability of becoming leaders and living by an exemplar virtuous behavior. As we will explain shortly in more depth a truly visionary organization requires leaders from the executive to the supervisory who set the example of authentic coherent rational moral overt behavior. This authentic coherent behavior is the result of the diffusion of virtuous organizational behavior.

We return to psychologist FOWER'S explanation of the promise of virtue and the integrated life:

> Virtue begins with a focus on what is good for human beings as the particular creatures that we are. Thus, virtuous life is a life lived well as a whole, with coherent, integrated set of aims, strength of characters necessary to pursue those ends, and the social bonds that give place and purpose to our activities. It is integrative in taking the agent's entire life as the domain of interest, not just some particular incidents or experiences. The concept of virtue encompasses essential features of individuals' psychological lives-dispositions, cognitions, affect, motivation, goals, behavior, relationships communities—and show how these elements of life can be brought into an integrated whole.[556]

When executives and leaders are recruited for the emerging visionary organizations of the so-called disruptive economy, it is necessary to recruit the virtuous visionary who is interviewed about their life and what brings such a person to this organization. SHAW finds that visionary successful companies are

---

[556] FOWERS, *Virtue and Psychology*, 5.

most careful about selection of new employees based on their interests, aims, what is their cultural and team fit, career motivation and an integrated lifestyle of purpose.[557]

Next to continuously being a prudent decision-maker, the second most important responsibility of executive leadership is the recruitment and development of exemplar (virtuous habits) leaders. The task is to use the knowledge of an Aristotelian-Thomistic behavioral psychology of good character in the art and practice of selecting candidates with the character suitable for leadership. In this process of searching for the right person with the disposition to become a virtuous leader, it is best to follow the Aristotelian-Thomistic description on four kinds of character: virtuous, continent, incontinent and vicious, as FOWERS explains.[558]

As an act of will, the *continent character* behaves morally because, even though he/she is somewhat reluctant to choose what is the better or best in a given situation, he/she understands what the better or best choice is to make. He or she exercises self-control and resists temptation to do evil.

The *incontinent character* knows what they should do but cannot bring themselves to do it. They are less praiseworthy than the continent because they do not decide to act well even though they understand how to act properly, but desire (sense appetite) wins out over moral responsibility. This type of person is not suited for leadership positions.

The *vicious character* is improperly focused and a disordered will pleasure seeker. The pleasures loved by vicious persons are: 1) acquired through habitual use of corrupt habits; 2) result from the habitual exercise of imprudent choice, 3) are not healthy by natural inclination. ARISTOTLE claims the vicious person pursues unnatural pleasures that are the behavioral signs of an unhealthy estimative sense, unhealthy passions, and a bad will.

FOWERS describes the vicious character in contemporary usage:

> Vicious often refers to malicious or mean behavior, but in virtue parlance, the vicious are greedy, deceitful, exploitive, or self-indulgent in a

---

[557] SHAW, *Extreme Teams*, Chapter 7.

[558] FOWERS, *Virtue and Psychology*, 71-73

characteristic way. Individuals with vicious characters seek external goods such as power, social status, pleasure, and wealth exclusively. Moreover, they pursue their goals with every available means, with success as their primary criterion for choosing means.[559]

It is with the vicious character that executive recruitment and selection for leadership and upward movement in an organization must exercise much caution. As we presented in chapter two, it is the vicious character that is capable of appearing as the hard driving industrious, intelligent, shrewd, and crafty organizational leader. He/she is seen as the "can do" profile of leading a competitive, winning, focused and efficient organization. Yet it is his vicious character "dark soul" that leads to organizational pathological behavior.

The *virtuous character.* Throughout this dissertation we have basically argued the executive function of an organization is to serve as an active, existential exemplar of leadership. Quite simply, we arrive at a description of an organizational exemplar in the Aristotelian-Thomistic concept of the virtuous as opposed to the vicious character. REDPATH explains an exemplar virtuous leader as the opposite of a vicious leader pursues thanks to the possession of particular reason and intellectual reason, by nature, to some extent (unlike brute animals), all human beings have the ability to distinguish between real and apparent goods and greater and lesser goods. Even in wicked man some desire for really good might still be probable because even in them some natural inclination to the real good still remains by nature to be desired as a real human good. As REDPATH explains:

> Thanks to the possession of particular reason and intellectual reason, by nature, to some extent (unlike brute animals), all human beings have the ability to distinguish between real and apparent goods and greater and lesser goods. Even in wicked man some desire for real good might still be probable because even in them some natural inclination to real good still remains by nature to be desired as a real human good.
>
> Just as virtue improves, strengthens, and perfects, more intensely unifies, and harmonizes, natural composite whole (a real nature), moral

---

[559] Ibid., 72-73

virtue improves, strengthens, and more intensely unifies a human composite with a qualitatively greater, more intense, and unbreakable strength of organizational unity and action.

Moreover, vice, on the contrary, is a corruption, fragmentation, pluralization, and imperfecting of a natural, concrete, composite wholeness, unity/harmony (integrity), and organizational strength and action. *Qua* vicious, evil men become fragmented, divided, from each other as organizational natures, parts, and civic beings—doers of good deeds. Vice, *not pleasure,* divides. By nature, pleasure inclines to unite, not pleasure properly understood and considered as such, fragments evil men and causes them to lose touch with reality.[560]

Contemporary psychology has given much attention to the issue of emotional intelligence and the impact on leadership. However, a premodern virtue psychology thinks in terms of the habits of the virtuous person and emotional concordance. FOWERS points out from a classical virtue, perspective self-constraint is not a virtue at all, because it requires the individual to overcome contrary desires to act well. Virtue, after all, is supposed to be the capacity to have the right emotions from the start. If you have emotions that need to be controlled, you are already in trouble. FOWERS makes some crucial observations about the importance of emotional concordance that readily applies to executive leadership and organizational exemplar models of overt behavior:[561]

1) One of the chief signs of excellence in character, then, is for one's emotions to be in harmony with the actions that are most fitting in the circumstances.

2) Virtue ethics focuses on one's attraction to what is good as the source of motivation for acting well rather than the notion that morality is a life harassed and persecuted everywhere by 'imperatives' and disagreeable duties, and that without these you do not have morality.

---

[560] REDPATH, *The Moral Psychology of St. Thomas,* 474.
[561] FOWERS, *Virtue and Psychology,* 73–75.

3) Experimental evidence suggests that intrinsically motivated individuals have greater interest, excitement, confidence, vitality, self-esteem, and general wellbeing.

4) When the situation facing the individual is one that has grave import or requires significant deliberation to arrive at a clear sense of what is best under confusing or difficult circumstances, the attendant emotion will not likely be spontaneous joy in the action. Yet once an individual with good character decides on the best course of action, he or she pursues it freely, ungrudgingly, and resolutely, and this whole heartedness is a key to virtue. It is this ability to firmly and willingly take a stand that grows out of the clarity of purpose derived from pursuing an important good.

6.2.4 Thomistic Organizational Molar Behavior and the Structure and Diffusion of Virtuous Habits of Leadership

We have presented the argument in these last two chapters that traditional Thomistic rational psychology is in many ways compatible with certain schools of non-radical Skinnerian and materialistic behaviorism. Furthermore, we have established in developing a Thomistic faculty-behavioral-psychology that it is best to enter into a "trading zone of behavioral principles" with behaviorist rather than introspective-brain, neuro, psychoanalytical and cognitive psychology. Thomistic faculty psychology of the soul holds that we know cognitive and sense powers. Yet, we turn to neo behaviorist like RACHLIN (teleological behaviorism), HOLT (purposive behaviorism) and BAUM (molar behaviorism) because these schools of behaviorism are most compatible with a Thomistic faculty behavioral psychology. Thomistic faculty-behavioral-psychology holds, as Richard Thomas LAMBERT states:

In Aquinas' view, the essential definition of the soul in psychological science would prove to be a clarification of self-perception. Secondly, the science of the soul has a peculiar brand of certainty, grounded in the infallibility of the knowledge that we are alive (In IDe An., Lect.1, n.6) since this latter knowledge belongs to singular perception of the soul, that experience does form some kind of basis for psychology. Thirdly, experience of one's soul (normally, if not always) make probable an impact of the former upon the latter, or at least means that the self-experience was available for use in the scientific attempts to understand the soul. Unless. we had experienced the fact of soul; we would probably have no guidelines to discover what the soul was. If self-perception did not provide us with the appearance of the concrete thing to which we point if we wish to identify what we mean by "soul," we would probably have a very difficult time identifying the subject matter of psychology. Self-perception assures us of the reality of the subject under discussion and gives us a set of concrete experiences to which we may constantly refer as exemplifications of the soul and as helps in our procedure in psychology.[562]

We have so far given attention to RACHLIN's Aristotelian teleological behaviorist method of final causation and meta discriminative stimulus and suggested a trading zone exchange that allows for the construction of a type of Thomistic method. We will now continue in this line of development by turning

---

[562] Richard Thomas LAMBERT, *Self-Knowledge in Thomas Aquinas: The Angelic Doctor on the Soul's Knowledge of Itself* (Bloomington: Author House, 2007), 224–225. In chapter 9 Understanding the Soul's Nature, Part 2, Methodological Consideration, LAMBERT touches upon Aquinas a credible justification for a Thomistic faculty-behavioral psychology, as he refers to: "Mark Jordan has discounted the place of introspection in Aquinas' methodology. Jordan claims that the only method that Thomas uses, and could have used for psychology was that of external observation and third person account; introspection can at most be a negative check against philosophical absurdities (e.g., the denial that thinking occurs), and cannot provide any evidence upon which positive theory can be constructed. Jordan's claim is, in a very general way, correct concerning the way in which Aquinas' typical presentations in psychology are phrased. Unlike Franciscan 'interiorists' like Duns Scotus and Peter Olivi, Thomas almost never uses his own experience of himself as a datum for a claim about human knowledge or affection (or for any other type of claim, for that matter). Aquinas does occasionally cite human experience as proof, or at least as conformation, of some psychological claim; and sometimes these appeals mention what people will presumably discover if they look 'inside' themselves."

our "trading zone" efforts to the William BAUM behavioral school of "Molar Behavior Analysis."

6.2.5 Organizational Behavioral Psychology and Everyday Organizational Molar Behavior

Thomas FLEMING writes, "In that land of once upon a time, the duties of ordinary people were restricted to the tiny sphere of everyday life."[563] He maintains that no one better than the amateur philosopher PLUTARCH does a better job summing up common wisdom.

> What is good and what is base, what is just and what unjust, what generally is chosen and what avoided; how one ought to deal with the gods, with his parent, with his elders, with the laws, with strangers, with ruler, with friends, with women, with children, with servants; that one must revere the gods, honor one's parents, respect one's elders, obey the laws, give way to rulers, love one's friends, exercise restraint toward women, be affectionate with children, and not mistreat slaves.[564]

FLEMING adds that "Plutarch's attitudes appealed to common sense of the ancient worlds, but his biographies and essays were widely read even in frontier America. The emphasis on particular responsibilities—as opposed to 'duty' is not exclusive to Plutarch. It is as commonplace as proverbs and Mother Goose rhymes."[565] As NOVAK pointed out, successful executive leaders consider themselves to be practical, realistic. Along with this identity of being a practical realist, the typical organizational executive is cautious what he/she would perceive as an esoteric organizational psychology. Despite this carefulness about esoteric knowledge, organizations readily accept many of the principles and methods of academic business ethics and various testing methods derived from introspective,

---

[563] Thomas FLEMING, *The Morality of Everyday: Rediscovering an Ancient Alternative to the Liberal Tradition* (Columbia and London: University of Missouri Press, 2004), 21

[564] Ibid. FLEMING Reference Plut. Moralia 7 d-e, 22.

[565] Ibid., 21–22.

neuro and cognitive psychology. DEMING, who was one of the founders of the quality movement, when asked to define quality would respond, "I don't know what quality is until I see it."

It is the same with esoteric knowledge we know it when we hear it. We sense it is accessible to a select few. On the other hand, we know everyday knowledge when we hear it. This is the everyday we hear in the above quote from PLUTARCH. Therefore, the challenge of a dissertation on presenting a premodern Aristotelian-Thomistic organizational psychology is to avoid the esoteric and present clearly the everyday organizational and moral psychology of the premodern Aristotelian-Thomistic age, as we find it presented in the NE. It is for this reason, like AQUINAS, we prefer to give attention to the everyday organizational expressions of virtuous and non-virtuous behavioral habits. We propose to achieve this "everyday behavior" by the methodology of 1) from the work of BAUM's description of the nature of molar behavior, and 2) his description of the diffusion of exemplar behavior in terms overt molar habits of virtuous and non-virtuous behavior.

6.2.6 Molar Behavioral Analytics

In his formative paper in behavioral psychology in 2002, "From Molecular to Molar: A Paradigm Shift in Behaviorism Analysis," William M. BAUM describes a change in basic assumptions that has developed in neo behavioral analysis over the past 30 years. He calls it "molar view because molar carries the connotation of aggregation or extendedness, and the molar view is based on the concept of aggregated and extended patterns of behavior."[566] Summarizing this work, we highlight the following pertinent points:

1) Molecular Behavioral View: The molecular view of behavior originates from 19th century psychology with the focus on the association of ideas, sensations, and movements as a sound scientific basis of psychology in the effort to measure consciousness. The chief principle is the law of contiguity

---

[566] William M. BAUM, "Form Molecular to Molar: A Paradigm Shift in Behavior Analysis," *Journal of Experimental Analysis of Behavior*, 2002, 78, 95-116, November 1 (July), 95.

that two events that occurred close together in time (i.e., in temporal contiguity) would tend to recur together. The association of ideas became less popular in the 20th century, the original atomism continued to use the concepts of stimulus (discrete event) in the environment and a response (a discrete response in behavior). In a classic paper, "The Generic Nature of the Concepts of Stimulus and Response," SKINNER (1935/1961) attempted to create definitions of stimulus and response that would serve as the basis for a science of behavior. SKINNER's stimulus and response, however, were classes of discrete events, the same sort of events as the previous century's ideas, situated at moments in time and explained by contiguity between events in time. A reflex for SKINNER was a correlation between two classes, meaning that when a member of the stimulus (as class) occurred, it would be followed by a member of the response (as class). Conditioned reflexes were created by the repeated contiguity of members of two classes.[567]

2) The Molar Behavioral View: Whereas the central ontological claim of the molecular view is that behavior consists of discrete responses, the central ontological claim of the molar view is that behavior consists of temporally extended patterns of action; BAUM calls these activities. Besides the concept of an activity, the molar view is based on the concept of nesting, the idea that every activity (e.g. playing baseball) is composed of parts (batting) that are themselves activities. The notion of activity takes for granted the possibility of quantification, extending it beyond discrete responses and contiguity. The key difference lies in the recognition that activities take up time. In such a case reinforcement it produces, e.g. the baseball team wins the game or the players' sense of joy from winning.[568]

3) Observed Behavior and the Time Issue: Like instantaneous velocity in physics, instantaneous behavior cannot be measured at the moment it is supposed to have occurred but must be inferred from a more extended pattern. That is why it might fairly be called an abstraction. That is why

---

[567] Ibid., 96.
[568] Ibid., 97.

one may argue that it is impossible to reinforce a momentary response; one can only reinforce some activity with some duration.[569]

4) Behavioral Activity as a Whole and Parts: Because every activity is composed of other activities-that is, because every activity is a whole constituted of parts-every activity itself contains an allocation of behavior. In the molar view, the appearance that behavior might be composed of discrete units arises because activities often occur in episodes or bouts. Task completion provides many examples: completion of a fixed ratio run, of a house, of writing a paper, of reading a book. In the molar view, an activity like building a house entails a pattern of activities such as pouring the foundation, framing the structure, insulating, putting in windows and doors, and finishing the interior. House construction seems like a unit only because it is labeled as such, as on my call an episode of napping a nap or a bout of walking a walk.[570]

5) Molar Behavior Reinforcement: In the molar view, reinforcement is like starting and stoking a fire. Special materials and care get the fire going and throwing on fuel every now and then keeps the fire going. In the molar view, a discriminative stimulus signals more frequent reinforcement of one activity or allocation than another, and its presence increases the time spent in that activity.[571]

6) Behavioral Nesting Activities: activities like species are parts of more extended activities. Getting to work each day may be part of working each day. Working each day may be part of holding a job. Holding a job may be part of making a living. Making a living may be part of gaining resources. Gaining resources may end with retirement, and all such parts make up a whole, e.g., dividing life activities personal satisfaction (health, maintenance), job (gaining resources) and family (resources, reproduction, and child rearing).[572]

---

[569] Ibid., 98.

[570] Ibid., 99–100.

[571] Ibid., 104.

[572] Ibid., 110.

We see that molar behavior is about activities that are extended in time and receive some form of pleasurable reinforcement, as BAUM states, one may question whether the notions of intermittent and continuous reinforcement have any meaning in relation to extended activities. In the molar view, reinforcers coincide with various parts of the activity in various forms. We are not suggesting that AQUINAS is a molar behaviorist, but we do see grounds for a trading zone with the molar view of behavior and a Thomistic faculty-behavioral-psychology. It is interesting that when AQUINAS gives attention to the nature of happiness and pleasure, he also gives attention to molar activity. He explains activities of mind or intellect differ from activities of the senses from one another because they are differentiating according to the faculties which are principles of activities. Consequently, pleasures that perfect activities differ specifically.[573] The pleasure that perfects activities the molar behaviorist would see as the pleasurable reinforcement. Aquinas continues, "He [Aristotle] observes first that this difference among pleasures corresponding to activities is evident from the fact each pleasure is ascribed by a kind of affinity to the activity it perfects, because each activity is intensified by its own pleasure."[574] Then, we see BAUM's molar behavioral principle of intermittent and continuous reinforcement. This issue of molar behavior reinforcement is so important that we quote the complete passage.

We notice that people who do any intellectual work with pleasure can judge each point better and investigate accurately the questions which pleasantly engage their attention. For example, a geometrician who takes pleasure in the study of geometry can grasp more clearly each problem of his science because his mind is detained longer by that which is pleasant. And the same reason holds for all others (similarly occupied), for instance, those who love music and delight in it, those who love architecture, and so on—because they find pleasure in such work, they make great progress in their art. Evidently then, pleasures intensify activities. But it is clear that what intensifies an action is proper to it. Consequently, things that are different are intensified by different things. Therefore, if activities, which are intensified by pleasure,

---

[573] AQUINAS, *Commentary on Aristotle's Nicomachean Ethics*, Book 10, Lecture 7.
[574] Ibid.

differ in kind—as we have shown—the intensifying pleasures themselves should be specifically different.[575]

6.3 Thomistic Faculty- Behavioral Psychology, the Executive Diffusion of Virtuous Habits and HEFT

It is pointed out that we are not discussing the nature of an organizational virtue psychology or a virtue ethics, as important as these disciplines to organizational excellence might promise. With a faculty-behavioral-psychology and the treatment of virtue, we take a drastically different approach to virtue ethics and/or a virtue psychology than modern positive psychology of virtue and character. An excellent treatment of positive psychology on character strengths and virtues is in the article "Positive psychology on character strengths and virtues: A disquieting suggestion," by Konrad BANICKI.[576] We will only give attention to the salient issues of his critique of positive psychology on virtue and character. As BANICKI argues, SELIGMAN called for a resurrection of character as the central concept to the scientific study of human behavior. This resulted in the development of the Values in Action (VIA) classification of character. BANICKI main criticism, with which we wholeheartedly agree, is the following:

> The thesis of the unity of virtue, importantly, is not only absent from the VIA classification but effectively contradicted by it. It is explicitly stated that some individuals may be creative and authentic but are neither brave nor kind. [...] In fact, it does not seem to be an accident that the VIA conceptual scheme involves virtues and character strengths but does not explicitly identify any unified virtuous character. The only weak trace of the unity of virtue thesis seems to be the author's speculation that all the core virtues must be present at above-threshold values for an individual to be deemed of good character.[577]

---

[575] Ibid.

[576] Konrad BANICKI, "Positive psychology on character strengths and virtues: A disquieting suggestion," *New Ideas in Psychology* 33 (April 2014), 21–34.

[577] Ibid., 26.

A faculty-behavioral-psychology of the executive function of leadership is concerned about the character and strengths of leadership, but rather than examining individual character traits we look upon executive leadership as a unity of intellectual and moral virtues. We have defined the function of an executive leader which includes in the organizational level of authority the Chief Executive Officer, various senior vice presidents and often key members of the executive staff as exemplar of virtuous habits. Being an exemplar of virtuous habits means, AQUINAS would suggest, being known for praiseworthy habits called virtues. An exemplar is not praised for good morals alone but for the habit of wisdom. He/she is praised for the moral virtues (habits), but also "intellectual virtues like wisdom, understanding and some others of this kind."[578]

The virtuous person passes judgment on things that pertain to human activity as good and pleasurable. AQUINAS says that "Those things are agreeable to the habit of virtue that are in fact good because the habit of moral virtue is defined by what is good with right reason."[579] From the perspective of behavioral activity we would say the activities nested in the habit of a virtue are pleasurable because the best activities and the end are in accord with right reason.[580] In other words, the moral end and the activities are in harmony with the soul.

We have put forth that an executive exemplar must be known by a unity of virtuous habits, but especially by the habit of prudent decision making and strategy making. If, as we have insisted, exemplar virtuous habits of leadership are spread by diffusion from top to senior and middle levels of leadership, it will be by means of formal learning and informal overt behavioral activities. In an environment where organizations from profit to nonprofit must develop an entrepreneurial, meaningful, competitive rational and moral vison, the executive function is to develop the unifying strategy of what needs to be decided, done, and become everyday activities. The exemplar, consequently, is known for his/her decisions making and strategy making knowledge. We call this ability of an exemplar HEFT. We use the acronym HEFT because it has a sense of the virtual quantity of an organization. It suggests that the executive exemplar must know and sense the

---

[578] AQUINAS, *Commentary on Aristotle's Nicomachean Ethics*, Book 1, Lecture 20.

[579] Ibid. Book 3, Lecture 10.

[580] Ibid. Book 6, Lecture 2.

perfection of the organization and at the same time carry the responsibility of this weight.

The acronym HEFT stands for the virtuous habits and spiritual power of the executive soul, and "a habit is a disposition determining a power in reference to something. When the determination is made conformable to the nature of the things, there will be a good habit which disposes a thing be done well."[581]

We have previously in terms of behavioral psychology said that behavioral habits seek to focus, measure, and target the passions and powers of the soul on union with a formal object. HEFT stands for the moral virtues (habits) that focus on the passions and powers of the soul, namely four operative powers (potencies) in a person which are habit forming the possible intellect, the will, the concupiscible (propelling) and the irascible (contending) appetite. There are four principal virtues: prudence, temperance, fortitude, and justice. We will use a metaphor to explain the importance of these four virtues known in Thomistic terminology as the cardinal virtues. Cardinal means a person's moral life depends on these virtues, as a door hangs on it hinges. We use another metaphor to get a sense of importance of heft; we will use the metaphor of the core muscles of the body and the importance of a robust physiological structure. If we go to a physical trainer, we are told that we must begin by exercising our core muscles of abdominal area (mid-section, back and sides, traverse abdominis, erector spine, obliques, and lower back); it will give our body more heft. If we want to develop the faculties required for executive exemplar leadership, then we must exercise the moral virtues. We must remember that the Latin word *virtus* (virtue) means potency, which is perfected, that it is in a condition of peak capacity. Heft means: H stands for habits of justice; E stands for estimative intelligence, i.e., prudence and particular reason; F stands for fortitude (courage, confidence); and T stands for temperance (self-mastery, mastery of the passions).

As BOURKE Points out, there is a fourfold division of moral virtues because every virtue must be the source of a human act which is done with right knowledge (the work of prudence); properly ordered in regard to external things to the moral agent (the work of justice); well measured in regard to the sensible goods (the work of temperance); and done with firmness and strength in the face of sensible evils

---

[581] Ibid. Book 2, Lecture 5.

(the work of fortitude). Each of the moral virtues is specific to the perfection of moral potency (power). Prudence, right practical reasoning, estimative intelligence, belongs especially to the practical intellect. Justice pertains to the will. Temperance (reasonable moderation) pertains to the concupiscible (propelling) passion resides in the concupiscible appetite. Fortitude, or reasonable firmness in one's irascible (contending) passions, perfects the irascible appetite.[582]

6.4. The Unity of Virtue and Prudence and Decision Making: The "E" Habit

"One must be able to 'nip things in the bud' before they grow and turn into invaluable and possibly destructive forces within the workplace. All these components make up decisive behavior techniques and flow out forces with the workplace."[583] BARNARD claimed, "A broad purpose and a broad decision require fragmentation of purpose into detailed purposes and of principal general decisions into detailed decisions."[584] Both MASON and BARNARD realize that the outstanding characteristic of the exemplar executive must be the power of his decision and strategy making ability and his ability to reproduce decision making acumen at all levels of leadership. It is important in organizational leadership to put organizational decision making and strategic making together. Organizational leadership is a matter of facing a contingent reality; we have explained previously that the order of an organization is always one of the desired order and the emergent order. The executive command and control of this uncertain order (variation) requires everyday tactical decision making and higher level organizational visionary strategic decision making. It is here that we start with the most important HEFT habit E, which ARISTOTLE calls estimative. As REDPATH explains,

---

[582] BOURKE, *ETHICS,* 264

[583] Moya K. MASON, "Thoughts on Leadership: How Important is Decision Making?", http://www.moyak.com /papers/leadership-qualities.html

[584] BARNARD, *The Functions of the Executive,* 206.

He calls "estimative" that part of the rational soul whose formal object is contingent beings. He maintains that estimating, deliberating, refer to the same formal object, which is changeable, contingent beings. He maintains that estimating, deliberating, refer to the same formal object, what is changeable, contingent. Because no one deliberates about what acts, exists, in only one way, he says that deliberation is an inquiry not yet concluded, like argumentation.[585]

REDPATH gives the reason for defining the confluence of particular reason and the habit of prudence as an "estimative intelligence" applicable to organizational decision making and the implementation of abstract strategy into everyday leadership of contingent and tactical decision making. He explains contingent organizational strategy and tactical decision making in two ways:

Abstractly, we understand contingent natures according to fixed part/whole relations in terms of their organizational parts being capable of generating their generic acts. Concretely considered, we understand contingent natures according to the way they operate, exist, in the contingent situation.

Abstractly considered is the way speculative sciences like physics and the division of physics like astronomy study necessary and contingent beings: as abstractly considered movers/agents.

Concretely considered is the way practical sciences like prudence and art proceed. Prudence and art consider things as they concretely exist, composite wholes as generating, causing, specific acts in individual circumstances. They do this through use of particular reason, the estimative sense, which, initially, individually collates, mnemonically *specifies* into a quasi-nominalistic sensory, experiential universal, some multitude into a temporal, generic relation [...]. Thus understood, contingent beings and operational universals can be formal objects of speculative intellect.[586]

---

[585] REDPATH, *The Moral Psychology of St. Thomas*, 342.
[586] Ibid., 342–343.

Prudence is an intellectual virtue (insofar as it perfects the practical intellect) and it is a moral virtue because it is necessary to the good life and in regard executive strategy and leadership decision making. It is necessary for the common good and rational moral perfection of the organization (virtual quantity). Therefore, prudence is one of the moral virtues. Throughout this dissertation we use the terminology of a Thomistic rational moral organizational psychology because we hold that there is always in leadership strategic and operational decision making a confluence of strategy, rationality, and ethics. It seems that organizational makers make implicit choices between rational and moral principles while using particular concepts in their strategic thinking.[587] Richard T. DeGeorge goes so far to affirm being moral is the same as being rational and we would add when it relates to organizational decision making.[588] Therefore, prudence in its essence is an intellectual virtue (again, insofar as its subject is the practical intellect), but in the object to which it applies, it is a moral virtue. If we want to get directly to the primary function of the executive leader, then we get to it directly when we look at the definition of the "prudent man," who is the exemplar executive. Applying AQUINAS:[589]

1) He/she by the power of habit can give good and useful advice about particular matters, but for the benefit of the total life; or we could say, as an executive leader gives advice for the common good of the organizational whole.

2) Therefore, it follows that an exemplar will be absolutely prudent who gives good advice about things touching the whole of life. Thus, we learn that for an executive leader there are two domains of organizational action and knowledge that he/she must possess, as per the next point.

3) In Aristotelian terminology, the practical intellect of the executive must prescribe right reason for art (about making) and prudence (about doing).

---

[587] A. SINGER, "Strategy as Moral Philosophy," *Strategic Management Journal,* 1994, 15, 191–213.

[588] Richard T. DeGeorge, *Business Ethics,* 3rd ed. (New York: MacMillan, 1990).

[589] AQUINAS, *Commentary on Aristotle's Nicomachean Ethics,* Book 6, Lecture 4; Lecture 6.

Thus, in an organization, we would say the executive must prescribe right reason for operations and product development and prudence for strategic planning and successful execution.

4) Prudence is concerned with things worthy of deliberation as a person who gives good counsel.

5) Prudence is concerned about things good and bad for man himself.

6) The principles of prudence are ends in regard to which rectitude of judgment is preserved by moral virtues. Hence prudence, which is concerned with things good for man, necessarily has joined with it the moral virtues preserving its principle. This is a point that really explains the meaning of the unity of the intellectual and moral virtues, as they are presented in the expression HEFT. We could say that when an exemplar executive has the quality of HEFT, he/she is a person in the Aristotelian-Thomistic concept of character of the virtuous person who possesses the desire to live by wisdom and be good.

The virtuous man especially wishes himself life and conservation in being chiefly for the part of the soul where wisdom resides.[590] If a man is virtuous, he must want what is good for himself because everyone desires good things for himself. But the good of a virtuous man is that he be virtuous.

We might say that an executive exemplar having found the wisdom of the soul as a leader has executive HEFT (Big Soul). It is expressed in his/her behavioral activities as a leader that he/she deliberates well about rational-moral decisions and strategy. They give good executive counsel and deal with the various means to a given end and are emulated for their discursive reasoning. Most important, they are known as leaders of successful activities that order the action to be done (or omitted) and are executed in a reasonable way.

---

[590] Ibid, Book 9, Lecture 6.

6.4.1 The Executive Exemplar Heft, Decision Making, the Unity of Virtue and of Dysfunctional Organization Leadership Habits (Vices) and Activities

As a behavioral faculty psychology study, we must give some attention to patterns of molar overt behavior over time. As the activities of the moral virtues are examined, it is unfortunately usually to describe dysfunctional behavioral activities and the lack of prudence, justice, temperance, and fortitude. AQUINAS would remind a virtuous exemplar leader that one of the everyday functions of leadership is to guard against the vices opposed to virtue.

> Since virtue ought to restrain vices, the aim of virtue is to curb more effectively those vices to which we have a stronger inclination. For this reason, those vices, which are in any way somewhat innate in us are more opposed to virtue. As from birth we more readily follow pleasures than flee from them, we are very moved to self-indulgence.[591]

What ARISTOTLE and AQUINAS call vice, we will refer to as dysfunctional leadership behavioral habit at any level of decision making, strategic planning, operational sense-making and interpersonal relationships expressed in overt behavioral activities. We are using in the outline Thomas AQUINAS's definition of vices, as they relate to the moral virtues discussed by BOURKE.[592]

6.4.2 E: (HEFT): Estimative Intelligence: Prudence, Practical Reason and Executive Decision-Making Activities

As we understand and apply BOURKE,[593]

1) In good rational moral reasoning or counselling, one must remember past experience, understand the present situation, and make an estimate of

---

[591] AQUINAS, *Commentary on Aristotle's Nicomachean Ethics*, Book 2, Lecture 10.

[592] BOURKE, *Ethics*, Chapter Nine, *Problems within the Moral Agent.*

[593] Ibid., 301–303.

future consequences, all are brought together into an orderly sequence of inference (estimative intelligence). Omitting essential steps is to be an imprudent decision maker by way of precipitation (haste, rush). For example, we mentioned in the study *Refining Leadership for a Digital Age* that organizations want agile leaders who are not afraid to commit to a new course of action when the situation warrants. In a disruptive, competitive, and digital culture, prudent decision-making becomes critical. For example, decision-making behaviors of the agile leader necessary in the digital age are 1) hyperawareness (constant scanning of the internal and external environment for opportunities and threats), 2) Moving quickly yet prudently and to the confident execution of doable deeds, 3) prudent and temperate use of qualitative and quantitative data and information to make evidence-based decisions, and 4) if required prudently moving quickly away from the doable deed or waiting for better circumstances.

2) There is the dysfunctional habitual failure of inconsideration, i.e., to make good judgments. Often, workers complain about leaders who continuously go to decision meetings and hear the issues but fail to make any judgment leading to action. Usually, in an organization such a leader may engage in such behavior because of political reasons or out of fear to take a risk.

3) There is the dysfunctional habit of inconstancy which is the failure to carry though a rational moral decision to its proper conclusion. Again, this dysfunctional behavior is usually affected by a lack of mastery of the irascible passions (contending emotions).

4) There is the dysfunctionality of negligence which is a lack of promptness in directing one's actions which arises from a negative influence of the will. The agent has no real desire to move on the decision. It is the type of thinking that "if I forget about it, then it will go away."

St. Thomas related the above dysfunctional (bad) habits as swayed by the passions, and he pointed out at some length the influence of lust (*luxuria*) that impacts the practical intellect. St. Thomas also gave attention to two expressions of excessive prudence. It is when we give too much attention to matters which are relatively unimportant:

1) There is a dysfunctionality of astuteness it is the habit of planning, to attain some end, whether morally good or bad, by the use of improper means. It is a habit usually found in the shrewd and crafty leaders

2) There is the dysfunctionality of the solicitude for temporal things. It consists in the habit of giving excessive consideration to the finite goods of this world. It is the type of leader who is always concerned about what is in it for me if I make this decision or take this risk. It is the disposition of "what can you do for me!"

Executive leadership must be concerned with more than drawing attention to imprudent dysfunctional behavior, it is the function of executive leadership to remove individuals who do not in their everyday behavior and specifically in decision making activities display heft (moral virtue). However, the executive human resource screening requires a nesting understanding of dysfunctional habits. For example, one of the most noticeable dysfunctional habits in organizations under the pressure of digital age leaders is the need for decisions to be made right now. Decisions makers can easily fall into the habit of precipitation, i.e., hasty and rushed behavioral activities. It is very important for employee reviews and promotion to have clear descriptions of dysfunction hasty and rushed dysfunctional imprudent decision making. Furthermore, a faculty-behavioral-psychology requires for the purpose of heft (moral virtues in action) education, best- and worst-case examples of prudent leadership behavioral activities. For example, in this situation we identify behavioral patterns that of the worst-case activities in a meeting of hasty and rushed activities.

6.4.3 Justice and Unjust (Heft, cardinal moral virtues) and Executive Organizational and Everyday Decision-making Leadership

Using an explanation of justice from BOURKE we define simply justice as a habit of will enabling a person to fulfill moral rights:

If we consider justice in a very general manner, simply as moral righteousness, then justice covers all moral virtues. This is true of all four of the cardinal virtues. Each share in the essential character of the other three. So, it is right and just, in a general way, to be prudent, temperate, and brave. Thus considered, general justice is not a special habit or virtue of the human will but is a broad moral condition of rightness in relation to any species of virtuous action. This general condition of rightness is not the cardinal virtue (for it is not a virtue at all) but approximates to the notion of moral goodness. Since justice, as special virtue, consists in a habitual willing to do what is right in regard to one's neighbors individually or collectively; and to avoid doing anything harmful to one's neighbors, individually or collectively.[594]

We should draw attention to the fact that in the field of empirical organizational psychology over the past approximate 30 years organizational justice has become one of the most popular research domains in organizational behavior. It is most important research because justice perceptions have shown to have effects on people's motivations, wellbeing, performance, attitudes, behaviors, and other relevant organizational outcomes.

Primarily, the organizational behavioral justice research has been focused on the domain of organizational justice. Marion FORTIN describes it as a perception of fairness in decision making contexts and the procedural behavioral activities deployed in the decision perception contexts.[595] He examines the perception of fairness under the categories of: 1) as a matter of distributive fairness of outcome distributions according to norms of allocation, 2) a matter of decision contexts and procedures are perceived as consistent across people over time, 3) interpersonal justice regard the quality of personal treatment, respect and sensitivity during decision making procedures.

From a perspective of Thomistic moral rational moral psychology most of the major concerns in terms of the executive function are referred to as "common legal

---

[594] Ibid., 331.

[595] Marion FORTIN, "Perspectives on Organizational Justice: Concept clarification, social context integration, time and links with morality," *International Journal of Management Reviews* 10(2), 2008, 93–126.

justice." It is the habit of the will whereby an employee is inclined to will and do what is for the common good of others with ordinary interpretation of the moral and legal code of the organization and terms of employment.

Here are examples of types of procedural activity fairness perception questions adapted from those developed by organizational psychologists:[596]

> Procedural Justice: The questions refer to the procedure your supervisor uses to make decisions about pay, rewards, evaluations, promotions, assignments, etc.

> 1) Are you able to express your views during the procedure?
> 2) Can you influence the decisions arrived at by those procedures?

> Distributive Justice: the questions below refer to the outcomes you receive from your supervisor, such as pay rewards, evaluations, promotions, assignments, etc.

> 1) Do those outcomes reflect the effort you have put into your work?
> 2) Are those outcomes justified, given your performance?

> Interpersonal Justice: the questions below refer to the interactions you have with your supervisor as decision making procedures (about pay, rewards, evaluations, promotions, assignment, etc.) are implemented.

> 1) Does he/she treat you with dignity?
> 2) Does he/she refrain from improper remarks or comments?

We can observe from these questions on organizational justice as "fairness perception" in the context of decision-making that they are based on the observation of supervisory behavioral activity. Of course, over time the

---

[596] T. Senthil MURUGAN and N. PANCHANATHAM, "Interpersonal Conflict Management styles on Conflict Sources in Services Settings," *IOSR Journal of Business and Management* 18(9), September 2016, 16–24.

instrumental method of supervisory behavioral activity shows a record of supervisors as being just or unjust in the evaluation process. A faculty-behavioral-psychology concerned with justice as an expression of leadership heft (cardinal moral virtues) is concerned about justice from the perspective of a leader's fairness in judging another. Therefore, judgment means the determination of what is right, and it follows that judgment is an act of reason. Questions of justice need to be decided by a judge who possesses not only the virtue of prudence to make a correct and practical intellectual judgment but also the appetitive, or voluntary, inclination to will what is right. The appetitive inclination is supplied by the virtue of justice. In terms of the importance of justice and the exemplar character, there are five virtues AQUINAS associates with justice. They are important in an organizational context for leaders to be perceived as just; they are the leadership activities of friendliness, veracity, vindication, gratitude, and respect for persons.[597] These virtues, connected to justice, are also overt behavioral activities of leaders that display an exemplar character of justice. We could say the existential activity of leadership heft is amplified, thereby increasing the perfection of the organization (virtual quantity).

Friendliness is the habit to speak and to act in regard to other persons in a fitting way. We are not talking about executive etiquette or superficially good manners. The friendly person observes the mean between fawning adulation and churlishness. Robert SOKOLOWSKI has written a paper on the "Phenomenology of Friendship" that requires a separate study in itself far beyond the scope of this chapter. He writes:

> But there is still another crest to be reached beyond justice in the study of moral virtue. It is reached in books 8 and 9 of the *Nicomachean Ethics*, which discusses friendship. Friendship should not be taken as a mere appendix to ethics; it completes justice and the other moral virtues. [...] Practical reason finds its highest employment, therefore, not in justice but in friendship. Friendship exceeds justice as a human perfection; Aristotle says, "Friendship seems to hold cities together, and lawgivers seem to care for it more than for justice; for concord is like friendship, and this they aim for most of all [...]

---

[597] BOURKE, *Ethics*, 340–343.

and when men are friends, they have no need of justice, while when they are just, they need friendship as well."[598]

GOLEMAN, the founder of emotional intelligence, in his work *Focus: The Hidden Driver of Excellence*, seems to put the ability to have empathy and empathic knowledge of others as the core of exemplar leadership: "empathy let us take people's perspective, comprehend their mental state, and at the same time manage our own emotions while we take stock of theirs."[599] He speaks of what he calls cognitive empathy as the elixir of organizational psychology. If we read carefully into the ingredient of the empathy elixir, as Thomists we once again find that it reads like the Rousseauian "Disordered Will."

SOKOLOWSKI in the confluence of friendship and justice finds a reality much more promising for organizational harmony than the elixir of empathy and sentiment. It is the habit and organizational activities of the virtue of justice and friendship. It is the heft of the just and friendly behavior of the executive at all levels of leadership and workers. He writes:

> Since friendship is the highest moral excellence, support even to the individual virtues and justice, this particular categorical form, this form of moral intelligence, is the highest kind of moral thinking. Friendship is not just an impulse or feeling; like justice, it involves calibration, but a different kind. It demands that in the contingencies and vicissitudes of life we possess the insight and the character to achieve truly the good of another. [...] Friendship, therefore, requires an act of intelligence; it has to understand the needs, inclinations, and emotions of the friends so that it can calibrate the equation that is the friendship between them.[600]

---

[598] Robert SOKOLOWSKI, "Phenomenology of Friendship," *The Review of Metaphysics* 55, March 2002, 452–453.

[599] Daniel GOLEMAN, *Focus: The Hidden Driver of Excellence* (New York: Harper, 2013), 98.

[600] SOKOLOWSKI, "Phenomenology of Friendship," 462.

In terms of organization friendship and justice, we can be just and friendly in the administration of corporate codes even when we do not share in the reciprocity and intimacy of close friendship. Organizational friendship is not a best friend and clique system. It is a friendship that is grounded on a common allegiance of mission. It is best expressed as camaraderie of serving a purpose and serving with workers besides, below, and above us and respecting their rights as friends at work.

Fred KOFMAN in *The Meaning Revolution* presents a telling story about the power of executive friendly behavior and the staggering impact on organizational leadership dysfunctionality. It is about Doug Conant who was recruited from Nabisco to become CEO of the old Campbell Soup company. By 2001 the one-time great company was hemorrhaging. It was rated as the poorest performing food company in the world. Gallup in a survey found 62 percent of the company managers were not actively engaged in their jobs, and another 12 percent felt actively disengaged. KOFMAN points out by 2009 the company was in a turnaround condition. Old managers were replaced, half the new leaders were promoted from within and morale had increased tremendously. Earnings climbed as did earnings per shares. Employees and managers became actively engaged with only 3 percent disengaged. Conant's maxim and vision for Campbell Soup was, "To win in the marketplace you must first win in the workplace." Conant made showing that he cared about employees a priority, and KOFMAN describes his personal commitment by his executive every day, friendly activity of a diffusion of leadership character:

> He always inquired after everyone. In the employee cafeteria—where he regularly ate his lunch in order to be with folks—he asked how the cooks were doing, how their kids were. He shook hands. He put an arm around people. The place felt more like a home than a big company—which made a lot of sense, since the brand is closely associated with moms and home. He knew the names of thousands of employees and personally wrote thirty thousand thank-you notes to them. He mentored hundreds of people. He sent roughly twenty thank-you notes a day to staffers on all levels. "And every six weeks," he said, "I had lunch with a group of a dozen or so

employees to get their perspective on the business, to address problems and to get feedback."[601]

This is a powerful little case study on the habit of executive friendship as a behavioral activity that reinforces on a continuous basis to create an atmosphere of sincere friendship with employees. It is because of this friendship that there is a diffusion of a perception of fairness in the company. The attitude is, yes, we trust this CEO as a prudent and fair decision maker because he sincerely respects and listens to us. A leader is not recognized as having a character of heft (habits of moral virtue), unless it is expressed in every day behavioral activities. It is what BAUM calls the molar behavioral principle of starting and stoking by positive reinforcement by means of an exemplar heft behavioral activity.

As organizations move into a structure where executive moral authority becomes more important than formal authority, we are reminded of the prophetic genius BARNARD in the 1930s. It was BARNARD who made the necessary connection between moral rectitude, friendship, and employee loyalty:

> "Loyalty," "solidarity," "esprit de corps," "strength" [it appears Barnard had a sense of virtual quantity] are the chief issue. Although they are indefinite, they relate to intensity of attachment to the "cause," and are commonly understood to refer to something different from effectiveness, ability, or value of personal contributions.[602]

BARNARD on the issue of an organizational philosophy was very much a moral realist. He realized that the basic executive function was the responsibility for an "esprit de corps," but he realized this "loyalty" required the blending of contraries. This contrariety was most apparent in the complexity of various personal, individual moral codes of conduct and work performance. The executive challenge was to align these personal codes with the objective, agreed upon organizational code of conduct. Thus, "the distinguishing mark of the executive responsibility is that it requires not merely conformance to a complex code of morals but also the

---

[601] KOFMAN, *The Meaning Revolution*, Chapter 2, 51.

[602] BARNARD, *The Functions of the Executive*, 84.

creation of moral codes for others. The most generally recognized aspect of this function is called securing, creating, inspiring of 'morale' in an organization."[603] The responsibility of the creative exemplar executive, according to BARNARD, is inculcating points of views, fundamental attitudes and minor dictates of personal codes to an objective organizational code.

BARNARD claims that the creative aspect of executive responsibility is the highest exemplification of responsibility. As an executive decision maker, he finds that the greatest proportion of organizational decisions requiring executive attention, are technical conflicts that also involve a clash of personal moral codes of execution and performance compared to an objective organizational code worthy of attention and respect. It is in these particular decisions of opaque technical moral situations that he sees the need for the executive type creative leader.[604] He makes the case that in conflict decision making situations that there must be attention to the organizational moral code. In other words, in conflict decision making the organizational code is owed the right of a prudent and just respect of objective authority. It demands what BARNARD calls handling exceptional cases of conflict, "the appellate function," "the judicial function." He explains as follows:

> This function is exercised in the cases that seem "right" from one point of view, "wrong" from another. The solution of such cases lies either in substituting a new action which avoids the conflict, or in providing a moral justification for exception or compromise. We are accustomed to call the first solution "executive," the second "judicial". They are both executive functions in the broad sense used in this essay. [...] The judicial process, from the executive point of view, is one of morally justifying a change or redefinition or new particularizing of purpose so that the sense of conformance to moral code is secured. [...] The invention of the constructions and fictions necessary to secure preservation of morale is a severe test of both responsibility and ability, for to be sound they must be "just" on the view of the executive, that is, really consonant with morality of

---

[603] Ibid., 279.
[604] Ibid., 282.

the whole; as well as acceptable, that is, really consonant with the morality of the part, of the individual.[605]

We suggest from the viewpoint of Thomistic heft and organizational conflicting decision-making that BARNARD's creative executive is the exemplar of prudential judgment. In the case of BARNARD's "judicial process" (or we might better call it judicial observable bouts of activity) his creative aspect of judicial decision-making is really about ARISTOTLE's virtues associated with prudence, i.e. *eubulia, eustochia, synesis,* and *gnome.* An *eustochia* decision maker is a person with a vivid imagination, sensitive to external situations, quick, accurate and reads situations well. It is the type of person who makes good on the line everyday decisions, good at sales, customer satisfaction, street police officers etc. Whereas the *eubulia* decision maker is known for excellence in deliberating like a wise attorney or a financial analyst. He/she takes time to develop and analyze. St. Thomas teaches that prudential matters should be quickly executed but deliberated slowly beforehand. For St. Thomas *eubulia* has four properties of rectitude in practical matters: 1) right deliberation, 2) about an absolutely good end, 3) by suitable means and 4) at the right time. ARISTOTLE also distinguished *synesis* from common sense, opinion *gnome* and *eustochia. Synesis* is concerned about practical matter like prudence about which we can doubt and deliberate. *Synesis* judges well about matters already well deliberated and investigated. It judges in an un-prescriptive way whereas prudence is predictive, *synesis* is descriptive, prudence is prescriptive.[606]

Basically, BARNARD's exemplar creative executive is defined in terms of a Thomistic faculty-behavioral-psychology as he/she is known for the exercise of estimative intelligence and decision-making heft, particularly in conflict contexts of fairness. We should note that the activity of executive judicial process of authority also comes under the associated virtue of respect.

There are for AQUINAS, dysfunctional habits (vices) opposed to the habit of friendliness. Adulation is the habit of paying excessive honor of others, most often authority figures, by words or deeds. It is really a political technique of the

---

[605] Ibid., 279–281.

[606] REDPATH, *The Moral Psychology of St. Thomas,* 362.

disingenuous use for organizational promotion. Adulation activities are very overt and visible in organizations and are cause of disharmony and a negative impact on the organizational esprit de corps. Second is quarrelsomeness (*litigium*), it is the habit of making oneself as disagreeable as possible to other people, by contradicting them continually. The fawning practitioner of adulation is too friendly; the quarrelsome person is not friendly enough. Both types of employee are not suited for a supervisory or leadership position, and definitely completely excluded from the executive level.

Veracity is the habit of speaking or acting in accord with the truth. A leader does not have to express all his thoughts or feelings, but when an executive level leader speaks in fairness to employees his thoughts and policy statements should be the truth. It is not possible to trust leaders as fair if they are known constantly by their behavior not to speak truthfully of and to employees. Today, we are learning in organizational behavioral research that there is an issue of informational justice, i.e., workers feel that they are owed truthful organizational information. This is especially true with the truthful disclosure of financial information. It is a major issue of distributive justice. The most blatant failure of distributive financial information justice was the Enron crisis of the 1980s. In organizations, the practice of lying is often associated with political intrigue and the machination for promotion and political purposes. It is usually practiced by the shrewd and crafty leader. There is no organizational activity like corporate political lying that destroys organizational loyalty, trust, and the bond of friendship. It also erodes, when practiced by leaders, an organizational belief in a bond of trust. It leads to what employees refer to as destructive political games.

Vindication is the habit of willing that another person who committed a moral offense be rightly punished for his own sake and the good of the organization. It is for the preservation of the perception and practice of justice for the whole organization. Vindication is an extremely dysfunctional habit (vice) if it is used to punish because of hatred or revenge. For example, I hate an employee because of his/her political views. The basic moral principle is that revenge arises from bad intentions, vindication from good motives. There is nothing that will destroy the perception of organizational fairness more than revengeful acts of behavior.

Gratitude is the habit enabling one to be duly thankful for some benefit received from another person. We have discussed the executive style of Southwest Airlines and the attitude of gratitude to employees. However, it must be a gratitude that is justified; otherwise, it comes across as management etiquette at best. When it is gratitude that is earned and justified, then it is the respect of the benefactor who is aware of the employee's everyday contributions. We stress that gratitude is not just expressed for great deeds.

Respect for persons is the habit of will enabling an exemplar leader to acknowledge with respect individuals worthy of such honor. The executive position is also worthy of respect, but in any organization moving to perfection there are individual and groups who should be given respect for their knowledge, skills, office, rational moral behavior, and loyalty. There is also just respect for those in immediate authority over one. AQUINAS calls it *dulia*, and obedience is a willingness to carry out just commands expected by all members of an organization.

6.4.4 T: Temperance (Exemplar Heft)

PIEPER describes temperance as the habit of selfless preservation.[607] He explains that AQUINAS's first meaning of temperance is much deeper than practicing moderation in eating and drinking. *Temperantia* is one of the unity of the cardinal virtues. AQUINAS explains it thus:

> The matter indeed of every moral virtue is that on which reason imposes a norm. Thus, justice treats dealing with others, fortitude treats of fears and aggressiveness, [...] temperance of certain pleasures. But pleasure is the principal end of all moral virtues.[608]

---

[607] JOSEF PIEPER, *The Four Cardinal Virtues* (Notre Dame, Indiana: University of Notre Dame Press,1966) 148

[608] AQUINAS, *Commentary on Aristotle's Nicomachean Ethics*, Book 2, Lecture 3.

Temperance in the Aristotelian-Thomistic understanding is more than the current concept of moderation which is dangerously close to fear of any exuberance. It is more than curtailment, bridling or repression. The Greek *sophrosyne* and the Latin word *temperantia* embrace the idea of directing reason. Temperance is the good habit of the concupiscible appetite enabling it to be moderated by reason. Moderation or reasonable self-restraint is the essence of temperance.

Previously, we had mentioned FARBER's description of the modern age as the age of the "distorted will." FARBER was suggesting that modern society views will power as a straightforward exercise of self-restraint based on the feeling of need. The problem for FARBER is that he argued that modern psychotherapy and psychiatry had no concept, as Aristotelian-Thomistic psychology holds, that the will is the appetite of the intellect. AQUINAS teaches that movements of sensitive appetite are directed (rebel) against reason because of the lack of moderation. It could be said that temperance is about a rational emotional moderation of the concupiscible (propelling) appetite. It is important to note the virtue of temperance is not an act of disordered will. As AQUINAS states:

> It belongs to moral virtue to moderate those passions which denote a pursuit of the good. [...] when a man flies from sensible and bodily evils, which sometimes accompany the good of reason, the result is that he flies from the good of reason. Hence it belongs to moral virtue to make man flying from evil to remain firm in the good of reason.[609]

It is this flying from evil pleasures and remaining firm in the movement to good reason that according to PIEPER, is the meaning of selfless preservation.

PIEPER points out that for AQUINAS the second meaning of temperance is "serenity of Spirit." AQUINAS in one beautiful and concise line in his teaching on temperance says temperance is concerned with the things that have the most disturbing effect on the soul, and then he states, "Hence tranquility of the soul is ascribed to temperance by way of excellence; although it is a common property of

---

[609] AQUINAS, *Summa theologiae* II-II, q. 4 a. 3.

all virtues."[610] In this one line, AQUINAS describes the purpose of the unity of virtues is to give man a serenity of a soul with faculties directed to a life of virtuous honor and excellence of character. It is for this reason that PIEPER maintains, "The purpose and goal of *temperantia* is man's inner order, from which alone this serenity of spirit can flow forth."[611] The objects of the intellectual appetition (the will) are universal goods or evils. Temperance is concerned about the concupiscible (propelling passions) that stimulated by an object which is simply attractive or repulsive. In themselves the concupiscible passions are morally neutral. They become good or bad by voluntary action and by the addition of suitable or unsuitable circumstances.

BOURKE gives this succinct definition of temperance as the good habit of the concupiscible appetite enabling it to be moderated by reason.[612] Moderation or reasonable self-restraint is the essence of all the natural virtues, and as we argue in this dissertation this habit of moderation and reasonable self-restraint also must be the essence of the organizational "exemplar leader." Furthermore, this disposition to moderation and self-restraint is cultivated by the confluence of habits of the cardinal virtues, i.e., reasonableness (prudence), moderation (from temperance), firmness (from fortitude) and a general rightness in view of the common end (from justice).[613] All four conditions are found in the exercise of any virtue. This is the meaning of the unity of virtue. It means that an executive or indeed any level of exemplar leadership must have a disposition to unity of the cardinal virtues, otherwise they will attempt to decide and do the next right thing by sentiment and a disordered will.

Temperance, as a virtue, must have a definite type of a problem differentiated from the other virtues. In Thomistic moral psychology the greatest problem in the concupiscible (propelling) appetite is the sense of touch.[614] The great moral difficulty is the stimulation by the pleasure of the sense of touch. Therefore, humankind is most vehemently and inordinately attracted by pleasures of

---

[610] AQUINAS, *Summa theologiae* II-II, 23,7.

[611] PIEPER, *The Four Cardinal Virtues*, 147.

[612] BOURKE, *Ethics*, 306.

[613] Ibid.

[614] AQUINAS, *Summa theologiae* II-II, q. 142 a. 4.

reproduction and of taking food and drink, and in a secondary manner other objects of the senses stimulate passions requiring the use of temperance.

Regarding the nature of touch and the impact upon the concupiscible (propelling) appetite we must give some brief attention to the phenomena of touch in the digital age. It is regarding the impact of touch and self-preservation that we must understand the confluence of touch, digital-electronic technology, self-preservation, and identity. It is here that we should give attention to two post-modernists, Marshal McLuhan, and Jean Baudrillard. As with much postmodernism, it is not a philosophy as much as a sociological criticism of the media culture dominated by materialistic consumerism.

McLuhan, especially in his early writings as a devout conservative Roman Catholic, was basically optimistic about the "electronic culture." He wrote mostly about the impact of the electronic culture, primarily the impact of television and the impact on the external senses. He saw the end of the hot message print dominated culture and the beginning of the cool culture. Exploration of this topic would require a separate dissertation in and of itself. He proclaimed that in a cool media culture that "hot linear communication" of a reading culture is replaced by the cool touching and hearing of the electronic age. McLuhan, as a man of the Renaissance, believed that the cool culture would lead to a return to a more traditional mystical premodern culture.

Baudrillard, who had been very influenced by McLuhan, was pessimistic about the implications of media technology and its relationship with a consumer driven culture on humanity. McLuhan maintained that the electronic media massages the senses. Of course, the massage concept immediately becomes a rational moral issue of touch, as it relates to the virtue of temperance and human authentic self-preservation. It was perhaps the more critical Baudrillard who was aware of the existential threat to authentic self-preservation. Baudrillard did not use the concept of massage; rather he created the idea of the study of *semiurgy* that studies the powerful forces reshaping the social experience.

Baudrillardian semiurgy is a disruptive force which traps, breaks, collapses, reduces and stimulates experience and communication, it is alienating. Technological massage also can be numbing, exhausting, and bewildering and requires protective ablations. [...] Semiurgy is, however, finally involved with itself and the relations of a closed system.[615]

Culture becomes a system of fetishism where the real, concrete, personal and conflictual differences between persons are abolished. In other words, the real every day of human touch disappears with a social media system of consumer touch homogenization. The media touch age becomes where the media abstraction of differences is industrially produced for mass consumer markets.

> The consumption of differences involves a strategy of personalization requiring affiliation with an abstract model of combined possibilities constituting, or instances, a fashionable "look" or adherence to a model of masculinity in which one can exclaim that "He can't be a man because he doesn't smoke the same cigarettes as me.[616]

In the present age of social media and smart phones consumers are in a constant psychosomatic stimulation with electronic and social media. It is a continuous sense of touch media where identity is based on the vicarious touch of social media that stimulates the propelling appetite of pleasure. Humankind is most passionately and exceedingly attracted to the pleasure of the act of reproduction and taking of food and drink. Therefore, the most obvious application of temperance is in sexual disorders and lack of moderation in eating and drinking. Yet, it does seem that there is the real possibility that an intemperate excessive use of digital social media has evolved, similarly to other forms of mental and physical addiction. We might argue without the virtue of temperance there is a possibility of a "consumer social media junk food addictive behavior." We begin to lose our rational moral sense of self-preservation identity in a world of the everyday, addictive touch of a social media reality.

Need for the Aristotelian-Thomistic golden mean is visible in the activities of temperament and intemperate behavior. The mean is to find a rational moral

---

[615] Gary GENESKO, *McLuhan and Baudrillard: The Masters of Implosion* (London and New York: Routledge, 1999), 69.

[616] Ibid., 66.

balance in the desires of the concupiscible sense. Excess or defect as measured by the mean is vice, whereas "the mean is the target of virtue because men are simply good."[617]

We explore this issue of the Aristotelian mean as it relates in a rather significant way to the nature of executive exemplar leadership behavior. We turn to RACHLIN, the Aristotelian teleological behaviorist, and his treatment of the relationship of the mean and the development of a coherent rational moral development. He takes the position:

> Aristotle's golden mean is not a midpoint between two extremes, as is often understood, but rather a wider perspective (a final cause) different from either of the extremes. For example, the extremes of the rashness and cowardice are resolved by courage. The extremes of surliness and obsequiousness are resolved by friendliness.[618]

Another Aristotelian psychologist, Daniel N. ROBINSON, takes the same approach to behavior and the mean: of vice as excess or deficiency and virtue as a higher rational moral end. As we observe in the following table:[619]

Table 7: Temperance

Vice (Excess)	Vice (Deficiency)	Virtue
Intemperance	*Insensibility*	*Temperance*
Loss	*Gain*	*Justice*
Shamelessness	*Shyness*	*Modesty*
Luxuriousness	*Submission to evils*	*Endurance*

RACHLIN continues his behavioral analysis of the mean and the behavioral resolution of conflicting behavioral patterns:

---

[617] AQUINAS, *Commentary on Aristotle's Nicomachean Ethics*, Book 2, Lecture 7.

[618] RACHLIN, *The Escape of The Mind*, 188.

[619] Daniel N. ROBINSON, *Aristotle's Psychology* (New York: Columbia University Press, 1989), 114.

"Actions are called just and temperate when they are such as the just and temperate man would do; but it is not the man who does these that is just and temperate, but the man does them as just and temperate men do them." (Nicomachean *Ethics,* chapter four). For example, two people may perform in the same just act (say they are storekeepers who return an overpayment to a customer), but both acts are not necessarily just. To be just, the act has to appear in the context of a series of other acts that form a pattern—a habit. A particular act done merely to win praise (as determined by other acts in the pattern), or in the context of a promotional campaign, or by compulsion, or by accident, would not be just—no matter how closely it resembled a particular act within a just pattern.[620]

While an executive-exemplar leadership is the virtuous person. He/she is not virtuous on all occasions. Virtue is not an executive promotional campaign. How to become a virtuous leader cannot be learned on a one-week seminar.

ARISTOTLE and AQUINAS tell us that "the virtuous man strives always to do what is reasonable. It is evident then that he always wishes for himself the absolute good."[621] The virtuous-exemplar leader is committed to be a person of virtue. As a leader he/she does not intend to do "the next right thing" because the occasions are advantageous to his/her career image and promotional aspirations.

Regarding the diffusion of executive leadership, character-coherence of behavior is critical. "Coherence" means an exemplar-leader appears consistently authentic way. Every day, on and off the job, the leader's behavioral activity emanates tranquility and clear consistency of good character. The exemplar displays rational decision-making and emotional mastery. Behavior is consistent in all types of situations of contending passions.

As leader exemplars do not fear under stress of conflict the shame of morally ugly (*turpis*) and reprehensible behavior. It is most important to note very well that in a Thomistic faculty-behavioral-psychology shame is a good passion (emotion), or as we would say today a trait of emotional intelligence. AQUINAS teaches that shame is a rational moral preventive feeling detector of the virtuous person,

---

[620] RACHLIN, *The Escape of The Mind,* 189.

[621] AQUINAS, *Commentary on Aristotle's Nicomachean Ethics,* Book 9, Lecture 4.

"Shamefacedness lays the first foundation of temperance, by inspiring man with the horror of whatever is disgraceful."[622] In terms of the diffusion of executive exemplar, there is a related virtue of uprightness (*honestum*), which is a love of the spiritually beautiful for its own sake. Honesty, as used by AQUINAS, is an attraction to what is morally beautiful (*decorum*) while shame is repulsion from the morally ugly. AQUINAS says that temperance holds in check the vices most deserving of reproach.

We could argue from the perspective of behavioral activities that in an organizational everyday environment the lack of temperance is the most obvious of leadership behavior. The virtuous behavior of the executive exemplar leader appears to workers as always calm. The temperate leader is an example of a person who has a rational moral inner sense of proper calm and coherent order, i.e. heft. AQUINAS, in a way, refers to the exemplar temperate and honest (coherent) leader, when he says, "our uncomely parts have more abundant comeliness, which namely destroys whatever is uncomely."[623]

BOURKE draws attention to important divisions of temperance that apply to executive leadership character, especially the ability of a leader under various conditions to steadily master the violent emotions of fear and anger. Gentleness (*mansuetudo, clementia*) is the good habit of the will enabling a leader to control the passion of anger.[624] *Clementia* is particularly concerned with moderating the visible behavioral activities associated with anger. Affability is a good habit of feeling kindly to others; the external manifestation of such social agreeableness is also a part of justice.[625] Principally, related to coherent leadership behavior is veracity (*veracitas*) as a good habit of wanting to signify one's true thoughts to others and to appear as one is. Executive veracity is of the utmost importance to the credibility and trust of the executive function and various levels of organizational leadership.[626]

---

[622] AQUINAS, *Summa theologiae* II-II, q. 144 a. 1 ad 3.

[623] Ibid., q. 145 a. 4.

[624] Ibid., q. 157 aa. 1–4.

[625] Ibid., q. 60 a. 5.

[626] Ibid.

In the digital age, executive leadership should give attention to the virtue of study (*studiosias*) which is a good habit of will controlling the unreasonable desire for knowledge (curiosity). In the age of the internet the availability of information can enhance organizational knowledge, but it is also easy to become addicted to information from a sense of novel intemperate curiosity.[627]

6.4.5 F: Fortitude (Exemplar Heft)

We have discussed in some depth the irascible (contending) passions as these passions relate to the function of executive leadership. We introduced that organizational leaders must prove their worth as a leader by their virtuous character over time in the contending behavioral zone. All levels of organizational leadership every day are challenged by excessive and ill-founded fears, tempted to engage in unreasonable daring and bursts of uncontrolled anger. Unless controlled by a habituation to behavior mastered by the unity of virtue, these overt behavioral activities turn into organizational dysfunctional leadership.

As stated, the virtue of fortitude primary organizational leadership purpose is a rational behavioral expression of fear to achieve an end as opposed to a dysfunctional expression and irrational, sometimes brute like, expression of fear. Fortitude (courage) is the name of the habit of propelling firmness in the face of the challenging, the difficult, the threatening and the arduous. BOURKE maintains, "It is to be emphasized that firmness is the essence of fortitude; the word means strength literally. A man must be prepared to remain calm and reasonable, even in a situation in which his life appears to be in danger."[628] In an organization, workers over time come to admire and trust the truly courageous and wise leader who is especially firm when the organizational future is under threat and calls for wise and courageous decision making for the common good. Again, as we see with the inner sense of orderly heft (leading by the habits of the moral virtues) a leader is able to remain calm, serene, and reasonable as he/she faces threatening events and situations.

---

[627] Ibid., q. 167 aa. 1–2.

[628] BOURKE, *Ethics*, 315.

BOURKE points out that four inclinations of the irascible (contending) appetite combine to constitute natural fortitude. These inclinations are the core feelings of an exemplar leader's daring and self-confidence. They deal with the challenge of facing a threatening situation. In summary:[629]

1) Confidence is a strong hope, based on firm opinion, prompting one to attack danger.

2) Magnificence is a strength within the irascible appetite, impelling one to execute a great deed. It is not the external doing of the deed but the internal "greatness" of daring which makes the difficult action possible. On the other hand, for the act of suffering danger, two integral parts may be found, as follows.

3) Patience is a condition of the concupiscible appetite, where sorrow is felt. This moderated feeling of sorrow is a sort of the concupiscible adjunct to fortitude. It is not identical with the virtue of patience.

4) Perseverance is a condition of the irascible appetite enabling one to persist firmly through a long period of suffering. The length of the suffering is the special difficulty faced by this feeling.

As BOURKE points out, there are virtues related to fortitude that bring out the full organizational leadership power of fortitude. They are: 1) Magnanimity, which means "great-mindedness." It strengthens the aspiration of honors reasonably possible.[630] 2) Magnificence is the capacity to make something great. It allows a person to face a special project with strong hope and courage.[631] 3) Patience is a virtue enabling a person to bear up under the impact of evils other than death, e.g., the loss of job, money, position, etc. It moderates against excessive sorrow.[632] 4) Perseverance enables one to persist in a reasonable way when the difficulty is really the length of time to be endured. It is the passion of sorrow that requires the need

---

[629] BOURKE, *Ethics*, 316-317

[630] AQUINAS, *Summa theologiae* II-II, q. 129 aa. 1–4.

[631] Ibid., q. 137 a. 1.

[632] Ibid., q. 135 aa. 1–2.

for patience.[633] 5) Longanimity is literally long-mindedness. It enables a person to keep one's attention fixed on some distant objective and against roadblocks and long-lasting obstacles, e.g., negative, and dysfunctional attitudes and behavior.[634] 6) Constancy enables a person to persist in the quality of good work and a doable deed and remain firm despite circumstantial difficulties, e.g., the loss of a key employee, insufficient budget funding, etc.[635]

BOURKE applies the power of fortitude to Louis Pasteur. It is a passage that any executive exemplar leader would do well to read in order to comprehend the importance of creative, innovative, and virtuous entrepreneurial leadership.

> Thus we would say that a pioneer in the development of some new scientific technique, such as Louis Pasteur, might be *magnanimous* in aspiring to the fame which might come with the accomplishment of his great work, *magnificent* in devoting his personal fortune to the discovery of something which might be of help to all future men, *persevering* in his refusal to be daunted by the continued lack of success of his early experiments, *longanimous* (long-minded) in his realization that it would take years to convince other scientists even after his experiments had been brought to a successful termination and *constant* in his refusal to be swayed from his work by the discouraging criticism of other scientists.[636]

BOURKE's description of Pasteur as a scientist exemplar of the virtue of fortitude is also a description of BOURKE's molar courageous magnanimous, magnificent, persevering, long minded and constant molar behavioral activities over time.

---

[633] Ibid., q. 137 a. 1.

[634] Ibid., q. 136 a. 5.

[635] Ibid., q. 136 a. 1.

[636] BOURKE, *Ethics,* 319

6.5 Verification of Exemplar Diffusion of Leadership Character and Moral Virtues

We have discussed that a Thomistic faculty-behavioral- psychology focuses on virtuous habits. Yet we have argued from the beginning of this dissertation that it is the responsibility of the executive level (here we include the chief executive and senior level, usually senior vice president levels) to set the example of an exemplar leadership character. It is this exemplar character of every virtuous habitual behavior worthy of emulation, enculturated by formal and informal learning and an objective code of rational moral character that enables the diffusion of the virtuous habits of leadership throughout the organization. We have addressed the intellectual virtues and focused on habits of cardinal virtues in all situations of organizational rational moral decision making, operational procedures and formal and informal rational moral codes of behavioral conduct. It is more important that organizational leadership is not a matter of persuasion by rhetoric. In an organization, there must exist some method of formal and informal learning of expected observable behavioral activities related to rational moral virtuous leadership. It means, in term of molar behavioral psychology, there must be nested observable prudent, just, temperate, and courageous activities. Quite simply, it requires verification of the diffusion of character.

We will select one case study of virtue-based measurement of activity; however, there are many possible qualitative and quantitative methods of measuring the executive diffusion of leadership character. We have selected a study by Ronald E. RIGGIO, Weichun ZHU, Christopher REINA and James A. MAROOSIS of Fordham University that has developed a suitable method of measuring organizational ethical leadership based on the observation and measurement of moral virtue behavioral activities.[637] The purpose of the study was to develop a reliable and valid scale to measure ethical leadership. We summarize and apply it here.

---

[637] Ronald E. RIGGIO, Weichun ZHU, Christopher REINA and James A. MAROOSIS, "Virtue-Base Measurement of Ethical Leadership: The Leadership Virtues Questionnaire) *Consulting Psychology Journal: Practice and Research*, 2010 Vol.62, No. 4, 235–250.

Ethics and Leadership. The study had developed from a previous interest and research on the part of the research team on the difference of ethical and unethical transformational leadership. The researchers had concluded that unethical transformational leadership was really pseudo transformational leadership. Based on other research in organizational ethical behavior, they defined organizational behavior for the purpose of the ethical leadership study as, "demonstration of normatively appropriate conduct through personal actions and interpersonal relationships and the promotion of such conduct to followers through two-way communication, reinforcement and decision-making."[638] Their prior research established (as we have suggested in this dissertation) that social learning theory suggest that leaders develop ethical leadership behaviors by emulating admired, ethical leader role models. Of course, the danger is the emulation of unethical leaders who exhort followers to behave ethically, while privately behaving unethically.

The Cardinal Virtues. In the study, values were defined as the "guiding principles in our lives with respect to the personal and social ends we desire, and virtue as something we practice at all times."[639] They worked within an Aristotelian-Thomistic moral philosophical understanding of the moral virtues. In terms of leadership, they described prudence as the wisdom that manages between doing too much or dictates a proper balance between two extremes in a world of shifting contexts and priorities. Prudence therefore is critical; a leader cannot be ethical unless he or she is prudent.

The psychologists, as they constructed the virtue questionnaire, interacted in study and dialogue with Aristotelian-Thomistic philosophers, as to the content validity of the measurement instrument being developed. The content validity was basically "prudence does what is just, while temperance and fortitude protect prudence from inner and outer threats. Temperance and fortitude seek to make someone a good person, while it is only the specific aim of justice to make a person a good citizen." Similar to the approach of this chapter, they held, according to ARISTOTLE, the virtues form a unified whole, with prudence playing a critical leadership role. It is prudence that interprets, evaluates, develops a plan of action,

---

[638] Ibid., 236.

[639] Ibid., 237.

and executes the virtues making one's actions just, courageous, and temperate. Therefore, the four virtues are substantially intercorrelated. Specifically, they wanted to move away from an emphasis purely on ethical behaviors and focus on the positive character of leaders.

Scale Development. Behavioral items were developed for each virtue and turned into questions. After many revisions, a preliminary pool of 40 items (10 items for each virtue) seemed to best represent the concept were reduced finally to form the LVQ.

Exploratory Factor Analysis I: They administered a 36-item survey online to 60 managers form a wide variety of industries (36% male, mean age 47.3 years, 33% 1st level managers, 46% mid to upper, 20.1% upper level). Exploratory Factor Analysis II administered 19 items to another sample of 140 managers from a number of companies and characteristics were similar to Analysis I. Confirmatory Factor Analysis (CFA) used a sample of 200 managers. Using the LVQ survey managers were asked to rate their direct leaders.[640]

Figure 3: The Leadership Virtues Questionnaire (LVQ)

Prudence Items

1. Does as he/she ought to do in a given situation.
2. Does not carefully consider all the information available before making an important decision that impacts others. (R)
3. Boldly jumps into a situation without considering the consequences of his/her actions. (R)
4. Does not seek out information from a variety of sources so the best decision can be made. (R)
5. Considers a problem from all angles and reaches the best decision for all parties involved.

---

[640] Ibid., 241–243.

Fortitude Items

1. Would rather risk his/her job than do something that was unjust.
2. May have difficulty standing up for his/her beliefs among friends who do not share the same views. (R)
3. Fails to make the morally best decision in a given situation. (R)
4. May hesitate to enforce ethical standards when dealing with a close friend. (R)
5. Ignores his/her "inner voice" when deciding how to proceed. (R)

Temperance Items

1. Seems to be overly concerned with his/her personal power. (R)
2. Is not overly concerned with his/her own accomplishments.
3. Wishes to know everything that is going on in the organization to the extent that he/she micromanages. (R)

Justice Items

1. Gives credit to others when credit is due.
2. Demonstrates respect for all people.
3. May take credit for the accomplishments of others. (R)
4. Respects the rights and integrity of others.
5. Would make promotion decisions based on a candidate's merit.
6. Does not treat others as he/she would like to be treated. (R)

Note. R reversed item. Response scale: 1 Not at all; 2 Once in a while; 3 Sometimes; 4 Fairly often; 5 Frequently

The psychometrics methodology and the tested reliability and validity of the measuring instrument were conducted by the psychology department of Claremont McKenna College known for their competence in organizational theory and testing. It is a robust instrument based on an understanding of the cardinal virtues and a careful question item reduction related to the theoretical content. It does demonstrate the importance in organizational behavioral studies of virtue and the advantages of giving attention to concrete items of behavioral activity nested within each virtue.

There are some findings that relate directly to this study of the function of executive leadership and the diffusion of organizational leadership, specifically on the diffusion of exemplar leadership.

> Based on the findings, there are a few practical implications we want to note for this study. First, our findings suggest that to be able to promote follower's positive outcomes such as developing follower moral identity and identification with the organization, leaders will need to demonstrate virtues. One specific example is that when leaders demonstrate justice and fairness in the decision process and treat employees with the same level of dignity and respect they deserve, followers are more likely to develop follower moral identity and positive outcomes. The second practical implication is to develop leaders' virtues leads to the development of follower moral capabilities and other positive outcomes.[641]

In practice, this means organizations could provide their managers with virtues development and training with respect to key characteristics or behavioral dimensions of virtuous leadership, namely prudence, temperance, justice, and fortitude.

> Third, it verified that follower of leaders to be more virtuous are likely to report higher levels of moral identity, and higher levels of identification with their organization. Also, it was verified that leaders rated higher on the cardinal virtue reported greater levels of psychological empowerment.[642]

In relation to the theory of diffusion of organizational executive- leadership character, most surprising in the LVQ study, was the strong interrelationship among measures of "good" leadership ranging from the "Ethical Leadership Scale," the "Authentic Leadership Scale," the "MLQ measure of Transformational

---

[641] Ibid., 248–249.

[642] Ibid.

Leadership" to the LVQ ethical leader scores. The interrelationship indicates that if a person scored high on ethical leadership then the same person scored high on authentic-leadership trait scales. This signifies that the truly virtuous person is most fit for positions of leadership.

Especially worthy of note that persons with a high rate on the LVQ scale also rated high on the "Authentic Leadership Scale." The authentic leadership and eudaemonic well-being are most concerned with the understanding of leader-follower behavior. Authentic leadership theory builds on an individual's experience in his or her daily engagements with life.

From a moral perspective, how he or she approaches these experiences and what he or she learns from them has profound implications for his or her personal and professional growth and the worthiness of personal life. Authentic leadership theory is basically a social learning measure to the nature of the authentic self. The construct also borrows from the Aristotelian concept of eudaemonia. ARISTOTLE's view of human happiness that assesses the goodness of life based on living in a manner that actively expresses excellence of character.

The LVQ researcher conducted very strong intercorrelations among the different measures of ethical, virtuous, and authentic leadership. For example, the balanced processing dimension of authentic leadership is similar to the virtue of prudence. Both involve considering multiple perspectives about an issue and weighing different information before acting. The authentic leadership component of self-awareness has some relationship to the virtue of temperance, which requires self-knowledge in order to understand and accept one's shortcomings,[643] (though the real assessment of a person as an organizational leader is not achieved in understanding his or her motives or sharing in a training session).

We come to know exemplar leaders only after we have observed their overt patterns of behavior of behavior over time. Crucial are their patterns of behavior in difficult and threatening times. The exemplars are known for the most excellence of habits, especially in habits of the moral virtues as nested and observed in everyday acts and activities. For such an observation, an executive-exemplar self-assessment instrument is advisable, For example:

---

[643] Ibid., 247.

1) Did I do the right thing today, the right way, for the right reason?
2) Was I fair in my decisions today?
3) Do I master my passions of fear and anger?
4) Do I aspire to excellence of character on a daily basis?
5) Am I patient when facing the arduous?
6) Do I properly focus on my priorities every day?
7) Do I set reasonable and doable goals and deeds for myself and others?
8) Do I appear to the people as a coherent and authentic leader over time?

This idea of coherence is an inclusive behavioral first principle of exemplar leadership in a Thomistic faculty-psychology. As we have argued, similar to the Claremont, LVQ and Authentic Leadership study, an exemplar leader is one who inspires followers to a state of emulation of the exemplar's leadership character. Consequently, it is important for a person who aspires to become a leader, let alone to the executive exemplar level that he/she is known in an organization as expressing coherent habits of behavior over time. Coherence basically means that a person expresses a characteristic goodness which is found in virtuous habits and everyday behavioral activities. In an organization, a leader's coherent behavior is particularly observed by followers under demanding threatening, stressful and competitive situations. It is in times of arduous situations that a leader's sense of inner rational-moral order and the tranquility and confidence associated with said inner order is observed and emulated. Followers will use expressions such as he/she can really keep it together under fire. They keep their cool.

We suggest, furthermore, the virtues of prudence and temperance on an everyday basis are most observed by followers, i.e., prudent good decision-making and problem-solving activities and temperate activities of continence, gentleness, humility, affability, and veracity. It is leadership of everyday heft: H habits of justice, E prudence (estimative Intelligence), T temperance F, and fortitude. It is necessary that leaders always have honest and respected feedback about the perception of their quality of coherent behavior in various situations. As RACHLIN explains:

Any superiority of a person's perception of his own mind over another person's perception of his mind lies in the quantity of his observations of his own behavior (he is always there when he is behaving), not in their quality. There is nothing inherently superior in a first-person perspective on the mind over a third-person perspective. In fact, because your behavior is more clearly seen by an observer than by you, a third person perspective may be more accurate. The meanings of mental terms (expectancy, belief, purpose, feeling, etc.) are, after all, socially learned.[644]

6.5.1 Verification of Thomistic Faculty-Behavioral-Psychology of Passion, Virtue and Emulation of Exemplar Grit

We return to our discussion of the concupiscible (propelling) appetite and the irascible (contending) appetite and the passions of the soul. We could use the modern terminology of emotions, but we prefer to stick with expression "propelling and contending passions." We used a case study of a medical student who had a vision (meta discriminative stimulus) that moved the propelling passions of his soul into, what we explained as a contending behavioral zone over a long period of time. There was the need for the propelling vision that at the same time stimulates the contending passions. It is the passion of love for the vision that gives one hope, audacity, and mastery of fear. Angela DUCKWORTH is not a Thomist, but her well-received work *Grit: The Power of Passion and Perseverance* is worthy of entering into a trading zone exchange about the nature of grit and the Thomistic psychology of vision, propelling and contending passion and exemplar leadership behavior followers emulate.[645]

DUCKWORTH's book has been hailed over the past few years as a classic treatment of the nature of success. She is a psychologist at the University of Pennsylvania and advises fortune 500 companies, the World Bank, NBA, and NFL teams of the nature of grit and success. She developed and verified the Grit Scale

---

[644] RACHLIN, *The Escape of The Mind*, 181.

[645] Angel DUCKWORTH, *Grit: The Power of Passion and Perseverance* (New York: Scriber, 2016).

Measuring Instrument. Much of her early work was on West Point candidates comparing Whole Candidate Score and the Grit Scale. She was interested in candidates who had completed the West Point program, since the drop our rate was so high. She discovered that graduates showed one major characteristic that she described as grit. It was not the highest IQ, the most athletic or the best previous academic record. It was candidates that rated with the highest grit score. Her explanation of grit is as follows:

> To be gritty is to keep putting one foot in front of the other. To be gritty is to hold fast to an interesting and purposeful goal. To be gritty is to invest, day after week after year, in challenging practice. To be gritty is to fall down seven times and rise eight.[646]

Pursuant to previous comments on temperance and media, DUCKWORTH's research indicates that in contemporary society in the measured cluster of virtues related to grit that self-control, particularly as it relates to resisting temptations like texting and video games, stand out. "What this means is that gritty people tend to be self-controlled and vice versa."[647] In her research, similar to an increasing number of empirical psychologists, she gives attention to the relationship of virtue and character.

She finds virtues which make possible the accomplishment of personally valued goals that have also been called "performance character" or "self-management skills." Her results point out that grit character includes gratitude, social intelligence, and self-control over emotions like anger. In the relationship of virtues and exemplars of character worthy of emulation, she mentions a concept of "eulogy virtues."

> Eulogy virtues because, in the end, they may be more important to how people remember us than anything else. When we speak admiringly of

---

[646] Ibid. 275

[647] Ibid., 273.

someone being a deeply good person, I think it is a cluster of virtues we're thinking about.[648]

DUCKWORTH arrives in her discovery of the Grit Scale that there is something other than IQ or personality traits, and she hints at an element of deep character. Albeit, not wholeheartedly, she turns to a mild expression of virtue and a psychology of character.

> So, grit isn't everything. There are many other things a person needs in order to grow and flourish. Character is plural. One way to think about grit is to understand how it relates to other aspects of character. In assessing grit along with other virtues, I find three reliable clusters. I refer to them as the intrapersonal, interpersonal, and intellectual dimension of character. You could also call them strength of will, heart, and mind.[649]

We draw attention to the Grit Scale because Thomistic faculty-behavioral-psychology finds the Grit theory and implications a complimentary trading zone. In the Grit Scale there are many items similar to the Thomistic habit of fortitude. However, we argue that the understanding of the grit is more pertinent to the nature of leadership when placed in the Aristotelian-Thomistic description of the virtuous person, faculties of the soul, the unity of virtues and everyday heft. Second the Grit Scale is supportive of a faculty-behavioral -psychology of exemplar leadership because the scale draws focus to observable overt activities. Although these overt acts and activities are always nested activities within the habits of the cardinal and associated virtues of AQUINAS presented in this chapter, we could call it Thomistic Grit.

---

[648] Ibid., 274.
[649] Ibid., 273.

6.6. The Exemplar Executive Methodist Pastor of the Church of the Resurrection, a Story of Vision, Courage and Virtuous Entrepreneurship

In chapter two we presented a short case study on Pope Francis and described his executive task as one of transformational leadership of the Roman Catholic Church, one of the world's most influential, longest lasting organizations facing the challenges of a disruptive age. We proceed in this chapter with another case study about the executive leader of another church organization. He is Adam Hamilton who is the Pastor of the United Methodist Church of the Resurrection in Leawood, Kansas, commonly known by the acronym COR. We have selected this church because it is one of the powerful stories of exemplar executive entrepreneurial-intrapreneurial leadership in the United States in church growth since the 1990s.

The golden era for the growth of mainline Protestant churches began in the United States after the Second World War when veterans returned home. American culture in those years was an ardent culture of three fundamental values, i.e., God, family, and country. Furthermore, after the war years, it was a period of strong demographic growth as the birth rate rapidly increased. It was a matter of building a church in a family community when church development began to grow in 50s into the 80s. It is really starting in the late 80s that a disturbing decline in the growth of mainline Protestant churches began to appear; by the nineties it had become alarming. Where there was growth it appeared in the independent mostly conservative evangelical mega churches. There are many sociological theories put forth to explain this social-cultural decline, but one of the most obvious, beyond the present scope of exploration, was the impact of electronic media and the impact on styles of worship, i.e., music, hymn selection, screens, etc.

In the midst of the distressing decline in mainline Protestant denominations like the United Methodist Church, a young minister came on the scene in Leawood Kansas, named Pastor Adam Hamilton. He was an ordained a Methodist minister, fresh from seminary with a burning passion for a style of ministry most needed when the disruption of the desired order of the United Methodist Church was becoming increasingly apparent and the quest for an emerging order was pressing and shaking the foundational organizational institutions of mainline religion.

Adam Hamilton approached his bishop with a passionate desire for a visionary ministry. He had a vision to build a Christian Community for non-religious and nominally religious who might enter into a journey of becoming deeply committed Christians.

As he often mentions, when speaking on church leadership, it is a vision that began in his seminary days. With his emerging vision of a Christian community for the non-religious and the nominal Christian, he began his ministry with the encouragement of his bishop to start a new congregation in Leawood, Kansas. The reason Adam Hamilton is so interesting as a case study as the exemplar executive entrepreneur is that he and his wife started their congregation in a well-located Johnson County Funeral Home using their chapel on Sunday morning. The first congregation was comprised of Pastor Adam, his wife, and their children. It began in 1990s and by 2018 had grown to 23,000 members under his leadership. Pastor Hamilton is a devout and theologically educated Methodist minister. He is not an Aristotelian-Thomistic student of virtue psychology, metaphysics of organization or Thomistic faculty psychology. However, we do think that many of the principles of a Thomistic psychology of virtuous character and the concept of the virtuous exemplar entrepreneur shed light on the phenomenal growth from a few members in 1990s to 23,000 in 2018.

We start with the observation that the idea of an entrepreneur is usually associated with business. Although for the greater part, it does apply to the person attracted to the competitive world of business, it also may apply to a religious institution facing if we might carefully suggest, the demand for members requiring the strategic mindset of the entrepreneur. The application of the entrepreneurial character is even more appropriate to a religious institution if we are referring to the virtuous exemplar entrepreneur. Therefore, we are examining Pastor Hamilton and his leadership style as a spiritual Pastor and as a virtuous leader from the perspective of a Thomistic psychological understanding of a virtuous executive exemplar worthy of follower emulation and the diffusion of the exemplar character throughout the emerging community.

First, we start with asking how does a leader become a virtuous leader? It does not start by taking a course on Thomistic psychology or virtue psychology. AQUINAS teaches:

Now, the first principle of reason, no less in moral than in speculative matters, has been given by nature. Therefore, just as by means of previously known principles a man makes himself understand by personal effort of discovery, so also by acting according to the principles of practical reason a man makes himself actually virtuous.[650]

We have explained in this dissertation one of the advantageous of Thomistic psychology is that it explains organizational leadership better than the efforts at practical intelligence, intuition and sense making by empirical psychology. Practical reason is a faculty of the soul and is much deeper than practical intelligence and intuition. For Thomists, practical reason is a lot more than being intelligent and pragmatic. Practical reason, AQUINAS teaches, is "the rule for the rectitude of the appetitive faculty in regard to the means."[651] "Practical reason is an intellectual appetite for the truth; it is a passion to pursue the things that reason calls true."[652] Adam Hamilton, for a number of years in formal and informal learning, had developed an intellectual appetite to understand the first principles of growing a community for the non-religious and nominally religious. DUCKWORTH says that the highly successful have a ferocious determination in two ways:

> First, these exemplars were unusually resilient and hardworking. Second, they knew in a very, very deep way what it was they wanted. They not only had determination, they had direction. It was this combination of passion and perseverance that made high achievers special. In a word they had grit.[653]

Yes, a successful Pastor like Adam Hamilton would obviously score high on the Grit Scale, but there is a reality much deeper with the virtuous exemplar. Adam Hamilton as the virtuous exemplar entrepreneur Pastor has passion, but it is the passion and appetite of the soul that hungers for the truth. He must intensely focus

---

[650] AQUINAS, *Commentary on Aristotle's Nicomachean Ethics*, Book 2, Lecture 4.
[651] Ibid., Book 6, Lecture 2.
[652] Ibid.
[653] DUCKWORTH, *Grit*, 8.

his soul on the formal and experiential study of how to build a community for the non-religious and nominally religious. He selects a subject domain of the non-religious and the nominal and begins to ponder and learn from various abstract and experiential probes into "who are the non-religious and nominal, where are they, what are they thinking, and what should we try?" He must believe that his inquiry will be pleasing to God, and he accepts the arduous task in the hope of a vision becoming in time a reality. In this journey, he must have the contending passions of hope and daring and the power of his contending (irascible) appetite to overcome despair by a rational mastery of fear.

Next, when Adam Hamilton talks about the beginning days of his bold ministry, one becomes aware of the importance of his wife, family, and his early followers. It is easy to detect that he has the virtuous exemplar character that draws his followers to his vision. This is at the heart and soul of the executive entrepreneur that the follower must live the vision. It means not just hearing the vision, not just believing the vision; rather, it is an embodiment of the vision as a formal object that draws forth the powers of the soul. The vision is the constant, everyday organizational behavioral meta-discriminative stimuli that provides the abstract spiritual and moral rules that direct an organization.[654] As an organizational meta-discriminative stimulus, it must be repeated constantly in formal and informal spoken, printed, digital media, advertising media of various types etc. When Adam Hamilton talks about the importance of vision and mission, he also mentions the importance of imagery. It means the vision must become concrete and communicated in an everyday language that people are able to visualize. For example, as they grew toward a capacity of 23,000 there was the need to expand throughout the Kansas City area and build a larger church with a huge worship and education capacity. It was not just a matter of fund-raising campaign; rather, it was the reinforcement of the vision of new non-religious and nominally religious filling the seats and attending worship and religious education classes. Virtuous exemplar leadership characteristics, as we have seen in the LVQ and authentic leadership surveys, inspire followers to emulate not only the vision, but the behavioral patterns of the exemplar moving toward a perfection of the vision. It is the emulators who move to emerging leadership roles in the organization.

---

[654] RACHLIN, *The Escape of The Mind*, 81.

Adam Hamilton had to be able to inspire the emulators into a core team that were mentored in his style of leadership.

In her extensive study of entrepreneurs, EHRINGER discovered, as did Pastor Hamilton, the critical importance of the executive "core team." EHRINGER writes, "The greatest influence on the decision thinking of these entrepreneurs came from their key people and management team."[655] An entrepreneur wrote the following:

> I would talk to my management team [...] I won't make that kind of decision myself because I don't own it [...] they would really have to own it with me [...] I always try to make sure that there is an indigenous team or core [...] Seeking other people out to talk has helped me a lot, been critical (to my success) I would get [my management team] together an say, "Well, I'm thinking about doing this, what's your reaction, do you think, it's a good idea."[656]

At COR, printed media is given to every member and it states COR's purpose and vision. It reads:

> Our purpose: To build a Christian community where non-religious and nominally religious people are becoming deeply committed Christians
> Our vision: To be used by God to change lives, strengthen churches, and transform the world.[657]

DEMING in his 12 principles of organizational leadership held that number 1 is "constancy of purpose." However, in the executive exemplar entrepreneurial organization, the vision is a dream introduced by the leader and the followers decide to participate in turning the dream to a vision, then to a strategy, then to operational tactics by continuous creative experimentation, emerging principles, and dedication to excellence. In many ways, there are also elements of the quality improvement model in his leadership style. There is also the Thomistic

---

[655] EHRINGER, *Make Up Your Mind*, 157.

[656] Ibid., 157.

[657] Marketing brand collateral materials provided by COR.

metaphysical organizational sense of virtual quantity and the continuous amplification of organizational perfection, harmony, beauty, and truth.

To go from a start up in a funeral home chapel of four members to 150, to 2000 in a school gym to now a 23,000-membership capacity on four campuses takes strategy. We, therefore, look at Hamilton as a virtuous entrepreneurial strategist that explains COR's leadership and in many ways growth. We approach this issue with four principles of the psychology of entrepreneurial decision-making from MINTZBERG, AHLSTRAND and LAMPEL.[658]

A) In the entrepreneurial mode, strategy making is dominated by the active search for new opportunities. The entrepreneurial organization focuses on opportunities; problems are secondary. Problem solvers are managers and administrators. The executive entrepreneur wants leader emulators who are deployed on finding opportunities. One of Hamilton's organizational mantras is Change, Innovate, Improve, or Die.

B) In the entrepreneurial organization, there is a sense of the Thomistic metaphysical organization principle of the equality of inequality. The best way to describe the rational and moral authority of the virtuous exemplar is with the metaphor we used in chapter three of the conductor of a volunteer community symphony. The conductor takes seriously the input from the lead musicians in all the different instrument sections. He is the conductor (maestro) who leads, arranges, and conducts the performance. The entrepreneur is the virtuous exemplar, and he is also the coach, as explained in chapter three, leads the organizational players "to touch the divine." Adam Hamilton is Pastor and the executive coach who is pragmatic, orchestrating the practical achievements by means of concrete smart goals: Specific, Measurable, Ambitious, Realistic and Time specific.

C) Strategy making in the entrepreneurial mode is characterized by dramatic leaps forward in the entrepreneurial organization by the taking of large decisions-those "bold strokes." The chief exemplar executive seeks out and thrives in conditions of uncertainty, where the organization can make dramatic gains. There is one principle that Adam Hamilton stresses when

---

[658] MINTZBERG, AHLSTRAND and LAMPEL, *Strategy Safari*, 133–136.

he is giving seminars to church ministers and lay people on leadership. It is what he calls a principle of nauseous decision making in times of pressing doubt and uncertainty.

Hamilton tells this story to illustrate one of his leadership principles. He tells how in the early days in the funeral home chapel that the evolving community had about 150 members. They needed space to grow and add a second service. Close to the funeral home chapel was a small empty church for sale at an agreeable price. It would have given them pews, a sanctuary and a pulpit, teaching rooms and a pastor's office. They would look like a traditional church except the church was hidden in a residential area behind the funeral home. The members of his new ministry were excited, except Adam Hamilton thinking in the entrepreneurial mode began to feel the growth vision was at risk. Yes, he thought that we could look and feel like a regular church. We would increase our seating capacity to 250. He could have an office. But he feared that we would be hidden in a small church hard to locate place. There was another option of moving into a school gym with great parking that was near the expressway. Hamilton and his team were appealing to the non-religious and nominal person, and the gym location would be more accessible and appealing. The downside was that Hamilton and his "core team" would have to arrive early every Sunday to set up and tear down for worship. There was a highly important decision to be made and the movement to their own little church was appealing to most of the members of the new and growing congregation. It was to play it safe and move to the available church.

It is here that Hamilton speaks to his leadership nausea principle. It is a principle where it is decision time where the meaning and courage of the vision is tested. Hamilton argues often that churches do not grow because the executive leadership is afraid to make the courageous choice. The virtuous executive entrepreneur is driven to take reasonable risk, but he/she also possesses the contending passions of hope and daring. Adam Hamilton, the executive entrepreneur seeks out and knows that his vision will only happen and thrive in conditions of uncertainty. He sensed the safe decision was the wrong decision because it was not true to the vision.

He sensed, deliberated, prayed, judged, and made the courageous decision to move to the gym. He states if they had moved to the small church that they would still be there as a small church as opposed to a congregation of 23,000 members and still growing. It is the reason he speaks about the virtue of courage as demanded by a great vision. He says there are times when it is necessary to feel queasy as an exemplar executive decision maker. It is the time to take the courageous path that leads to church growth.

D) Growth is the dominant goal of the entrepreneurial organization. The executive entrepreneur is motivated above all by the need for achievement. It is EHRINGER's phenomenological research method of how entrepreneurs see business as related to life decisions that provides a rather positive view of the entrepreneur's meaning of achievement, here are the comments of one entrepreneur that are somewhat representative of entrepreneurial patterns on the meaning of achievement:

> The particular blessing, I have is the capacity to speak and articulate what my vision is […] and mission is. [I like to] teach personal skills. Public speaking skills based upon the idea that people succeed because they like themselves, have a sense of self-worth, know they can relate to someone else […] I hope I am going to be a good teacher.
>
> I really enjoy helping people, I really get off on it, it's a kick for me and so to have the opportunity to do it and especially to help your friends.
>
> In terms of being introspective, what do I want written on my gravestone? My early message used to be "He was smart, he worked hard, and he was rich." And I put the eraser to that five or ten years ago, and now it would say "He helped me achieve what I wanted to achieve." That's really my whole self-image.[659]

When Adam Hamilton is interviewed or speaking in public, this same sense of achievement is obvious. It is clearly obvious when he gives workshops to other

---

[659] EHRINGER, *Make Up Your Mind*, 259.

Methodists ministers and laity on church leadership and growth in the 21st century. It is that entrepreneurial desire to teach the lesson of recognition of self-worth, the ability to truly communicate to others as a leader and doer. It is the same enthusiasm for achieving for Christ that he preaches to his large congregation each Sunday. It is a message that followers readily hear, take to heart, and emulate. Adam Hamilton, the executive exemplar entrepreneur, takes joy in the diffusion of the vision.

Finally, Hamilton has a DEMING sense of quality, or we could say that he has metaphysical sense of an organizational perfection (virtual quantity), continuously moving to the organizational formal object (purpose and vision) of unity, harmony, and rational-moral perfection. Similar to a commitment to quality it is in the continuous process of achieving excellence. COR is successful because it is committed to excellence in worship, education, and outreach to the community. COR listens attentively to the voices of the non-religious, the nominal religious and members in the congregation. These voices of spiritual questions, doubts, fears, and hope are blended into thematic, Biblical, existential solution sermons. Definitely, the success of COR is multivariable, but the most dominant factor is the quality of the preaching and teaching in an everyday language of excellent existential solution sermons. Furthermore, everything must be done with excellence, e.g., the beauty and architecture of their new worship center, education wings, music from contemporary to traditional executed with excellence, operations, and volunteers greeting people as they enter. COR verifies that people are attracted to excellence and relevance. For example, Pastor Hamilton will give approximately 35-minute sermons based on a theme such as "What would Jesus say about firearms?" and he holds the congregation's attention with a unique style of defining a problem and presenting a Biblical solution with refined, fitting, and appropriate blend of media and a coherent preached Biblical word. We might say that COR seems a type of contemporary solution place community.

6.7 Virtuous Exemplar Executive and Intrapreneurial and Sensing Something More Than Big Picture

The entrepreneurial style of executive leadership is described as the visionary school that is dependent on the vision of the entrepreneur and moving the vision by means of an ordered flexibility and strategy-making to completion. The danger is that an organization is constructed completely on the vision and the charism of the visionary entrepreneur. On the other hand, the proper executive function is to create and develop a visionary organization. We hold that in a world of evolving hierarchical and heterarchical organizational contrariety, the most appropriate organizational structure is one similar to the above case study of the Methodist pastor. It is where the executive entrepreneurial exemplar seeks to develop a core team of, what is called in current organizational theory, intrapreneurs. These intrapreneurs are senior level leaders. They share in entrepreneurial decision, strategy making and implementation. They are often assigned to critical new risk-taking products that require high leadership skills, especially the ability to lead a team in a demanding contending behavioral zone. In the contemporary organizational scene, intrapreneurs must have high aptitudes for team sense making, especially their findings for staying ahead of their competitors. It is, moreover, the responsibility of the executive to seek out workers who have the natural ability in terms of estimative intelligence and the virtuous habits to become an intrapreneurial leader. A Thomistic faculty-behavioral-psychology would recommend that a person considered for the position of an intrapreneurial leader is not selected on the basis of being a crafty-shrewd risk taker; rather, a person selected as an intrapreneur must be known as a prudent risk taker with a proven history of an "estimative intelligence." It is quite simple; the intrapreneurial organization is the result of the diffusion and emulation of the virtuous executive exemplar character.

When we talk about the organizational vision, purpose, and mission, we usually think that it means seeing the big picture. It is really more than the entrepreneur and his intrapreneurial team seeing the big picture. The entrepreneurial mode of thinking is a continuous exercise of individual and team estimative intelligence. If we express the idea in the language of a metaphysics of organization, it is the rational sense of the organizational whole and a blending of all the creative and estimative powers of the one and the many to sense beyond the "whole." It is the ability to go beyond the whole that defines organizational perfection, the genus.

The executive function is to develop and maintain in an extraordinary competitive environment an entrepreneurial-intrapreneurial team that as individuals has a psychological team sense of how to do new things or doing things already done in a new way. DRUCKER identifies entrepreneurship as central to the business enterprise is "the entrepreneurial act, as an act of economic risk taking."[660] This psychological sense is best explained and developed by means of the Thomistic understanding of psychological sensing and risk taking. REDPATH describes this psychological sense, based on the behavioral faculties that enable him/her to do the following:

a) Estimate one's personal strengths and weaknesses (be able to judge on the sense level whether or not a contemplated deed is doable within in existing circumstances).

b) Experience the emotions of hope and fear (locate in the contending irascible appetite within cogitative reason).

c) Possess a sense of time, especially related to the future which deepens upon possession of memory located within particular reason.

d) Possess some sense of prudence motivating a person to escape from the real dangers that ignorance of causes can generate in a person's life (a sense of prudence also located within particular reason).[661]

With an executive entrepreneurial-intrapreneurial in a competitive environment, the successful execution of the organizational vision is dependent upon a dynamic entrepreneurial-intrapreneurial team of continuous strategic decision sense making. It is an estimative sense making that must relate to six levels of the organization strategic estimative intelligence.

---

[660] MINTZBERG, AHLSTRAND and LAMPEL, *Strategy Safari*, 133.

[661] Peter A. REDPATH, "Standing on the Shoulders of Giants to Refine Gilson's Teaching about Christian Philosophy," unpublished at the time of writing.

6.8 Exemplar HEFT, the Organizational Vision, and the Courage to Grow

From the work of BARNARD, we use a generic definition of an organization "as a system of consciously coordinated activities or forces of two or more persons."[662] Although we have used examples and cases from business, we have mainly focused on entrepreneurial driven enterprises. This approach has been taken because we contend it is most aligned with an organizational psychology of an executive exemplar leadership character. The exemplar is the virtuous person since we learn from AQUINAS that "the virtuous man is perfect in the human species, this should be taken as the measure in all man's affairs."[663] In other words, we could say the exemplars are known for their "behavioral heft" and it this heft that the best of followers emulates. We focus on the entrepreneurial virtuous exemplar because we believe the virtuous entrepreneur is most compatible with a Thomistic metaphysics of the organizational first principle of the equality of inequality. In this virtuous, exemplar entrepreneurial application, there is one organizational first principle that every leader and supervisor and indeed every follower must accept, i.e., the organizational vision (formal object). This vision tends to be a kind of image more than a fully articulated plan (in words and numbers). A verbal image leaves it flexible, so that the leader can adapt it to his or her evolving experiences. This suggest that the executive exemplar strategy, goal setting and everyday decision and sense making is one of desired order and emergent order.[664] It this virtuous executive exemplar vision that is most suited for even nonprofit and religious organizations facing the impact of the disruptive culture and the quest for an emerging contemporary hierarchical-heterarchical organization.

6.9 The Contending Thomistic Faculty-Behavioral. Psychology HEFT Executive Leadership

We started this thesis with the intention to develop a Thomistic behavioral organizational psychology. We explained the metaphysical importance of

---

[662] BARNARD, *The Functions of the Executive*, 271.

[663] AQUINAS, *Commentary on Aristotle's Nicomachean Ethics*, Book 9, Lecture 4.

[664] MINTZBERG, AHLSTRAND and LAMPEL, *Strategy Safari*, 124.

organizational whole as a one and a many, referred to roles equality of inequality, virtual quantity, and contraries within an organizational whole, or "real genus."

We then described that, within human organizations, a tension of desired and emergent order always exists. While this is a simple principle, it is crucial to understand to comprehend the nature of executive leadership.

If we ask a CEO how business is, he/she might say, "it has been good for three months, but right now something strange is going on. I hope it does not last for long. This response evinces the contrariety tension existing within all desired and emerging organizations. In his Summa theologiae, St. Thomas explains why this is so: "Hence, the object of the irascible power is said to be the difficult (*arduum*), because the irascible power tends toward overcoming contraries and winning out over them." [665]

When the irascible tension is high and driven by the violent passions of fear and anger (which so easily go together), one of three behavioral patterns will kick in because fear: 1) inclines most of us to forget everything and run; 2) tends to cause false evidence to appear as real; or 3) causes a person to face everything and recover the rational powers of his or her soul.

Option 2 is very important because, when it is in a high state of irascible tension, executive leadership will often spend much time and money collecting false evidence, information, data that only increases the tension in the long run. The virtue of prudence and temperance allow an executive to pay attention with an appropriate level of tension (option 3).

Take option 1 and the agent looks for an escape route. We have given a great case study [Mann Gulch Disaster] that establishes the principle of the leader and "controlling irascible tension." Another way of putting the principle is: "Really competent leaders can give maximum attention with minimum tension and really incompetent leaders give minimum attention and maximum tension."

Organizational harmony will collapse in an environment of continuously high-irascible- tension because, in such a situation, estimative attention decreases. We submit this claim as a Thomistic organizational- behavioral principle of leadership in irascible situations of emergent to chaotic order [generic collapse].

---

[665] AQUINAS, *Summa theologiae*, 1, 81,2

In this situation, the basic behavioral contrariety-tension is, that "all the passions of irascible power take their origin from passions of the concupiscible power and terminate in the latter. For instance, pursuit of justice rises from an already-inflicted conviction of the existence of pain. If just revenge is gained the sense of vengeance, terminates in joy. For this reason, St. Thomas tells us that "among animals struggles are over concupiscible things like food and sexual pleasure."[666]

Therefore, so long as the irascible passion is engaged (which, to some extent is every moment that a real, human organization is operating) to some extent, the issue of irascible tension always exists within the organizational genus of the leaders' soul, and within his or her interaction with the organizational whole [genus] irascible tension of contrariety [the *arduum*].

Also, in the same passage referred to above, Aquinas teaches this irascible tension principle, "the soul resists opposing things ...the irascible power tends toward overcoming contraries and winning out over them."

Of course, the tension is only resolved only by focus on rational thought and principles of action. However, first the emotions calmly ordered by the support of the habits of the virtuous leader (his/her HEFT) H is justice, E estimative sense + particular reason habit of prudence, F is fortitude (courage) and T is temperance.

As a result, from the many, different ways we have considered in which modern organizational science examines the structure and functioning of the emerging organization in the disruptive age, we have reasonably concluded that a Thomistic organizational psychology of exemplar, soulful leadership is more compatible than any other known teaching with a visionary and intellectually-sound learning philosophy and psychology of organizational leadership in the present day.

---

[666] Ibid.

Conclusion

Chapter One: Behavioral Soul

Starting with chapter one, and continuing through chapter four, we established that a Thomistic faculty-behavioral-psychology is the foundational psychology for the art of organizational, soulful leadership. Having done this, in chapters five and six, we were able to expand and apply a Thomistic, faculty-behavioral-psychology to the art and practice of organizational soulful leadership

Chapter Two: The Small, Dark Soul

We presented the small, dark soul as a metaphor for a dysfunctional, pathological, organizational mode of leadership. In the analysis of this type of organizational leadership, we maintained that the executive levels of an organization allow, tolerate, promote, or resist, this soulless, toxic, dysfunctional-leadership-syndrome. Therefore, a primary responsibility of executive leadership is to *detect and eliminate* the dysfunctional-leadership-syndrome from the organization.

We contended that, by means of exemplar executive leadership, a Thomistic organizational psychology begins to immunize the organization against dark-soul leadership psychological disorder. We defined the exemplar executive as a leader responsible for rational, moral goodness in all organizational affairs. In turn, the exemplar becomes the virtuous role model for emulation by members of the organization. We put forth and explained that, beyond the other cardinal moral virtues of temperance, courage, and justice, the virtue of prudential and organizational self-understanding (that, by nature generates personal and organizational humility and opposes personal and organizational arrogance, hubris) is the most important virtue for an executive exemplar to develop.

Chapter Three: The Virtual Soul

Next, we established that a sense of a metaphysics of organization is essential for executive-exemplar, soulful leadership. We defended this position by defining basic metaphysical principles and applying these principles to organizational leadership situations and practical cases. We used a case method that applied metaphysical principles to a small, volunteer organization to demonstrate the essential principles of organizational, soulful leadership.

We elucidated that the wise exemplar knows and embodies the essential principles of: 1) the one and the many (part/whole relations) that generate and move an organization; 2) equality of inequality (command and control, and diffusion, of leadership); 3) contrariety (co-ordination and communication of opposites a continuous blending of conflicting forces); and 4) within the organizational whole (genus and members), an existential participation in the diffusion of rational-moral goodness of exemplar character and leadership.

Chapter Four: The Sensing Soul

From respected organizational scholars, we surveyed the evolving nature of organizations in modern culture. Many different ways exist to describe the evolving organizations and present-day culture (for example, information, digital, electronic, or disruptive age). We chose to use the terminology of the impact of the "disruptive age" upon organizational leadership.

We proposed the theory that the impact of creative, smart, and fast disruptive leadership is changing organizations from a hierarchical leadership structure to heterarchical network structure. We observed that in leadership education today much attention is given to the developing practice of organizational sensemaking in a disruptive culture where leaders are expected to act as smarter, harder, and faster decision-makers and risk-takers. In this disruptive organizational age, we claimed and described a common sensemaking based on Aristotelian-Thomistic inductive reasoning and the resting of principles in the soul of the rational sensing leader and exemplar of craft knowledge.

Chapter Five: The Estimative Soul

We focused intensely on the art and practice of organizational soulful leadership. If one behavioral, psychological principle exists essential and critical to the nature of organizational, soulful leadership, it is the Thomistic principle of the estimative soul. Thomistic behavioral psychology is essentially constructed on the principle that a person possesses an animal rationality. We are the highest of the animal species because we are rational *animals.* We know in a rational way, "*in, and by means of, the senses,*" including the human passions.

Like the rest of the animal genus, for human beings, to sense means to estimate. In his *de Anima* (4, 1) AVICENNA said animals have an internal estimative sense. In his *Summa theologiae* (1, 78, 4, *sed contra*) AQUINAS applies this insight to elaborate on human nature as man possessing an estimative intelligence (particular or cogitative reason) capable of estimating with an animal intelligence danger, threat, risk. Based on the scholarship of REDPATH, in this chapter, we were able to develop a confluence of practical reason, the habit of prudence and the cogitative sense (estimative soul) and develop the practical concept of "estimative intelligence."

Subsequently, we established development and application of estimative intelligence to be the essential leadership power of an executive-exemplar, especially in terms of organizational decision-making and risk-taking in difficult and often-threatening, contingent situations. We also paid attention to the interaction between estimative intelligence and the need for a leader to master the passions in order to deliberate and make rational, moral decisions and take rational risks. Finally, we applied mastery of the passions and the propelling and contending passions over extended periods of time engaged in organizational difficult and arduous individual and team activities.

Chapter Six: The Big, Enlightened Soul

Thomistic faculty behavioral psychology of soulful leadership was further clarified as *virtus* (Latin word meaning "strength"). We claimed that *virtus* is an essential perfecting of the exemplar leader and followers for peak performance.

Simply put, we explained the dynamics by which, chiefly under the influence of excellent estimative intelligence and the moral virtue of prudence, virtuous moral habits enhance leadership's capacity for peak rational and moral decision-making, problem-solving, strategic-planning, tactical-execution, and continuous-peak-performance of operational activities. We referred to these moral virtues with the acronym HEFT, ("H" sands for habits of justice," E," for prudence, particular reason, and the cogitative sense (we defined as estimative intelligence), "F" is for fortitude, and "T" is for temperance).

By returning to a faculty, behavioral-genus of virtuous habits and molar behavior, we established that the neo-behavioral principle of WILLIAM BAUM'S theory of molar behavior is compatible with a Thomistic organizational, faculty-behavioral psychology. We proposed that BAUM's principle of molar behavior as bouts, or episodes, of activities nested in a behavioral genus over time is most useful for locating leadership and worker moral activities within a virtue genus using methods of qualitative and quantitative observation of virtuous activity over time.

Finally, as in chapter one, we stated that the dissertation is not an exercise in *speculative*, organizational science. Even though we used many references, research, and case studies taken from for-profit business that the study of organizational soulful leadership is applied to profit, nonprofit, and government organizations, we stressed that *this thesis is chiefly a study of the practical function of the executive soulful leader and the diffusion and emulation of exemplar leadership throughout an organization*. In the process, in the age of disruptive organization, we analyzed the transformational style of Pope Francis executive leadership of the Roman Catholic Church; and, in the final chapter, we presented a case study on the entrepreneurial style of Adam Hamilton of the United Methodist Church of the Resurrection (the largest Methodist church in the USA). As a result, from the many different ways we have considered in which modern organizational science examines the structure and functioning of the emerging organization in the disruptive age, we have reasonably concluded that a Thomistic organizational psychology of exemplar, soulful leadership is more compatible than any other known teaching with a visionary and intellectually-sound learning philosophy and psychology of contemporary organizational leadership.

Conclusion Summary

The primary purpose of this dissertation has been to address organizational, soulful leadership from the perspective of a Thomistic, organizational, faculty-behavioral-psychology. The topic was approached despite the obvious, foremost, difficulty that no previous Thomistic, philosophical-psychological research had existed on the subject of a Thomistic, organizational, behavioral psychology of soulful, organizational leadership. Since the 19th century Thomistic neo-scholastics had developed a Thomistic rational psychology. This neo-scholastic psychology was firmly grounded on a Thomistic, faculty-of-soul psychology.

With the development of modern, experimental psychology, the soul was dismissed as a proximate principle of an understanding of human psychology. While 19th–century, Neoscholastic, Thomistic rational psychologists had a strong desire for a synthesis of rational and modern psychology, this objective of a robust application of rational and empirical psychology did not happen. Eventually, coming into the 1960s, even among Catholic, academic, and practicing, professional psychologists, the soul was dismissed as the foundational principle of psychological research and practice. Therefore, the paramount challenge of this dissertation has been to construct a Thomistic, organizational, faculty-behavioral psychology with the faculties of the soul as proximate first principles of an organizational, faculty, behavioral psychology.

Since a synthesis of Thomistic, rational and empirical psychology never came to realization, mainly over the issue of the faculties of the soul as a foundation for a science of human behavior. It was argued that, even to the present day, the best approach to entering into a trading zone (transitional genus) with the principles and methods of scientific psychology is by avoiding all expressions of past, present, and future introspective psychology, and brain mentalism; and turning to a trading zone transitional genus with teleological, behavioral principles and Aristotelian-Thomistic faculties-of-soul psychology.

We presented concisely and evaluated the principles and practices of the discipline of empirical organizational psychology from the work of E. SCHEIN. As one of the founders of organizational psychology, he defined the discipline as a multi-perspective, incorporating theory and principles of human and organizational psychology from different social science schools. He also had established five domains of scientific inquiry for organizational psychology: 1) the individual and the organization, 2) motivation and assumptions about human nature, 3) leadership and participation, 4) groups and organizations, and 5) organizational structure and dynamics.

In this dissertation, as the title of "Soulful Organizational Leadership" indicates, the focus was on the topic of executive leadership and organizational, follower participation. Throughout the chapters, we touched on issues of organizational motivation, the Aristotelian-Thomistic assumption about the rational-moral nature of human character in organizational settings, and the changing nature of organizational structure in disruptive environments. Yet all organizational topics of investigation continuously returned to the dominant factor of the thesis: (the nature of the executive function of soulful leadership and the diffusion of executive leadership as an exemplar of virtuous rational and moral character throughout the organization).

Most important was to establish that a fundamental disagreement exists about the nature of an empirical and Thomistic, organizational psychology of soulful leadership. The basic difference is that Thomistic organizational psychology is grounded on an ARISTOTELIAN-THOMISITIC metaphysics of human nature and organization. Since empirical organizational psychology does not claim a metaphysical foundation, or a meta-philosophical foundation, empirical psychology approaches the study of organizational behavior as a method of skill-set instrumentalism.

Consequently, we established that, without a premodern ARISTOTELIAN-THOMISTIC metaphysics of organization and a faculty psychology, the concept of executive leadership competence becomes defined as skill-set leadership competencies. *The practice of skill-set Instrumentalism generally portrays individuals' and groups' strategic expertise in reaching their goals as independent of the kinds of persons they are. Strategies, techniques, methods, skill sets, and so on are spoken of as tools that can be acquired by anyone with the resources to do so.*

Furthermore, we brought attention to the inadequacy of empirical organizational psychology to respond to the cultural, pejorative perception of profit and nonprofit organizations as under the influence of "toxic leadership," where individuals and groups are increasingly confronted with workplace narcissism caused by leadership. For example, the U.S. Army defines toxic leaders as those who put their own needs first, micromanage subordinates, periodically behave in a mean-spirited manner, and display poor decision-making.

The argument was made that empirical organizational psychology is not prepared to respond to the anxiety and boredom of workers who feel disengaged from their organization because of a lack for existential spiritual meaning in, as DURKHEIM held, a culture of moral erosion. We defined and described the concept of the "small dark soul." of an organization which is really a term about the dark side leadership character of the organization. The "dark soul and dark side" metaphors were used to describe an organization where individuals experience an everyday sense that this organization does not respect and treat its people well.

Special attention was given to the demotivating leadership of the "Narcisstic Toxic Leader." Furthermore, we expanded the concept of dark-side leadership by studies from psychologists, CONRAD BAARS, MANFRED F. R. KETS DE VRIES, and KAREN HORNEY. HORNEY described authoritarian and corporate settings as controlled by leaders who are the self-centered, perfectionist, un-empathetic, manipulative personality types of the modern age. DE VRIES thoughts referred to the "dark side" of leadership as the Darth Vader aspect of leadership which grows out of personality traits such as narcissism, self-deceit and abuse of power and leaders are unwilling to face and acknowledge their weaknesses. BAARS'S writings were about the individuals in authority and the neurotic fear of the feelings of failure and inappropriate behavioral defense mechanisms.

ALBERT Z. CARR was presented as representative of a hard-driving, competitive, business-culture philosophy of the American 1960s to the present: a psychology and ethics built on the principle that business is like a poker game. Everyone involved in business knows that it is a game where bluffing is expected. Therefore, the norms of good and bad conduct of everyday social morality are different in business.

Business develops its own species of ethics. CARR represented the school of executive thinking that the business of business is making a profit. Making a profit is the primary function of executive responsibility and leadership. Consequently, it requires a skillset, instrumental, behavioral psychology. Executives and leaders must have the values and skills that support the organizational purpose of profit by means of organizational goal setting, efficient and effective co-operation, and co-ordination, of human and non-human resources.

We established a Thomistic organizational psychology of soulful leadership as the most suitable psychology to respond to the ever-present threat of a dark soul, dysfunctional, pathological organizational behavior. For this reason, we introduced the observations of organizational consultants Roger LEWIN and Birute REGINE from their book, *Soul at Work.* They did not approach the phenomena of the leadership and the absence of the soul as a philosophical or theological issue. They refer to the soul as metaphor for careful interactions, instead of we could not care less about others. The soul at work is a double-entendre metaphor for an individual's soul being truly engaged in the workplace, and the emergence of the collective soul of the organization.

We presented two contradictory metaphors of the "dark soul" and "soulful" organizational leadership. The emerging Thomistic, organizational psychology of chapter two reconstructed the organizational psychology of leadership of three recognized foundational scholars of the science of organizational management: CHESTER I. BARNARD, W. EDWARDS DEMING, and PETER DRUCKER. We, also, established a link between Thomistic organizational psychology and the Japanese school of knowledge management and the spiral of knowledge.

We addressed BARNARD as the original thinker of an organization as a structural-functional system. Heavily influenced in his thinking by Talcott PARSON's sociological structural functional systems theory, Barnard adapted this structural-functional theory to an organizational structure maintained by three basic interacting systems of 1) communication, 2) co-ordination, and 3) co-operation. While BARNARD was a philosopher of organization and author, he was mainly a practitioner as president of New Jersey Bell Telephone. Pertaining to insights on the nature of executive exemplar leadership, the organizational diffusion of leadership and emulation of exemplar character, his major work, *The Functions of the Executive*, was critical to chapter two and throughout other chapters.

Because of his principles on the function of the executive, BARNARD'S earlier thinking was crucial to the construction of a Thomistic organizational psychology. BARNARD remains unique in his organizational philosophy of executive leadership in his first principle of "the executive responsibility for the moral rectitude of the organization." While BARNARD does not approach the executive function as an ARISTOTELIAN-THOMISTIC organizational psychologist, in many ways, he shares the reflections and principles that blend with moral psychologist PETER A. REDPATH'S work *The Moral Psychology of St. Thomas Aquinas: An Introduction to Ragamuffin Ethics.* From this full title of REDPATH'S work, from the metaphor of the "Ragamuffin," we learned of the affinity between REDPATH and BARNARD.

REDPATH'S Ragamuffin metaphor is about a Thomistic organizational and moral psychology of contending, flourishing, adapting, ordering, and organizing in a concrete, every day, promising-yet-arduous environment of technical doing and rational, moral decision-making behavior. Barnard went so far as to insist that the basic responsibility of the executive function is to accept the responsibility for the moral rectitude of the concrete, everyday technical-moral activities of workers and leaders.

According to BARNARD, the main responsibility of executive leadership is the right rational-moral ordering of the organization. For BARNARD the organizational system of co-ordination, co-operation, and communication requires continuous, daily, leadership attention. Because leadership always involves moral focus, executive leadership involves more than technical attention. For BARNARD, like DEMING and DRUCKER, moral rectitude is not achieved by implementation of ethical-type systems as taught in MBA programs. Nor is it a matter of human-resource-monitoring and policy statements. It is a matter of moral conviction and leadership. As did DEMING and DRUCKER, BARNARD believed in the innate, noble character of leaders and workers. Consequently, the responsibility of executive leadership is to oversee hiring and nurturing of morally good people and to recognize among them those with the aptitude for leadership.

As argued throughout this dissertation, if we are to understand the nature of organizational leadership, we must start with the executive function. In chapter two, we maintained that a psychology of leadership is grounded on an ARISTOTELIAN-THOMISTIC metaphysics of organization. A critical principle of such a metaphysics is an equality of inequality: a principle that holds for an insistence of a clear order of leadership and authority in an organization. Again, like DEMING and DRUCKER, BARNARD knew only too well that the quality and style of leadership and mode of authority is established at the executive level.

While BARNARD was a structural functionalist organizational scientist, he had a belief in the nobility of the executive character. In this dissertation, we have taken BARNARD's insistence that the essence of the executive function is the creative ability to comprehend the moral aspects of technical decisions. If an organization hopes for long-term success, such success will depend primarily on an executive leadership and diffusion of such leadership of "creative moral" comprehension and concrete practice. The diffusion of this mode of leadership occurs mainly as a result of worker-followers emulation of the creative morality of leaders and supervisors. These creative leaders are selected and mentored for leadership because of their proven creative moral character. This is a Thomistic psychology of leadership that we developed: *a virtuous-exemplar, executive-leadership character,* and a *follower-behavioral- emulation.*

The same philosophy constituted of a moral psychology is found in DEMING and DRUCKER. As much as he appreciated sociology, BARNARD had maintained the social sciences were far too general and academically esoteric for purposes of exemplar leadership. He called for a commonsense, every day, practical knowledge: a behavioral knowledge. Nowhere is this more indispensable than in the executive arts. He saw that organizations needed leadership knowledge nurtured by persistent, habitual experience and what is often called "intuitive behavior." In chapters three to six we have outlined and explained that BARNARD's search for an organizational, behavioral psychology is best found in a Thomistic organizational, faculty-behavioral-psychology of executive leadership.

We held and defended that a Thomistic organizational psychology is applicable to profit, non-profit, and governmental agencies. We noted that organizational life has an incredible impact on a person's individual and social identity. Increasingly, it shapes one's personal identity and sense of personal worth. We pointed to the reflections of ROBERT FOGEL that organizational life has become essential to the Western sense of self-realization. Also, as technology changes with the reduction of the number of work hours and early retirement, nonprofit organizations will become more in need of outstanding exemplar leadership. In chapter two we introduced that, presently, both the nature of the organizational structure and leadership are in the process of major transformation. Therefore, the approach of a Thomistic organizational psychology is the appropriate response to the emerging organizational structure and the nature of emerging leadership.

We presented REDPATH's concept of a *Ragamuffin Ethics*, and established principles from REDPATH'S Aristotelian-Thomistic metaphysics of organization. Because the Ragamuffin is always contending with a rational-moral sense understanding of the reality of causation, order, and organization, for REDPATH, the Ragamuffin philosophical metaphysician is not a logician. He examines the nature of things that stimulate his/her senses to wonder and draw forth the powers of his /her intellect, will, and emotions to examine the utility of things. He/she is concerned primarily with the probing into the causes of things. The Ragamuffin philosopher wants to know how this and that relates to each other and why this and that are in a group. ARISTOTLE and the Greek philosophers are, above all else, driven in wonder to observe and, by means of inductive reasoning know, the order, organization, of nature from the perspective of the problem of the one and the many. As we quoted REDPATH:

> "All reasoning, right as well as wrong, starts with, presupposes, some organizational whole that we know; with an induction of some chief relation that harmonizes, orders, some disparate multitude into being parts of a whole that we immediately, recognize!"[667]

We strongly contended that, to achieve perfection, a Thomistic organizational psychology of the executive leadership function must have an Aristotelian-Thomistic metaphysical organizational foundation. For the greater part, REDPATH had introduced this approach to this metaphysical foundation. Therefore, we read Thomistic metaphysics through the eyeglasses of a moral philosophical psychology.

Because he/she wants to live and lead by first principles, a metaphysics-of-organization-philosopher wonders about first principles. While the science of

---

[667] REDPATH, *Moral Psychology of St. Thomas*, 214

metaphysics is often perceived as the most esoteric of the philosophical disciplines, such an identity is not the case with ARISTOTELIAN-THOMISTIC metaphysics as presented in this dissertation.

We argue a realistic and common-sense metaphysical philosopher immediately has the metaphysical sense that happiness, human flourishing, and organizational excellence require some knowledge of the highest and universal principles of perfection: *perfect operation*. Therefore, we refer to this as the executive exemplar character of "touching the divine." We proposed the claim that the executive exemplar has a metaphysical sense of wisdom. We stressed that we are talking about a realist sense of wisdom. It is not a sense of wisdom that a person gets from an MBA degree from Harvard or Wharton. We used the example of Herb Kelleher the founder and Chief Executive Officer of Southwest Airlines as the exemplar executive with a metaphysical sense of the one and the many in the strategic and concrete daily activities of business.

Executive leadership, as expressed by Kelleher in chapter three, is a vast mosaic of a thousand pieces put together daily. It comes from the heart and the head. He maintains that followers cannot long emulate a leader they do not perceive as authentic. No such thing as programmatic leadership exists for Kelleher because he considers leadership essentially to be about communication and mutual participation in a common good.

It is to diffuse throughout the organization, as a great entrepreneur, leader, Kelleher believes that it has to be of the fabric of the soul. Alongside Kelleher's teaching about the importance of organizational leadership as a fabric of the executive's soul, we turned attention to Aristotelian scholar JOE SACKS and his brilliant phenomenological description of the existential experience of the soul.

We continued to develop a reconstruction of BARNARD's philosophy of organization along the lines of a Thomistic organizational psychology and metaphysics of organization. BARNARD maintained that the executive function required individuals who have a special gift of an intellectual sensing of the aesthetic and moral sense of fitness of the organization. We emphasized that BARNARD's description of the aesthetic and moral sensing executive was more completely explained in terms of REDPATH's concept of the truly wise leader with a metaphysical grasp of the fundamental universal principles of organizational leadership and participation. Chapter three proposed the argument that an exemplar executive leader is one who has a metaphysical sense of organizational wisdom, albeit it might be a tacit knowledge.

In the case study "Touching the Divine" and the teachings of the rowing coach philosopher George Pocock and the novel *Boys in the Boat* by John Rantz, we gave an existential description of the metaphysical organizational sense of participation in its intensive greatness: "touching the divine." When grasped for its metaphysical, organizational, psychological significance, this case study allowed for a most powerful, concise, and accurate definition of exemplar leadership. The exemplar leader is the person who leads the members of the organization in all their affairs in the habit of continuously to touch the divine. Furthermore, the *virtus* (power) of this executive is what is emulated, as a result the character of rational-moral goodness and constancy of purpose that diffuses throughout an organization.

We explained the necessity of a metaphysics of organization with special emphasis on: 1) the fact that a "wise person knows the essential principle of the one and the many (part/whole relations) that generate this or that organization"; 2) the organizational principle of equality of inequality; 3) the coordination and communication of opposites (principle of contrariety); 4) within the organizational whole (genus and members) an existential participation in the diffusion of rational-moral goodness and executive leadership; and 5) the Thomistic principle of metaphysical participation (virtual quantity).

Sections 7 C. and 8 of chapter three gave special attention to the crucial issue of virtual quantity. In line with REDPATH'S insistence on the importance of the Thomistic metaphysics of virtual quantity we focused on the way to measure quantity of virtue (*quantitas virtutis*) within an organization. We also gave attention to O'ROURKE, *Pseudo-Dionysius and the Metaphysic of Aquinas,* and CROWLEY, O.P., *Aristotelian-Thomistic Philosophy of Measure and the International System of Units.* Like REDPATH, O'ROURKE and CROWLEY develop AQUINAS'S teaching on the virtual intensity of being as it applies to organizational leadership. In section 7C. we discussed the work of CROWLEY and its significance to the measurement of an organization's capacity to receive organizational greatness: perfection of its form, organizational existence, unity, and action.

The capacity to receive greatness of organizational form became crucial in chapters four and five, as we developed the principles and methods of a Thomistic organizational faculty-behavioral-psychology. On the issue of organizational measurement of virtual intensity, we brought attention to CHRISTIAN MADSBERG'S thinking on organizational sense-making and suggested CROWLEY'S measurement of virtual intensity is of importance in an age of statistical engineering, huge base datamining, and power algorithms.

The changing nature of emerging organizational structures in the modern world was examined. We used the term "modern" primarily in terms of organizational structure and psychology of leadership in the present and into the future. We did not use "modern" in terms of the organization as influenced by modern enlightenment philosophy. Different organizational and management scientists use various cultural concepts to describe evolving organizational structure and psychology of leadership as adapting to the impact of the Information Age, the Digital Age, Age of the Emerging Organization, or the Disruptive Age.

In chapter two, we suggested that western culture is moving from the Industrial Age organization to the Awakening Spiritual Age. We explained this movement as a humanistic, philosophical, and cultural quest for a spirituality of self-realization. This quest for self-realization is having, and will continue to have, incredible impact on how workers and organizational volunteers consider the existential meaning of work and organizational commitment. We maintained that self-realization in the workplace is one of the most important contexts in which people come together daily to accomplish what they cannot do on their own, that is to realize their full potential as human beings.

We then developed the proposition that we live in an age of a most puzzling paradox. On one hand, we are observing an increasing skepticism regarding traditional institutions of spiritual and moral formation; and, at the same time, we are looking for a new mode of spiritual self-realization in the workplace, and in political and volunteer organizations. Therefore, we concluded that today is essentially a disruptive age. Because it is driven by information-digital technology, machine learning artificial intelligence, and statistical engineers analyzing huge data sets of thin data looking for thick-narrative and spiritual meaning with robotic advisors, for leaders to understand this disruptive age is extremely difficult. At the same time, we are looking for a new mode of humanistic spirituality and organizational flourishing. Therefore, we addressed the consequences for executive leadership of facing a digital disruptive-spiritual-quest-generation and the need for a Thomistic faculty-behavioral psychology.

A disruptive age is an environment that easily lends itself to deconstructive, skeptical nihilism of the post-modernist. However, we argued, an element of truth exists in the ultra-modernistic rejection of the enlightenment modernistic assumptions that have shaped the industrial bureaucratic organization. In chapters two and three we started to explain why a Thomistic organizational psychology of leadership is the most proper, fitting, response to the disruptive-spiritual-quest-organization issued in by the paradoxical, digital, disruptive age. Furthermore, we suggested that organizational development requires an executive level of leadership grounded on a post-postmodern Thomistic organizational-moral psychology: precisely put, a premodern Aristotelian-Thomisitic organizational solution.

Paradoxical is that speedy, machine-learning, digital technology, the quest for humanistic-spiritual meaning, and responding to competitive disruptive forces impacting profit, non-profit and governmental organizations are requiring leaders to make decisions and work smarter, harder, and faster. The preceding sentence is composed of an important choice of words. The mindset of working harder and longer was a common mindset of the authoritarian bureaucrat of the pre-digital age. While, like their predecessors, digital age executives and employees have to work hard and sometimes extremely hard, in the disruptive age, as individuals and teams, for leaders and followers the challenge is to also work much smarter than ever was required in the past. To work faster, harder, and smarter with the support of unbelievably fast digital technology requires every day, virtuous-exemplar leadership. To achieve this blend of hard-to-extremely-hard-and-always-smart (never making a mistake) activity requires a new mode of executive-distributed leadership.

Workers have to be especially rationally-and-morally trustworthy about their commitments, promises, and tasks. They must be highly trusted as team players. Most of all, more than in the pre-digital age, leaders and followers must be trusted to exercise common sense. This trust issue is a reciprocal rational-moral bond between the executive leaders and the followers. For this reason, we wrote of the executive leader as the exemplar in the manner of Herb Kelleher of Southwest Airlines. We believe that the more successful profit and non-profit organizations will move to a distributed, decentralized, leadership practice in which increased operational and decision-making authority will have to be given to down-the-line leaders, supervisors, and teams.

At the same time, since we proposed a Thomistic organizational psychology grounded on a metaphysics of organization, we hold to the principle of equality of inequality. Thomistic organizational psychology maintains that executive leadership in the contemporary disruptive age must be based upon a respected command and control voice of harmony, rooted in a moral code of prudent decision-making, *commutative and distributive justice*, and respect for workers' rational and moral participation in accomplishing the organizational aim.

Given the requirements of harder, faster, and smarter decision-making and effective and efficient execution of tactical operations, absolutely necessary is to have the command and control leadership authority in the digital disruptive environment where executive authority and leadership is decentralized and prudently and justly distributed. This distributed command and control organization depends on the commitment of a rational moral authority based on faculties-of-the-soul psychology that was opened up in greater detail in chapters five and six.

There we introduced and clearly defined from AQUINAS'S *Commentary on the Nicomachean Ethics* that the executive leader must be known and emulated as a virtuous person. The virtuous person leading by virtuous habits must serve as exemplar of habits of behavior for all levels of leadership. Chapter four focused on the current concern by organizational psychologists for education of individuals and teams in distributed leadership as it relates to the practice of sensemaking by individual leaders and teams.

We identified the current theory and importance of organizional sensemaking by empirical organizational psychologists. A paradox of the digital, disruptive age is that, even more so than in prior times, the faster, harder, an organization moves does not mean it necessarily becomes smarter. We argued with other organizational psychologists that executive-to-on-the-line-level leadership demands education in leader-team sensemaking. Furthermore, the digital-disruptive economy requires continuous need for a diffusion of leadership sensemaking.

We discussed empirical organizational psychology's approach to sensemaking, and we found much of the practice is based on the concept of "intuition." Then, from the perspective of a Thomistic psychology, we recommended that a Thomistic understanding of inductive reasoning, particular reason, and knowledge of first principles is a much more intelligible and robust method of sensemaking. We defined Thomistic sensemaking as "organizational common sensemaking;" and proposed it as a more suitable psychological option for contemporary leadership and team formation. After establishing a Thomistic definition and inductive method of common sensemaking, we put forth the concept that, aside from being a moral exemplar, an exemplar leader must be known and respected for his/her mastery of the subject domain pertaining to their organization. We defined and described it as the practice of a craft knowledge required for executive leadership.

We identified the shift from a modernistic, bureaucratic organization of a top-down hierarchy of centralized authority, decision-making, stable-and-specialized classification of roles, standardized processes, and routines to a more flattened hierarchical organization of decentralized authority and decision-making; fast, smart teamwork; and flexible, orderly, tactics and processes. This change in basic organizational structural assumptions was identified as the major opposition of evolving, organizational, executive leadership in the post-modernistic organizational era: the "hierarchical-heterarchical tension."

We presented evolving organizational definitions of individual and team accountability, relationships; leader-follower roles and boundaries; work process and composition; and performance criteria and reward. In responding to this hierarchical-heterarchical tension we upheld that a Hierarchical-Heterarchical Organizational Contrariety (H-H O C) is the fundamental opposition for executive exemplar leadership. As developed in chapters four, five, and six, to operate with utmost perfection, we maintained that this H-HOC tension requires a Thomistic, organizational, faculty-behavioral-psychology.

A profound issue of leadership exists behind this H-HOC tension and the required emerging- executive-function and diffusion of virtuous leadership character. In addition, need exists for a rational-moral bond of trust between the executive and down-the-line levels of leadership. This deeper bond is based on technical and moral trust that allows for an increase in decentralized decision-making; operational design; work monitoring and measurement; employee assessment; tactical strategy; and goal setting participation. Understanding this emerging hierarchical-heterarchical paradigm, we argued, requires a more profound grasp of a metaphysics of organization as one of desired and emerging order.

Supported by long-term systems theory and field research of a wide and varied base of organizations over an extended period of time, the IBM systems research division concluded that organizational science has turned to a new awareness of complexity science and the dynamics of contrary states of "desired order" and "emergent order." They maintained that KANT had separated things that can be known empirically from things that are the province of God. In so doing, supposedly, KANT had helped to section of all-but-efficient causes to epiphenomena that could be safely ignored. Fueled by the positivism of COMTE and the advances in physics and biology, a social science [sociology] developed, maintaining the theoretical possibility of discovering laws like those of physics that could explain the behavior of people in societies. Because of the Kantian-Comte impact on the science of society, they described the growth of a management science as incapable of understanding, let alone responding to, the issue of organizational chaos and emerging organization.

We proposed that AQUINAS'S metaphysics of organizations accommodates both an all-powerful God and free human beings. With AQUINAS'S general observation that all the beings we perceive are limited in their being, are organizational wholes, he strikes a surprisingly modern insight that not only regard human free will but the whole of creation, including its material aspect that possess relative autonomy from God. In terms of an organizational whole, an opposition of desired order and emergent order always exists.

St. Thomas's *Summa Contra Gentiles* (3, 74) is foundational to his argument of fortune and chance (organizational randomness) as a fundamental challenge to the executive leadership of a system. Based on the IBM Cynefin study, we predicted five emerging forces that will continue to cause disruptive change in society, profit, and non-profit organization the forces are:

1. Exponential pattern of technological change: Disruptions caused by technological breakthroughs and rapid adoption of new technology will bring job loss and skill obsolescence.

2. Social and organizational reconfiguration: Increased autonomy and decision-making authority, structured social networks, and work organization and less hierarchy. Employment based on highly team-oriented purposeful descriptions.

3. All-inclusive, more diverse, talent market: Minority segments will become majorities. Leadership style will respond to varied cultural preferences in policies, practices and worker engagements, reward, and benefits.

4. A truly connected world: Information is more abundant and available to everyone. Digital media will enable seamless global real-time communication. Shorter go-to-market and product development strategies will increasingly develop.

5. Human and machine collaboration: Analytics, algorithms, and artificial intelligence will solve harder, smarter, and faster market/sales, customer service and operations problems, and enable humans to become faster and smarter at making harder decisions.

Having established that powerful technological, social, cultural, and environmental forces are changing the structure of organizations and executive leadership to the often-called flat organization of decentralized team authority and decision-making, we described the situation as the hierarchical-heterarchical tension. We then proposed that an emerging responsibility is the blending between the contrary tension of maintaining a command and control hierarchical-heterarchical authority.

/

Furthermore, the deeper and more pressing issue for profit and non-profit organizations is that the executive function is responsible for leading their organizations as adaptive systems in the age of the disruptive economy. No longer is it possible to look upon organizations as well-structured and mechanical functioning pyramids of desired order. In the disruptive age, under executive leadership, organizations are structured as dynamic systems ready to respond to emergent order that has become the new normal for organizational success. Increasing need exists for organizational structures and leadership designed to exist and adapt to the dialectical tension of the desire and emergent order.

In section 5.4 of chapter five, we began to focus more precisely on the exact nature of a Thomistic, organizational, faculty-behavioral-psychology of executive leadership and the diffusion by means of follower-emulation and structured formal and informal social learning. We proposed the thesis necessarily constructing a Thomistic organizational, faculty-behavioral psychology as a better alternative to modernistic empirical organizational psychology.

We eventually presented 10 Core teachings of a Thomistic faculty behavioral-psychology, especially behavior and the internal senses with special emphasis on the cogitative sense that REDPATH expands into a confluence of the practical intellect and particular reason. This confluence of faculties was defined as estimative intelligence as it relates especially to the irascible appetite and decision-making behavior under arduous contingent situations. Basically, we presented REDPATH's brilliant confluence of the faculties of the soul as they relate to behavior as compatible with recent neo-behaviorists HOLT, BAUM, and the Aristotelian teleological-behaviorist RACHLIN.

In terms of a Thomistic, organizational behavioral-faculty-psychology we paid special attention to the nature of the concupiscible and irascible passion. Following what REDPATH says in *The Moral Wisdom of St. Thomas,* we referred to the concupiscible as the "propelling passions" and the irascible as the "contending passions." Modern empirical psychology uses the terminology of emotions instead of passions; but we suggested that advantages exist to the terminology of the passions, especially when explaining the intensity of the dynamics of organizational psychology.

We used an important case study "The Mann Gulch Disaster" that appears in several texts on organizational leadership and psychology. This is a case study used to examine organizational sensemaking when organizations enter into states of extreme, emergent disorder that falls into chaos. The case describes the disintegration of desired order when leaders and followers are no longer able to engage in team sensemaking under chaotic conditions.

We used this case chiefly to introduce the importance of the Thomistic confluence of the faculties of the soul in emergent situations where desired order under contingent situations disintegrates. From this case study, we continued to develop the theory of exemplar leaders and extreme teams as individuals most capable of responding to contingent-and-emerging, arduous challenges over long time periods. We called this ability of individual leaders and teams entering into a state of contending passions over time the "Contending Behavioral Zone" (CBZ).

In line with the contending behavioral zone, from the Aristotelian neo-behaviorist RACHLIN, we proposed the notion of a "meta-discriminative stimulus" We explained that RACHLIN's concept of the meta-discriminative stimulus was compatible with the Thomistic concept of the "formal object" as a stimulus of individual, and team, organizational behavior. As a result, we paid careful attention to elucidating the organizational vision as an organizational formal object and meta-discriminative stimulus. We continued this investigation of vision into chapter six.

As much as we agreed with empirical psychologists that, for a more meaningful and moral environment, contemporary organizations must direct attention to emerging expressions, we contended that emerging schools of organizational psychology represent a psychology grounded on a modernistic HUMEAN-ROUSSEAUIAN social science of moral psychology, constructed on the Rousseauian error of the "Disordered Will."

The Rousseauian error is that the first principle of the organizational diffusion of unity and meaning is achieved by "the revelation of enthusiastic feeling" that drives the individual and organizational will. *On the contrary, we proposed the Thomistic solution that, because the vision is the formal object and meta-discriminative stimulus that is, by nature, in intense harmony with (proportionate to, naturally suitable for) the rational, behavioral faculties of souls of the organizational leaders and followers, a human organization naturally moves toward union with the proper end and perfection of its virtual intensity inclination.* This issue is a fundamental one that clearly differentiates Thomistic organizational and moral psychology from empirical, social-scientific, organizational, and moral psychology.

We established that the main task of a Thomistic, faculty, behavioral psychology of leadership is elucidation of *virtus*, which essentially involves perfecting the exemplar leaders and followers for peak performance. Simply put, we explained the dynamics by which the virtuous habits of the moral virtues enhance the leadership's capacity for: 1) peak rational and moral decision making, 2) problem solving, 3) strategic planning, 4) tactical execution, and 5) continuous peak performance of operational activities. Throughout this chapter, we continued the insistence of this dissertation that the primary responsibility of the executive function of an organization is preservation and guidance of organizational rational moral rectitude.

We maintained an organization may have short-term success with a utilitarian, crafty leadership; but the long-term success demands a virtuous, exemplar leadership at the helm. An imposed Kantian type of management ethics of duty and human-resource monitoring does not provide the necessary organizational faculty psychology, everyday virtuous habits of prudence, justice, fortitude, and temperance that contemporary organizations crucially need. Once again, we identified these virtues with the anacronym HEFT: "H" is habits of justice prudence. "E" stands for prudence, particular reason, and the cogitative sense (the combination of which we defined as "estimative intelligence"), "F" signifies fortitude and "T" represents temperance.

We explained how these virtuous habits (HEFT) especially enhance executive decision-making and problem solving. Furthermore, we concluded the final chapter by returning to a transitional, faculty-behavioral genus of virtuous habits and molar behavior. We proposed that the behavioral principles of BAUM's neo-behavioristic theory of molar behavior are compatible with a Thomistic, organizational, faculty-behavioral-psychology. We proposed that BAUM's principle of molar behavior as bouts of activities nested in a behavioral genus over time is most useful for nesting leadership activities and worker activities within a virtue genus, using methods of qualitative observation and quantitative measurement of virtue behavioral activity over time.

The chief aim of this dissertation has been to study and set forth a psychology of organizational leadership based on a Thomistic, organizational, faculty-behavioral psychology. While we have dedicated much of the dissertation to defining and explaining the nature of a soulful organizational leadership, we are primarily concerned with proposing an approach to an application of a Thomistic psychology of organizational leadership. Many theories of organizational leadership have been developed in organizational and management sciences today. Also, growing numbers of leadership-training and certifications sprung up. Many books have been written on the topic by academics and consultants that offer well-developed, applied theories and methodologies about leadership.

In this dissertation, on many levels, we have explained the uniqueness of a Thomistic psychology of the soul (faculty-behavioral psychology) as it applies to organizational leadership. The uniqueness of a Thomistic solution to the issue of organizational leadership is based on two fundamental and crucial issues that differentiate a Thomistic, organizational, faculty-behavioral psychology of leadership from empirical and organizational psychology. One, in some depth, we explained in the dissertation that a Thomistic, organizational psychology is more accurately known as a Thomistic, organizational, faculty-behavioral psychology. Two, an organizational psychology of leadership must be grounded on Thomistic metaphysical principles of organization and Thomistically-understood rational-moral order that takes into consideration how particular, or cogitative, reason functions to help generate prudential leadership within individuals and corporate leaders.

The dissertation, grounding leadership on a metaphysics of organization and faculty-behavioral psychology, is basically about the applied, craft knowledge of experienced leadership. The executive-exemplar's function is to lead as the most virtuous practitioner of the craft of leadership. The exemplar-leader in his/her organizational activities must express the soul of the exemplar, virtuous leader. From a Thomistic perspective we have made clear in this dissertation that executive-exemplar leadership is not a matter of acquired functional skillsets. Exemplar leaders are not the result of training work sessions on leadership or classroom education. We have argued that exemplars are leaders who elect to lead as persons of virtuous, especially of prudential and just, character. Most crucially, exemplars are leaders who have made an existential decision to live, work, and lead by virtuous habits, rational principles in touch with reality, and consistent and coherent moral behavior.

Exemplar executive leadership requires a craft-knowledge leader who is a rational, inductive experienced, leader: someone who possesses the intellect and the will to lead as perfectly as possible. In chapter four, section 4.9, we gave much consideration to an Aristotelian-Thomistic craft knowledge. Such knowledge is based on a profound type understanding and application of the inductive reasoning potential of the exemplar practitioner of a craft. We could, also, refer to craft knowledge as a practical knowledge or knowledge of an art. As stressed in the dissertation, the concept of Aristotelian-Thomistic induction is much better at explaining leadership decision-making than is "intuition." The main reason this is so is that Thomistically-understood inductive reasoning is not an emotional feeling. It is an intellectually enriched, sensory habit of the soul that allows the student of a craft to acquire first principles of causation from his/her leadership experiences over time. These principles rest in the psychological constitution of the exemplar leader (chiefly in the intellect, will, intellectual and sense memories, particular reason, and imagination) to constitute a "commonsense rationality" that guide him/her to choose to do the next right thing, in the right way, for the right motive, at the right time. Thomistic organizational principles are causal in that they move the exemplar leader in his/her activities to move the organization toward its purpose, aim, vision on a continuous basis in all promising, contending, and arduous situations. Therefore, we conclude our dissertation with six Thomistic craft leadership principles that should rest in the soul of an exemplar leader.

Craft Knowledge Principle One: An Organizational, Faculty-Behavioral Psychology

With the awareness that, in order to study the nature of organizational, soulful leadership, we must approach the challenge from the perspective of a metaphysics of organization and a Thomistic faculty- behavioral Psychology:

The Thomistic solution to the issue of organizational leadership is grounded on a well-developed Thomistic faculty-behavioral psychology. Therefore, we have articulated an organizational, faculty- behavioral psychology as foundational to the study and practice of soulful leadership.

Craft Knowledge Art Principle Two: Soulless Executive/Soulful Executive and a Return to Virtuous Character

We deliberately began with an examination of the "dark soul." Unfortunately, we seldomly think in terms of organizations as domains of soulfulness. The history of the "soul" in relationship to leaders and workers in organizations is, as a rule, one that has often had pejorative connotations. More frequently expressed and believed is that organizations, especially business and governmental, are perceived as being "soulless" as opposed to "soulful."

Such perceptions and attitudes suggest the sense of workers feelings of discontent with their organizational existence is more often than not justified. We argue that the main reason for soulless, organizational discontent is the result of dark, soulless leadership. We contend that the primary reason for soulless leadership is the lack of properly understood executive leadership. Therefore, the issue of the small, dark-soul organizational syndrome is fundamentally a lack of executive soulful leadership and appropriate attention being paid to nature of personal and organizational virtues required in the character of executive, exemplar leaders.

Craft Knowledge Principle Three: Metaphysical Sense of Organization and Wisdom

Most needed is that the study of organizational soulful leadership be grounded on metaphysical principles and a faculty psychology of the powers and acts of the soul. We focus attention to the issue of metaphysics. Unfortunately, drawing attention to metaphysics as foundational to the study of organizational leadership is unusual, not the norm.

A metaphysics of organization, especially, the topic of organizational, soulful leadership, is fundamental to the understanding and practice of organizational leadership. Furthermore, executive leadership must discover a new respect for a Thomistic metaphysics of organizational leadership that helps accurately to identify and articulate the true nature of soulful leaders. Such a metaphysics is one of order *and participation*: *mutatis mutandis*, exemplars of soulful character must be multiplied throughout in the organizational genus emulated by the members of the organization. To be able to do this, the nature of soulful leaders must first precisely be identified. Only a metaphysics of organization and participation can do this.

Once executive leaders with the prudential moral character master such metaphysical principles, on a daily basis, as exemplar leaders, they can diffuse and amplify virtuous powers of harmony, cooperation, that bring a social group to perfection throughout the organization. This process of diffusion of virtual intensity of organizational power must begin with the soulful executive who has a metaphysical sense of organizational perfection.

Craft Knowledge Principle Four: Common Sensemaking Induction

Exemplar executives must pay special attention to the growing interest in the relationship between leadership and spirituality. Increasingly in the present age, it has become acceptable to refer to leadership in terms of spirituality and the soul at work. This development appears to represent a discontent with the impact of enlightenment "philosophy" upon Western organizational concepts of leadership.

In the search for more spiritual and soulful modes of leadership, in this dissertation we argue that a Thomistic organizational applied psychology of soulful leadership is highly appropriate for the disruptive age.

One of the more interesting phenomena developing in the education of present-day organizational leaders is the attention given to the evolving discipline of leadership and sense-making. There is a recognition that contemporary leaders must have highly developed sense-making abilities. On this issue we argue that empirical psychology and leadership education has an inadequate understanding of the intellect and intuition to generate such sense-making abilities. We maintain that Thomistic faculties-of-soul psychology that we have articulated in this dissertation serves as a much more accurate understanding of common sense-making than does the essentially flawed, soulless, caricatures of such sense-making that currently exist in contemporary empirical psychology and leadership education.

Craft Knowledge Principle Five: The Diffusion of Exemplar and Follower Organizational Learning of Estimative Intelligence and Emotional Master

As any successful executive knows, leadership is about achieving the organizational aim. Every successful leader is a sense realist because, at the very least, he/she has real, physical goals and objectives that need to be satisfied on a daily basis. Since the organizational environment is not predictable, every student of business learns quickly that he/she must lead under the tension of a desired order and an emerging order.

Every organizational leader must, to some extent, daily confront variation, contingencies, and is responsible for the response and control of such variation, contingencies. Leading an organization in conditions of desired and emerging order requires that a leader have a highly developed estimating sense of the soul. This power of the estimating soul is the result of a confluence of internal powers of the soul.

We defined this confluence of estimative powers as an estimative intelligence that is essential to the practical art of soulful organizational leadership. Second, the ability to lead by means of the confluence of the estimative powers of the soul requires a mastery of the faculties of the soul, especially of the human passions.

On a daily basis organizational leadership is challenging. Over extended, arduous periods of time, it is physically and psychologically exhausting. The requirements of decision-making and risk-taking demand mastery of the human passions. We hold that the estimating soul and mastery of the passions is a more crucial factor for soulful leadership than is even an understanding of emotional intelligence. Understanding and nurturing of the proper emotional responses related to estimative intelligence throughout the organization is one of the most valuable and essential leadership virtues in the digital age, where leaders must make decisions and work harder, smarter, and faster than ever before.

Craft Knowledge Principle Six: The Moral-Molar Nested Behavioral HEFT

The exemplar leader is the organizational role-model of virtuous habits. The behavioral dynamics of the moral virtues enhance a leader's capacity for rational and moral decision-making, problem-solving, strategic planning, tactical execution, and operational activities. As opposed to an imposed Kantian type of management top-down ethics of duty and human-resource monitoring, we present an everyday, faculty-behavioral-psychology of soulful leadership based on a unity of the intellectual and moral virtues.

We hold for a trading-zone Thomistic, faculty-behavioral psychology with the work of the neo-behaviorist BAUM's theory of behavior and the observation of molar behavior as compatible with a Thomistic, faculty-behavioral psychology. Most importantly, we will apply this concept of the observation of molar behavior and nesting activities to the moral virtues. We suggest the practice of developing thin and thick data moral-molar observational methods for the continuous improvement of leadership virtuous character and observable organizational activities.

Bibliography

Adler, Mortimer J. *Intellect Mind Over Matter* (New York: Macmillan Publishing Company, 1990).

_____. *The Time of Our Lives* (New York: Fordham University Press, 1996)

_____. *Desires Right & Wrong, The Ethics of Enough* (Mount Jackson, VA 2282: Axios Press, 1991).

Agor, Weston H. *Intuition in Organizations, Leading and Managing Productively* (Newbury London New Delhi: Sage Publications, 1989).

_____. *The Logic of Intuitive Decision Making, A Research-Based Approach for Top Management* (New Work: Quorum Books,1986).

Ajanwachukwu, Okoro Edward. "Reason as the Guide in Human Action: Aquinas' Ethics," ISOR journal of Humanities and Social Science Volume 20, issue 10 Ver. III (Oct. 2015): 61-66.

Alaa, Ghada. "Derivation of Factors Facilitating Organizational Emergence Based on Complex Adaptive Systems and Social Autopoiesis Theories," *E:CO issue* Vol.11 No. 1 (2009): 19-34.

Allers, Rudolf. *The Psychology of Character* (New York: Sheed & Ward, 1939)

Álvarez, Mar. Echavarría, Martín, F. and VITZ Paul C. "A psycho-ethical approach to personality disorders: The role of volitionality," *New Ideas in Psychology*, 47 (2017), 49–56.

_____. "Re-conceptualizing Neurosis as a Degree of Egocentricity: Ethical issue in Psychological Theory," *J Religion Health* 2015 Oct. 54 (5): 1788-99.

Ancona, Deborah and Backman Elaine, MIT Leadership Center. (October, 2017). "Distributed Leadership. From Pyramids to Networks: The Changing Leadership Landscape." http://problemledleadership.mit.edu/wp-content/uploads/MIT_Whitepaper-From_Pyramids_to_Networks.pdf

Ancona, Deborah, MIT Leadership Center. (n.d.) "Sensemaking, Framing and Acting in the Unknown," *The Handbook for Teaching Leadership*. https://www.sagepub.com/sites/default/files/upm-binaries/42924_1.pdf

Aquinas, St. Thomas. *Commentary on Aristotle's Metaphysics*. Trans. John P. Rowan. (Notre Dame, Indiana: Dumb Ox Books, 1961.

———. *Commentary on Aristotle's Nicomachean Ethics*. Trans. C.J. Litzinger, O.P. (Notre Dame, Indiana: Dumbo OX Books, 1964).

———. *The Summa Theologiae*, Trans. Fathers of the English Dominican Province. (Benziger Bros. edition, 1947).

———. *Commentaries on Aristotle's "On Sense and What is Sensed" and "On Memory and Recollection."* Trans. Kevin White & Edward M. Macierowski. (Washington: The Catholic University Press of America, 2005)

———. *Commentary Posterior Analytics of Aristotle*. Trans. by Fabian R. Larcher, re-edited html formatted by Joseph Kennedy, dshspriory.org/thomas/

———. *Questiones Disputatae Veritatae*. Trans. Robert Mulligan, S.J. Q 1-9, James V. McGlynn, S.J., Q 10-20, Robert W. Schmidt, S.J., Q 21-29 (Chicago: Henry Regency Corporation,1952-1954).

Arnold Magda B, Gasson John A, S.J. *The Human Person an Approach to An Integral Theory of Personality* (New York: The Ronald Press Company, 1954).

———. *Story Sequence Analysis, A New Method of Measuring Motivation, and Predicting Achievement* (New York and London: Columbia University Press, 1962).

Ashley, Benedict, M., O.P. *Healing for Freedom, A Christian Perspective on Personhood and Psychotherapy* (Arlington, Virginia: The Institute for the Psychological Sciences Press, 2013).

———. *A Companion to Albert the Great* (London Boston: Brill, 2013).

Assagioli, Roberto M.D. *Psychosynthesis, A Collection of Basic Writings* (Amherst, Massachusetts: The Synthesis Center edition, 2000).

Atkinson, Timothy N. and Butler, Jesse W. "From Regulation to Virtue: A Critique of Ethical Formalism in Research Organizations." Journal of Research Administration, Volume XLIII, Number 1, 2012 17-30.

Baars, Conrad W M.D. *Feeling & Healing Your Emotions A psychiatrist takes a positive look at negative feelings* (Plainfield, New Jersey: Logos International, 1970).

Baars, Conrad W. &. Terruwe Anna A. *Psychic Wholeness & Healing, Using All the Powers of the Human Psyche* (Eugene, OR 97401: Wipf and Stock Publishers, 1981).

Banicki, Konrad. "Positive psychology on character strengths and virtues. A disquieting suggestion," New Ideas in Psychology, 33 (2014): 21-34.

_____. "The character-personality distinction: An historical conceptual, and functional investigation," *Theory & Psychology* Vol. 27 (1) (2017): 50-68.

Barnard, Chester I. The Functions of the Executive (Cambridge, Massachusetts and London, England: Harvard University Press, 1938 and 1968).

Baum, William M. *Understanding Behaviorism, Science, Behavior and Culture* (New York: Harper Collins College Publishers, 1994).

_____. "From Molecular to Molar Behavior A Paradigm Shift in Behavior Analysis," *Journal of the Experimental Analysis of Behavior*, 2002, 78, Number 1 (July): 95-116.

Bennis, Warren. *Why Leaders Can't Lead, The Unconscious Conspiracy Continues* (San Francisco: Jossey-Bass Publishers, 1989).

Bergquist, William. *The Postmodern Organization* (San Francisco: Jossey-Bass Publishers, 1993).

Blondel, Maurice. *Action (1893) Essay on a Critique of Life and a Science of Practice*, Trans. Oliva Blanchette (Notre Dame, Indiana: University of Notre Dame Press).

Boardman, Craig, and Ponomariov, Branco. "Organizational Pathology," *Global Encyclopedia of Public Administration, Public Policy, and Governance.* (January 1, 2017). https://works.bepress.com/craig_boardman/35/

Bolman L.G. and Deal T.E. *Leading with Soul: An Uncommon Journey of Spirit* (San Francisco: Jossey-Bass, 1996).

Boring, E.G. *A History of Experimental Psychology*, Second Edition (New York: Appleton, 1957).

Bourke, Vernon, J. *Ethics, A Textbook in Moral Philosophy* (New York: The Macmillan Company, 1951).

_____. *St. Thomas, and The Greek Moralists* (Milwaukee: Marquette University Press, 1947).

Bowditch, James L. and Buono, Anthony F. *A Primer on Organizational Behavior* (New York: Jon Wiley & Sons, Inc., 2001).

Brennan, Robert Edward O.P. *Thomistic Psychology, A Philosophical Analysis of the Nature of Man* (New York: The MacMillan Company, 1941)

Briskin A. *The Stirring Soul in the Workplace* (San Francisco: Jossey-Bass, 1996).

Brooks, Carder and Marilyn, Monda. "Deming's Profound Knowledge and Leadership We Are Still Not Out of Crisis" *Human Development Leadership Division ASQ* asqhdandl.org/uploads/3/4/6/3/34636479/2013_profound.pdf

Brown, Daniel James. *Boys in The Boat: Nine Americans and Their Epic Quest for Gold at the 1936 Olympics* (New York: Penguin Books, 1951).

Brown, Ruth. "Four sheriffs' deputies hid during Florida school shooting," *New York Post, February 23, 2018, https://nypost.com/2018/02/23/four-sheriffs-deputies-hid-during-florida-school-shooting/*

Bushlack, Thomas J. "Mindfulness and the Discernment of Passions: Insights from Thomas Aquinas," *Spiritus: A Journal of Christian Spirituality*, Volume 14, Number 2 Fall 2014, 141-165.

Butera, Giuseppe. "Thomas Aquinas and Cognitive Therapy: An Exploration of the Promise of the Thomistic Psychology," *Philosophy, Psychiatry, and Psychology*, 17 (4):347-366 (2010). https://philpapers.org/rec/BUTTAA

Carr, Albert Z. *Business as a Game* (New York, New York: Signet Book, 1968).

_____. "Is Business Bluffing Ethical?" *Harvard Business Review*, January, 1968 (4). https://hbr.org/1968/01/is-business-bluffing-ethical

Chappell, T. *The Soul of a Business: Managing for Profit and the Common Good* (New York: Bantam Books, 1994).

Clegg, Stewart R. *Modern Organizations, Organization Studies in the Postmodern World* (London: Sage Publications, 1990).

Collins, Jim. *Built to Last, Successful Habits of Visionary Companies* (New York, New York: Harper Business, An Imprint of Harper Collins Publishers, 1994.)

Colquitt, Jason A., and Rodell Jessica B. "Measuring Justice and Fairness." *The Oxford Handbook of Justice in the Workplace*, Edited by Russell S. Cropanzano and Maureen L. Ambrose. (Oxford: Oxford Handbooks, 2015).

https://media.terry.uga.edu/socrates/publications/2015/01/ColquittRodel l2015.pdf

Crowley, Charles Bonaventure O.P. *Aristotelian-Thomistic Philosophy of Measure and the International System of Units (SI), Correlation of International System of Units with the Philosophy of Aristotle and St. Thomas,* *edited* with a prescript by Peter A. Redpath (Lanham, Maryland: University of America Press, 1996).

Dalio, Ray. *Principles* (New York: Simon & Schuster, 2017).

Damasio Antonio R. *Descartes Error, Emotion, Reason, and the Human Brain* (New York: G P Putman's Sons, 1994).

_____. *The Feelings of What Happens, Body and Emotion in The Making of Consciousness* (San Diego: A Harvest Book, Harcourt, Inc., 1995).

Darry, Bruce. "On the Origin of the Term Neuropsychology," *Neuropsychologia*, 23 (6), (1985): 813-814.

DeGeorge Richard T. *Business Ethics*, 3rd ed. (New York: MacMillan, 1990).

De Haan, Daniel D. and Meadows, Geoffrey A. "Aristotle and the Philosophical Foundations of Neuroscience," *Proceedings of the ACPA,* Vol.87 213-230

De Haan, Daniel D. "Delectatio, gaudimm fruitio Three Kinds of Pleasure for Three Kinds of Knowledge in Thomas Aquinas." https://www.brepolsonline.net/doi/abs/10.1484/J.QUAESTIO.5.108628

Deely, John N. "In the Twilight of Neothomism, a Call for a New Beginning: A review of the Way toward Wisdom," *American Catholic Philosophical Quarterly Vol. 83, 2, 2009, 268–277.*

Deming, Edwards W. *Out of the Crisis* (Cambridge, Mass: Massachusetts Institute of Technology, 1986).

_____. *The New Economics, For Industry, Government, Education* (Cambridge, Massachusetts: MIT Press, 1994).

De Roberts, Eugene. "Metaphysics and Psychology: A Problem of the Personal," *Journal of Theoretical and Philosophical Psychology*, Vol.25, No. 2005.

Dimitrov Vladimir and Lloyd Fell. "Autopoiesis in Organizations," *http://www.biosong.org/Dimtrov.pdf*

Doherty, William J. *Soul Searching, Why Psychotherapy Must Promote Moral Responsibility* (New York, NY: Basic Books Publication, 1996).

Doris, John M. & the Moral Psychology Research Group. *The Moral Psychology Handbook* (Oxford, UK: The Oxford University Press, 2012).

Drucker, Peter F. *Managing the Nonprofit Organization, Principles and Practices* (New York: Collins Business, 1990).

Duckworth, Angela. *Grit The Power of Passion and Perseverance* (New York: Scribner, 2016).

Echavarria, Martin F. "Esse et Intelligere In Thomas Aquinas according to the 'Thinking Realism' of Francisco Canals Vidal," *Portuguese Journal of Philosophy*, 2015, Vol. 71 (2-3) 545-566.

Ehringer, Ann Graham. Make Up Your Own Mind, Entrepreneurs Talk About Decision Making (Santa Monica: Merritt Publishing, 1995).

El Khachab, Chihab. "The Logical Goodness of Abduction in C.S. Pierce's Thought", Transactions of the Charles S. Peirce Society: A Quarterly Journal in American Philosophy, Volume 49, Number 2 (Spring 2013): 157-177.

Ellis, Albert. *Executive Leadership, A Rational Approach* (New York, New York: Institute of Rational Living, 1978).

_____. *Reason and Emotion in Psychotherapy, A Comprehensive Method of Treating Disturbances revisited and updated* (New York, New York: Carol Publishing Company, 1994).

Elsberg, Barbara Roche Teresa, and Lovergan, Susan. "Emergent Leadership. Executive Summary, Five Forces of Change, Emerging Trends in Leadership Development," CHREATE, June 2016, 3.

Erturk, Ramazan. "Thomas Aquinas on Knowledge of other Minds," *The Journal of International Social Research* Volume 3/11 (Spring 2010).

Etzioni, Amitai. *A Comparative Analysis of Complex Organizations revised and enlarged edition* (New York, New York: Macmillan Publishing Co., Inc., 1975).

Farber, Leslie H. *The Ways of the Will, Essays Toward a Psychology and Psychology of Will* (New York & Evanston: Harper & Row, Publishers, 1966).

Feser, Edward. *Philosophy of Mind* (London, England: Oneworld Publications, 2006).

Findlay, Edward F. C*aring for the Soul in a Postmodern Age, Politics, and phenomenology in the thought of Jan Patocka (*Albany New York: State University of New York Press, 2002).

Finlay, Steve. *Artificial Intelligence and Machine Learning for Business* (Great Britain, Relativistic Books, 2017).

Flaherty, James. *Coaching, Evoking Excellence in Other*s (Amsterdam. Boston. Heidelberg. London. New York. Oxford. Paris. San Diego. San Francisco. Singapore. Sydney. Tokyo: Elsevier Butterworth Heinemann, 2005).

Fleming, Thomas. *The Morality of Everyday, Rediscovering an Alternative to the Liberal Tradition* (Columbia and London: University of Missouri Press, 2004).

Fogel, Robert William. *The Fourth Great Awakening & The Future of Egalitarianism* (Chicago: The University of Chicago Press, 2000).

Forester, Paul. *Peirce and the Threat of Nominalism* (Cambridge CB2 8RU, UK: Cambridge University Press, 2011).

Fortin, Marion. "Perspectives on Organizational Justice: Concept clarification, social context integration, time and links with morality." onlinelibrary.wiley.com/doi/abs/10.1111/j.1468-2370.2008.00231

Fowers, Blaine J. *Virtue Psychology* (Washington DC: American Psychological Association, 2005).

_____. "The Promise of a Flourishing Theoretical Psychology," *Journal of Theoretical and Philosophical Psychology,* American Psychological Association, 2015. http://dx.doi.org/10.1037/a0038646

Freeman, Walter J. *How Brains Make Up Their Minds* (New York, New York: Columbia University Press, 2000).

Freiburg, Kevin and Freiburg, Jackie. *Nuts! Recipe for Business and Personal Success* (Austin: Brad Press, 1996).

Gabor, Andrea, and Mahoney, Joseph T. "Chester Barnard and the Systems Approach to Nurturing Organizations" (2010). https://andreagabor.files.wordpress.com/2010/10/barnardoxfordpressgabor.pdf

Galison, Peter. "Trading with the Enemy," In *Trading Zones and International Expertise: Creating New Kinds of Collaboration*, edited by Michael E. Gorman, 25-52. Cambridge: The MIT Press, 2010. https://galison.scholar.harvard.edu/publications/trading-enemy

Gasser-Wingate, Marc. "Aristotle on Induction and First Principles" *Philosophers Imprint* Volume 16 No.4 (February, 2016).

Gavetti Giovanni and Rivkin Jan W. "How Strategists Really Think: Tapping the Power of Analogy," *Harvard Business Review, https://hbr.org/2005/04*

Genosko, Gene. *McLuhan and Baudrillard The Masters of Implosion* (London & New York: Routledge, 1999).

Gill, Michael J. "The possibilities of phenomenology for organizational research," *journals.sagepub.com/doi/10.1177/1094428113518348*

Gilson, Etienne. *Thomist Realism and the Critique of Knowledge*, trans. Mark A. Wauck (San Francisco: Ignatius Press, 1986).

Goerner, Sally J. "Autopoiesis in Organizations, Chaos and the Evolving Universe," *World Futures General Evolution Studies* (8), 1988.

Goleman, Daniel. *Focus, The Hidden Driver of Excellence* (New York, New York: Harper Collins Publishers, 2013)

_____. *Working with Emotional Intelligence* (New York: Bantam, 1998),

Griffin, Douglas. *The Emergence of Leadership: Linking Self-Organizing and Ethics* (London: Routledge, 2002).

Guzie, S.J., Tad. *The Analogy of Learning, An Essay toward a Thomistic Psychology of Learning*, (New York: Sheed and Ward, 1960).

Hancock Curtis L and. Redpath, Peter. A *Recovering a Catholic Philosophy of Elementary Education* (Mount Pocono: Newman House Press, 2006), 82–83

Harak, Simon. S.J. *Virtuous Passions, the formation of character.* (Eugene OR 97491: Wipf and Stock Publishers, 1993)

Harman, Sidney. *Mind Your Own Business: A Maverick's Guide to Business, Leadership, and Life* (New York: Currency Doubleday, 2000).

Harmon, Francis L. *Principles of Psychology* (Milwaukee: The Bruce Publishing Company, 1938).

Harack, S.J., G. Simon. *Virtuous Passions, the formation of Christian character* (Eugene OR: Wipf and Stock Publishers, 1993).

Hartman, Edwin M. *Virtue in Business, Conversations with Aristotle* (Cambridge, UK: Cambridge University Press, 2013).

Haslam, Nick Prudence. "Aristotelian perspectives on practical reason," *Journal for the Theory of Social Behavior*, 21:2 0021-8308

Hebb, Donald O. *The Organization of Behavior: A Neuropsychological Theory* (New York: John Wiley & Sons, 1949).

Hill, Russ. *Teach Internal Locus of Control, A Positive Psychology Application* (Beach Haven, NJ: Will to Power Press, 2011).

Hillman, J. *The Soul's Code: In Search of Character and Calling* (New York: Random House, 1996).

Holt, Edwin B. *The Freudian Wish and Its Place In Ethics* (New York: Henry Holt and Company, 1915 NJ: Power Press, 2011).

Horney, Karen. *New Ways in Psychoanalysis* (W. W. Norton: London, 1939).

Ilies Remus, Morgenson Frederick P., Nahrgang. "Authentic Leadership and Eudemonic well-being: Understanding Leader-Follower Outcomes," *The Leadership Quarterly*, Quarterly 16 (2005) 373-394

Inglehart, Ronald. "The Meaning of Life Is on Most People's Minds," *Spirituality & Health*, March/April 2004.
Modernization and Postmodernization: Culture, Economic and Political Change in 43 Societies (Princeton: University Press, 1997).

Jackson, Michael C. *Systems Approaches to Management* (New York, New York: Kluwer/Plenum Publishers, 2000).

Janowitz, Morris. "Changing Pattern of Organizational Authority," *Military Establishment Authority Science Quarterly* (1959): 481–639.

Kantor, J.R. *The Scientific Evolution of Psychology*, Volume 1 (Chicago: Principia Press,1963), 161.

Kärkkäinen, P. *Internal Senses.* Lagerlund H. (eds) Encyclopedia of Medieval Philosophy. (Springer, Dordrecht, 2011).

Kase, Larina. *The Confident Leader* (New York, New York: McGraw Hill, 2009).

Kellogg Katherine C., Orlikowski Wand J., and Yate JoAnne. "Life in the Trading Zone: Structuring Coordination Across Boundaries' in Post-Bureaucratic Organizations," *Organization Science*, Vol.17 No. 1 (January-February 2006): 22-44.

Kelly, George A. *A Theory of Personality, The Psychology of Personal Constructs* (New York. London: W.W. Norton & Company, 1963).

Kemple, Brian. "The Preeminent Necessity of Prudence," *Studia Gilsoniana* 6:4 (October-December 2017), 549-572.

Kets de Vries Leaders. *Fools and Impostors, Essay on the Psychology of Leadership* (New York: iUniverse, Inc., 2003).

Kima, Gyula. "Saint Thomas Aquinas: On The Principles of Nature," https://www3.nd.edu/~afreddos/papers/Aquinas-principlesofnature-klima.htm

King, Peter. "The Nature of the Passion*," Aquinas Moral Theory* (Cornell 1999): 101-132. *individual.utoronto.ca/pking/articles/Aquinas_on_the_Passions.pdf*

Kluver, Heinrich. *Behavior Mechanism in Monkeys* (www.Literary Licensing, Sept 21, 2013).

Kofman Fred. *The Meaning Revolution, The Power of Transcendent Leadership* (New York: Currency, 2018).

Kohak, Erazim. *The Embers and The Stars, a philosophical inquiry into the moral sense of nature* (Chicago, London: The University of Chicago Press, 1984).

Kolzow, David R. *Leading from Within: Building Organizational Leadership Capacity* (ideconline.org client uploads, 2014).

Kontos, Pavlos. *Aristotle's Moral Realism Reconsidered, Phenomenological Ethics* (London: Routledge Taylor & Francis Group, 2011).

Krause, Donald G. *The Book of The Five Rings for Executives* (London: Nicholas Brealev Publishing, 2001).

Kugelmann, Robert. *Psychology and Catholicism, Contested Boundaries* (Cambridge CB2 8RU UK: Cambridge University press, 2011).

Kupers, Wendelin. "A Phenomenology of embodied passion and the demotivational realities of organizations," *St. Gallen Switzerland: Institute for Leadership and H-R Management, 2001. Retrieved from*

*http://www.mngt.waikato.ac.nz/ejrot/cmsconference/2001/Papers/Passion%2
0for%20Organising/Kupers.pdf*

Kurtz, C.F., Snowden D.J. "The New Dynamics of Strategy: Sense-making in a Complex and Complicated World" *IBM Systems Journal* Vol 42, NO 3, 2003

Kurzynski, Marci. "Peter Drucker: Modern day Aristotle for the business community," *Journal of Management History* Vol.15. 4, 2009, 357–374.

Lambert, Richard Thomas. *Self-Knowledge in Thomas Aquinas: The Angelic Doctor on the Soul's Knowledge of Itself* (Bloomington, Indiana: Author House, 2007).

Larchet, Jean-Claude. *Mental Disorders and Spiritual Healing* (San Rafael, CA: Angelico Press/Sophia Perennis, 2005).

Leonard, George. *Mastery* (New York: Dutton Penguin Books,1991): xi–xii.

Lewis, M. Clarence Irving. *Mind and The World Order, Outline of a Theory of Knowledge* (New York: Dover Publications, 1929); P.W. BRIDGMAN, *The Logic of Modern Physics* (New York: Macmillan, 1928).

Lewin Roger and Regine Birute. *The Soul at Work, Embracing Complexity Science for Business Success* (New York: Simon & Schuster, 2000).

Lichtenstein, Benyamin, B. and Plowman, Donde Ashmos. "The leadership of emergence: A complex systems leadership theory of emergence at successive organizational levels," Leadership Quarterly, 20:4,(August 2009) 617-630

Lincoln, James R. and Guillot. "Durkheim and Organizational Culture," *IRLE working paper No. 108-04 http://irle.berkeley.edu/workpapers/108-04.pgf*

Lohrenz, Cary D. *Fearless Leadership: High Performance Lessons from the Flight Deck* (Austin: Greenleaf, 2014).

Lombardo, Nicholas E O.P. *The Logic of Desire, Aquinas on Emotion* (Washington, D.C.: The Catholic University of America Press, 2011).

Lucier, Chuck. "Herb Kelleher: The Thought Leader Interview," https://www.strategy-business.com/article/04212?gko=8cb4f.

Luthans, Fred, Youssef Carolyn M and Avolio Bruce J., *Psychological Capital, Developing the Human Competitive Edge (*Oxford, UK: Oxford university press, 2007)

Madsbjerg, Christian. *Sensemaking, The Power of the Humanities in the Age of the Algorithm* (New York Boston: Hachette Books:2017).

Malcolm, Susan B. "Peter Drucker" ethics scholar par excellence," *Journal of Management History*, Vol.15 No. 4 2009 375-367.

Mango, Peter J. "Philosophical Tensions among Leadership, Efficiency, Community-and What It Means for the Academy," *Studia Gilsoniana*, 3 (2014): 567–568.

Mason, Moya K. "Thoughts on Leadership: How Important is Decision-Making?" www.moyak.com/papers/leadership-qualities.html

Maurer, Armand. *St. Thomas Aquinas, The Division and Methods of The Sciences* (Toronto, Canada: The Pontifical Institute of Mediaeval Studies, 1963).

McVey, William A. "Thomistic Scientific Leadership and Common-Sense Triad of Organizational Harmony," *Studia Gilsoniana*, 3 (2014): 586.

Mele, Domenec. "Practical Wisdom in Managerial Decision Making," *Journal of Management* Vol.29 No. 7/8 2010 637-645.

Mercier, Joseph. *The Origins of Contemporary Psychology* (New York: P.J. Kenedy & Sons, 1918).

Miller, Lisa. *The Spiritual Child, The New Science on Parenting for Health and Lifelong Thriving* (New York: St. Martin's Press, 2015).

MIT Leadership Center. "Making a Difference by Making Sense." *www.mineducacion.gov.co/cvn/1665/articles-112257_archivo_pdf2.pdf*

Mintzberg Henry, Ahlstrand, Bruce, and Lampel, Joseph. *Strategy Safari, A Guided Tour Through the Wilds of Strategic Management* (New York London Toronto Sydney: Free Press, 1994).

Mirvis, Philip H., "Soul Work in Organizations," *Organization Science* https://doi.org/10.1287/orsc.8.2.,192.

Mitroff, Ian I. and Denton, Elizabeth A. *A Spiritual Audit of Corporate America*, (San Francisco: Jossey-Bass Inc. Publishers, 1999).

Moore, T. *Care of the Soul: A Guide for Cultivating Depth and Sacredness in Everyday Life* (New York: Harper Perennial, 1994).

Morgan, Gareth. *Images of Organization* (Newbury, California: Sage Publications, 1986).

Moss, Jessica. "Virtue Makes the Goal Right," www.nyu.edu/gsas/dept/philo/faculty/moss/VirtueMakesTheGoalRight.pdf

_____. "Aristotle's Ethical Psychology," Reason's Role in Virtue and Happiness," https://www.nyu.edu/gsas/dept/philo/.../moss/Aristotles%20Ethical%20Psychology.pdf

Murugan, Senthil, and Panchanatham, N. "Interpersonal Conflict Management styles on Conflict Sources in Services Settings," *IOSR Journal of Business and Management* 18(9), September 2016, 16–24.

Neenan, O.P. Sr. Mary Angelica. *The Nature of the Human Soul, Philosophical Anthropology & Moral Theology* (Washington, DC: Cluny Media edition, 2017).

Neubauer Rainer, Rarling Andrew and Wade Michael. "Redefining Leadership for a Digital Age" www.imd.org/globalassets/dbt/docs/redefining-leadership

Nolop, Bruce. "The Experts," https://blogs.wsj.com/experts/2014/04/29/four-qualities-of-successful-executives/

Nonaka, Ikujiro, and Takeuchi, Hirotaka. *The Knowledge Creating Company, How Japanese Companies Create the Dynamics of Innovation,* (New York Oxford: Oxford University Press, 1995).

Novak, Michael. *Business as a Calling, Work, and the Examined Life* (New York: The Free Press, 1996).

Novogrodzka, Bernice Josephine. "The Problem of Intuition in Saint Thomas Aquinas," (194), Master's Thesis Paper 788. http://ecommons.luc.edu-thesies/788

Nutt, Paul C. *Making Tough Decisions, Tactics for Improving Managerial Decision Making* (San Francisco Oxford: Jossey-Bass Publishers, 1990).

Olmstead, Abraham. "8 Herb Kelleher Quotes That Will Teach You Everything You Need to Know About Life." *CO* (March 21, 2014). https://www.freeenterprise.com/8-herb-kelleher-quotes-will-teach-you-everything-you-need-know-about-life/

O'Rourke, Fran. Pseudo-Dionysius and the Metaphysics of Aquinas, (Notre Dame, Indiana: University of Notre Dame Presse, 2005).

Pieper, Josef. *The Four Cardinal Virtues* (Notre Dame, Indiana: University of Notre Dame Press, 1996).

Pink, Daniel H. *A Whole New Mind, Moving from the Information Age to the Conceptual Age* (New York: Riverhead Book, 2005).

Pixton, Pollyanna, Gibson, Paul and Nickolaisen, Niel. *The Agile Culture, Leading Through Trust and Ownership* (New York: Addison-Wesley, 2014).

Polanyi, Michael. *The Tacit Dimension* (Chicago: The University of Chicago Press, 2009).

Prusak, Larry. "What Can't Be Measured." *https://hbr.org/2010/10/what-cant-be-measured*

Rachlin, Howard. *Judgment, Decision and Choice* (New York: W.H. Freeman and Company, 1989).

_____. *The Escape of The Mind* (Oxford London: Oxford University Press, 2014).

_____. "About Teleological Behaviorism," *The Behavior Analyst/MABA* (October 2013): 209-222.

_____. *Introduction to Modern Behaviorism* (San Francisco: W. H. Freeman and Company, 1970).

_____. "A Behavioral Science of Mental Life: comments on Foxall's "Intentional Behaviorism," *Behavior and Philosophy, Cambridge Center for Behavioral Studies*, 35 (2007): 131-138.

_____. "Behaviorism in Everyday Life." (Englewood Cliffs, New Jersey: Prentice-Hall, Inc., 1979).

Randall, H. *Aristotle* (New York: Columbia University Press, 1960).

Redpath, Peter A. *A Not- So Elementary Christian Metaphysics* (St. Louis, MO: En Route Books & Media, 2015).

_____. *The Moral Wisdom of St. Thomas, An Introduction* (Lanham New York London: University of America Press, 1983).

_____. *The Moral Psychology of St. Thomas Aquinas, An Introduction to Ragamuffin Ethics* (St. Louis, MO: En Route Books & Media, 2015).

_____. *A Simplified Introduction to the Wisdom of ST. Thomas* (Lantham. New York. London: University of America Press, 1980).

_____. *Masquerade of the Dream Walkers, Prophetic Theology from the Cartesians to Hegel* (Amsterdam: Rodopi Press, 1984).

_____. *A Thomistic Tapestry, Essays in Memory of Etienne Gilson*, edited by Peter A. Redpath (Amsterdam: Rodopi Press, 2003).

_____. "Virtue as Intensive Quantity In Aristotle," *International Journal of World Peace,* Vol, 18, No. 1 (March 2001).

_____. "The Essential Connection between Common Sense and Leadership Excellence," *Studia Gilsoniana*, 3 (2014): 605–608.

Reid, Heather L. *The Philosophical Athlete* (Durham, North Carolina: Carolina Academic Press, 2002).

Riggio, Ronald E., Zhu Weichun, Reina Christopher, and Maroosis James A. "Virtue-Based Measurement of Ethical Leadership: The Leadership Virtues Questionnaire," *Consulting Psychology Journal and Research,* Vol. 62, No.4 (2010): 235-250.

Robinson, Daniel N. *Aristotle's Psychology* (New York: Columbia University Press, 1989).

_____. *Philosophy of Psychology (*New York: Columbia University Press, 1985).

Romme Georges, A., Avenier, Marie-Jose, Denyer David, Hodgkinson Gerard P. Pandza Krsto, Atarkkey Ken and Worren Nicolay "Toward Common Ground and Trading Zones in Management Research and Practice," *British Journal of Management*, Vol. 26. (2015): 544-599.

Rosenthal Sandra B.& Buchholz Rogene A. Rethinking Business Ethics, A Pragmatic Approach (New York Oxford: Oxford University Press, 2000)

Sachs, Joe. *On the Soul and On the Memory and Recollection* (Santa Fe, New Mexico: Green Lion Press, 2004).

Sajjadi, Adollah and Mehrpour, Mohammad. "New Emerging Leadership Theories and Styles," *Technical Journal of Engineering and Applied Sciences* (2014): 180-188.

Sandelands, Lloyd E. "The Argument for God from Organization," *Journal of Management Inquiry*, Vol. 12 (2) (2005/6): 68-177.

Scarani, Valerio. "The Universe Would Not Be Perfect Without Randomness: A Quantum Physicist's Reading of Aquinas," Proceedings of the Conference Quantum (Vienna, 19–22 June 2014).

Schein, Edgar H. *Organizational Psychology 3rd edition*, ed. Richard S. Lazarus (Upper Saddle River, N.J. 07458: Prentice Hall, Inc., 1994).

Schuurman, Derek C. *Shaping a Digital World* (Downers Grove, Illinois: InterVarsity Press, 2013).

Scott, Richard W. *Organizations Rational Natural, and Open Systems* (Upper Saddle River, New Jersey: Prentice Hall, 1998).

Seidman William and McCauley Michael. "Rediscovering the Corporate Soul." (2003). www.cerebyte.com

Seligman, Martin E.P. *Flourish, A Visionary New Understanding of Happiness and Well-Being* (New York London Toronto Sydney New Delhi: Atria, 2013).

Diamond Sharp. "Sloan, Man in the Gray Flannel Suit." *Reading Journal*. https://diamondsharp.wordpress.com/tag/sloan-wilson/

Shaw, Robert Bruce. *Extreme Teams* (New York: American Management Association, 2017).

Singer, A. "Strategy as Moral Philosophy." *Strategic Management Journal*, 15, (1994): 191–213.

Sokolowskı, Robert "Phenomenology of Friendship," *The Review of Metaphysics* 55 (March 2002).

Sorkin, Andrew Ross. "Wall Street Titan Demands Good "Deeds, Andrew Ross Sorkin," The Week (January 26, 2018): 31.

Spadaro, Antonio. "A Big Heart Open to God: An Interview with Pope Francis," American Jesuit Review (2017). https://www.americamagazine.org/faith/2013/09/30/big-heart-open-god-interview-pope-francis

Spencer, Karl. *The Neuro Psychology of Lashley. Selected Papers of K.S. Lashley*, ed. Frank Beach (New York: McGraw Hill, 1960).

Stacey Ralph D, Griffin Douglas and Shaw, Patricia. *Complexity and Management: Fad or Radical Challenge to Systems Management* (London and New York: Routledge, Taylor & Francis Group, 2000).

Staddon, J.E.R. *Adaptive Dynamics, The Theoretical Analysis of Behavior* (Cambridge, Massachusetts: MIT Press, 2001).

Staw, B.M. Sandelands L.E and. Dutton J. E. "Threat-rigidity effects in organizational behavior: A multilevel analysis*," Administrative Science Quarterly* (1981).

Sternberg, Robert J. *Wisdom, Intelligence & Creativity Synthesized* (New York, NY: Cambridge University Press, 2003).

_____.*Why Smart People Can Be So Stupid* (New Haven & London: Yale University Press, 2002).

_____. *Practical Intelligence in Everyday Life* (Cambridge: University Press, 2000).

_____. *Cognitive Psychology,* (Australia: Wadsworth Cengage Learning, 2009).

Sticher, Matt. "Practical Skills and Practical Wisdom in Virtue*," Australasian Journal of Philosophy*, DOI: 10. 1080/ooo4802.2015.10

Strumia, Alberto. *The Sciences and The Fullness of Rationality*, trans. By Philip Larrey and Peter Waymel (Aurora: The Davies, 2009).

Sullivan Kevin, Craig, Tim, and Wan William. "'People are angry': Pain turns political in Parkland after school shooting," *The Washington Post* (February 17, 2018). *https://www.washingtonpost.com*

Synder, C.R. *The Psychology of Hope (New York London Toronto* Sydney Tokyo Singapore: The Free Press: 1994).

Tallis, Frank. *Hidden Minds: A History of the Unconscious* (New York: Arcade Publishing, 2002).

Titus, Craig Steven. "Aquinas, Seligman, and positive psychology: A Christian approach to the use of the virtues in psychology," *The Journal of Positive Psychology, DOI: 10. 1080/17439760.2016.1228005*

Tong, Benjamin R. "Karen Horney and the Psychopathology of Culture," *paper presented at the conference of the International Karen Hornet Society*, New York (April 17, 1993).

Twenge, Jean M. *Generation Me, Why Today's Americans Are More Confident, Assertive, Entitled and More Miserable Than Ever Before* (New York London Toronto Sydney: Free Press, 2006).

Vannio, Olli-Pekka. *Virtue an Introduction to Theory and Practice* (Eugene, Oregon: Cascade Books, 2016).

Vermiebe, Roland. https://www.soz.ukdnivie.ac.at/fileadmin/user_upload/inst_soziologie/Perso nen/

_____.Institutsmitglieder/Verwiebe/Social-Institutions-in-Encyclopedia-of-Quality-of-Life-Research.pdf

Ward, John William. *The Ideal of Individualism and the Reality of the Organization*, The Business Establishment, ed. Earl F. Cheit (New York: Wiley, 1964).

Warfield, John N., and Cardenas, A. Roxana. *A Handbook of Interactive Management,* Second Edition (Ames: Iowa State University Press, 1993, 2002).

Weick, Karl E. "The Collapse of Sensemaking in Organizations: The Mann Gulch Disaster," *Administrative Quarterly,* 38 (1993): 628-652.

_____. *Making Sense of the Organization* (Oxford: Blackwell, 2001).

Welter, Brian. Book Review. "Peter A. Redpath, The Moral Psychology of ST. Thomas Aquinas: An Introduction to Ragamuffin Ethics," *Studia Gilsoniana* 6:4 (October-December 2017): 6.

Wheatley, Margaret J. *Leadership, and the New Science: Learning about Organization from an Orderly Universe* (San Francisco: Berrett-Koehler, 1992).

Wilson, Sloan. *The Man in the Gray Flannel Suit* (Cambridge, MA: DaCapo Press, 1958): 33-677.

Wippel, John F. "Maritain and Aquinas On Our Discovery of Being." *Studia Gilsoniana* 3 (2014): 415-443.

Wittmer, Carrie. "WHAT IS BILLIONS ABOUT?" *Business Insider.* (MARCH, 2017). *www.businessinsider.com/what-is-billions-show-about-2017-3*

www.ingramcontent.com/pod-product-compliance
Lightning Source LLC
Chambersburg PA
CBHW080128270326
41926CB00021B/4388